T0305155

TAXATION AND SOCIAL POLICY

Edited by
Andy Lymer, Margaret May and
Adrian Sinfield

P

First published in Great Britain in 2023 by

Policy Press, an imprint of
Bristol University Press
University of Bristol
1–9 Old Park Hill
Bristol
BS2 8BB
UK
t: +44 (0)117 374 6645
e: bup-info@bristol.ac.uk

Details of international sales and distribution partners are available at
policy.bristoluniversitypress.co.uk

British Library Cataloguing in Publication Data
A catalogue record for this book is available from the British Library

ISBN 978-1-4473-6417-7 hardcover
ISBN 978-1-4473-6418-4 paperback
ISBN 978-1-4473-6419-1 ePub
ISBN 978-1-4473-6420-7 ePdf

The right of Andy Lymer, Margaret May and Adrian Sinfield to be identified as editors of
this work has been asserted by them in accordance with the Copyright, Designs and Patents
Act 1988.

Cover design: Nicky Borowiec
Front cover image: Adobe Stock/Andrey Popov
Bristol University Press and Policy Press use environmentally responsible print partners.
Printed and bound in Great Britain by CPI Group (UK) Ltd, Croydon, CR0 4YY

Contents

List of figures and tables

Figures

List of abbreviations

BEIS	Department for Business, Energy and Industrial Strategy
BtL	Buy to Let
CCC	Climate Change Committee
CCL	Climate Change Levy
CGT	capital gains tax
CJRS	Coronavirus Job Retention Scheme
CPAG	Child Poverty Action Group
DB	defined benefit
DC	defined contribution
DEL	Departmental Expenditure Limits
DLUHC	Department for Levelling Up, Housing and Communities
DWP	Department for Work and Pensions
EEE	exempt, exempt, exempt
EET	exempt, exempt, tax
ESOs	Energy Savings Obligations
ETB/ETBHI	effects of taxes and benefits on household income
ETS	Emissions Trading System
EU	European Union
FRS	Family Resources Survey
GAO	Government Accountability Office (US)
GDP	gross domestic product
GEIA	Gender Equality Impact Assessment
GHG	greenhouse gas emissions
GRB	Gender Responsive Budgeting
GTED	Global Tax Expenditure Database
H&SCL	Health and Social Care Levy
HMRC	His Majesty's Revenue and Customs
HMT	His Majesty's Treasury
IEA	Institute of Economic Affairs
IfG	Institute for Government
IFS	Institute for Fiscal Studies
IHT	inheritance tax
IMF	International Monetary Fund
IPPR	Institute for Public Policy Research
ISA	Individual Savings Account
JRF	Joseph Rowntree Foundation
LCF	Living Costs and Food Survey
LIT	local income tax
LVT	land value tax
MAR	maximum available resources

MIRAS	Mortgage Interest Relief at Source
MMT	modern monetary theory
NAO	National Audit Office
NHS	National Health Service
NI	National Insurance
NICs	National Insurance contributions
NIT	Negative Income Tax
OBR	Office for Budget Responsibility
OECD	Organisation for Economic Co-operation and Development
OTS	Office of Tax Simplification
PAC	Public Accounts Committee
PIT	personal income tax
SDLT	Stamp Duty Land Tax
STE	Social Tax Expenditure
TDEL	Total Departmental Expenditure Limit
TET	tax exempt tax
TNCs	transnational corporations
TTE	taxed, taxed, exempt
TUC	Trades Union Congress
UBI	Universal Basic Income
UK	United Kingdom
UN	United Nations
VAT	value added tax
WBG	Women's Budget Group
WPC	House of Commons Work and Pensions Committee

Notes on contributors

Paul Bridgen is Associate Professor of Social Policy in the School of Economic, Social and Political Sciences, University of Southampton. He is currently working on the distributive impact of UK environmental taxation; domestic energy efficiency policy and fuel poverty; and the impact of welfare regimes on the development of eco-social policies. Recent publications include 'Sustainability' (2022, with Shoyen) and 'Eco-social policy development in liberal capitalism' (2023).

Milena Büchs is Professor of Sustainable Welfare at the University of Leeds. From 2005 to 2016 she was lecturing in sociology and social policy at the University of Southampton. Milena's research focuses on sustainable welfare and low carbon transitions. Milena is Co-Investigator of the Horizon Europe project "Towards a Sustainable Wellbeing Economy" (2022–2025), and of the UKRI-funded Centre for Research on Energy Demand Reduction (2018–2023). Recent publications include: "How socially just are taxes on air travel and 'frequent flyer levies'?" (2022, with Mattioli), "Fairness, effectiveness and needs satisfaction" (2021, with Ivanova and Schnepf) and "Sustainable welfare" (2021).

Kevin Caraher is Lecturer in Social Policy at the School for Business and Society, University of York. His research interests mainly focus on the interaction between the labour market and social policies in both a UK and international context. His current research interests are focused on the relationship between solo self-employment, wellbeing and social protection in the UK. Recent publications include 'Risk privatisation and social investment' (2020, with Reuter) and 'Mind the gaps' (2019, with Reuter).

Micheál L. Collins is Assistant Professor of Social Policy at the School of Social Policy, Social Work and Social Justice, University College Dublin (UCD), Ireland. Prior to joining UCD, he was Senior Economist at the Nevin Economic Research Institute. His research and teaching interests focus on income distribution and poverty, taxation, fiscal welfare, pensions, economic evaluation and public policy. Recent publications include 'Private pensions and the gender distribution of fiscal welfare' (2020) and 'Taxation and social policy' (2022, with Ruane and Sinfield).

Kevin Farnsworth is Professor of International Social and Public Policy, University of York. He has written extensively on the political economy of the welfare state, including on taxation and the mixed economy, corporate power and corporate welfare. Recent publications include 'Retrenched, reconfigured and broken' (2021) and 'Towards a whole-economy approach to the welfare state' (2019).

James Gregory is Teaching Fellow in the School of Social Policy, University of Birmingham. He was previously Senior Research Fellow at the Fabian Society, where he first worked on housing policy, and prior to that completed a PhD in political philosophy at the London School of Economics. His book, *Social Housing, Wellbeing and Welfare*, was published by Policy Press in 2022. Other recent publications include 'Personal savings for those on lower incomes' (2022, with Lymer and Rowlingson) and 'Does housing tenure matter?' (2021, with Angel).

Susan Himmelweit is Emeritus Professor of Economics at the Open University, a feminist economist whose research focuses on the gender implications of economic policy, the economics of care and intra-household inequalities. The founding Chair of the UK Women's Budget Group, she is currently their leading expert on tax, writes their annual briefings on tax policy and is on the advisory board of Tax Justice UK. Recent publications include 'Taxation and social security' (2020, with Bennett) and 'A short guide to taxing for gender equality' (2019, with Coffey and Stephenson).

Andy Lymer is Professor of Taxation and Personal Finance at Aston University, where he is also Director of the Centre for Personal Financial Wellbeing (CPFW). He was the Director of the HM Treasury Tax Development programme 2006–11 and is currently the Chair of the international Tax Research Network. His research interests lie at the intersection of the practices and policies of taxation and all aspects of personal finance. He is the co-author (with Oats) of the textbook on UK taxation, *Taxation: Policy and Practice* (30th edition 2023) and of *Comparative Taxation* (2nd edition forthcoming 2023, with Evans, Hasseldine, Ricketts and Sandford).

Margaret May is External Associate at the Centre on Household Assets and Savings Management at the University of Birmingham. Past Chair of the Social Policy Association, she has over 40 years' experience of teaching, examining and researching in social policy and human resource management. Her research interests include employment policy, occupational welfare, taxation, social security and comparative social policy. She co-edited *The Student's Companion to Social Policy*, 6th edn (2022, with Alcock, Haux and McCall).

Stephen McKay is Professor of Social Research at the University of Lincoln. He conducts research on living standards, including employment, taxes and social security benefits. In pursuit of these topics, he often conducts quantitative analysis of large datasets. Recent publications include 'The rationality of "rainy day" savers' (2022, with Cuismano, Donegani and Jackson) and 'How do you shape a market?' (2022, with Needham et al).

Michael Orton is Assistant Professor at the University of Warwick. He previously worked in a local government finance department during the poll tax and the introduction of council tax. In addition to his interest in local taxation, Michael's research is concerned with social security. In particular, his current focus is the Commission on Social Security led by Experts by Experience. Recent publications include 'The Commission on Social Security and participatory research during the pandemic' (2022, with Morris et al) and 'Guiding principles for social security policy' (2022, with Summers and Morris).

Chris Pond is Chair of the Financial Inclusion Commission and of the Lending Standards Board. Previously Director of Financial Capability at the Financial Services Authority, he has been CEO of two national charities (the Low Pay Unit and Gingerbread) and trustee of many others. Between 1997 and 2005, he was a Member of Parliament, serving on the (then) Social Security Select Committee, as Parliamentary Private Secretary in the Treasury and as Work and Pensions Minister. He was later a member of the Ethics and Responsibility and Tax Committees of the HMRC Board. Chris has held Honorary Visiting Professorships with Surrey and Middlesex Universities and teaching positions with the Civil Service College, Kent University and the Open University. He was co-editor of *Taxation and Social Policy* (1980, with Sandford and Walker) and co-author of *To Him Who Hath* (1977, with Field and Meacher).

Enrico Reuter is Senior Lecturer in Public and Social Policy at the School for Business and Society, University of York. His research interests are changes in wage-labour conditions and labour market policies, in particular regarding self-employment, and the social protection challenges they create, as well as questions of state capacity and legitimacy, notably regarding public services. Recent publications include 'Risk privatisation and social investment' (2020, with Caraher) and 'Mind the gaps' (2019, with Caraher).

Karen Rowlingson is Professor of Social Policy and Dean of the Faculty of Social Sciences at the University of York. Her research focuses on economic inequality spanning poverty and debt to riches and wealth with a particular interest in policies on social security and taxation. Recent publications include 'Want: still the easiest giant to attack?' (2022, with McKay) and 'Attitudes to a wealth tax' (2021, with Sood and Tu).

Sally Ruane is Reader in Social Policy at De Montfort University, Leicester. Her research interests include health service reform and the role of taxation in social policy. She co-convenes the Social Policy Association-endorsed Taxation and Social Policy Group with Adrian Sinfield and Micheál Collins. She co-authored *Paying for the Welfare State in the 21st Century* (2017, with Byrne) and *Data in Society* (2019, with Evans and Southall).

Adrian Sinfield, Professor Emeritus of Social Policy, University of Edinburgh, has worked on the social division of welfare, especially fiscal welfare, social security, unemployment, poverty and inequality. Past Chair and President of the Social Policy Association, he received its first lifetime achievement award; also co-founder of the Unemployment Unit and Chair for its first ten years, Vice-Chair of the Child Poverty Action Group for eight years. Publications include *What Unemployment Means* (1981) and *The Workless State* (with Showler, 1981) and *Comparing Tax Routes to Welfare in Denmark and the United Kingdom* (with Kvist, 1996).

Carlene Wynter is Lecturer at Aston Business School. She is a chartered accountant with over four decades of management, teaching and research experience in the UK, the United States and Jamaica. Her research interests include taxation in housing, tax policy, tax culture, tax enforcement and compliance. Recent publications include *Property Tax Management and Its Impact on Social Housing* (2021, with Manochin et al) and 'Knock, knock! The taxman's at your door!' (2021, with Oats).

Acknowledgements

The editors would like to thank the authors for their contributions, especially given the pressures arising from the COVID-19 pandemic and the many fiscal changes being made just as the chapters were being submitted to Policy Press.

We would also like to thank Laura Vickers-Rendall, Jay Allan, Dawn Preston and the team at Policy Press and Newgen Publishing for their support, the anonymous reviewers for their insightful comments and advice, and James Smith and Mohit Dar for their administrative and research assistance.

The editors are particularly grateful for the advice and support they have received from Bruce May, Dorothy Sinfield and Lorna Lymer throughout the production of the book.

Introduction: The case for considering taxation and social policy together

Andy Lymer, Margaret May and Adrian Sinfield

Taxation and Social Policy aims to fill significant gaps in both the social policy and tax literature by providing an overview of the role of tax in shaping UK social policy, broadly defined, and examining its distributional and behavioural significance.

Social policy analysts have long touched on aspects of taxation or on specific taxes in their work but have seldom sought to place taxation centre-stage or offer a broad-based approach to exploring the interactions between it and social policy. Indeed, though the interplay between the two was highlighted in the discipline's founding literature (Titmuss, 1958, 1962), and the first volume of the *Journal of Social Policy* included a call for joint research (Atkinson, 1972), direct interest in doing this has been patchy.

A key study that did address the interrelationships between the two, and the inspiration for this text, was *Taxation and Social Policy*, edited by Cedric Sandford, Chris Pond and Robert Walker. Greeted with much enthusiasm when it was published in 1980, it opened up many important questions and crucially emphasised the role of taxation as an instrument of social policy. After 40 years, it is, unsurprisingly, in many respects quite dated and long out of print. The impetus behind it, however, has not lost its saliency. Both taxation and social policy, its editors suggested, had 'developed in an independent and largely ad hoc manner. This process of separate development has created an overlap and interaction between the two systems which makes it impossible to consider satisfactorily either system in isolation from the other' (Sandford et al, 1980, p vi). In this volume, we seek to revisit this concern, explore the extent to which it remains unresolved and provide a basis for a long overdue consideration of the social policy–tax interface.

At best, this complex interface between taxation and social policy has since received only fitful attention, as Chapter 2 indicates. In the last few years, however, the linkages between the two have begun to attract increasing interest among social policy analysts (Hills, 2015; Byrne and Ruane, 2017). In 2018, Sally Ruane initiated the Social Policy Association's Taxation and Social Policy Group, which facilitates workshops, symposia and research, including a themed section in *Social Policy and Society* (2020). Proposals for change have also been set out in Jonathan Bradshaw's compendium for the Child Poverty Action Group (2019), itself stimulated by John Hills' work (1988) – a notable example of an attempt to raise the focus of this linkage in its time.

With growing recognition of the many ways in which taxation affects society, its institutions and groups within it, and is in turn affected by them, it is clearly time to look again at taxation through a social policy lens. The purposes, level and forms of taxation are now high on the political agenda and have gained added significance in the light of Brexit, the COVID-19 pandemic, the rising costs of energy and the climate crisis. COVID-19 and energy price rises have already forced temporary, unparalleled peacetime levels of government intervention and cast a spotlight on the scale of the multiple systemic inequities and inequalities in UK society. Moreover, combined with recent government changes and the rising living costs exacerbated by the war in Ukraine, there is significant heightened concerns over the continuing impact of a decade of austerity, recharging interest in longstanding debates over the nature and core principles of the UK's tax regime. Crucially, it has also spurred new thinking on the role of taxation as a form of social policy, its structure and place in the UK's mixed economy of welfare.

This publication is designed to further this emerging area of social policy analysis, serving in part as a textbook and a reader for those wanting to include issues of taxation in their teaching but primarily as a resource to stimulate further research in policy development and beyond. By continuing to break down the walls between tax and social policy discussions, we hope it will also provide a basis for research within areas related to social policy and be similarly of use in accounting, economics, business, law and cognate subjects as well as to policy makers.

Above all, we hope it will encourage debate about how both systems can and should be considered much less in isolation from each other than is still commonly the case four decades on from the attempt of Sandford et al to foster a more holistic approach. Their study focused mainly on direct taxation, particularly income tax. But it was felt that today we should take account of a wider range of taxes, the ways they interact throughout a spectrum of policy domains, their impact on the quality of life across society and where relevant the implications of devolution.

Setting the scene for this in Chapter 2, Chris Pond, one of the editors of, and a contributor to, the 1980 volume, reflects on the impact of changes in the political climate on the many developments in tax and social policy over the decades since.

Andy Lymer (Chapter 3) then sets out the dimensions of the current tax and social policy landscape, outlining the key features of the UK tax system, such as it is, the linkages between its underpinning principles and operation, and its use for social benefit as a key, but not the only reason, for tax raising.

Extending this contextual overview, a fourth anchoring chapter of the text presents an analysis by Adrian Sinfield of fiscal welfare and tax expenditures (Chapter 4). Despite increased data since they were explored by Pond in the 1980 book, these remain subject to continuing government reluctance to incorporate them into wider policy making and are still generally overlooked in public debate. Yet the UK's particular use of tax expenditures has considerable implications for the distribution of resources and the common wealth across society.

A second part of the text then follows exploring the linkages between the tax system and tax policy and specific aspects of social policy. In the first of these chapters, the ramifications of the different fiscal regimes for employment and self-employment are examined by Kevin Caraher and Enrico Reuter (Chapter 5). They discuss the implications of the many failures to establish consistency of fiscal treatment and possible ways forward.

The related subject of taxation and pensions is then scrutinised by Micheál Collins and Andy Lymer (Chapter 6). Few areas of social welfare have been changed so directly by tax policy in recent years, and the chapter sets these connectivities in perspective, highlighting the significant tax-advantaged position long-term savings in the form of pension provision has in the UK and its implications for a fairer society.

Steve McKay (Chapter 7) focuses on those of working age and their children, where relevant, threading his way through the broad field of tax, benefits and household income. Revisiting a central issue of the 1980 volume, he examines the implications of the interactions between taxes and benefits and the challenges arising from the increasing reliance on means-testing and the erosion of the contributory principle.

Sally Ruane (Chapter 8) considers the very different ways in which health services and social care are funded, helping to maintain a division between the two that successive governments have promised to tackle. As critically, she also engages with the broader question of how taxation might contribute to reducing the health gap across society.

In Chapter 9, on homes, housing and taxation, James Gregory, Andy Lymer and Carlene Wynter examine the changes in tax treatment of different housing tenures over time, consider the continuing effects of fiscal preference for owner-occupation on the widely accepted goal of achieving decent homes for all and offer possible reform options.

Karen Rowlingson's examination of wealth taxation (Chapter 10) spells out the persisting preferential taxation of certain forms of wealth compared to employment, the deepening of this gulf and the extent of mythmaking that results in sustained opposition to change. She considers how this, and other barriers, might be challenged to enable fiscal measures to tackle the effects of increased wealth inequalities.

In Chapter 11, Susan Himmelweit draws particularly on a gender responsive budgeting approach to reveal how gender inequalities are implicitly absorbed and maintained within taxation and sets out the importance of concentrating on how taxation interacts with other policies to bring about change.

Michael Orton's analysis of local taxes (Chapter 12) uncovers the interconnections between taxation and social policy at a local level and the inequities it can give rise to while also pointing to the remarkable persistence of problems and reform proposals over time.

On a different front, in considering corporate taxation and corporate welfare, Kevin Farnsworth (Chapter 13) reveals the extent to which tax policy discussion of social problems and available resources fails to take account of the significant fiscal subsidies to businesses, especially transnational corporations, and the ways in which these can shape the wider social environment.

Finally, looking at an issue that was only beginning to gain attention in 1980, the climate crisis and taxation, Paul Bridgen and Milena Büchs (Chapter 14) expose the generally ad hoc and unconnected development of different environmental taxes in the UK. Their own analyses demonstrate the distributional impact of these measures before they consider how a more systematic and effective response can be developed.

In differing ways, each chapter of the book unveils the importance of cross-cutting analyses bringing together disparate debates and taking account of the full range of society's resources, including that forming part of the hidden, little scrutinised and discussed wiring of taxation. Reflecting the limitations both of available data and political debate, this has involved new research, re-examining existing sources and highlighting their flaws and omissions, particularly relating to gender and ethnicity.

There are, of course, many other areas where tax and social policy interact that could have provided the basis for additional chapters. However, it is hoped the areas chosen for this text will at least stimulate debate in these key social policy areas.

This text's motivation of stimulating debate is picked up in the conclusion (Chapter 15), which discusses the main issues raised by the chapters and the effects of not taking a wider view of taxation. Here we also consider the key themes running throughout the book and the challenges these set for the development of better-integrated tax and social policy planning, especially in a context in which tax is so often simply held to be a burden.

References

Atkinson, A.B. (1972) 'Income maintenance and income taxation', *Journal of Social Policy*, 1(2): 135–48.

Bradshaw, J. (ed) (2019) *Let's Talk about Tax*, London: CPAG.

Byrne, D. and Ruane, S. (2017) *Paying for the Welfare State in the 21st Century: Tax and Spending in Post-industrial Societies*, Bristol: Policy Press.

Hills, J. (1988) *Changing Tax*, London: CPAG.

Hills, J. (2015) *Good Times, Bad Times*, Bristol: Policy Press.

Ruane, S., Collins, M. and Sinfield, A. (eds) (2020) 'Themed section: taxation and social policy', *Social Policy and Society*, 19(3): 431–520.

Sandford, C., Pond, C. and Walker, R. (eds) (1980) *Taxation and Social Policy*, London: Heinemann.

Titmuss, R. (1958) 'The social divisions of welfare: some reflections on the search for equity', in *Essays on 'the Welfare State'*, London: Allen & Unwin, pp 34–55.

Titmuss, R. (1962) *Income Distribution and Social Change*, London: Allen & Unwin.

2

Fiscal and social policy: two sides of the same coin

Chris Pond

The persistent lack of co-ordinated policy

There has been no shortage of public and policy debate about both taxation policy and social policy in recent decades. The vacuum has been in bringing these two together. Both economic efficiency and fairness have suffered from this absence of coordinated policy development, reducing the ability of even those governments that wished to do so to challenge rising inequality. Is there a way forward in some of the radical proposals for merging the two systems? Has the COVID-19 pandemic, requiring unprecedented levels of public support for jobs and incomes, changed attitudes in such a way as to make such radical reforms more likely?

By the time of the first volume of *Taxation and Social Policy* (Sandford et al, 1980), the interaction between taxes and benefits had been the subject of policy debate for some years. The Right had been keen to explore integration of tax and social security through some form of negative income tax or tax credits (as proposed by the Conservative government of 1972), while some on the Left had highlighted the similarity between social security and 'tax expenditures' (Sinfield, 1978; also Chapter 4). But there was still considerable scepticism in official circles about the parallels between the two systems.

When two of the first volume's editors (Robert Walker and I) were teaching economics at the Civil Service College (now National School of Government), we brought together officials from the Treasury and Inland Revenue with those from 'spending departments', including the (then) Department of Social Security. We wanted to explore with them how the two sides of fiscal policy might be considered together. The discussions, amid the rhododendrons of Sunningdale, were to help us shape our thoughts for the forthcoming volume.

We soon discovered that this was the first time many of these officials had met, let alone worked together, and the suggestion that tax allowances and reliefs might perform similar functions to social security benefits was met with disdain by many of the senior civil servants present. That some of the better-off might be in receipt of state support via such reliefs was considered a somewhat offensive idea.

Such attitudes spurred us on to explore further the ways in which the two wings of fiscal policy performed similar functions, albeit in different ways and with different levels of generosity. We sought out Cedric Sandford, whose valuable *Social Economics* (Sandford, 1977) explored the interaction between economics and social policy. He had been a member of the Meade Committee with its highly influential report, 'The structure and reform of direct taxation' (Meade, 1978). This highlighted the shortcomings of the existing direct tax and benefits system and proposed some radical reforms, especially of the taxation of income and wealth. Many of its ideas found their way into *Taxation and Social Policy*.

Between the three of us, we identified those who were best equipped to explore the ways that the two wings of fiscal policy interacted in several different areas of government activity – housing, health, transport, pensions and the family.

Fiscal policy comes under the spotlight

The potential to use the tax system to deliver social welfare to the poorest had long been of interest, particularly among Conservative policy makers. Free-market think tanks, such as the Institute of Economic Affairs (IEA), had promoted the idea of a negative income tax for some years (IEA, 1970). The delivery of welfare through 'negative taxes' to those below a poverty line would be mirrored by the withdrawal of income through 'positive taxes' for those above the line.

The concept of negative income taxes was built on the selectivist principle that help should be concentrated on the poorest, with benefits withdrawn rapidly as income rises. Hence most models of negative income tax included high marginal tax/withdrawal rates.[1] A more universalist approach to integration saw the introduction in 1977 of Child Benefit, bringing together child tax allowances and a cash benefit – Family Allowance – into a single cash payment.

The proposal to introduce Child Benefit would have been abandoned had Malcolm Wicks (a civil servant and later MP for Croydon and Minister for Pensions) not leaked the contents of Cabinet minutes discussing the plan to scupper it, passing these to Frank Field, then Director of the Child Poverty Action Group (later also a Labour MP and Department of Work and Pensions [DWP] Minister). Although I had been Malcolm's colleague at the Civil Service College and later at DWP and had written a book on taxation jointly with Frank Field, such was the discretion of both that I never found out who had been the source of the leak until Malcolm's memoirs were published posthumously. Nor, fortunately, did the official inquiry into the leak (Wicks, 2014).

Aside from these limited but important initiatives, the wider interaction between the two wings of fiscal welfare remained unexplored. The original edition of *Taxation and Social Policy* found its way into a world in which this was a neglected corner of public policy.

However, a period of increased scrutiny of fiscal policy was to follow. The Institute for Fiscal Studies (IFS), which hosted the Meade Report (1978) and the later Mirrlees one (Mirrlees et al, 2010), had grown in size and influence in the decades that followed with its journal, briefing and Green Budgets. An array of economic policy think tanks such as the Centre for Policy Studies and the Adam Smith Institute joined the IEA on the Right.

Parliament was also beginning to increase scrutiny of taxation. The Joint (Lords and Commons) Tax Rewrite Select Committee (charged with scrutinising the letter of tax legislation) replaced the Joint Select Committee on Tax Simplification (of which the present author was a member), whose responsibilities were subsumed in 2010 into the Office of Tax Simplification, an official advisory body, as part of the Treasury but still stated to be independent until 2023 when it ceased to exist.

These bodies were not charged with making tax policy but only with advising on the legislative presentation of that policy. Only much later did other parliamentary select committees, nourished by the output of the fiscal think tanks, become more vociferous. The Public Accounts Committee (PAC), the Social Security Committee, later Work and Pensions Committee, and the Treasury Select Committee of the House of Commons began to scrutinise every Budget and more aspects of welfare policy. The PAC, in particular, began scrutinising the activities of government departments, following the 'taxpayer pound' with an often-ruthless tenacity against government resistance. It paid particular attention to what it perceived as HMRC's lack of motivation in closing the 'tax gap' (Hodge, 2016).

The shifting burden of taxation

The past 40 years have therefore seen increased, but generally spasmodic, scrutiny of the two wings of fiscal policy. There has been much change to scrutinise. *Taxation and Social Policy* struggled to life during the final years of the Labour Callaghan administration (1974–79). The Conservative governments of Margaret Thatcher and John Major then held power for the following 18 years and shifted the balance decisively from direct to indirect taxation while implementing welfare changes that contributed to rising inequality and poverty.

The structure of taxation, welfare provision and public spending changed significantly over the decades that followed, with consequent shifts in the distributional impact, but the overall level of tax receipts has changed relatively little as a proportion of the nation's income. When the original volume of *Taxation and Social Policy* was published in 1980, total UK tax receipts accounted for 31.2 per cent of gross domestic product (GDP), compared with 33.4 per cent in 2019/20 (before the impact of the COVID-19 pandemic). In between, it had fallen rapidly in the Thatcher/Major years, to 28.4 per cent in 1992/93, remaining fairly stable during the Blair/Brown years but rising back to 34 per cent during the Coalition and May governments of 2010–19. The Office for Budget Responsibility stated that taken together with previously announced changes, the overall tax burden would rise to 36.3 per cent of GDP in 2026/27, its highest level since the 1940s (OBR, 2022).

However, this apparent stability in the overall level of tax receipts concealed significant changes in the make-up of taxation. Income tax accounted for about a third of all tax revenue in 1980, falling to a quarter a decade later as a result of the sharp reductions in direct taxes under Margaret Thatcher (1979–90) and then rising again during the 1990s but stabilising through the first decade of this century.

In contrast, National Insurance contributions (NICs) – essentially another tax on earnings – have been creeping up over time from around 17 per cent of tax revenue in the early 2000s to around 20 per cent today. The balance between income tax and NICs matters because there are some notable forms of income that are not subject to NICs, including some investment income, pension income and income earned above the state pension age (IFS, 2021).

This significant rise in NICs took another twist during the government of Boris Johnson (2019–22) due to the introduction of an additional 1.25 per cent surcharge ostensibly to pay for the backlog in NHS funding and, in due course, to contribute to funding of social care. It fell more heavily on those of working age than on the likely beneficiaries mainly in retirement (Adam, 2021) but was cancelled in the September 2022 tax changes and not restored since. We will have more to say about the impact of this on generational inequality later in this chapter.

However, IFS reports that the biggest change over the past 40 years has come from changes in taxes on spending. Revenue raised from value added tax (VAT) doubled as a proportion of the total between 1978–79 and 2021, bringing in 18 per cent of total tax revenue in the later year (IFS, 2021).

These changes in the structure of taxation, within the relatively stable envelope of overall tax receipts, were reflected in the changing distributional impact:

> Back in 1977, the composition of taxation was relatively equal across the income distribution (partly reflecting lower income inequality). But by 1997 the taxes that were most important for the poorest were very different from those for the richest. Among the lowest income decile, VAT and tobacco/alcohol/betting duties were 47 per cent of total taxes, with income tax just 7 per cent; whereas in the top decile

income tax accounted for 56 per cent, and those consumption taxes only 17 per cent. (Corlett, 2019, p 24)

There had been much interest in distributional issues during the 1970s, reflected in the establishment in 1974 by the Labour government of the Royal Commission on the Distribution of Income and Wealth, chaired by Lord Diamond. The commission generated a mass of data, much of it new, detailing the extent of inequality and the changes that had occurred in the post-war period. While this exposed the considerable extent of inequality that persisted, despite the extension of the post-war welfare state in the preceding decades, it was also cited by conservative commentators as evidence that equality had progressed too far, stifling incentive and innovation (Kelsey, 2018).

One of the earliest acts of the incoming Conservative government in 1979 was to abolish the commission, reflecting changing public policy priorities with respect to distributional issues. The Thatcher/Major years that immediately followed the publication of *Taxation and Social Policy* were characterised by a significant shift in the incidence of taxation from the highest- to the lowest-income groups, while social security policy – described as 'welfare reform' – consisted of restrictions in access to benefits through additional conditionality requirements together with reductions in the value of some benefits.

These Conservative governments believed that using fiscal policy as an instrument of redistribution stifled incentives and wealth creation. Adapting the 'trickle-down' rhetoric popular in the United States at the time, they argued that increased incentives for the better-off would – in the fullness of time – enhance the wellbeing of poorer sections of society as well. Inequality was perceived to be the driving force of economic enterprise and vitality. The economic stimulus it generated would act as 'the tide that would lift all boats'. The proponents of this belief failed to notice that many of the 'boats' were waterlogged by the backwash from the power craft of the rich (Vine, 2016).

Inequality rose faster in the UK during this period than in any other major industrialised country. In the year that Margaret Thatcher became prime minister, the richest tenth of households' disposable income was 3.1 times that of the poorest tenth. By the time she left office in 1990, it had increased to 4.4 times, falling slightly during the subsequent period of office of John Major (Belfield et al, 2016, p 25).

The top marginal tax rate was reduced from 83p in the £ on earned income to just 60p in the first Budget of the Thatcher administration, and to 40p in 1988. The (unearned) 'investment income surcharge' of 15p in the £ (added to the highest marginal rates) was abolished in 1985, so the top rate of tax on the highest investment incomes fell from 98p in the £ to 60p and then 40p.

Meanwhile, the marginal rates at the lower end of the income distribution were increased during the period of Thatcher's premiership (1979 to 1990), both by removing the reduced rate of tax and increasing NICs. The starting rate of tax of 25p in the £ was abolished in the 1980 Budget, meaning the marginal rate at the bottom of the income tax scale increased to 30p. Meanwhile, basic employee NIC rates increased in steps from 6.5p in 1979/80 to 9p in the £ in 1983/84. This increase in marginal tax rates on the lowest incomes further exacerbated the increase in effective (average) rates created by declines in the real value of tax thresholds (IFS, 2005).

Inequality worsened even further after this as a result not only of fiscal changes but of stagnation in the growth of real wages, while the 'uber rich' enjoyed stratospheric increases in their wealth. It is 'the Haves and the Have Yachts' said Rachel Johnson, the sister of a later prime minister (Johnson, 2007). As Sarah Vine, then wife of the later Conservative Secretary of State for Levelling Up, Michael Gove, wrote in *The Times*:

> In Britain, the economic circumstances are even more conducive to such a vast gap opening up between what are already, by most people's standards, vast fortunes. Not only is London the undisputed centre of the world's markets, it also has a cultural climate that is most congenial towards wealth, and in particular multicultural wealth. Perhaps most importantly, Britain has one of the most business-friendly tax environments on the planet, exemplified by the non-domicile (or 'non-dom') tax laws. In simple terms, these allow wealthy foreign nationals to hold their main liquid assets in tax-free offshore environments while operating freely within the UK – largely untroubled by the Exchequer (the same is not true of British nationals). (Vine, 2016)

The Deaton Review of inequality reported in 2022 that the 'top 1% of adults received 15% of fiscal income in 2018–19. This is more than flows to the bottom 55% of adults combined, and is an increase from the 6% income share flowing to the top 1% in 1980' (IFS, 2022).

The evolution of tax credits

Despite the change in 1988 of the means-tested Family Income Supplement to Family Credit, largely an exercise in rebranding rather than replacement, interest in the interaction between the two wings of fiscal policy diminished during the 1980s. There was certainly little interest in government in the concept that tax allowances and reliefs might form an element of welfare, albeit for the better-off, whose wellbeing was to be nurtured as the driver of national prosperity. However, interest in the link between taxation and social policy began to re-emerge outside government (Hills, 1988; Ruane et al, 2020).

One of the key members of the Meade Committee in its early deliberations and of the Royal Commission on the Distribution of Income and Wealth in its later years was the formidable A.B. Atkinson, who continued to drive the academic and policy debate on inequality through some 24 books and 350 research papers. Towards the end of the 1980s, he chaired the Fabian Society's Taxation Review Committee (Atkinson, 1990). A decade later, the Fabian Society established their Commission on Taxation and Citizenship (2000).

Such academic thinking undoubtedly influenced the development of Opposition policy leading up to the 1997 General Election. The Labour governments of the 1960s and 1970s had seen taxation as the main tool for reducing inequalities of income and wealth. However, their emphasis on marginal tax rates (rising to 83p in the £ on earned and 98p on unearned income), while nominally fiercely progressive, was less so in effect, largely because of their neglect of the impact of tax expenditures. Despite apparently eye-watering levels of marginal tax rates, the richest tenth of households paid no more than a third of their income in direct taxes. The regressive distributional effects of tax allowances and reliefs significantly reduced the average (effective) tax rates on the better-off far more than those affecting lower-income groups (Pond, 1980).

The Blair/Brown governments married fiscal policy with an approach of direct market intervention, including the national minimum wage, promotion of employment, investment in education and childcare provision. The approach was to address the underlying causes of inequality rather than using fiscal means to adjust for the symptoms after the event. Fiscal measures were used to supplement the incomes of non-market participants – the elderly, children and those with disabilities – but, to the extent that these were directed at the working-age population, the focus was on enhancing incentives and rewards from participation in the labour market (Pond and Cowburn, 1999).

In 1999, Family Credit was replaced by the substantially more generous Working Families' Tax Credit, which reduced the taper from 70 per cent to 55 per cent and introduced a Childcare Credit of 70 per cent of actual childcare costs up to £150 per week. In 2003, two new tax credits replaced this. Child Tax Credit effectively merged several parts of the existing tax and benefit system that support families with children. Separately, the Working Tax Credit was intended to support adults with or without children in low-paid work, as well as providing subsidies for certain childcare expenditure for some working parents (Brewer, 2003).

The increased generosity of the new tax credits for families and pensioners, pioneered by the then Chancellor Gordon Brown, significantly reducing the scale of child and pensioner poverty, also represented the first real attempt to integrate the tax and benefits systems since the creation of Child Benefit in the late 1970s (Millar, 2003).

In 2005, the Inland Revenue, traditionally the home of both direct tax collection and policy, was subsumed, along with Her Majesty's Customs and Excise, into the new Her Majesty's Revenue and Customs (HMRC). HMRC was essentially operational, administering both direct and indirect tax collection, together with the national minimum wage and major elements of welfare provision such as the tax credits. It was stripped of responsibility for tax policy, most of which moved to the Treasury. New Labour's ambitions for a tax system that combined fairness with efficiency required expertise to be concentrated in a single institution. As Tuck et al pointed out:

> New Labour had big ambitions for the tax system centred on this central value of efficiency and its enhancement to enhance fairness, something that was thought to require expertise to be concentrated in a single institution. All of the taxes needed attention and new ones had to be introduced, admittedly a process begun under the Conservatives before 1997. High marginal rates of income tax for those on low incomes needed to be mitigated. All of this involved a blurring of the boundaries between tax and social security, a blurring that was quite deliberate. The idea was that if a wider range of people could conceivably be both potential income taxpayers and benefits claimants, the social stigma associated with welfare might be reduced, along with popular opposition to greater generosity towards claimants. (Tuck et al, 2019, p 9)

The Working Tax Credit was paid by employers, with the self-employed being paid direct by the Inland Revenue. While the merging of the different tax collection departments had merits, particularly in cost savings, it carried with it a significant disadvantage, which revealed itself with the introduction of the new system of tax credits. The IFS Mirrlees Review explained that the tax credits

> based entitlements on circumstances in the current year, like income tax. It was intended to be responsive, with claimants encouraged (and, in some cases, obliged) to notify HMRC when their circumstances changed. But since claimants did not usually inform HMRC of changes in circumstances as they happened, provisional payments were based on past information, generating underpayments and overpayments to low-income families on a large scale. When actual circumstances had

been confirmed, typically at the end of the year, these underpayments and overpayments were corrected. The recovery of overpayments in particular gave rise to widespread discontent and in many ways undermined the whole tax credit system, providing a salutary warning of the dangers of relying on an 'approximate now, reconcile later' approach to support for low-income families. (Mirrlees et al, 2011, pp 140–1)

Families whose circumstances had changed found themselves deemed to have been overpaid and liable to repay or have subsequent payments reduced, sometimes by quite substantial sums. The failure was to realise that people's circumstances and incomes, especially those in low-paid jobs, were often in a constant state of flux, changing almost weekly, with the result that large numbers were caught in an overpayment trap.

Fiscal policy in the age of austerity

The Coalition/Conservative administrations that followed in 2010 adapted the tax credit approach by introducing Universal Credit, an integrated working-age credit of a basic allowance with additional elements for children, disability, housing and caring. It replaced Working Tax Credit, Child Tax Credit, Housing Benefit, Income Support, income-based Jobseeker's Allowance and income-related Employment and Support Allowance. The Mirrlees Review had advocated such integration, citing numerous proposals by policy makers and commentators in the previous few years (Mirrlees et al, 2011, p 136). The principle of Universal Credit was generally but not universally well received as a sensible merging of several benefits into one.

However, Universal Credit, introduced in the era of austerity following the financial crisis of 2008/9, was further undermined by Treasury insistence that this should generate savings in expenditure, compromising the promise issued at its introduction that no-one making the transition from legacy benefits to Universal Credit would be worse off.

Austerity was delivered overwhelmingly through spending cuts rather than tax rises. Indeed, the government's target was to balance the fiscal budget by implementing cuts in spending and tax increases in a ratio of 80:20 – four times as much saving was to be achieved through spending cuts as through tax rises. In fact, IFS calculated that, by 2013, the ratio had been 85:15, meaning that taxes had increased by £6 billion less – and spending had been cut by £6 billion more – than the government's own target (IFS, 2013).

The tax rises implemented through the austerity programme of the Coalition government (2010–15), driven by Chancellor George Osborne, were achieved by withdrawing or reducing some tax expenditures in the form of reliefs and allowances, rather than through increasing tax rates.

What remained of tax reliefs for homeowners, largely phased out during the Thatcher/Major years, were further curtailed, as were those for the growing number of Buy to Let landlords and pensioners. Child Benefit was effectively confiscated for those paying tax at the higher rates. Osborne also adopted a version of the 'vanishing exemptions' mentioned in Sandford et al (1980) and previously promoted by Field et al (1977). Standard tax allowances, exempting the first tranche of income, were of greatest value to those with the highest marginal tax rates, who were able to exempt a larger proportion of their income from tax altogether. The idea of vanishing exemptions was that these would diminish in value the higher the taxpayer was on the income scale.

With respect to household incomes, therefore, the Coalition did much to restrict social welfare, and less so fiscal welfare, as part of the austerity regime justified as a means of repairing the damage to the public finances generated by the 2008/9 financial crash. However, fewer restrictions were imposed with regard to corporate tax reliefs and exemptions (Hodge, 2016).

Horizontal versus vertical inequalities

The austerity economics of the Coalition and May administrations, following the 2008/9 downturn, undoubtedly widened income, gender and generational disparities. The first edition of *Taxation and Social Policy* principally focused on inequalities of income and wealth – aspects of the vertical distribution of resources. However, greater recognition of gender inequalities has led to more attention to gender differences in taxation, and there is also a growing awareness of racial disparities, especially following the increased prominence of the Black Lives Matter movement. The differential impact of fiscal policy on different groups is a product of their different circumstances and patterns of employment, household composition and income – indirect discrimination, perhaps, but powerful nevertheless. Unless tax and welfare policies acknowledge these differences, that differential impact will inevitably be negative (see Chapter 11).

Generational disparity has also become increasingly prominent. In the first edition, we pointed out that public spending on health and education, in particular, could have a regressive effect, mainly benefitting the higher socio-economic groups who use these services most. We focused less on the intergenerational aspects of this disparity, vividly highlighted by former Conservative Cabinet Minister (Lord) David Willetts and the Resolution Foundation, which he chairs (Willetts, 2011; Resolution Foundation, 2018). While post-war 'Baby-Boomers' benefitted most from free education, a comparatively well-funded health service, full employment, generous private pension provision and an almost permanently buoyant housing market, younger generations have been disadvantaged in all these respects.

The policy shift to more stress on individual rather than collective provision and more responsibility on the individual than on the state or commercial provision that Thatcher began has exacerbated this trend (Hills, 2015).

Some of the changes in the fiscal context resulting from the greater devolution of tax and other financial powers within the UK have been more substantial for Scotland and have led to significant variations in Wales and Northern Ireland. These are examined in Chapter 3 and will not be covered here.

The way forward: Universal Basic Income?

The concept that the state should provide a basic subsistence income for every citizen, regardless of circumstances, is not new. Over time, it has emerged under different guises as a Basic Income, Citizen's Income, Social Credit, National Dividend, Demogrant, Negative Income Tax or Guaranteed Minimum Income (Floyd, 2022).

Strictly, the last two in the list – Negative Income Tax and Guaranteed Minimum Income – are not Universal Basic Income (UBI) but forms of means-tested top-ups to other income. UBI, by contrast, would represent a universal grant to every individual or household. It would incorporate all personal tax allowances and all benefits and tax credits, with tax payable from the first pound of income. In that respect, it would be the ultimate merging of the tax and benefit systems.

Floyd reminds us that as long ago as 1797, Thomas Paine proposed a 'ground rent' of £15 be paid to every individual upon turning 21, followed by £10 every year after turning 50, payable to rich and poor alike. A century later, Henry George called for 'no taxes and a pension for everybody' via a public land fund. James Meade, the Nobel Prize-winning economist whose Committee on the Structure and Reform of Direct Taxation was referred to earlier, had proposed a 'social dividend' funded by income tax or corporate profits as long ago as 1935 (Meade, 1935).

While the idea of a Basic Income has meandered through the decades, a combination of circumstances has brought it back from the sidelines of public policy debate with pilots of various forms carried out and underway here and in other countries. The COVID-19 pandemic resulted in the suspension of normal work for millions, whose subsistence was guaranteed for a period by the state; the pandemic also exacerbated the longer-term trend of increasing job and income insecurity. Once again, the development of artificial intelligence and robotics seemed to herald a time when traditional employment would no longer be an option for many, although the average time workers have been in their present jobs has not changed from 60 months in three decades (Bell, 2022).

These factors have once again ignited the debate about UBI. The Welsh government has begun trialling it for young people leaving care, the Scottish government has invested in the feasibility of pilots, and several English cities are keen to test it out. The Labour Party included a commitment to UBI trials in its 2019 manifesto, and the policy was subsequently adopted in the programmes of the other main opposition parties.

However, the Joseph Rowntree Foundation (JRF, 2021) remained unconvinced: the costs are high and the impact on child poverty limited. JRF concluded that, given the considerable costs of UBI, many if not most of the benefits could be accessed in other ways, through reform of the existing tax and benefit system to provide higher rates of benefit, less conditionality and a more progressive tax structure.

This less radical approach may also be more easily digested by the British public. The latest edition of the British Social Attitudes Survey available at the time of writing in late 2022 concludes that, while the tendency for people to be more supportive of the provision of welfare for those of working age held steady during the pandemic, despite unprecedented government support, this view didn't become more popular: 'The only new shift of any note is some sign that slightly more people now regard Britain as an unequal society … Even so, the proportion who now feel that Britain is too unequal is far from being the highest it has been over the last four decades' (Curtice et al, 2021, p 2). The Deaton Review of inequality concluded that a 'large and stable majority of people, around 80%, say they are worried about inequalities. But concern about inequality does not translate into widespread support for redistributive policy, at least through the direct means of taxation and income transfers' (IFS, 2022). The hope in some quarters that the apparently unifying impact of the pandemic, following the divisive effects of Brexit, might result in a more egalitarian appetite among the public, opening the door to more radical reforms, seems to have been over-optimistic.

Conclusion: Where next?

Has debate or policy moved on since the first edition of *Taxation and Social Policy* four decades ago? Sadly, less than the authors of that volume might have hoped – or those of this volume might have liked. It is necessary to recognise how impervious to each other the different divisions of tax and social policy have continued to be.

In particular, and with few exceptions, the disciplines and professions concerned with taxes have proved very successful in treating and defending taxation as their own special subject, in part because of the financial rewards they derive from advising on it. While advice on individual and corporate tax planning is expensive, it is in plentiful supply. Advice on benefits is sparse, falling mainly on the shoulders of poorly resourced charities and local authorities. The same is true of access to other public services: witness the struggle that so many parents have in accessing support for children with special needs, patients in accessing primary care or young adults accessing training or apprenticeships.

This 'division of welfare' has been matched and assisted by the reluctance of HMRC and the Treasury to publish data on tax expenditures. In his 1980 concluding chapter, Sandford explicitly complained of this reluctance and noted that 'the harm of not allocating tax expenditures to programmes seems greater than any possible harm from so doing' (Sandford, 1980, p 231). The general degree of cooperation and coordination between the tax authorities in the Treasury and HMRC with the spending departments has remained very one-way, as noted throughout this book.

Margaret Hodge's memoir on her time as Chair of the PAC reinforces the point by documenting the ways in which her committee was obstructed in their attempts to investigate the work of fiscal administration (Hodge, 2016). She also highlights increasing concern with and revelation of the ways in which HMRC and the Treasury have routinely made use of professional tax accountants and lawyers to advise on legislation and practices that result in their being left more exposed to advice on tax planning and mitigation by the same firms that have frustrated attempts to control inequalities.

In the final section of the 1980 Conclusions chapter, Sandford called for a 'Royal Commission on Taxation and Social Policy' that could command the powers and resources to carry out a thorough review of the way in which the two wings of fiscal policy interact. Nearly 40 years since the Beveridge Report and some 25 since the Royal Commission on the Distribution of Income and Wealth, an assessment of the two together was long overdue, even then. The criticism that Royal Commissions and Committees of Inquiry 'take Minutes and last years' was not lost on Sandford. He recognised how often governments disregarded such commissions but nevertheless felt it could help to create the more open and public discussion that was needed to move forward.

Today, Royal Commissions have lost much of their glamour, but many other ways to open up discussion exist. Think tanks and research institutes such as the IFS with its Deaton Review, the Resolution Foundation and the Centre for Social Policy have begun to undertake or commission their own inquiries into the interaction between the different aspects of state fiscal policy and wider society, but much more needs to be done. The select committees of both Houses of Parliament and the devolved authorities, such as the PAC, the Treasury Select Committee or the Work and Pensions Committee, have increased powers to influence policy. The House of Lords Select Committee on Financial Exclusion registered little in public perception but achieved the appointment of two ministers of financial inclusion and the establishment of a Policy Forum on the matter (House of Lords, 2017).

Twenty-first-century governments have demonstrated that much can be achieved in increasing or reducing redistribution even without pulling hard on the levers of fiscal policy. The post-1997 Blair–Brown governments, as noted, married non-fiscal measures – the minimum wage, employment and investment in public services – with reform of taxes and benefits to reduce inequalities. The Coalition government that followed oversaw a long-term freeze in the level of real wages, alongside welfare and tax changes, resulting in a shift in the opposite direction. This was itself a prelude to steep and regressive increases in taxation and cuts in benefits as the second decade of that century ended.

However, if future governments are to satisfy the apparently increasing public appetite for a fairer, more productive and more prosperous economy, then fiscal policy must play its part. The failure to acknowledge and document the role that taxation, its tax expenditures and other arrangements play in shaping our economy and the distribution of its rewards within society will continue to cost us dearly. We hope that this volume does more than the first to raise awareness in public and policy debate of the need to take the impact of taxation on the individual and the wider society seriously – in all its aspects.

Postscript: October 2022

'Trickle-down' under Truss

The concept of 'trickle-down' economics, the much-criticised idea that increased incentives for the richest would, in the fullness of time, enhance the incomes of the poorest, was resurrected by the government of Liz Truss, which succeeded that of Boris Johnson in September 2022. While all previous governments, with the possible exception of that of Margaret Thatcher, expressed an aspiration to close the gap between rich and poor (while often doing the opposite), the Truss government was proudly inegalitarian. Soon after being appointed as prime minister, Truss asserted: "The economic debate for the past 20 years has been dominated by discussions about redistribution. And what has happened is, we have had relatively low growth … and that has been holding our country back" (BBC, Sunday with Laura Kuenssberg, 11 September 2022).

The new administration acted to scrap the cap on bankers' bonuses as part of its 'fiscal event' (so-called to avoid a legal requirement for budgets to be scrutinised by the Office for Budget Responsibility). Involving £45 billion of tax cuts – the biggest such reduction in 50 years – the benefits were strongly focused on higher-income households. The additional 45p rate of income tax, payable by those earning more than £150,000 a year (about 1.1 per cent of all adults or 600,000 people), was to have been scrapped, alongside associated cuts to dividend tax. Someone earning £200,000 gained £5,220 a year, with the gain rising to £55,220 for a £1 million earner. Those on £20,000 gained just £157, according to the Resolution Foundation (Bell et al, 2022). Under these plans, almost half (47 per cent) of the gains were to go to the richest 5 per cent of households, compared to 12 per cent for the entire poorer half. Meanwhile, the cost of the otherwise unfunded tax cuts, which caused panic in the markets, pushing down the value of sterling and pushing up interest rates, was to be funded by cuts in welfare benefits and public services. Ten days later the Chancellor, Kwasi Kwarteng, was forced to abandon the plan to abolish the 45p rate of tax and soon afterwards was dismissed and replaced by Jeremy Hunt. The Prime Minister, Liz Truss, herself resigned a few days later to be followed by Rishi Sunak

Further fiscal changes are briefly covered in the Editors' postscript at the end of Chapter 15.

Note

1   The marginal rate of tax is the tax payable on an additional £1 of income; the average rate of tax is the amount payable as a proportion of income of total income.

Further reading

- Hodge (2016) – an account of the misuse of public funds and millions lost in unpaid tax by the Chair of the PAC, both the oldest and the most powerful of the parliamentary select committees. Written by someone on the front line of politics for many decades, it provides invaluable insight into the way that tax policy operates in practice.
- Mirrlees et al (2011) – the final report from the IFS's Mirrlees Review, providing a thorough and forensic analysis of the workings of the UK tax system in the first decade of the 21st century, examining its incentive and distributional effects and setting out proposals for realistic reform. Chapter on the interaction of benefits and taxes is particularly relevant.
- Sandford et al (1980) – the original volume highlighting the interaction between the 'two wings' of fiscal policy, and a salutary reminder that there is still much to be done to develop policy that is coherent, taking account of the impact of both.

References

Adam, S. (2021) 'Pensioner families would provide ten times more of the revenue from an income tax rise than from a NICs rise', IFS Observation. Available from: https://policymogul.com/key-updates/18669/ifs-pensio ner-families-would-provide-ten-times-more-of-the-revenue-from-an-inc ome-tax-rise-than-from-a-nics-rise

Atkinson, A.B. (1990) 'Reform of direct taxation: report of the Fabian Taxation Review Committee', London: Fabian Society.

Belfield, C., Cribb, J., Hood, A. and Joyce, R. (2016) 'Living standards, poverty and inequality in the UK: 2016', London: Institute for Fiscal Studies.

Bell, T. (2022) 'Forget all you've heard about working life in modern Britain: it's wrong', *The Guardian*, 20 February.

Bell, T., Broome, M., Cominetti, N., Corlett, A., Fry, E. and Handscomb, K. et al (2022) 'Blowing the budget: assessing the implications of the September 2022 fiscal statement', London: Resolution Foundation.

Brewer, M. (2003) 'The new tax credits', Institute for Fiscal Studies, briefing note no 35.

Commission on Taxation and Citizenship (2000) *Paying for Progress: A New Politics of Tax for Public Spending*, London: Fabian Society.

Corlett, A. (2019) 'The shifting shape of UK tax: charting the changing size and shape of the UK tax system', Resolution Foundation, November.

Curtice J., Abrams, D. and Jessop, C. (2021) 'New values, new divides?', *British Social Attitudes 38*, London: NatCen Social Research.

Field, F., Meacher, M. and Pond, C. (1977) *To Him Who Hath: A Study of Poverty and Taxation*, Harmondsworth: Penguin.

Floyd, D. (2022) 'The long, weird history of Universal Basic Income – and why it's back', Investopedia, February. Available from: https://www.investopedia.com/news/history-of-universal-basic-income/

Hills, J. (1988) 'Changing tax: how the tax system works and how to change it', London: Child Poverty Action Group.

Hills, J. (2015) *Good Times, Bad Times*, Bristol: Policy Press.

Hodge, M. (2016) *Called to Account: How Corporate Bad Behaviour and Government Waste Combine to Cost us Millions*, London: Little, Brown.

House of Lords Select Committee on Financial Exclusion (2017) 'Tackling financial exclusion: a country that works for everyone?', HL paper 132, session 2016–17, 25 March.

Institute of Economic Affairs (1970) 'Policy for poverty', London: IEA.

IFS (Institute for Fiscal Studies) (2005) 'FiscalFacts2000: Current tax rates and past rates, 1973–2000', London: IFS.

IFS (2013) 'IFS Green Budget 2013', London: IFS.

IFS (2021) 'How have government revenues changed over time?', IFS TaxLab, Available from: https://ifs.org.uk/taxlab/taxlab-key-questions/how-have-government-revenues-changed-over-time

IFS (2022), 'Inequality/themes: the IFS Deaton Review', ifs.org.

Johnson, R. (2007) *Notting Hell*, London: Penguin.

JRF (Joseph Rowntree Foundation) (2021) 'Is Universal Basic Income a good idea?', JRF research report, 27 May. Available from: https://www.jrf.org.uk/report/universal-basic-income-good-idea

Kelsey, T. (2018) 'An unexpected cut: revisiting the Diamond Commission and assessing inequality in post-war Britain', London: Resolution Foundation.

Meade, J.E. (1935) 'Outline of an economic policy for a labour government', in Howson, S. (ed) *The Collected Papers of James Meade, Volume I: Employment and Inflation*, London: Unwin Hyman, 1988, pp 33–78.

Meade, J.E. (1978) *The Structure and Reform of Direct Taxation*, London: Allen & Unwin.

Millar, J. (ed) (2003) *Understanding Social Security: Issues for Policy and Practice*, Bristol: Policy Press.

Mirrlees, J., Adam, S., Besley, T., Blundell, R., Bond, S. and Chote, R. et al (2011) *Tax by Design*, London: IFS. Available from: www.ifs.org.uk/publications/mirrleesreview

OBR (Office for Budget Responsibility) (2022) 'Economic and fiscal outlook', March, CP 648.

Pond, C. (1980) 'Tax expenditures and fiscal welfare', in C. Sandford, C. Pond and R. Walker (eds) *Taxation and Social Policy*, London: Heinemann, pp 47–63.

Pond, C. and Cowburn, R. (1999) 'Welfare', in M. Linton, K. Raymond and A. Whitehead (eds) *Beyond 2002: Long Term Policies for Labour*, London: Profile Books, pp 235–55.

Resolution Foundation (2018) 'A new generational contract, final report of the Intergenerational Commission', London: Resolution Foundation.

Ruane, S., Collins, M.L. and Sinfield, A. (2020) 'The centrality of taxation to social policy', *Social Policy and Society*, 19(3): 437–53.

Sandford, C. (1977) *Social Economics*, London: Heinemann.

Sandford, C. (1980) 'Conclusions', in C. Sandford, C. Pond and R. Walker (eds) *Taxation and Social Policy*, London: Heinemann, pp 228–36.

Sinfield A. (1978) 'Analyses of the social division of welfare', *Journal of Social Policy*, 7(2): 129–56.

Tuck, P., de Cogan, D. and Snape, J. (2019) 'A tale of the merger between the Inland Revenue and HM Customs & Excise', in P. Harris and D. de Cogan (eds) *Studies in the History of Tax Law*, vol 9, Oxford: Hart Publishing, chapter 8.

Vine, S. (2016) 'The haves and have-yachts', *The Times*, 4 December.

Wicks, M. (2014) *My Life*, Leicester: Matador.

Willetts, D. (2011) *The Pinch: How the Baby Boomers Took Their Children's Future – and Why They Should Give It Back*, London: Atlantic Books.

3

Tax and the social policy landscape

Andy Lymer

Introduction

Taxation is an important feature of a modern democracy. It serves two key objectives that enable countries to operate effectively. First, it provides a key source of revenue to support government expenditure plans. Secondly, it is used as a 'lever' to deliver government policy as a tool to correct what may otherwise occur if left unchecked. It achieves this primarily by changing the prices of goods and services to motivate changes in the behaviour of taxpayers.

This chapter provides an overview of the UK's tax system, with a particular reference to its relationship with social policy. It reviews the tax system in its current form and provides some historical perspective to help understand the current system. It seeks to outline what a tax is, why tax is an important feature of a modern democracy and how it is administered for social benefit. It discusses what are known as the three 'tax bases' – the broad classifications under which taxes are created and operated. It will also discuss how tax policy is set and how taxes are administered in the UK – in general terms but also in terms of some of the key features of the policy-setting process and administration that have evolved over the 40 years since the book was published upon which this title looks to build (Sandford et al, 1980).

The UK is primarily used as the context for this chapter, but selected other international comparators are included with similar large, developed democracies to illustrate areas of commonality and key differences.

What is a tax?

All taxes have common features, namely they are 'a compulsory levy, imposed by a government or other tax raising body, on income, consumption, wealth or people, for which nothing directly is received in return' (Lymer and Oats, 2022, p 3). It is a required payment (a 'compulsory levy') of those captured by a tax jurisdiction (usually individual or corporate citizens of a country for which tax paying is one of the responsibilities of citizenship – but it can include non-citizens of a tax jurisdiction too for some taxes and in some circumstances) to pay sums to their government (or 'other tax-raising bodies' given this power to raise taxes is usually held by national, regional, local or sometimes supranational, government bodies, but can be given to other entities to manage on the behalf of one of these).

There is usually therefore the need for a legal basis for the powers to raise taxes and to raise them in a particular manner. This requires, ideally, clear legislation, supported by suitable enforcement processes and agreed upon procedures and rules to set out how these taxes will be computed and how they will be paid when due.

This last part of the definition makes clear that tax payments are unrequited (OECD 2021a) – that is, what is provided by a government in return for payment of tax is not normally directly in proportion to the payments made. In other transactions, goods or services are transferred in return for what both parties agree is a suitable payment, or the transaction would not usually occur. Taxes are different in this respect, as governments have the power to demand payment of these sums in return for citizenship rights, and this is key to their definition to differentiate a tax from other payments made to a government for the services it provides.

However, in practice this final element of the definition does have to be taken with some latitude. Some payments to a government can have features that are partly or potentially unrequited but that might lead to entitlement of a share of a government resource (such as a benefit) immediately, or at some future point in time. A good example of this is found in social security payment systems – in the UK called National Insurance contributions (NICs). These 'contributions' produce varying degrees of entitlement to current or future benefit – or may lead to no benefit at all in practice despite payments being made. Some payers may therefore receive back what they pay in, some more, some less, the point of the payment being to contribute towards the costs of national provision of services for the common good – not to buy 'insurance' for your own needs in the conventional sense, as the name may imply.

As such, these forms of payment to government may look and feel like a tax (often compulsory payments charged on an income base in practice) but do produce something directly in return for at least some payers. Many nevertheless consider it suitable to classify these payments as a tax for the purposes of most analyses – even if politically this may not be deemed to be ideal practice where a distinction can be used to serve political ends (see Chapter 5 for more on this debate in the UK).

Why do we tax?

At the most basic level, governments tax to raise revenue to support their spending plans. A clear link is often made between the ability to raise tax and the spending desires of a government. As such, it is typically for us to see tax demands changing in line with a government's spending plans.

Politicians will typically make this link very explicit in seeking support for their policies.

There is, however, a line of argument that suggests that this link is not in reality necessary – at least for countries, such as the UK, that print their own currency. According to what is known as modern monetary theory (MMT), where a government controls the money supply of a country, it can, according to this theory, print and issue as much money as it wants into its economy in support of its plans. This is only constrained in practice by the need to control the inflation that printing too much money could create. This ability to control the economy via the money supply has been a key tool for governments for a long time – and occasionally becomes a more visible policy tool, such as in response to the financial crisis from 2007 onwards, where money was printed to stop the economy imploding following a significant banking crisis.

Under such instances, tax can be viewed as the mechanism by which money is returned to the supplier of money, usually the national bank, to cancel out the debt created by its printing – and as such the link between tax raising and spending may be in fact less direct than is often explained politically or even in many introductory economics courses.[1]

Either way you wish to see this relationship between tax and government spending, there is a clear link between tax-raising activity and a government's plans to spend or to otherwise influence its economy in delivering its political objectives.

Link between taxation and government spending

Taxes form the context for much of the government spending that occurs in the UK – directly or via its role in repaying borrowing that has occurred to help fund the country in the past. They are not the only source of money for spending, however, and governments look to use other sources where these can be earned or generated. These include profits made from selling services to their citizens – something some countries do more of than others (for example, utility provision historically in the UK) or by directly owning and receiving income from the operation of businesses, either as a monopoly provider (for example, mineral extraction is a government-owned activity in many countries around the world) or in open market engagement as one of a number of competitors in a market.

How money raised by governments is spent is subject to regular review, and the various departments of the UK government are subject to a detailed process for determining their annual budgets (revenue and capital) each year – with a longer-term so-called 'Spending Review'[2] occurring less frequently (usually every two to four years). In the latter case, these provide opportunity for more in-depth consideration of the balance of government spending across its activities. The Spending Review's focus is on costs that can be planned longer in advance and forms 'Departmental Expenditure Limits' (DELs) that make up about half of all government spending each year. The less predictable spending, which changes on an annual basis, called 'Annually Managed Expenditure', makes up the other half. It is in this latter category that much social security-related spending sits.

The UK's Spending Reviews are government-led activity – Parliament has no direct legislative role in them. The latest Spending Review was held in the autumn of 2021 and set budgets for revenue and capital spending from 2022/23 for two years. Table 3.1 summarises the details of these plans.

This data shows, at a high level, that funding of issues related to social policy forms most of the planned spend. Health and social care, education and work and pension department costs alone amount to 50 per cent of the total departmental budgets in 2021 – and social policy-related costs will be incurred in other areas too, pushing this total to well over half of all government spending.

In the UK, very little spending is directly linked to a specific tax source (called 'hypothecated'), that is, where a tax revenue stream is directly linked to promises to spend on a specific area (although the proposed Health and Social Care Levy that was to have been introduced in April 2023 was going to do exactly that before it was scrapped by the Liz Truss government in September 2022) – but this is rare. There can be political expediency to do this – it helps politicians to sell taxation increases – but it is often not favoured by those who manage the process of developing tax policy as it can constrain future allocation of tax to spending needs.

Behavioural tool

Taxation forms part of the cost of engaging in many activities. This fact can be used by governments to change behaviours they wish to affect by either encouraging (by lowering taxation on a specific activity to lower costs or increase returns from doing it) or discouraging particular behaviour (by increasing taxes).

An example of this second key motivation for taxation can be seen in the way a government may seek to manage environmental damage from human activity. For example, applying taxes more heavily on non-renewable energy generation, such as using oil, gas or coal, relative to renewable generation, such as using wind, wave or water, can help to deliver more demand for the then relatively cheaper provision (see Chapter 14).

That taxes can be used as a behaviour-influencing 'lever' for a government, as well as a source for revenue, highlights the challenges involved in the tax system design process. Changing taxes does not just change revenues yielded but can change how people may act, for example changing their buying

Table 3.1: Selected departmental budgets: total DEL (TDEL) excluding depreciation

£ billion (current prices)				Average annual real terms growth (%)
	Outturn 2020–21	Baseline 2021–22	Plans 2024–25	2021–22 to 2024–25
Health and Social Care	144.9	156.4	188.6	4.10
Education	71.5	76.3	86.7	2.00
Home Office	13.6	14.6	16.5	1.90
Law Officers' Departments	0.6	0.7	0.8	2.10
Defence	42.4	46	48.6	−0.40
Foreign, Commonwealth and Development Office	12.5	9.7	11.8	4.40
DLUHC Local Government	5.3	8.5	12.8	9.40
DLUHC Levelling up, Housing and Communities	11.4	9.7	8.9	4.10
Levelling Up Fund	–	0.2	1.4	–
Transport	20.5	23.2	26.2	1.90
Business, Energy and Industrial Strategy	20.9	17.9	23.8	7.50
Environment, Food and Rural Affairs	5	5.6	7	5.30
Work and Pensions	6	5.9	7.2	4.40
HM Revenue and Customs	4.7	4.8	5.2	0.00
Scotland	35.5	36.7	41.8	2.40
Wales	15.8	15.9	18.2	2.60
Northern Ireland	13.6	13.4	15.2	2.20
Others	18.3	38.1	44.9	
TDEL ex depreciation and ringfenced COVID-19 funding	*442.5*	*483.6*	*565.6*	*3.00*
Ringfenced COVID-19 funding	127	70.3	–	
TDEL ex depreciation including ringfenced COVID-19 funding	*569.5*	*553.9*	*565.6*	

Source: HM Treasury (2021, p 182, table E2)

behaviours. When designing tax policy, officials therefore need to attempt to estimate the revenue impacts a change will create but also how taxpayers may react and change their behaviour.

An 'Impact Assessment' report is often produced alongside enacted tax policy changes that attempts to show what assessment of change has been estimated by the government. While they are rarely followed up to confirm if this estimate proved accurate with hindsight, it has become a welcome feature of the UK tax system to at least attempt this and make this assessment public.

However, making these assessments accurately is not an exact science, as how people will react to tax changes is notoriously difficult to predict. A good example of this can be seen in the way financial markets reacted to the significant changes to taxation (significant unfunded cuts for many, particularly those arguably more able to pay the taxes) implemented by the Truss government in September 2022 in the name of driving growth as their proposed solution to the cost-of-living crisis. Within several days of the cuts being announced, there were very adverse reactions to these changes. This created a situation where sterling dropped to its lowest ever rate against the US dollar, which in turn had huge impacts on things like the cost of mortgages and of imports, potentially fuelling cost-of-living increases further – a very significant reaction to a tax change showing a severe lack of confidence in the government's plans and necessitating the Bank of England to intervene in the market to stop a further slide in the value of sterling occurring. While this specific situation was short-lived and corrected (largely) with confidence returning to the markets following a further change in UK political leadership, this is a good example of how difficult forming and delivering effective tax policy can be.

Other motivations for taxation

In addition to raising revenue and influencing behaviour, other objectives for taxing are likely to be in evidence. Most prominent among these is the role of government in reducing inequity in society that is not corrected naturally by the market.

At its most basic, levying taxes on one part of society to provide funds to support another part creates a redistribution of wealth that may not otherwise occur. Careful use of taxes for this purpose is called for, however, as this can sometimes be done in more sophisticated ways through use of other aspects of the tax or benefits system. In the former case, selectively not collecting taxes that might otherwise be due (the so-called 'tax expenditure' system – see Chapter 4) can be used to improve redistributive effects. The application, in the latter case, of the benefits system could be even more suitable for better targeting of any redistributive aim. The suitable balance between using the tax and the benefits systems for redistribution and inequality addressing aims has long been a debate in the UK.

Administering the tax system

The effective administration of the tax system requires careful design to enable taxes to be collected in ways that optimise the costs of collection (so the most money possible can go to the spending purposes for which the taxes were collected) and maximise the revenue collected while not adversely changing behaviours in unexpected ways. As such, several key administrative principles underpin all tax systems designed to achieve these goals – that of the direct versus indirect nature of the design of a tax, how to share the 'burden' of paying taxes around various taxpayers, and more general 'good design' characteristics that a well-constructed tax or tax system should exhibit.

Direct versus indirect

The design of all taxes can be said to fall into one of two types – those applied on taxpayers directly and those that are applied indirectly. Neither is implicitly better than the other, but the choice of which to use in designing the different aspects of your tax system does create implications for how the tax is constructed and applied to taxpayers.

In a direct tax design, the taxpayer has a direct responsibility to pay their tax obligations to the government. These may be handled by third parties on their behalf (for example, an employer withholding taxes due on wages via a 'Pay-as-You-Earn' system), but the obligation to pay the tax due remains with the taxpayer.

It is typically the case that income and capital taxes are administered as direct taxes. For example, for personal income taxes a taxpayer will be required to file an annual tax return in many countries to summarise their different sources of income and compute any taxes due on that income.

This has some advantages over indirect taxes in that the government is given direct access to data on its taxpayers; however, this can make it more costly to administer, as the government must maintain that link to all taxpayers in its jurisdiction to ensure they file their returns and pay the taxes due.

Indirect taxes are those that are administered via a third party that is given the legal responsibility to collect the taxes due from the taxpayer on behalf of a government. These third parties then periodically pay the collected sums over to the relevant tax authority. As such, the taxes are collected indirectly, and no direct link is required between the government and the taxpayer.

The indirect approach can be a more cost-effective approach to collecting taxes from a government's perspective, as their costs of managing this process is reduced where they are only dealing with those who have collected the taxes on their behalf (usually fewer in number than the taxpayers themselves). However, it is a matter of debate as to whether costs of collection are truly 'cheaper' overall for society, as some costs are then incurred by those who are (unpaid) tax collectors on the government's behalf.

Indirect administration of taxes is often the approach used for the design of consumption taxes – as we see in the operation of value added tax (VAT) in the UK. Similarly, excise duties are applied 'up stream' in a production process of a good and passed on in the price to the final consumer – so again an indirect design is being used.

Progressivity versus regressivity versus proportionality

The determination of the spread of the tax 'burden' is a key feature of how tax systems are designed and administered. Three broad metrics can be applied to assess how this burden falls on taxpayers. Is the tax proportional, progressive or regressive in how the tax burden is shared between the taxpayers?

Proportional taxes are applied constantly across a tax base. For example, all taxpayers on the same income would pay the same percentage of tax on that income.

At one level, an initial analysis might suggest this should be a favoured approach to be 'fair'. However, this takes no account of how able to pay these taxes a taxpayer is and could therefore be considered less than fair if one taxpayer, for example, had much higher disposable income than another. In such a case, while they may pay the same sums in percentage terms, one would be paying tax out of sums of money that may be needed to cover more basic necessities than the other.

A tax system could therefore be designed to seek to ensure more equality of the overall burden – so that those more able to bear taxes, or who perhaps can be considered to have been more favoured in some way by the economic system they find themselves in, pay a higher percentage on their tax base than others. For example, someone on a higher income might pay an average of 25 per cent of their income in taxes whereas someone on a lower income may pay 20 per cent. This would be an example of a tax or tax system that is deemed progressive.

The opposite applies if the tax system is regressive, that is, as the tax base rises, they pay a smaller proportion of the base in tax. For example, someone on a higher income pays an average of 20 per cent on their income but someone on a lower income pays 25 per cent on average.

Determining the right balance for the sharing of the total tax burden a government wishes to impose is a key social policy issue with wide-reaching implications.

Principles of good tax system design

In designing a tax system, we also need to think about the key characteristics we wish the overall system to exhibit and embody. Getting these principles right can have a significant impact on the levels of compliance with the system (compliance being an important feature, as a government needs the taxes they are imposing to be collected to bring in the revenues they seek to spend).

These are not new challenges. As long ago as the 1700s, the same issues were being debated, and solutions to how to do this became formed at that time into what have become known as the 'canons of taxation'. These were captured in the work of Scottish political economist Adam Smith in his book *The Wealth of Nations* (Smith, 2012 [1776]). Smith described four key characteristics that should be considered as fundamental in the design of a tax system – and these are still the measures against which we can assess tax systems today.

Equity

Smith proposed that a tax needs to be seen by taxpayers as being equitably applied. That way, taxpayers are more likely to pay it as they feel the obligation on them is fair.

Convenience

Second, the tax should be convenient to pay. This implies easy to compute but also to know when it should be paid. As such, the tax system therefore needs to be designed to be as simple as possible to aid understanding and thereby increase compliance.

Certainty

Third, the principle of certainty was proposed. Taxpayers should know what the taxes are that they are likely to be obligated to pay in the future and should not be surprised later by changes that would have altered the decisions they made with hindsight.

Efficiency

The fourth characteristic proposed is that of efficiency. Taxes should be designed to cost as little as possible to collect so that a government is not just raising taxes to pay to collect the taxes.

This principle also implies that taxes should not unduly change people's activity or behaviour – at least not beyond the way it was designed to deliver if that was the motivation for the tax. This idea is captured in the concept of 'tax neutrality' and is often seen in tax policy design where suspected impacts on one group that may be adversely affected by a proposed tax or welfare system change are 'corrected' elsewhere to compensate for this change. While this might not always create a tax neutral response, it can reduce this impact to acceptable levels.

Are all these characteristics equally important?

In practice, it is not possible to achieve all of these in any one tax, or even across an entire tax system, to desired levels that will satisfy all taxpayers. These are perhaps therefore best considered to be 'yardsticks' of assessment setting minimum bars of achievement to reach.

However, there is a hierarchy of these characteristics that should be considered by tax policy designers. Foremost among these four is equity – without the tax system being widely considered fair, even if not entirely so in all circumstances, tax systems can quickly become vulnerable to collapse. Correspondingly, a government's spending of tax revenue needs to be considered to be broadly appropriate. Without both of these in place, systemic failure is a real challenge that will eventually need to be faced (we will explore this issue further throughout this book – particularly in Chapter 10 related to wealth taxation).

Digitisation

A feature of the administration of tax systems, in particular since the early 2000s, has been the significant increase in digitisation of all aspects of its administration and operation (Granger et al, 2022). This has occurred both for taxpayers and for the tax authority.

Most UK taxpayers now file any tax returns due electronically. More than ninety six percent of all the UK's 2020/21 personal tax returns were filed electronically by the deadline of 31 January 2022 (HMRC, 2022). This automation has greatly aided efficiency of the tax system's operation for both taxpayers and the tax authorities but does require access to computers (or similar electronic tools like tablets) and some IT and tax-related expertise to do this. This creates difficulties for some taxpayers who may not have either of these available to them, nor the resources to pay for this where this is not publicly provided (as it isn't in the UK despite significant amounts of guidance from the tax authority also having been moved online in attempts to aid this process). Taxpayers are also likely to be increasingly communicated with electronically by the tax authorities (for example, annual taxpayer statements summarising a taxpayer's tax details are now only provided online). A digital divide of capability is therefore being created that leaves some excluded from the best support.

Application of tax bases and levels of UK taxes collected

Taxes can be classified into one of three types (referred to as 'bases') – taxes on:

- *Income*: being receipts that add to your wealth – for example, salary, pensions, benefits in kind (non-pay items received in reward of

employment), dividends, savings interest, self-employment income, rental income and so on;
- *Wealth*: the store, transfer or growth in value of things you own – based on a mixture of how much you own at a point in time, what is the value you have released from owning assets when you sell them, taxes on gifts and inheritances and so on; or
- *Consumption*: on what you take out of society for your use such as goods or services that you consume.

All taxes can be grouped into one of these three bases. In the UK, we can allocate the main taxes in our tax system to these bases as set out in Table 3.2.

To the extent NICs can be argued to be a tax – in this book, we will treat them as such for the reasons outlined earlier – they are a tax on incomes so would be a further example of the use of the income tax base.

A handful of UK taxes can be difficult to classify as they have features of more than one base – for example, council tax is a charge based on the value of the property you live in (or to be precise the value in 1991 in most parts of the UK – see more on this in Chapter 12) but is charged on the occupier not the owner. As such, it has features of both a wealth tax and a consumption tax.

Income

Income is a popular tax base for countries like the UK to use. In general, more than 50 per cent of all tax revenues received in the UK come from this base through a combination of personal income tax (PIT), corporation tax and NICs (Table 3.3). This level of reliance on income as a base is due to it being particularly well suited to the features of a tax that make it effective for use (in line with the canons of taxation detailed earlier). This includes being possible to apply fairly equitably, at least in theory: those on higher incomes can be made to pay more to enhance a progressive approach to taxation with the use of higher rates than those

Table 3.2: Classification of the main UK taxes by tax base

Income taxes	Personal income tax
	Corporation tax
Wealth taxes	Capital gains tax
	Inheritance tax
	Stamp duty
Consumption taxes	Value added tax
	Excise duties
	Customs duties
	Insurance premium tax and air passenger duty

Table 3.3: Sums raised from main UK taxes, 2000–19

(£ million)	1980	2000	2019
Total tax revenue	81,153	359,370	725,615
Taxes on income, profits and capital gains	30,651	142,197	251,489
Of individuals	23,868	104,136	200,486
On capital gains	492	2,211	9,187
Corporate	6,783	38,061	51,003
Social security contributions (NICs)	13,531	60,252	143,255
Employees	5,228	24,175	56,200
Employers	8,210	34,028	82,699
Self-employed or non-employed	317	2,049	4,356
Taxes on payroll and workforce (Apprenticeship Levy)	0	0	2,764
Taxes on property	9,774	41,134	90,258
Recurrent taxes on immovable property	8,665	30,552	68,748
Council tax	0	13,991	35,957
National non-domestic rates	0	14,966	28,928
Estate, inheritance and gift taxes	479	2,215	5,165
Taxes on financial and capital transactions (stamp duty)	630	8,367	15,962
Taxes on goods and services	23,699	115,787	237,849
Value added taxes	11,897	65,018	154,754
Excise duties	8,616	37,315	49,285
Customs and import duties	1,109	2,086	3,488
Taxes on specific services	456	5,826	17,043
Air passenger duty	0	940	3,810
Insurance premium tax	0	1,707	6,417
Other taxes	600	559	4,742
Landfill tax	484	461	784
Climate Change Levy	0	0	2,091
Aggregates Levy	0	0	396

Source: Based on OECD (2021b, table 5.37)

on lower incomes. It can also be set up to be administratively efficient – most people receive income periodically via wages or salaries and so periodic payments of tax via a Pay-as-You-Earn approach on the receipt of this income can be efficiently used to cover the bulk of a PIT liability.

Online filing of income details can then be used to conveniently provide the details for tax assessment on an annual basis to determine tax liability for any taxes not paid on receipt (such as income from self-employment or from rental incomes).

Despite these positive features, income is not however a perfect solution, which means that more than just this tax base is often needed to optimise application of the canon's design characteristics. For example, to set levels of taxation to create a progressive system, the thresholds at which different rates of tax will be applied must be created. However, the impact of inflation on the value of incomes means these thresholds need to be regularly changed to avoid them deteriorating in real-value terms (what can be bought year-on-year for the same value of money) over time. This ensures that those on lower incomes do not end up paying higher taxes as their wages rise just to keep up with inflationary price changes – what is referred to as fiscal drag. This constant need to change threshold levels means higher than ideal levels of uncertainty have to be part of any income tax system as it is never clear from one year to the next what these values will need to be.

As such, most tax systems have more than income as their sole tax base even though using more bases will increase complexity in the tax system.

Wealth

A second base often used for taxation is wealth – the value of the assets, minus any claims on those assets, that a taxpayer has. We explore wealth taxes more fully in Chapter 10, but such taxes can take one of three broad forms (Evans et al, 2017, p 102) as a tax based on:

1. the total value of someone's wealth at a point in time;
2. the value of this wealth at a point of transfer to another, such as when it is given away/received or when it is passed on at death; or
3. the change in the value of wealth over time.

Most countries include in their tax system taxes in at least the last two of these three categories, that is, in the case of a wealth transfer tax, either an inheritance tax (typically on what is inherited, so the rate of tax is determined by the recipient's financial position to enhance progressivity) or an estate duty (based on the value of the estate being passed on). Many countries, the UK included, also have taxes when wealth is given away during life – so-called 'gift taxes'. These are needed in a tax system where wealth is taxed on death to avoid the obvious tax avoidance strategy of giving away all of your assets just at the point of death.

The third category of wealth taxes are also very commonly used across the world. These are usually taxes on the changing value of wealth and are typically computed by taking the value of an asset at a point in time from its purchase or acquisition value. However, such taxes are usually paid only at the point at which this value becomes realised, that is, when a final sale of the item is made so the full change in value linked to ownership can be determined. This approach to collecting taxes due avoids administrative challenges of what happens when values go down while assets are owned – are taxes previously paid on any gains then rebated only then to have to be repaid later if the value rises again? In the UK, the main example of this tax is capital gains tax.

Wealth taxes of the first kind – on the value of someone's wealth at a point in time – are very much rarer to find used. An annual assessment of wealth for tax purposes does happen in various countries in the form of an 'annual wealth tax', such as applies in France on real estate, as well as Norway, Spain and Switzerland among others (Advani et al, 2020), but has not been a feature of the UK's tax system in modern tax history. Some are arguing it should be introduced in some form, but for the reasons detailed in what follows, this is proving elusive from a policy perspective.

Wealth taxes are typically only used for limited purposes – particularly to address equity and redistribution perspectives and to try to ensure periodic correction to the otherwise steady concentration of wealth in fewer and fewer people (which occurs if birth rates are less than death rates and grandparents/parents predominantly pass on their wealth to only a few children/grandchildren). Effective use of wealth taxes can reduce, even if not eliminate, this challenge. However, more generally these taxes suffer from several key challenges that significantly limit their wider use. These include challenges of administration – such as how to get the population to fairly and fully declare what wealth they hold (Troup et al, 2020), and also issues of valuation – once we know what wealth is held, how do we agree what value it represents so that an agreed tax burden can be computed (Daly and Loutzenhiser, 2020)?

For these reasons, wealth taxation therefore typically makes up less than 3 per cent of tax revenues in the UK (see Table 3.3).

Consumption

The third base for taxation in many tax systems around the world is consumption – attaching taxes to what taxpayers take out of society for their own use. This will typically be applied via taxes collected alongside points of sale such as when you buy something or order a service to be delivered to you physically or electronically. This can create an efficient and convenient means to collect taxes; however, it can also have undesired influences on consumption patterns by adding extra cost to purchases.

It may be argued that taxing consumption is the fairest way to apply taxation because a benefit approach is in effect being applied: those who take out more resources from their society to consume them personally will pay more in consumption tax for that privilege. This, in principle, may feel like a good and fair idea. However, applying this in practice can create a variety of challenges for setting good tax policy (Crawford et al, 2010). Those who have most need for support from society are most likely not to have the means to pay for their basic necessities, let alone the consumption taxes on top of this – and, as such, focusing taxation solely on consumption of resources will likely lead to an unfair tax burden falling on those in most need. Those who are richer and have disposable income that may not be immediately consumed will likely pay a lower proportion of their income in a consumption tax. Consumption taxes can therefore be regressive in nature, which can reduce their fairness and the overall fairness of the tax system, if not addressed suitably.

This may suggest some reflection of 'ability to pay' needs to be present elsewhere in our tax system to counter this issue. However, in making such adjustments to how consumption taxes operate, this adds complexity to the system used to address these failures – so consumption tax cannot be easily used as the sole tax base in an economy, at least one where fairness is considered to be important.

Despite these constraints, the UK is a significant user of consumption taxes. Table 3.3 illustrates, of all taxes raised, consumption taxes counted for 29 per cent in 1980, 32 per cent in 2000 and 33 per cent in 2019 of total taxes raised

Successive governments have attempted to balance the natural regressivity of this tax base by various means. This includes use of reduced rates of some consumption taxes on goods or services deemed to be disproportionately bought by those who have to consume higher percentages of their income or wealth to provide for their basis needs.

The UK has a number of consumption taxes. The main one is a so-called 'general' sales tax, VAT. This is applied at a rate of 20 per cent on most things bought, but it also has 5 per cent, 0 per cent and zero[3] rates that are used on certain specifically identified goods or services. The UK also applies excise duties – consumption taxes on specifically identified items that vary item-to-item, sometimes based on their value but often on other features of the item, such as its weight. Excise taxes are most commonly applied to consumption of three categories of goods – to fuel, alcohol and tobacco products.

The UK also has a range of other, much smaller, consumption-related taxes, including customs and import duties, betting and gaming taxes, insurance premium tax and air passenger duty. The UK's various environmental taxes (explored further in Chapter 14) are often also of the form of consumption taxes. These include landfill taxes, the Climate Change Levy and aggregates tax.

Given these details of the three bases of tax, it should be clear why tax systems are typically made up of a mix of taxes covering all three of the tax bases. This is exactly how the tax system in the UK operates, as Table 3.3 demonstrates.

Who pays what UK taxes?

Taxes in the UK typically fall on two groups – on individuals in the form of personal taxes, and on business/corporates in the form of taxes paid by various business entities on behalf of the individuals who own them.

Personal taxes

Personal taxes in the UK include PITs. These are paid by all who earn incomes as individuals from almost all sources, whether or not the income is earned (such as wages/salaries or via self-employment-related profits) or unearned (such as interest on savings, dividends from shareholdings, rental or pension income and similar). These taxes are paid at the rates set out in Table 3.4 (for 2022/23 – rates change year on year).

Table 3.4 shows that the rates of tax to be paid on personal incomes can differ depending on the type and amount of income received. All these rates apply after a personal allowance is used up. This provides an income tax-free sum to all individuals. For 2022/23, the personal allowance is £12,570, and this is planned to remain unchanged until 2025/26.[4]

PIT rates can differ based on location in the UK. The devolved governments in Scotland and Wales set their own tax rates, although they tend to be broadly similar to those for England.[5]

Table 3.4: Rates of tax on different forms of income for England for 2022/23 (after personal allowances)

Tax bands (£)	Rates (per cent)		
	Savings	Dividends	Other income
0–2,000	0	0	–
0 (or 2,000)–37,700	20	8.75	20
37,701–150,000	40	33.75	40
Over 150,000	45	39.35	45

Personal taxes also include NICs. These are based on employment earnings at 12 per cent of earned income (these normal rates of NICs are reduced to 2 per cent above a threshold of around £900/week).[6]

Personal taxes are also born by individuals in other ways – these include payment of consumption taxes on their purchases of goods and services (taxes that are not insubstantial, as VAT alone costs 20 per cent of most things bought), inheritance taxes (these can be up to 40 per cent of the sums received), capital gains tax (charged mostly at 10 per cent or 20 per cent currently) and a range of other smaller taxes (such as on insurance premiums and flights).

In the UK, as is the case in most developed countries, the largest burden of all taxes collected by the government falls on individuals across this range of taxes – as shown in Table 3.3. This can equate to 80 per cent or more of all taxes paid (for example, this amounted to 78 per cent in 1980, 80 per cent in 2000 and 82 per cent in 2019).

The changing trends on the key personal taxes paid can be seen in Figure 3.1. Of particular note is the fact that PIT in 2019/20 is at the same level that it was in 1999/2000 (at 9.2 per cent of GDP), albeit having risen in the middle of this period to 10 per cent of GDP in 2007/8 and fallen back again to lower levels before a rise again more recently (pre-COVID impacts) (Keep, 2021).

This pattern is similar for VAT (at a lower level than PIT), also rising to the middle of this period (from below 5 per cent of GDP after the 2008/9 recession to a peak of 6.1 per cent) before falling back slightly (to 5.5 per cent of GDP in 2020/21) (Keep, 2021). However, the pattern is different for NICs, which have seen a steady rise in use over this period, from 5.4 per cent of GDP in 1999/2000 to 6.7 per cent in 2020/21 (Keep, 2021).

Figure 3.1: Trends in the four largest UK taxes as percentages of UK gross domestic product

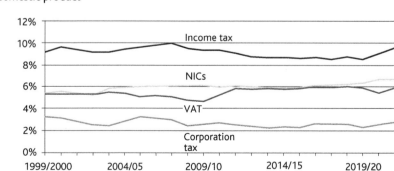

Source: Keep (2021, p 12)

Within this overall direction of travel, different taxpayers contribute to these levels of taxation at different levels. These are discussed in more detail in Chapter 7, which also brings in analysis of benefits to this assessment.

Corporate taxes

Corporate entities are also required to pay taxes in the UK. These include taxes on their profits (those earned inside the UK at least – see Chapter 13) and taxes on their capital gains (termed 'chargeable gains' when earned by a company). Both are paid in the form of corporation tax in the UK: there is no separate tax for chargeable gains that companies earn as there is for such gains made by individuals. Corporation tax has been paid at a flat rate of 19 per cent on all profits and capital gains received by corporations for several years. Larger businesses used to pay a higher rate than smaller businesses, however, this difference had been whittled away at until the differential rate was removed. From April 2023, businesses with taxable incomes less than £50,000 will continue to pay this tax at 19 per cent however, a differentiated rate will apply to large businesses again – rising to 25 per cent.

These taxes on corporates raised just over £51 billion in 2019 (see Table 3.3). This amounts to 7 per cent of all taxes paid. This is a sum that many find surprisingly low – at least when compared to the total taxes that individuals are expected to bare. This has been falling in the last 20 years, as shown by Figure 3.1 (from 3.3 per cent of GDP in 1999/ 2000 to 2.3 per cent in in 2019/20 – Keep, 2021). Companies may also be obligated to pay other taxes, including NICs on their employees (per Table 3.3, this amounted to more than £82 billion in 2019 or 11 per cent of all taxes paid).

It can perhaps be argued that corporations can also be considered to be the source for many personal taxes – as it is the profitability of corporations that enables salaries to be paid to their employees from which much of their taxes are paid. See more on corporate taxes in Chapter 13.

Tax policy-making structure and processes

The process of setting tax policy in the UK is complex. This is particularly the case when key systemic change is needed and tax policy development can be stymied by political processes and pressures for popularism over longer-term national benefit.

However, the process of setting tax policy is one that requires a constant refreshing. As the key objectives of tax include both revenue-raising and direct policy delivery functions to influence behaviours, and because revenue needs are always changing and policy needs are not static over often even short periods (as we have seen very clearly during the COVID-19 pandemic period), there is a need to constantly change the tax system or it will date quickly with resulting impacts on its ability to support government objectives.

Further, as the interactions of fiscal and welfare policy objectives are complex, this can create a significant challenge to ensure a tax change to deliver improvements in one area does not get undone with corresponding impacts elsewhere.

HM Treasury versus HM Revenue and Customs

HM Treasury has the remit in the UK for developing effective tax policy and seeing through a legislative process to develop the constantly evolving tax system. This is largely done via parliamentary process creating laws that can then be enforced. In turn, these laws become subject to review and amendment over time where they need updating for changed circumstances, or where their application in practice shows up less than perfect initial drafting.

A mix of administrative laws – giving powers to collect tax and determining how taxes should be collected – and substantive laws – explaining how tax should be computed across the range of taxes being operated at any point – is used to create these rules.

In the UK, this process is centred on an (at least) annual examination of the national Budget that brings together the spending plans for the government and how they plan to develop the tax system to create the revenue to enable the proposed spending to occur. A national Budget is typically published by the government in the autumn of each year as a single 'fiscal event' (so that tax rules are not churned too frequently, aiding certainty as a desirable characteristic of a good tax system), to be brought into effect the following April (or later – tax rules are very rarely adjusted retrospectively, also related to seeking to create improved certainty in system design). This annual process then subsequently creates a Finance Act for that year that amends tax-related law with the details of the Budget.[7]

Other administrative Acts can also be enacted periodically but often with large gaps in time between when there is examination of particular rules related to taxation, which can mean administrative processes are somewhat slow to evolve on occasions but does result in infrequent significant changes to tax operations (again aiding certainty for taxpayers).

Once these laws are enacted, HM Revenue and Customs (HMRC) is tasked with collecting taxes due according to these laws (or their interpretation thereof).

HMRC is typically responsible for managing almost all of the UK's various taxes – although it does not directly deal with taxation collected locally. In the UK, unlike most countries in the world, until recently only one tax was collected locally – council tax (Chapter 12). However, since 2012, devolved governments have been given greater powers under a unitary arrangement (one where tax is collected more locally to the taxpayer but still largely centrally controlled from the national parliament) to collect some taxes (Cheung and Paun 2020). As such, adjustments to the rules on how some taxes are computed and paid now exist in the UK for Scotland, Wales and Northern Ireland (although not for England, whose tax policy is entirely determined by the national government).

Department for Work and Pensions

Various aspects of the tax system are administered by the Department for Work and Pensions (DWP). These typically include those most closely associated with the welfare/benefit system. The DWP works with HMRC to help the latter correctly adjust their tax collection demands where suitable due to specific sources of income that arise via the work of DWP. These can include, for example, benefit receipts (Universal Credit for example is not taxable as income) and pensions where income tax liability has to include any money paid out from a pension as part of regular income.

Courts

All tax-raising and administrative rules are based in law. As such, any details of what that law requires, or may imply is required, is subject to challenge via the legal system. This can include case-by-case discussions initially via the lower level of UK tax courts – the tribunal system – to look at specific concerns of individual taxpayers about their specific tax affairs, through to matters of principle that need further debate, and maybe resulting in calls for significant tax law changes, at the highest court level – that of the UK's Supreme Court.

Conclusion

This chapter has sought to provide a high-level overview of the UK tax system as necessary to provide a context for its more detailed review later in this book.

The UK's tax system is a complex and constantly changing environment where both the revenue-raising needs of the tax system and its use as a direct 'lever' of government agency to change behaviour need to be carefully managed to fund and to deliver policy objectives. It is made up of various taxes that are paid by individuals and corporates alike and carefully administered to seek to achieve optimal mixes of the desired characteristics for effective taxation.

The following chapters of this book build on the contents of this chapter and apply the principles it has outlined to specific social policy-related issues, digging deeper into the relationships between taxes and the tax system and how it is used and has evolved over time in respect of these various social policy issues.

Notes

[1] Readers are encouraged to explore more on MMT by those who advocate for this way to revisit the role of taxes in society such as Hail, 2017; Mitchell et al, 2019; and Baker and Murphy, 2020, but also those who are sceptical of this reasoning, for example see Mankiw, 2019.

[2] Smith, 2020 – Spending reviews have been in operation in their current periodic form since 1998 under the Blair government, when it was introduced as a 'new strategic approach to public spending' (see The Stationery Office, 1998). A critique of the current Spending Review process by the Institute for Government can be found in Wheatley et al (2018).

[3] The UK has both 0 per cent and zero rates of VAT – related to the differences in who becomes the ultimate payer of these taxes as it progresses down a supply chain; see further discussion in Lymer and Oats, 2022, pp 363–7.

[4] For fuller details of the application of personal income tax rates, see chapter 4 of Lymer and Oats, 2022.

[5] For rates of income taxes applicable in Scotland and Wales, see chapter 4 of Lymer and Oats, 2022. Rates of tax in Northern Ireland are currently the same as those in England.

[6] An additional charge (pre-empting the introduction of a Health and Social Care levy that was due to be charged from April 2023) was added to NICs in April 2022 adding a further 1.25 per cent to these rates, but this was scrapped by the Truss government in September 2022. An additional charge of 13.8 per cent also falls on employers for most of their employees. No upper cap applies to these payments.

[7] Further details on the UK budgetary process can be found at HM Treasury, 2017 – although there are vocal critics of this current process, including the Institute for Government, Chartered Institute of Tax (CIOT) and Institute for Fiscal Studies (IFS), who have produced various proposals for changes to this system (for example, Rutter et al, 2017) that they argue will reduce taxpayer confusion, cut down on costly errors and avoid the periodic U-turns that occur not infrequently in the current process.

Further reading

- Evans et al (2017) – a textbook exploring the reasons tax systems around the world often follow common designs but also why they have key design differences.
- Lymer and Oats (2022) – a comprehensive introductory guide to UK taxation.
- HMRC statistics – latest statistics on the UK tax system, https://www.gov.uk/government/organisations/hm-revenue-customs/about/statistics
- House of Commons Library briefings – review and discussion of UK tax statistics, https://commonslibrary.parliament.uk/research-briefings/cbp-8513

- Institute for Fiscal Studies resources and videos – a resource providing summary reviews of key aspects of the UK tax system, https://ifs.org.uk/tools_and_resources

References

Advani, A., Chamberlain, E. and Summers, A. (2020) 'A wealth tax for the UK', London School of Economics Wealth Tax Commission, Available from: https://www.wealthandpolicy.com/wp/WealthTaxFinalReport.pdf

Baker, A., and Murphy, R. (2020) 'Modern monetary theory and the changing role of tax in society', *Social Policy and Society*, 19(3): 454–69.

Cheung, A. and Paun, A. (2020) 'Taxes and devolution', Explainers – Institute for Government, Available from: https://www.instituteforgov ernment.org.uk/explainers/tax-and-devolution

Crawford, I., Keen, M. and Smith, S. (2010) 'Value added taxes and excises: Chapter 4', in S. Adam, T. Besley, R. Blundell, S. Bond, R. Chote and M. Gammie et al (eds) *Dimensions of Tax Design*, vol 1, Oxford: Oxford University Press, pp 275–362

Daly, S. and Loutzenhiser, G. (2020) 'Valuation', Wealth Tax Commission Wealth and Policy working paper 109, Available from: https://www.weal thandpolicy.com/wp/109.html

Evans, C., Hasseldine, J., Lymer A., Ricketts, R. and Sandford, C. (2017) *Comparative Taxation: Why Tax Systems Differ*, Malvern: Fiscal Publications.

Granger, J., de Clercq, B. and Lymer, A. (2022) 'Tapping taxes: digital disruption and revenue administration responses', in N. Hendriyetty, C. Evans, C.J. Kim and F. Taghizadeh-Hesary (eds) *Taxation in the Digital Economy*, London: Routledge, pp 21–44.

Hail, T. (2017) 'Explainer: what is modern monetary theory?', *The Conversation*, 31 January, Available from: https://theconversation.com/explainer-what-is-modern-monetary-theory-72095

HM Treasury (2017) 'The new Budget timetable and the tax policy making process', Policy Paper. Available from: https://www.gov.uk/government/publications/the-new-budget-timetable-and-the-tax-policy-making-proc ess/the-new-budget-timetable-and-the-tax-policy-making-process

HM Treasury (2021) 'Annual Budget and Spending Review 2021', Available from: https://assets.publishing.service.gov.uk/government/uploads/sys tem/uploads/attachment_data/file/1043688/Budget_AB2021_Print.pdf

HMRC (2022) 'More than 10.2 million filed their self-assessment by 31 January', Press Release. Available from: https://www.gov.uk/government/news/more-than-102-million-filed-their-self-assessment-by-31-january

Keep, M. (2021) 'Tax statistics: an overview', House of Commons Library, Available from: https://commonslibrary.parliament.uk/research-briefings/cbp-8513

Lymer, A. and Oats, L. (2022) *Taxation: Policy and Practice*, Malvern: Fiscal Publications.

Mankiw, N.G. (2019) 'A skeptic's guide to modern monetary theory', paper prepared for American Economic Association (AEA) Meeting, January 2019 for session 'Is United States deficit policy playing with fire?', Available from: https://scholar.harvard.edu/files/mankiw/files/skeptics_guide_to_modern_monetary_theory.pdf

Mitchell, W.L., Wray, R. and Watts, M. (2019) *Macroeconomics*, London: Red Globe Press.

OECD (2021a) 'Glossary of tax terms', Available from: https://www.oecd.org/ctp/glossaryoftaxterms.htm

OECD (2021b) 'Revenue statistics 2021: the initial impact of COVID-19 on OECD tax revenues', Paris: OECD, Available from: https://doi.org/10.1787/6e87f932-en

Rutter, J., Dodwell, B., Johnson, P., Crozier, G., Cullinane, J., Lilly, A. and McCarthy, E. (2017) 'Better budgets: Making tax policy better', Chartered Institute of Tax, Institute for Fiscal Studies and Institute for Government Report. Available from: https://www.instituteforgovernment.org.uk/publi cations/better-budgets-making-tax-policy-better

Sandford, C., Pond, C. and Walker, R. (eds) (1980) *Taxation and Social Policy*, London: Heinemann.

Smith, A. (2012 [1776]) *The Wealth of Nations*, Classics of World Literature, Ware: Wordsworth Editions.

Smith, C. (2020) 'Budget and the spending review', In focus report. House of Lords Library. Available from: https://lordslibrary.parliament.uk/bud get-and-the-spending-review/

The Stationery Office (1998) 'Modern public services for Britain: Investing in report. Comprehensive spending review: New public spending plans 1999-2002', Cm411. Available from: https://assets.publishing.service.gov.uk/government/uploads/system/uploads/attachment_data/file/260 743/4011.pdf

Troup, E, Barnett, J. and Bullock, K. (2020) 'The administration of a wealth tax', Wealth Tax Commission Wealth and Policy working paper 111, Available from: https://www.wealthandpolicy.com/wp/111.html

Wheatley, M., Maddox, B. and Kidney Bishop, T. (2018) 'The 2019 spending review: How to run it well', Institute for Government. Available from: https://www.instituteforgovernment.org.uk/summary-2019-spend ing-review-how-run-it-well

4

Fiscal welfare and tax expenditures

Adrian Sinfield

Fiscal welfare and tax expenditures are means of running public policies through tax reliefs. They have been identified as policy instruments by some countries and international bodies for more than half a century. They 'are alternative policy means by which governments deliver financial support to individuals and companies' (IMF, 2019, p 7). While such explicit descriptions are now being used more often, the impact of tax reliefs on individuals, the economy and broader society is still much neglected, left hidden, if not secret, in comparison to that of direct public spending.

After introducing the concepts and their development, the chapter considers the particular HMRC classification of UK tax reliefs, the scale of UK tax expenditures and the growing available evidence on them. It discusses their distributive and behavioural effects, their political implications and the impact on the wider distribution of resources across society and the economy. Possible policies to promote greater transparency, accountability, equality and fairness are discussed before the conclusion.

The growing recognition of fiscal welfare and tax expenditures

The two terms, fiscal welfare and tax expenditure, are not identical but overlap. *Fiscal welfare*, a term introduced by Richard Titmuss in 1955 in the UK, is one of three elements in his *social division of welfare* (Titmuss, 1955 in 1958; Alcock et al, 2001, part 2, chapter 2). Resources are made available by government through tax reliefs and related subsidies and not only as benefits and services of *public* or *social welfare* through the welfare state. The final element is *occupational welfare*, with services accessible through employment, often subsidised by fiscal welfare. In the UK, this usually means provided or organised through employers but in other countries often by trade unions and other groups (Sinfield, 1978).

The term *tax expenditure* was first used in the United States in 1967 by Stanley Surrey, an academic tax lawyer working in the federal government, to mirror the term *public expenditure* to show spending policies being run through the tax system (developed in Surrey, 1973). Established as departures from the tax benchmark, the basic structure of the fiscal system, tax expenditures then 'represented about a quarter of the Federal Budget' but were 'outside the normal procedures of budgetary scrutiny' (Pond, 1980, p 51). From 1974, the US Federal Budget was legally required to include a list of tax expenditures, and the term has since come to be widely used (US Treasury, 2022).

The term is broader than fiscal welfare, with many industrial and other tax expenditures as well as primarily welfare ones. While social tax expenditure (STE) is often used for fiscal welfare, some elements of it are not necessarily recognised as tax expenditures. Much including non-monetary company benefits and services 'increase an individual's command over the use of society's scarce resources' but may not be considered for tax and so have no relief (RCTPI, 1955).

A third term, *tax breaks for social purposes*, developed in the Organisation for Economic Co-operation and Development's (OECD) Social Policy division, compares the costs of tax reliefs with public social spending to reach 'net total social expenditure' (Adema et al, 2014). However, as it excludes tax expenditures classified as part of some countries' tax benchmarks and others not sufficiently comparable to public benefits, it is not pursued here.

Tax reliefs can take many forms including allowances, exemptions, reductions, deferrals and credits. They are not part of the Tax Gap, monies that should by law be paid in tax but are not (Smith, 2021). The reliefs have been deliberately created by government and are intended to be used for specific purposes (Murphy, 2018). Using them is not non-compliance, avoidance or evasion, although, of course, they may be misused or abused.

From the start, both Titmuss and Surrey emphasised that tax reliefs tend to increase inequalities. These 'upside-down' benefits, in direct tax reliefs in particular, help those with higher incomes paying higher-rate taxes more than basic-rate taxpayers, since the former would otherwise pay more tax at their marginal, top rate (Surrey, 1973, p 37). Someone paying above the basic tax rate of 20 per cent gains 40 per cent of the relief, or 45 per cent, if paying the top rate, and not just 20 per cent. In Scotland, the basic rate remains 21 per cent, and the additional rate of 46 per cent has been retained. Someone with a very much lower income and tax bill may receive very little, if any benefit, from a tax relief.

The exception is tax credit, which reduces the tax due to be paid: the benefit is the same for everyone whose tax bill is as large as the credit. Credits may be refundable so that anyone with a tax bill smaller than the credit may receive the rest of the credit as a direct payment.

The reluctant unveiling of UK tax expenditures

For many decades, the UK government resisted providing an account of tax reliefs and their management. In fact, few staff were assigned to them, and, apart from occasional handing out as Budget 'lollipops', they seemed to be largely ignored until the 21st century. This institutionalised neglect, even disregard, combined with a Treasury-knows-best-so-leave-it-to-us attitude, has left a long legacy of unaccountability that still shapes government action.

Titmuss's raising of the issue in the 1950s and 1960s initially had very limited impact on the government, but by the mid-1970s the case for greater transparency and accountability was being made increasingly strongly in UK academic analysis and political and media campaigning (Pond, 1980). Under sustained pressure, official release of a few costed tax reliefs began annually at the end of the 1970s. These one-year lists took no account of the argument for putting comparable public and tax spending together, as it is 'difficult to form a coherent political discussion when ... the two halves of the argument are in different places' (House of Commons Expenditure Committee, 1976, quoted in Pond, 1980, p 61), even though brief HMRC accompanying texts each year noted this point.

Over four decades later, 'the two halves of the argument' still remain 'in different places', and there is no tax expenditure budget, argued for in 1978 and now routine in many countries (Willis and Hardwick, 1978, p 107; IMF, 2019). Tight control over the limited statistical releases remained with the Inland Revenue and the Treasury, with only small changes in what was published for over 30 years. Attempts to gain more information generally met with reluctance, if not opposition, as Margaret Hodge made very clear in her memoir on chairing the Public Accounts Committee (Hodge, 2016, especially chapter 9).

OECD's first report on tax expenditures was not officially well received in the UK (OECD, 1984). A senior member of the Treasury was quick to dismiss the report and the concept of tax expenditure (interview by the author, 1985). Any recognition of tax reliefs as tax expenditures, he warned, could lead to the relevant spending minister wanting to control it within their policy framework and to consider using those resources differently. That, he emphasised, could weaken Treasury control of the economy and lead to enormous difficulties in maintaining revenue flows.

Change began in 2011 with the newly established Office of Tax Simplification (OTS, 2011) revealing very many more tax reliefs than HMRC listed with costs estimated for less than a quarter of that list. The National Audit Office's (NAO) subsequent critical reports on the management of tax reliefs provoked opposition from the Treasury, and the Chancellor of the Exchequer, George Osborne, was reported to be incandescent. 'The Treasury's view is that the design and impact of a relief are questions of policy and therefore outside of the NAO's remit' (NAO, 2014a, para 10; 2014b). The 'Better budgets: making tax policy better' team reported that the NAO head confirmed that legal advice had made clear that its remit does extend to this sort of investigation and it concluded 'that no one in either the Treasury or HMRC is accountable for either the value for money or the cost of tax measures' (Rutter et al, 2017, p 31).

NAO continued to trenchantly criticise HMRC's lack of effective management, including weak or non-existent internal monitoring even when costs greatly increased (NAO, 2016, 2020). The Office for Budgetary Responsibility (OBR) added pressure with another scathing analysis of 'policy-motivated' tax expenditures (OBR, 2019). The Public Accounts Committee demanded 'a step change' from the government:

> Tax reliefs have an enormous impact on tax revenue but it is far from clear whether they deliver the economic and social objectives many are supposed to support. The full cost of tax reliefs that support government's economic and social objectives is not known. ... Despite our repeated examination of this topic since 2013, HM Treasury and HM Revenue & Customs (HMRC) have made unacceptably slow progress. ... It is staggering that they still have insufficient understanding of the cost and value for money of tax reliefs, as well as who benefits from them. (PAC, 2020, p 3)

Under continuing criticism, HMRC and HM Treasury eventually expressed a public commitment to develop the management and monitoring of tax reliefs and to publish considerably more, including impact reviews (HMRC, 2021b, section 2).

The official UK classification of tax reliefs

Before discussing the significant increase in data in 2021, it is necessary to examine the particular UK official designation of a tax expenditure. HMRC makes no use of any form of tax benchmark (IMF, 2019; see also 2016) but identifies reliefs as *structural* or *non-structural*, which it has also begun to call tax expenditures (HMRC, 2020). This distinction has changed little since the 1970s and is still only briefly explained (for a fuller discussion, see TARC, 2014, for NAO). The 'many' structural

> tax reliefs are largely integral parts of the tax structure. ... These reliefs have various purposes including: to define the scope of the tax, calculate income or profits correctly, and make the tax progressive or to simplify. For example, a number of the larger allowances operate as thresholds to make the tax system progressive, while others exist to avoid disproportionate compliance burdens, or define the tax base by recognising the expense incurred in obtaining profits. ... In contrast, the effect of non-structural reliefs is to help or encourage particular

types of individuals, activities or products in order to achieve economic or social objectives. (HMRC, 2020, p 5)

The distinction 'is not always straightforward' (Pond, 1980, p 54; NAO, 2014a, p 16, para 1.6). It is unclear why 'to make the tax system progressive' is not to achieve 'economic or social objectives'. Besides, many fiscal relief decisions make the system less progressive. Reliefs are apparently structural if applying to everybody, but value added tax (VAT) rates apply to everybody, and their deductions and exemptions are officially treated as non-structural. Both types of relief 'reflect policy decisions about how the tax system is designed' and so should be treated together 'to mean the same thing' (Lymer and Oats, 2020, p 486).

The number and scale of tax reliefs is significant. In 2020, NAO reported that HMRC identified 1,190 reliefs for all taxes, dividing them into 828 'structural' and 362 'non-structural' or tax expenditures. The total estimate for the 196 costed items was £426 billion, nearly two thirds structural and over one third non-structural (NAO, 2020, figure 2).

HMRC has constantly opposed adding the cost of separate reliefs to reach a total as misleading and inappropriate (HMRC, 2021b, section 3). Much the same argument could be made for public spending items, and it is important to have some sense of the scale (Surrey and McDaniel, 1985, p 52). However, the reliability of official estimates is not clear, with some labelled 'high uncertainty' and many structural reliefs not listed, let alone costed (HMRC, 2021b, section 4).

'Large in absolute terms – approaching 8 per cent of GDP – and also by international standards' is OBR's description of the total costed 'policy-motivated' tax expenditures alone (OBR, 2019, para 4.69). The UK's much greater use of tax expenditures than most countries has since been confirmed by the Global Tax Expenditure Database (GTED) in its cull of 'the hidden side of the fiscal contract' (von Haldenwang et al, 2021b, p 128). It only includes what each government identifies as such, so UK structural tax reliefs are not counted. Out of the 338 items in their UK records for 2020, the 151 costed came to £171.74 billion, 8.13 per cent of UK GDP and equivalent to some 30 per cent of the tax base in 2019 (GTED, 2022, country file).

Only three other countries of the 102 reporting, Netherlands 14.2 per cent, Finland 12.38 per cent and Ireland 10.38 per cent, had higher percentages of GDP than the UK. Australia 7.92 per cent, United States 6.55 per cent, Canada 6.53 per cent and Portugal 6.29 per cent were the only other countries well above the 4.7 per cent average for richer countries (2.3 per cent for poorer countries) (von Haldenwang et al, 2021a, p 9; GTED, 2022).

HMRC's 'Tax relief statistics (December 2021)' marked a significant step forward, with data on 339 non-structural tax reliefs including estimated costs for 220 (HMRC, 2021b) and for 247 in the latest release (HMRC, 2023a).

The time series was extended from two to six years for 102 reliefs while others had only been recently costed. This report and associated tables on both structural and non-structural reliefs provided more details than in the past including the number of recipients for many of the reliefs (HMRC, 2021b; for example of a fuller analysis, Canada, 2022).

However, the total number of tax reliefs has yet to be given by HMRC. It is not clear why as the NAO total of 1,190 for 2018-19 was reached with HMRC assistance (NAO, 2020, figure 2). At that time NAO designated 362 reliefs tax expenditures and 828 structural. It appears likely therefore that in the latest HMRC releases well below half of all tax reliefs have been costed – perhaps three-quarters of non-structural reliefs but below a tenth of structural ones (HMRC, 2023a and b). HMRC has chosen to give priority to analysing the non-structural/tax expenditure reliefs and only a subset of structural reliefs has been released with fewer cost estimates (HMRC, 2023a and b).

The HMRC aggregate of all costed tax reliefs was close to £480 billion in 2020–21. The non-structural part of this, a little below £200 billion, has been rising steadily, 'a gradual increase' (HMRC, 2021b, section 6.2), in contrast to persistent and substantial cuts to public spending in the decade before the COVID-19 pandemic. The most costly items in HMRC's published non-structural or tax expenditure list for 2021–2022 are shown in Table 4.1.

This chapter will focus on the tax expenditures, the non-structural allowances. However, changes to structural allowances clearly affect the scale and ability as well as incentive to use the non-structural. Above-inflationary lifts to tax thresholds increased the cost of the structural personal tax allowance by 25 per cent to £113 billion in the six years to 2020–21. This presumably reduced the total cost of many other reliefs as well as leaving many more people below tax thresholds and unable to benefit from them.

How comprehensive the picture is now remains unclear. In contrast to general practice internationally, HMRC does not accept tax reliefs to nine basic social security benefits as tax expenditures (HMRC, 2021b, section 3, tables 3 and 4). Their total disclosed cost of £1.8 billion is included among the costed structural income tax reliefs. The then estimate of over £1 billion for tax-free Child Benefit was omitted for revision when its high-income ceiling was introduced, but no figure has reappeared.

The cost of much-touted 'salary sacrifice' schemes has still not been given. These schemes allow workers to receive less pay in order to claim particular benefits, which reduces income tax and National Insurance contributions (NICs) for them and their employers, but their original pay remains the basis for earnings-related pensions. The schemes were being promoted to reduce liability for the Health and Social Care Levy before its cancellation (see Chapter 8). Many more accounting issues could also be documented.

Table 4.1: HMRC-defined tax expenditures over £2 billion, UK 2021–22, £ billion

Income tax and NIC	
Registered pension schemes *IT 26.9 net + NIC 24.7*	51.6
Individual savings accounts	3.5
Employment allowance *NIC*	2.6
Charitable donations	2.0
Capital taxes	
Private residence relief	37.3
Transfers between spouses and civil partners	3.3
Corporation taxes	
Research & development 5.0 and 2.7	7.7
Capital allowances – annual investment	3.2
Duty rate for certain gas & other fuel uses	2.4
VAT	
Food	20.8
Construction and sale of new dwellings	16.1
Temporary reduced rate for hospitality, etc.	5.5
Domestic fuel and power	5.2
Domestic passenger transport	4.1
Drugs and supplies on prescription	3.6
VAT registration threshold	3.0
Water and sewerage services	2.4
Zero rate for children's clothing	2.0

Source: HMRC (2023a, figure 1)

Government failure to examine distribution

Limited government monitoring of reliefs does not reveal much attention to who gets what and how. Only about half of taxpayers make claims for tax reliefs besides personal allowances, with the one in 14 with incomes over £50,000 making nearly half of these (latest data 2018–19). The one annual table provides no analysis of the value to the claimants, nor any breakdown by gender, age, area or any other dimension, although other tables showed those with incomes over £50,000 being twice as likely to be men as women (HMRC, 2021a, tables 3.8 and 3.3).

Pension-related reliefs are the most expensive items in fiscal welfare, over 2 per cent of GDP, including NIC exemptions (see Chapter 6). They were claimed by nearly nine out of ten tax-relief claimants, but no evidence of the value to them analysed by income was provided until some five years ago except in written answers responding to parliamentary questions and select committee requests. In 2016–17, the richest tenth of taxpayers received half the value of the pension reliefs, but the poorest half only one tenth (Treasury Committee, 2018, p 33, chart 5.1, possibly underestimated, omitting £8 billion relief on pension funds and all £16 billion NIC exemptions from the analysis).

The lack of regular evidence on distribution by any dimensions not only handicaps evaluation but conceals how upside-down and regressive most direct tax reliefs are at a time when more progressive public spending has been limited. The 'distributional analyses', appearing in the 2021 report for the first time, were brief, patchy and remarkably varied (HMRC, 2021b, especially section 6.6). Some indicated the proportion going to higher-rate taxpayers, others public and private recipients, while very few mentioned gender or other dimensions. Many only gave links to data elsewhere that readers themselves might analyse. This confirms that the government attached little importance to taking account of who benefits from particular tax reliefs compared to public spending.

'The distinctive political dynamics' of tax expenditures (Hacker, 2002)

By contrast, concern outside government with how tax reliefs affect distributional and behavioural impact has been considerable among the few studying tax reliefs. They examine reliefs in a broader social, political and economic context that includes comparisons with public social policies.

Taking account of tax reliefs as part of broader government policy requires an expansion to the traditional social policy distinction between universal and selective or means-tested benefits. Another form of selectivity needs to be recognised: *means-enhancing* as well as *means-tested*. The first applies to most income tax reliefs and many others, while the second applies to an increasing proportion of working-age public spending benefits. The first provides more generously for those with higher incomes whose tax liabilities would be greater without these reliefs, while the second limits benefits to those with resources beneath a certain level and often adds various behavioural conditions.

The extent of means-enhancing by income tax reliefs, contributing to widening inequalities, was clearly revealed in one Institute for Fiscal Studies (IFS) special analysis of basic HMRC records in 2004–5 (Brewer et al, 2008). While the average income taxpayer received £570 in reliefs in addition to personal allowances, the three groups with the highest incomes were 'racing away' from the rest. The top 10 per cent to 1 per cent gained £1,998 in such extra relief, the top 1 per cent to 0.1 per cent £8,103 and the very richest, the final 0.1 per cent, some £49,143 (author's calculations based on Brewer et al, 2008: table 1, NIC exemptions excluded). The value of income tax reliefs to the final 0.1 per cent was 86 times more than it was to the average taxpayer, although their pre-tax income was only 31 times more. It is not clear how much has altered since then with the many changes made to the tax system since this point, including greatly increased personal allowances, a higher top tax rate introduced, and more registered for private pensions but with annual and (until April 2024) lifetime caps on pensions tax relief (see Chapter 6).

While tax reliefs help the wealthiest to race away, they leave the poorest further behind. For those without sufficient taxable income, there can be no or very little benefit from direct tax reliefs unless they are refundable tax credits. In consequence, not only are tax reliefs unable to help reduce the increasing insecurity at the bottom end of the labour market but may serve to widen the growing inequalities (Giupponi and Machin, 2022). With the pandemic particularly affecting lower-paid workers, especially those in ethnic minorities, this exclusion has gained greater significance (Chapter 5).

Tax expenditures are 'an important pillar of the politics of taxation and the political economy of tax bargaining' (von Haldenwang et al, 2021b, p 129). This has been brought out more explicitly in the United States than in the UK. Early American analysts of 'taxation and its beneficiaries' argued that 'the political genius of those who benefit … lies in creating the impression that it is others who profit' (Corwin and Miller, 1972, p 200). Surrey wondered how the 'upside-down' benefits of tax reliefs could possibly be introduced if their real nature were spelt out in proposals to Congress (Surrey, 1973, p 37; Stern, 1974, chapter 7, satirical correspondence between the US Treasury and rich and poor citizens).

The most detailed analysis of these divisions in development, Jacob Hacker's *The Divided Welfare State*, concluded that 'the heavy distributional skew of tax breaks for private benefits cannot be treated as an analytic afterthought. It must be placed at the heart of any explanation of the distinctive political dynamics' (Hacker, 2002, p 39). 'In effect, tax expenditures allow public officials to address specific problems by cutting taxes, not raising them. That is a very seductive proposition to anyone aspiring to elected office, especially in a polity attuned to tax burdens.' Tax expenditures 'appear to reduce the size of government while enlarging the scope', so 'in some ways, [they] represent plan B for both [political] parties' (Howard, 2009, pp 88, 96, 99). The hidden wiring of the 'subterranean' workings of fiscal welfare (Hacker, 2002) conceals both scale and effects. A rare Scandinavian study similarly concluded that 'the invisibility of tax expenditures represents both a democratic problem and a problem of political steering' (Ervik and Kuhnle, 1996, p 93). Comparative studies also provide some supporting detail on tax expenditure policy making (Kvist and Sinfield, 1997; Avram, 2017; Morel et al, 2018, 2019).

Influence on private markets and the wider society

'By allowing deductions from the tax base, governments can allow any number of expenditures to claim priority over income tax' and public spending (Evans et al, 2017, p 77). Thus tax reliefs indicate government choices that 'automatically' take effect before governments make budgetary allocations to their own spending departments (Surrey and McDaniel, 1985, p 32). This effectively constitutes 'pre-distribution', used to describe activities taken before public spending decisions, such as employer wage policies (Hacker, 2011, p 35; Chwalisz and Diamond, 2015). (Curiously Hacker did not extend the term to include them despite his own major work [2002].)

These reliefs 'reshape the linkages between state and society' and groups within it, discriminating 'some taxpayers positively against the rest' (von Haldenwang et al, 2021b, pp 139, 130), but there has been scant official engagement with these broader issues. Even NAO, which is answerable to Parliament, and OBR, within the Treasury but classified as independent of government, tend to concentrate on costs and misuse.

The ways tax reliefs influence and promote private markets while depriving the Exchequer of public revenue deserve much further and sustained government and independent scrutiny to examine the impact on wider society (Byrne and Ruane, 2017). Behind-closed-doors policy development and control by the more powerful beneficiaries is illustrated by the major reform to pensions tax relief resulting in the 2004 Act (see Chapter 6). Consultation proposals were drawn up by an Inland Revenue-chaired committee that yielded to special representations and brought in tax professionals and representatives of the pensions industry but no members of trade unions or other stakeholders. Unsurprisingly, fiscal concessions to private pensions remained remarkably generous, with very high ceilings to contributions. Nevertheless, the very great majority of consultation responses, almost entirely from the tax professions and pensions industry, successfully argued for even higher and inflation-proofed limits to what was proposed.

Fiscal subsidies to private pensions aiding employers and the pensions and insurance industries are probably the greatest example in most countries, as Titmuss pointed out nearly 70 years ago (Titmuss, 1955 in 1958, chapter 3, also in Alcock et al, 2001, part 2, chapter 2; Titmuss, 1962). This wider impact with its subsidised transfer of power is particularly underlined in *The Cold War in Welfare*: '[P]rivatisation is about reducing the role of the state and expanding the role of stock markets, which is altogether a different proposition' from providing better pensions (Minns, 2001, p xv, italics in original; Blackburn, 2002).

Even less discussed are employers' and employees' gains from not having to pay NICs on payments into pensions by employers. The cost practically doubles the total subsidy to non-state pensions – some £12 billion to employers and some £6 billion to employees in 2021 (see Chapter 6). The scale was not revealed for many years, is still not included in NI accounts and has apparently never been discussed in government despite the detailed proposal in the Mirrlees Report to levy NICs on employed pensioners (Mirrlees, 2011, chapter 14).

These pre-distribution subsidies constitute a form of 'privatization [that] needs to be understood as a fundamental re-ordering of claims in society … [it] undermines the foundation of claims for public purpose and public service' with significant 'distributive implications', shifting 'power to those who can more readily exercise power in the market' (Starr, 1989, p 42). This 'individualisation of the social' (Ferge, 1997) can undermine, if not sabotage, the welfare state, as the hidden wiring of taxation weakens protection to those more vulnerable to poverty without wider recognition of its impact. This requires a broader view of fiscal welfare not solely confined to the fiscal activities strictly comparable to public spending social policy. The persisting neglect has significant political implications, a clear example of power 'at its most effective when least observable' (Lukes, 2005, p 1).

Other major affected markets include private health care, particularly in the United States, and the private housing market, which has a substantial influence on the building industry (see Chapter 8). Tax reliefs on interest on loans for house-buyers and/or landlords existed in the UK for a very long time and provided even greater support to owner-occupiers after the end of Schedule A in 1963 with the added benefit of no longer having to pay an imputed rent. Today, VAT relief of £16.1 billion supports the building industry and its suppliers in constructing and selling new buildings but not in maintaining, repairing and renovating. This gains additional societal significance with the need to increase sustainability and the considerable emission saving in restoring over building new.

Employers also benefit from many other reliefs generally only discussed in terms of the individuals benefitting, such as the employment allowance and the reliefs on termination payments that subsidise employers' costs. Their use and abuse has had to be scrutinised more carefully, with the cost of the accompanying NI exemption only recently acknowledged and costed (HMRC, 2021b, 7.10).

Both direct and indirect fiscal support to businesses helps to shape decisions on employment and much else in the communities in which people live and work, affecting the quality of life and access to resources across the whole of society (see Chapter 13). The UK is among the countries that have many tax expenditures at sub-national level that are seldom included, let alone costed, in national, and so multi-country, listings (von Haldenwang, 2021a). Nevertheless, many are costly and have an important influence on how communities develop and survive. For example, non-domestic rate reliefs may support service stations and shops in sparsely populated areas (Scotland), exempt registered childcare providers (Wales) or help small businesses more generally. How much they shape the community in these and many other ways appears little explored.

Finally, the use of tax expenditures can affect other countries and relationships with them. Richer nations' overseas development aid often comes with long-established requirements imposed on recipient countries to exempt from tax some or all forms of donor support. Its distributive impact there influences attitudes to, and behaviour in, their tax systems. The market-distorting effect of tax-free access available to resident expatriates and local subcontractors and their families creates privileged groups and undermines others' willingness to pay taxes (von Haldenwang et al, 2021, p 45; Steel, 2021).

Examining comparable public and tax spending together

The failure to analyse comparable public and tax spending together continues despite it being 'difficult to form a coherent political discussion when … the two halves of the argument are in different places' is at least as misleading and damaging today as it was nearly half a century ago (re-iterating the House of Commons Expenditure Committee, 1976, quoted earlier and in Pond, 1980, p 61). Still to be introduced in the UK, such budgetary comparisons of tax reliefs and public spending have been used in the United States, Canada and some other countries (GAO, 2016). However, they have generally been discontinued on changes of government. Bringing the two together in the UK shows, for example, that adding the £40 billion net cost of tax and NIC reliefs to the £106 billion spent on social security benefits increases total retirement income spending by nearly two fifths (2016–17) (Sinfield, 2020).

The insulation of taxes from other government interventions administratively and politically has largely been maintained, protecting political decisions on tax from closer scrutiny of their wider impact. While benefits were cut back as part of Thatcher's attack on 'welfare state dependency' (Thatcher, 1995, p 538), some fiscal welfare was made more generous. For example, bereavement tax allowances were extended to a second year in 1982, while earnings-related short-term social security benefits were being abolished. In 2015, when most public welfare benefits for people of working age were being kept below inflation under the Coalition's regime of austerity, changes were made to allow amounts remaining in some private pensions to be passed on tax-free to direct family (Chapter 6). While freezing benefits was presented as an inevitable economic imperative, these tax cuts, described as 'indefensibly generous' by the IFS, helped those well enough off to avoid drawing as much on their pensions to pass these savings on, means-enhancing their families (IFS, 2021).

In the United States, Christopher Ellis and Christopher Faricy's *The Other Side of the Coin* brings out the importance and value of examining STEs alongside direct spending at claimant level (Ellis and Faricy, 2021). Interviewing users of both STEs and social security showed many more people receiving STEs than public benefits and generally well aware of the support from the former – especially if asked about 'government subsidy programs' rather than 'government social programs' (Ellis and Faricy, 2021, pp 48–9, 116). While tax expenditures may be seen as hidden welfare in broader discussions, at individual level their value was realised and appreciated by most.

In contrast to negative perceptions of 'welfare' and its race-sensitivity in the United States, STEs were less politicised and more acceptable to supporters of small government and low taxes. They 'provide ways for both parties to get something they want – an expanded social welfare state for Democrats, a smaller amount of federal tax revenue for Republicans' (Ellis and Faricy, 2021, p 122). They 'have a built-in "framing advantage" in that it is easier for policymakers to persuade the public to support private rather than public solutions to social problems' (Ellis and Faricy, 2021, p 120). How far this is confined to the United States needs further research (see Hills, 2015). Very often, 'the public' are unaware of tax reliefs being built into many taxes.

Policy development, evaluation and change

'Why do governments insist in using costly fiscal policy mechanisms without any proof of effectiveness? What is to be gained from this specific mode of tax governance, which bypasses ordinary tax and spending politics?' (von Haldenwang et al, 2021b, p 129). In marked contrast to the regular scrutiny and debate on public spending provisions in the UK and many other countries, tax expenditures and how they are developed, implemented and monitored continue to be neglected. The conclusions of two major studies in the United States have received little attention – the historical analyses of the creation, development and impact of major social tax expenditures by Howard (1997, 2009) and Hacker (2002).

In the UK, there is still no official analysis of tax spending alongside public spending, and no tax expenditure budget. Yet 'the harm of not allocating tax expenditures to programmes seems greater than any possible harm from so doing' (Sandford, 1980, p 231). Such issues were first raised over 60 years ago. It has taken over 40 years since the first official response for substantially more of the necessary evidence to be regularly reported, but much more needs to be done. NAO, OBR and some select committees have at last begun to pursue elements of these questions more persistently, teasing out more data from HMRC (OBR, 2019; NAO, 2020; PAC, 2020). However, behavioural and distributive implications for the wider society and economy require much closer attention.

The burying of most fiscal welfare changes, often in the depths of annual budgets, without the opportunities for wider and more public discussion that accompany changes to public spending programmes, is part of the reason why tax policy making is not fit for purpose: '[N]o one in either the Treasury or HMRC is accountable for either the value for money or the cost' (Rutter et al,, 2017, p 31; see Chapter 15). There is also too much behind-closed-doors policy development and control by the more powerful beneficiaries of tax reliefs. This has already been well illustrated above when the Inland Revenue working group on the major reform to pensions tax reliefs resulting in the 2004 Act effectively excluded trade unions and others outside the pensions industry and their relevant professions from drawing up the consultation proposals. Time will tell if a similar story will emerge about the removal of the lifetime pension contribution cap in the 2023 Budget. Purported to be needed to keep senior doctors working within the NHS when much smaller and cheaper measures could have worked, it provides enormous tax benefit to all (not just senior doctors) with very large pension pots (and their beneficiaries).

HMRC and HM Treasury have long pleaded that their primary concern is with correctly implementing tax reliefs as if they only had a technical role, but they have been slowly cajoled into taking greater account of the revenue cost of a relief, the need to monitor changes, the value for money and the wider impact. However, doubts about how far they will do this and release control, providing tax expenditure-level data and giving a broader view of the operation and cost of all reliefs and their effects on other government activities, have led to demands for a separate minister and Ministry of Taxation directly accountable to Parliament (Murphy, 2017).

Internationally, the need for policy improvements has been made bluntly, with the World Bank noting tax expenditure 'violates' vertical and horizontal equity (WB, 2003, p 2). 'This incentive pattern might be judged absolutely perverse – giving the most inducement to those who need the inducement least – and yet it is the common practice in at least some countries.' Evaluating may be hard, but 'a more serious problem may be the failure to try. ... An out-of-sight, out-of-mind attitude can arise and continue to insulate inefficiencies from scrutiny for periods of years' (OECD, 2010, pp 28–9). 'Tax bases should be broadened first by removing or reducing tax expenditures that disproportionately benefit high income groups' to promote inclusive growth, helping 'achieve both greater efficiency and a narrower distribution of disposable income' (Brys et al for OECD, 2016, p 51; also OECD, 2018;

IMF, 2019; and von Haldenwang et al for GTED, 2022). A joint-OECD critique of tax expenditures in Colombia had some trenchant advice that might well be applied to the UK (Tax Experts Commission, 2022). The European Commission has required member states to provide tax expenditure data on a consistent basis since 2014, but there does not appear to have been any subsequent official report or analysis.

Strengthening transparency and accountability will enable more evidence-based policy making (Rutter et al, 2017). The case is made all the stronger by increasing arguments for a human rights-based approach to economic and fiscal policies and budget-making in particular:

> [A]s the government's main tool to realise rights on the ground ... human rights standards shape the goals of a budget, whilst human rights principles (of participation, accountability, transparency and non-discrimination) shape the budget process, in all of its stages. This can improve the impact of economic policy by making sure that financial decisions benefit those who are most in need. (O'Hagan et al, 2021)

The costs of tax reliefs would then be included in budgets and public accounts alongside public spending items.

More open accounting of tax expenditures would also meet the requirements of the UN's International Covenant on Economic, Social and Cultural Rights (ICESCR), which obliges governments to '"take steps ... to the maximum of its available resources, with a view to achieving progressively the full realization of the rights recognized in the present Covenant ... without discrimination of any kind" (ICESCR, article 2 (1))' (Nolan, 2018). Maximum available resources (MAR) should therefore be drawn on to avoid cutting basic human rights (Blyberg and Hofbauer, 2014, p 4). However, tax expenditures are not so far included in MAR analyses. By making the policy goal and impact of each tax expenditure clearer and more accountable, MAR can be identified and used to respond to such urgent needs as the pandemic and the cost-of-living and climate crises.

Conclusion

The very slow and partial official opening up on tax expenditures, 'an important means by which government pursues economic and social objectives' (NAO, 2020, p 12), raises important questions about democratic accountability and the influence still being exercised by powerful vested interests including employers and pension funds. More evidence, analysis and sustained questioning of the long-closed world of tax reliefs and its hidden wiring are helping to reveal and connect many issues that have so far received little attention, at least in the UK. Closer examination of tax reliefs in the broader context of society and economy reveals the upside-down benefits of much tax expenditure and a more broadly defined fiscal welfare with its tendency to greater generosity upwards in comparison to increasingly meaner social security benefits.

Outside government, who gets how much and how through taxes as 'alternative policy means' (IMF, 2019, p 7) to public spending is receiving more sustained attention, but how far a tax relief is universal, means-tested or means-enhancing in comparison to other government support needs more examination. More questions are being raised about the ways and extent that reliefs supplement, complement or undermine welfare state services and benefits, encouraging alternative provision and draining public support for state provision. 'We can see the play of powerful economic and political forces; the strength and tenacity of privilege; the continuing search for equity in a rapidly changing society' (Titmuss, 1958, p 54; 1959, 1962). Many decades later, we still know little about how far vested interests outside and within government influence the hidden fiscal wiring that continues to help maintain, if not increase, inequities and inequalities.

The wider implications of not only narrowly defined fiscal welfare or STEs but also many of the tax expenditures that are not identified as social deserve to be taken more account of in social policy analysis and policy making. With effective priority over taxing and public spending, their pre-distributive spending through taxes helps to shape, even determine, changes in local, regional and industrial development with subsidies that influence industrial structure, the availability of employment, the standard of living and the quality of life across society.

A human rights-based approach to budgeting and tax policy aligned with the ICESCR's requirement to identify and deploy Maximum Available Resources could help ensure better and wider access to human rights. It would challenge the current priority to tax reliefs and make the hidden wiring in taxation more visible, accountable and less regressive.

Tax reliefs can be as, or even more, important in their impact on living standards, shaping behaviour and the wider development of societal welfare as direct benefits and services in public spending programmes. Issues of power, equality, rights and social justice are becoming more recognised as explicitly relevant to fiscal welfare and tax expenditure policies, only strengthening the case for more research and better policy.

Further reading
- GTED (2022) – Global Tax Expenditure Database with country files providing access to available data from over 100 countries.
- HMRC (2023a) – the second much improved and fuller official account of UK tax expenditures.

- Hodge (2016) – vivid account of efforts to extract data and more from HMRC by a convener of the Public Accounts Committee, especially but not only chapter 9.
- Morel et al (2018) – good discussion of fiscal welfare with European analysis.
- NAO (2020) – fine analysis of the strengths and weaknesses of HMRC management of tax expenditures.

References

Adema, W., Fron, P. and Ladaique, M. (2014) 'How much do OECD countries spend on social protection and how redistributive are their tax/benefit systems?', *International Social Security Review*, 67(1): 1–25.

Alcock, P., Glennerster, H., Oakley, A. and Sinfield, A. (eds) (2001) *Welfare and Wellbeing: Richard Titmuss's Contribution to Social Policy*, Bristol: Policy Press.

Avram, S. (2017) 'Who benefits from the "hidden welfare state"? The distributional effects of personal income tax expenditures in six countries', *Journal of European Social Policy*, 28(3): 1–23.

Blackburn, R. (2002) *Banking on Death*, London: Verso.

Blyberg, A. and Hofbauer, H. (2014) 'The use of maximum available resources: Article 2 & governments' budgets', International Budget Partnership.

Brewer, M., Sibieta, L. and Wren-Lewis, L. (2008) 'Racing away? Income inequality and the evolution of high incomes', Institute for Fiscal Studies, IFS briefing 76.

Brys, B., Perret, S., Thomas, A. and O'Reilly, P. (2016) 'Tax design for inclusive economic growth', OECD taxation working papers 26, Paris: OECD.

Byrne, D. and Ruane, S. (2017) *Paying for the Welfare State in the 21st Century: Tax and Spending in Post-industrial Societies*, Bristol: Policy Press.

Canada (2022) 'Report on federal tax expenditures: concepts, estimates and evaluations 2021', Ottawa: Government of Canada, Available from: https://www.canada.ca/en/department-finance/services/publications/federal-tax-expenditures/2021.html

Chwalisz, C. and Diamond, P. (eds) (2015) *The Predistribution Agenda: Tackling Inequality and Supporting Sustainable Growth*, London: Tauris.

Corwin, R. and Miller, S.M. (1972) 'Taxation and its beneficiaries: the manipulation of symbols', *American Journal of Orthopsychiatry*, 42(2): 200–14.

Ellis, C. and Faricy, C. (2021) *The Other Side of the Coin: Public Opinion toward Social Tax Expenditures*, New York: Russell Sage.

Ervik, R. and Kuhnle, S. (1996) 'The Nordic welfare model and the European Union', in B. Greve (ed) *Comparative Welfare Systems: The Scandinavian Model in a Period of Change*, Basingstoke: Macmillan, pp 87–107.

Evans, C., Hasseldine, J., Lymer, A., Ricketts, R. and Sandford, C. (2017) *Comparative Taxation: Why Tax Systems Differ*, Malvern: Fiscal Publications.

Ferge, Z. (1997) 'The changed welfare paradigm: the individualisation of the social', *Social Policy and Administration*, 31(1): 20–44.

GAO (Government Accountability Office) (2016) 'Tax expenditures: opportunities exist to use budgeting and agency performance processes to increase oversight', Available from: https://www.gao.gov/products/GAO-16-622

Giupponi, G. and Machin, S. (2022) 'Labour market inequality', *IFS Deaton Review of Inequalities*.

GTED (2022) 'Country files', Available from: www.gted.net

Hacker, J.S. (2002) *The Divided Welfare State: The Battle over Public and Private Social Benefits in the United States*, Cambridge: Cambridge University Press.

Hacker, J.S. (2011) 'The institutional foundations of middle-class democracy', *Policy Network*, 6: 33–7.

Hills, J. (2015) *Good Times, Bad Times: The Welfare Myth of 'Them' and 'Us'*, Bristol: Policy Press.

HMRC (2020) 'Estimated cost of tax reliefs', London: HMRC, 30 October.

HMRC (2021a) 'Survey of personal incomes', London: HMRC.

HMRC (2021b) 'Tax relief statistics (December 2021)', London: HMRC. NB: only non-structural reliefs, but section 3 gives links in tables 3 and 4 to a very limited subset of structural ones.

HMRC (2023a) 'Non-structural tax relief statistics (January 2023)', London: HMRC. Available from: https://www.gov.uk/government/statistics/main-tax-expenditures-and-structural-reliefs

HMRC (2023b) 'Structural tax relief statistics (January 2023)', London: HMRC. Available from: https://www.gov.uk/government/statistics/minor-tax-expenditures-and-structural-reliefs

Hodge, M. (2016) *Called to Account*, London: Little, Brown.

House of Commons Expenditure Committee (1976) Fourth Report, HC 299, London: HMSO.

Howard, C. (1997) *The Hidden Welfare State: Tax Expenditures and Social Policy in the United States*, Princeton, NJ: Princeton University Press.

Howard, C. (2009) 'Making taxes the life of the party', in I.W. Martin, A.K. Mehrotra and M. Prasad (eds) *The New Fiscal Sociology*, New York: Cambridge University Press, pp 86–100.

IMF (2016) 'United Kingdom fiscal transparency evaluation', Washington, DC: IMF.

IMF (2019) 'Tax expenditure reporting and its use in fiscal management: a guide for developing economies', Washington, DC: IMF, March.

Kvist, J. and Sinfield, A. (1997) 'Comparing tax welfare states', in M. May, E. Brunsdon and G. Craig (eds) *Social Policy Review 9*, London: SPA, pp 249–75.

Lukes, S. (2005) *Power: A Radical View* (2nd edn), Basingstoke: Palgrave Macmillan.

Lymer, A. and Oats, L. (2020) *Taxation: Policy and Practice 2020/2021* (27th edn), Exeter: Fiscal Publications.

Minns, Richard (2001) *The Cold War in Welfare*, London: Verso.

Mirrlees, J., Adam, S., Besley, T., Blundell, R., Bond, S. and Chote, R. et al (2011) *Tax by design*, London: IFS.

Morel, N., Touzet, C. and Zemmour, M. (2018) 'Fiscal welfare in Europe: why should we care and what do we know so far?', *European Journal of Social Policy*, 28(5): 549–60.

Morel, N., Touzet. C., and Zemmour M. (2019) 'From the hidden welfare state to the hidden part of welfare state reform: analyzing the uses and effects of fiscal welfare in France', *Social Policy and Administration*, 53(1): 34–48.

Murphy, R. (2017) 'The Tax Gap and what to do about it', in W. Snell (ed), *Tax Takes: Perspectives on Building a Better Tax System to Benefit Everyone in the UK*, Bristol: Tax Justice UK, 2017, pp 20–1.

Murphy, R. (2018) 'Tax avoidance is not theft', Tax Research UK blog, 13 December, Available from: https://www.taxresearch.org.uk/Blog/2018/12/13/tax-avoidance-is-not-theft

NAO (2014a) *Tax reliefs*, HC 1256, session 2013–14, 7 April.

NAO (2014b) *The effective management of tax reliefs*, HC 785, session 2014–15, 7 November.

NAO (2016) 'Report by the Comptroller and Auditor General', in HMRC, *Annual report and accounts 2015–2016*, London: HMRC, R1-90.

NAO (2020) *The effective management of tax expenditures*, HC 46, session 2019–20, 14 February, Available from: https://www.nao.org.uk/report/the-management-of-tax-expenditures

Nolan, A. (2018) 'Making economic and social rights real', University of Nottingham video Available from: https://www.nottingham.ac.uk/hrlc/operationalunits/economic-and-social-rights-unit/videos.aspx

O'Hagan, A., Hosie, A., Ferrie, J., Mulvagh, L. and Corkery, A. (2021) 'Advancing human rights through the Scottish budget process', SPA conference working paper.

OBR (2019) *Fiscal risks report*, London: OBR, July, CP 131.

OECD (1984) *Tax Expenditures in OECD Countries*, Paris: OECD.

OECD (2010) *Tax Expenditures in OECD Countries*, Paris: OECD.

OECD (2018) *Financial Incentives and Retirement Savings*, Paris: OECD.

OTS (2011) *Review of tax reliefs: final report*, London: Office of Tax Simplification.

PAC (2020) *Management of tax reliefs*, HC 379, Public Accounts Committee, 12th report of session 2019–21, 20 June.

Pond, C. (1980) 'Tax expenditures and fiscal welfare', in C. Sandford, C. Pond and R. Walker (eds) (1980) *Taxation and Social Policy*, London: Heinemann, pp 47–63.

RCTPI (Royal Commission on the Taxation of Profits and Income) (1955) Report of the Royal Commission on the Taxation of Profits and Income (Cmnd 9474), London: HMSO.

Rutter, J., Dodwell, B., Johnson, P., Crozier, G., Cullinane, J. and Lilly, A. et al (2017) 'Better budgets: making tax policy better', Chartered Institute of Taxation (CIOT), Institute for Fiscal Studies (IFS) and Institute for Government (IfG).

Sandford, C. (1980) 'Conclusions', in C. Sandford, C. Pond and R. Walker (eds) *Taxation and Social Policy*, London: Heinemann, pp 228–36.

Sinfield, A. (1978) 'Analyses in the social division of welfare', *Journal of Social Policy*, 7(2): 129–56.

Sinfield, A. (2020) 'Building social policies in fiscal welfare', *Social Policy and Society*, 19(3): 487–99.

Smith, C. (2021) 'Unpaid taxes: the "tax gap"', House of Lords Library, 9 November.

Starr, P. (1989) 'The meaning of privatization', in S.B. Kamerman and A.J. Kahn (eds) *Privatization and the Welfare State*, Princeton: Princeton University Press, pp 13–48.

Steel, I. (2021) 'Three ways lower-income countries can use new UN guidelines on the taxation of aid', ODI: Think Change, 10 May.

Stern, P.M. (1974) *The Rape of the Taxpayer*, New York: Vintage Books.

Surrey, S. (1973) *Pathways to Tax Reform*, Cambridge, MA: Harvard University Press.

Surrey, S. and McDaniel, P. (1985) *Tax Expenditures*, Cambridge, MA: Harvard University Press.

TARC (2014) 'The Definition, measurement, and evaluation of tax expenditures and tax reliefs', Technical paper for NAO, London: NAO.

Tax Experts Commission (2022) 'Tax expenditures report: Colombia 2021', Paris: OECD.

Thatcher, M. (1995) *The Path to Power*, London: HarperCollins.

Titmuss, R. (1958) 'The social divisions of welfare: some reflections on the search for equity', in *Essays on 'the Welfare State'*, London: Allen & Unwin, pp 34–55.

Titmuss, R. (1962) *Income Distribution and Social Change*, London: Allen & Unwin.

Treasury Committee (2018) 'Household finances: income, saving and debt', HC 565, 26 July.

US Treasury (2022) Tax expenditures', Available from: https://home.treasury.gov/system/files/131/Tax-Expenditures-FY2022.pdf

Von Haldenwang, C., Redonda, A. and Aliu, F. (2021a) 'Shedding light on worldwide tax expenditures', GTED Flagship Report (preliminary version), Available from: https://gted.net/2021/05/shedding-light-on-worldwide-tax-expenditures/

Von Haldenwang, C., Kemmerling, A., Redonda, A. and Truchlewski, Z. (2021b) 'The politics of tax expenditures', in L. Hakelberg and L. Seelkopf (eds) *Handbook on the Politics of Taxation*, Cheltenham: Edward Elgar, pp 128–45.

Willis, J.R.M. and Hardwick, P.J.W. (1978) 'Tax expenditures in the United Kingdom', London: Institute of Fiscal Studies.

World Bank (2003) 'Why worry about tax expenditures?', PREMnotes Economic Policy, 77, January.

5

Employment, self-employment and taxation

Kevin Caraher and Enrico Reuter

Introduction: perceptions, politics and socio-economic implications

Taxes on income from employment are a substantive source of government revenue, a largely 'visible' and hence easily politicised form of taxation, and they have serious implications from a social policy perspective.

First, in the case of the UK, income tax (which is levied on income from employment, some benefits, most pensions, rental income, dividends and interest from savings) and National Insurance contributions (NICs) represent more than 40 per cent of the overall tax revenue of the UK government, well ahead of value added tax (VAT), corporation tax and any other remaining sources of revenue (see Chapter 3).

Second, taxes on employment are directly visible to anyone who is in employment, as deductions are highlighted on each payslip, whereas those who are self-employed receive tax bills on their profits after submitting an annual self-assessment. This is then a form of taxation operating in plain sight, and it is therefore not surprising that income tax and NICs feature prominently in the media coverage of spending reviews and budgets – notably when the impact of tax changes on individuals and households is assessed.

It is equally unsurprising that taxes on employment play a key role in political calculations, with the public perception of changes to personal allowances, thresholds and tax rates being regarded as relevant for a government's future electoral prospects and as indicative of its wider political ideology. A recent illustration of this political salience was the 2022 Spring Statement, at which the then Chancellor of the Exchequer, Rishi Sunak, found it politically useful to announce a planned future decrease of the standard income tax rate to create a counterpoint to an immediate increase in NICs, thus seeking to address the need for additional government revenue while being seen as committed to lower taxation – even though the potential gains of this future tax cut for households would be marginal in comparison to increased costs of living and higher NI payments.

In a similar vein, the then Chancellor Kwasi Kwarteng, used the 'mini-budget' in September 2022 to announce not only a reversal of the NIC increase but also to confirm for England, Wales and Northern Ireland a reduction of the standard income tax rate from 20 per cent to 19 per cent and the abolition of the 45 per cent tax rate from April 2023 onwards as part of a wider set of tax cuts in an attempt to underline the new government's ambition to establish 'low-tax' and 'small-state' as key characteristics of the Liz Truss premiership and as a visible differentiation from the previous administration. At the time of writing, the 45 per cent tax rate has been restored for England, Wales and Northern Ireland, and plans for a reduction in the standard rate have been reversed as part of Jeremy Hunt's emergency Budget in November 2022, which sought to close the funding gap left by the Kwarteng Budget. In the case of each of these changes to taxation in 2022, the question of income tax rates has attracted substantive attention and served as a key signal to citizens and financial markets. Furthermore, the Scottish government has increased the higher and top rate of income tax by 1 percentage point from 2023/24, whilst reducing the threshold for the top rate from £150,000 to £125,140.

Third, as wages and salaries are the only or main source of income for most, taxation of income derived from paid work substantially determines the disposable income of individuals and households. How much tax needs to be paid by whom, and what exemptions and reliefs are available, hence opens up questions of fairness and social justice, both vertically with regard to individuals on different levels of income and horizontally between persons with similar incomes but different life circumstances.

Depending on the nature of the welfare system, revenue raised from employment income will also define to different degrees entitlements to key elements of social protection, such as Universal Credit, contributory benefits and pensions. While the contributory principle is much less pronounced in the UK than in conservative-corporatist welfare regimes, a number of benefits remain linked to NI payments. In a wider sense, the increased reliance, over the course of the 20th century, on the taxation of income from employment can be regarded as a product of industrialisation and the expansion of democracy (Tanzi, 2020, p 77). How this form of taxation is organised thus allows for insights into the particular arrangement of welfare capitalism that prevails in a given country at a given moment in time.

The aim of this chapter is to discuss the taxation of income from paid work, both with respect to employment and self-employment. For this purpose, we will proceed in three steps. The first section provides an overview of the organisation of employment-related taxes in the UK to highlight the key features of a system that combines simplicity with complexity. In the second part, the fairness, equity and efficiency of this system are explored to identify some of the most salient problems of the existing system from a social justice perspective. It should be noted that as the focus of this chapter is on the individual taxation burden, it does not include explicit reference to corporation tax relief, nor a consideration of savings made by employers.

Finally, before a short conclusion, we look more closely at the political conflicts and tensions that underpin the taxation of income from paid work to shed light on why reform is difficult to achieve in the context of diverging interests.

Taxing employment: simplicity and complexity

The taxation of income from employment in the UK can be characterised as both simple and complex.

Simplicity manifests itself in the following ways. There is, in addition to income tax, only one type of social insurance contribution, which furthermore is only weakly hypothecated (see Chapter 3). In many conservative-corporatist welfare states, payments for health insurance, pensions and unemployment insurance are differentiated.

As Tables 5.1 and 5.2 indicate, in England, Wales and Northern Ireland, once income exceeds the tax-free personal allowance (£12,570 in 2022/23), only three tax rates are levied on income from employment; in Scotland, once income exceeds the same personal allowance limit there are four tax rates levied on income from employment. It is worth noting that in all four countries an individual's personal allowance will reduce by £1 for every £2 earned over £100,000. Therefore, once an individual earns £125,140 (in 2022/23) they will pay tax on all income and receive no personal allowance.

With regards to Class 1 NICs, employees whose income is above the primary threshold of £823 per month pay 12 per cent up to the point where they reach the upper earnings limit of £4,189 per month, above which the contribution is reduced to 2 per cent.

Class 1 NICs are also paid in the UK by employers and are set at a single rate of 13.8 per cent as soon as pay exceeds the so-called secondary threshold, an earnings level slightly lower than the primary threshold that applies to

Table 5.1: Income tax rates and bands 2022/23 (England, Wales and Northern Ireland)

Band	Taxable income	Tax rate (%)
Personal allowance	Up to £12,570	0
Basic rate	£12,750 to £50,270	20
Higher rate	£50,271 to £150,000	40
Additional rate	Over £150,000	45

Source: https://www.gov.uk/income-tax-rates

Table 5.2: Income tax rates and bands 2022/23 (Scotland)

Band	Taxable income	Tax rate (%)
Starter rate	£12,571 to £14,732	19
Scottish basic rate	£14,733 to £25,688	20
Intermediate rate	£25,689 to £43,662	21
Higher rate	£43,663 to £150,000	41
Top rate	Over £150,000	46

Source: https://www.mygov.scot/income-tax-rates-and-personal-allowances

Table 5.3: Class 2 NIC rates 2022/23

Small profits threshold amount per year	£6,725
Rate per week	£3.15

Table 5.4: Class 4 NIC rates 2022/23

Lower profits limit at which self-employed individuals start paying Class 4 NI	£11,908
Upper profits limit at which self-employed individuals pay a lower rate	£50,270
Rate between lower profits limit and upper profits limit	9%
Rate above upper profits limit	2%

Note: Table 5.4 presents the Class 4 NIC rates that take account of the abolition of the 1.25 per cent increase in rates as announced on 22 September 2022.

Source: Data for Tables 5.3 and 5.4 adapted from https://www.gov.uk/government/publications/rates-and-allowances-national-insurance-contributions/rates-and-allowances-national-insurance-contributions#historical-and-future-rates under consideration of the reversal of Health and Social Care Levy confirmed in September 2022 (see: https://www.gov.uk/government/publications/the-growth-plan-factsheet-on-cancellation-of-national-insurance-rise-and-health-and-social-care-levy/reversal-of-the-health-and-social-care-levy-factsheet)

employees themselves. Finally, there are no additional tax–free allowances for dependent children as can be a feature of other tax systems, nor age–related allowances (although this was the case in the UK until 2016).

In the main, those who are self-employed are liable for Class 2 and Class 4 NICs rather than Class 1, as set out in Tables 5.3 and 5.4.

Defining employment

An important first question to consider is just who are the 'employed', and how is this status defined both in terms of employment and for tax purposes in the UK? This matters, as the rules for determining tax due on income from employment differs to that due from self-employment in several key ways.

As HMRC (2016) note, employment as a status is defined by case law rather than legislation, and, as noted in a Law Society submission to the Taylor Review (2017, p 34), '[d]etermining whether you are an employee, a worker or genuinely self-employed requires the ability to understand complex legislation, which is spread over many Acts, and be aware of a mountain of case law'. In the context of this chapter, and as set out in the 1996 Employment Rights Act, in the UK there are three main types of employment status that determine an individual's rights under employment law and access to benefits. They are:

- worker
- employee
- self-employed or contractor.

HMRC (2016) guidance notes that

> [w]hether an individual is employed or self-employed will depend upon the nature of the relationship with the person for whom the services are provided. Where two individuals are engaged to carry out similar work, it is possible for one to be self- employed and the other to be an employee because they have been taken on under contracts with different terms and conditions.

Generally, an employee is offered greatest protection by their contract of service.

A worker is less well protected than an employee, although they are entitled to core employment rights, for example:

- getting the National Minimum/Living Wage
- protection against unlawful deductions from wages
- the statutory minimum level of paid holiday
- the statutory minimum length of rest breaks
- to not work more than 48 hours on average per week or to opt out of this right if they choose
- protection against unlawful discrimination
- protection for 'whistleblowing' – reporting wrongdoing in the workplace
- to not be treated less favourably if they work part time.

Workers may also be entitled to a range of benefits including statutory sick pay, statutory maternity/paternity/adoption pay and shared parental pay. All employees are workers, but they are entitled to additional rights over and above those classed as workers, such as: statutory maternity, paternity, adoption and shared parental leave (workers only get pay, not leave); minimum notice periods; protection against unfair dismissal; the right to request flexible working; time off for emergencies and statutory redundancy pay.

An individual is classed as self-employed if they run their own business and are responsible for the success or failure of that business. UK employment law does not cover those who are self-employed as they are classed as being their own boss and so have minimal legal protections limited to protection of their health and safety and protection against discrimination and rights as set out in any contract with a client.

Those classed as solo self-employed, that is, those who work for themselves and by themselves with no employees, are by far the most significant group within a broader definition of self-employment, with the solo self-employed accounting for 85 per cent of the self-employed (IFS, 2020). Within this group, occupations traditionally associated with solo self-employment – construction, agriculture and food preparation – form the largest segment and account for 25 per cent of solo self-employment (Toovey, 2022). Beyond this, individuals working for themselves operate in myriad fields across the economy, ranging from accountancy, management and data-analytic services to the media, entertainment, beauty, personal wellbeing, care and road transport industries.

In terms of access to employment-related benefits, the Department for Work and Pensions (DWP, 2022) defines self-employment as:

- your main job or your main source of income
- you get regular work from self-employment
- your work is organised – this means you have invoices and receipts, or accounts
- you expect to make a profit.

Returning to the question of taxation, the initial picture of relative simplicity turns into something more complex as soon as one looks more closely. Without providing a comprehensive summary, the following features of the taxation of income from paid work create complexity:

- The total sums of tax-free allowances for income tax can be variable – for example, in addition to personal allowances commonly received by (almost) all taxpayers (other than those on high earnings more than £125,000 per annum by which level the allowance has been phased out), some employees can benefit from the Marriage Allowance, which enables them to receive a small share of their partner's personal allowance if it is not fully used.

- The substantially reduced rate for NICs above the upper earnings limit (£967 per week or £4,189 per month for 2022/23) reduces the progressive nature of the taxation of employment income.
- Persons with children with an adjusted net income of more than £50,000 per annum see their Child Benefit payments reduced and either become liable for the High Income Child Benefit Charge or can choose not to receive Child Benefit with the risk of losing NI credits.
- While not being a tax in the strict sense, student loan repayments for young employees who have studied after the introduction of tuition fees and the abolition of maintenance grants face an additional reduction of their disposable income by 9 per cent above a certain threshold.
- With regard to employees, individuals can obtain reductions in their taxable income by subscribing to salary sacrifice schemes. Such schemes, which can also bring savings for employers, are contractual agreements involving salary exchanges to reduce an employee's entitlement to cash pay, usually in return for a non-cash benefit. The main examples include cycle to work and low emission/green car schemes, workplace nurseries, employer-provided pensions advice and payments into pension schemes, which offer the most generous savings (see Chapter 6). They also include childcare vouchers and directly contracted employer-provided childcare that commenced before October 2018.

Since the gains from these schemes are more substantial for higher-rate income taxpayers, they benefit middle- to high-income earners disproportionately. It is also worth noting that salary sacrifice schemes are not available to the self-employed and, though they are available, are not routinely offered to employees of small organisations (Brunsdon and May, 2016).

As highlighted by Tables 5.1 to 5.4, another complication is the difference in taxation of earned income between employees and self-employed persons. The latter pay much reduced NICs, either of a small fixed weekly amount if only small profits are achieved, or of 9 per cent for annual profits up to about £50,270 (2022/23 rates) and then 2 per cent for profits above this level.

A fair and efficient form of taxation

To unpack how fair and efficient the taxation of income from employment and self-employment is in the UK, we will highlight three key points: first, the balance between taxation of earned and other forms of income; secondly, the weaknesses in the system's progressiveness, with particular attention to the topic of tax reliefs and questions of horizontal distribution; and thirdly, the difference between employment and self-employment.

While income tax is raised on income from employment, some benefits, most pensions, rental income and interest from savings, income in the form of dividends, inheritance and capital gains is taxed at lower rates, with capital gains roughly taxed at half the rate of employment income. This imbalance between the taxation of income from paid work and the taxation of other sources of income is even more acute if NICs are regarded as a tax on earnings from employment – a plausible position, given the shift from contributory to means-tested social security benefits and the erosion of the links between contributions and entitlements (see Chapters 2 and 7), combined with NICs increases under successive governments since the 2000s, which have often been described as a stealth tax and led to a steady rise of NICs as a proportion of overall tax revenues. Moreover, taxation of earned income via the Pay-as-You-Earn system, despite the existence of a number of relief schemes and exemptions, allows for limited degrees of tax management by the individual taxpayer. This is at odds with other forms of taxation: for example, inheritance tax can be circumvented by gifting at least seven years before death.

It can furthermore be argued that land and property are 'under-taxed' in the UK, especially since '[n]one of these taxes adequately capture increases in land values, including those which occur when planning permission is granted' (IPPR, 2018, p 211, and see Chapter 9).

Overall, in many cases, the taxation of employment as a productive economic activity is heavier than the taxation of unproductive income derived from ownership. This not only raises questions about fairness but also about efficiency and effectiveness of the tax system to encourage those activities that lead to a more prosperous and productive national economy.

The overall progressive quality of the taxation of paid income is undermined by a number of factors, not least that employers are also liable for NICs, which in effect can be regarded as a tax on employment and a key impediment to any future proposed merger of income tax and NI. First and foremost, though, as mentioned earlier, NICs do not rise once an individual reaches certain levels of income as with the higher income tax rates. Instead, employee NIC rates drop by 10 percentage points, thus largely reducing the overall increase in taxation that is caused by crossing into the higher income tax rate of 40 per cent. The effect is similar with regard to profits from self-employment, even if the reduction in NICs is only 7 percentage points.

Second, Conservative government tax reforms, with their focus on raising the tax-free personal allowance first for income tax and in the 2022 Spending Review for NI, have benefitted those on middle and higher incomes more than those at the bottom of the income distribution, further eroding principles of progressive taxation. The short-lived 'mini-budget' in September 2022 continued this trend. While a decrease of the standard rate of income tax by 1 per cent was announced, benefitting a large segment of the UK population outside Scotland, the absolute gains from this reduction would have been more substantive for those on higher incomes. This 1 per cent increase was subsequently abandoned by Jeremy Hunt in his first budget as Chancellor in November 2022. Moreover, the planned abolition of the additional income tax rate of 45 per cent for those earning more than £150,000 per year would have meant that the biggest boosts to disposable income accrued to individuals at the very top of the income hierarchy, had it not been quickly withdrawn in reaction to adverse political and market responses. Finally, the decision in 2021 to freeze both the personal allowance and the 40 per cent threshold until 2026 will increase the number of people whose income crosses over those thresholds and who consequently pay a larger share of their income in tax. This further exacerbates the extent to which gains related to recent changes of employment-related taxes predominantly benefit individuals on very high salaries.

Third, the existing panoply of tax reliefs, be it for workplace pension contributions, certain types of expenses such as professional subscriptions or salary sacrifice schemes, enable those on higher incomes to achieve higher levels of savings, whereas those whose income is below the threshold for paying income tax are unable to benefit. These and related forms of tax relief hence appear as 'middle-class benefits' that not only advantage individuals on relatively higher incomes but also restrict the related incentives to a limited part of the population.

This creates obvious problems with regard to vertical redistribution, as those on higher incomes stand to gain more than those on lower incomes – and these types of allowances are hence 'means-enhancing rather than means-tested' given that they accrue largely to better-off persons (Collins et al, 2022, p 249). Moreover, many occupational welfare and voluntary benefit schemes remain at the discretion of employers, with smaller and medium-sized enterprises far less likely to offer them (May, 2022).

However, it can be argued that the problem extends further to also include a horizontal dimension over the life cycle of an individual (Sefton, 2008). As has been shown in detail by Hills (2015), the benefits of a collective social protection system do not necessarily fall to those most in need at a particular point in time. It is rather a holistic assessment across the entire life cycle that is needed to judge who benefits from social spending and the collective management of social risks.

Finally, the differences in tax treatment between those in employment and those who are self-employed leads to further questions about fairness and efficiency. On the one hand, the argument for reduced NICs by individuals who are self-employed appears reasonable in light of their limited access to certain benefits, such as statutory sick pay or contribution-based Jobseeker's Allowance. On the other hand, the self-employed qualify for the state pension, and the abolition of the partially incomes-related additional state pension in 2016 further aligned pension benefits between the self-employed and employees. Moreover, the self-employed have full access to Universal Credit and of course healthcare services on an equitable basis. Therefore, overall, the gaps in available social protection can, in normal circumstances, be seen as less relevant than the savings in NICs. However, as the COVID-19 pandemic has shown, even relatively small gaps in social protection for the self-employed can cause serious problems.

We now turn to the question of (solo) self-employment in more detail. Word limits pre-empt consideration of the ways in which some self-employed such as company owner-managers can take income in the form of dividends and benefit from capital gains tax, allowing tax savings compared to employees (Cribb et al, 2019; Miller et al, 2021). Similarly, we will not consider the specific circumstances in the gig economy (Woodcock and Graham, 2020) and the extent to which those working in these jobs can be regarded as genuinely self-employed. Hence the focus here is primarily on the largest group, sole traders.

Contrary to the late 1970s, when this form of employment was regarded as dwindling (Sandford et al, 1980), its relevance as a taxation and social policy issue has substantially increased due to the rise in self-employment since the 1990s.

State of play for self-employment in the UK

The number of those defined as self-employed in the UK increased over the first two decades of the 21st century, up from around 3.2 million in 2000 or 12 per cent of the labour force in 2001, with pre-pandemic levels in 2019 standing at over 5 million or around 15 per cent of the labour force (ONS, 2018, 2020; Caraher and Reuter, 2019, 2020). This rise in the numbers of self-employed in the UK mirrored the pre-pandemic EU average, which itself stood at a fraction under 15 per cent of the EU working population (Caraher and Reuter, 2019), and the increase in the numbers of the solo self-employed in the UK was among the highest in the Organisation for Economic Co-operation and Development (OECD) (Giuponni and Xu, 2020). Indeed, in the aftermath of the 2008 global financial crisis, the growth in UK self-employment 'outstripped growth in permanent employment by 3 to 1' (O'Leary, 2014, p 9) and represented 'nearly half of the increase in total employment since the recession' (Deane, 2016, p 7).

This significant growth in the levels of self-employment continued in the latter half of the decade, accounting for 47 per cent of overall increases in employment in 2018 (Resolution Foundation, 2019). However, as is to be expected, the COVID-19 pandemic has had a negative impact on the level of solo self-employment in the UK, with the Association for Independent Professionals and the Self-Employed (UK) (Toovey, 2020) reporting a decrease of 5 per cent, reducing the numbers of self-employed to around

4.4 million people, with figures from the Office for National Statistics (ONS) confirming a predicted continued reduction to 4.2 million at the end of 2021 with outflows from self-employment to both unemployment and paid employment as an employee (ONS, 2022). Despite such reductions, solo self-employment contributed £303 billion to the UK economy in 2021 (Toovey, 2022).

Who are the self-employed?

A feature of the growth in numbers of the self-employed in the aftermath of the 2008 global financial crisis was an increase in older self-employed individuals and women. This presents something of a 'mixed bag', as age is a factor related to the need to supplement inadequate pension provision for those nearing or beyond retirement.

Gender as a factor in the increase of solo self-employed was on the surface a more positive development, as the increases saw more women become self-employed with decisions often related to job satisfaction and self-determination. Gender has been an increasingly significant aspect of self-employment since the financial crisis. Citing the Labour Force Survey, ONS (2014) reported that although men dominate this sector of the labour market, accounting for 68 per cent of those who are self-employed, there has been a sharp increase of 34 per cent in the number of women who are now self-employed, with figures for the 2009–14 period standing at 1.4 million individuals, increasing to 1.7 million in 2019 (Toovey, 2020). Men still dominate those who are classed as solo self-employed with figures of 61 per cent of the overall rate, compared to the proportion of solo self-employed women standing at 39 per cent (Toovey, 2021).

This gender disparity is reflected in the sectors in which men and women find employment. As Toovey (2021) notes:

> Men continue to dominate in most of the occupational categories, such as in SOC5 [Standard Occupational Category] skilled trades occupations (88 per cent), SOC8 process, plant and machine operatives (87 per cent) and in SOC9 elementary occupations (61 per cent). However, women dominate SOC6 caring, leisure and service occupations (84 per cent) and SOC4 administrative and secretarial occupations (81 per cent).

Data from ONS (2014; 2018) makes clear that age was, pre-pandemic, a contributory factor in the increase in both full and part-time. So the overall picture is one of growth, with explanatory factors being gender, age and maintenance of self-employment status or a combination of such factors.

Ethnicity is also a factor that should be considered when defining who the self-employed are, and self-employment among ethnic minority groups has increased over the decade 2011–21. Data from the Annual Population Survey published by the UK government (2021) notes that the largest of these groups who were classed as self-employed were the combined Pakistani/Bangladeshi group at 23.2 per cent, increased from 2011 when the figure was 21.6 per cent. In contrast, the group with the lowest number of self-employed individuals was the Black community, which recorded figures of 8.2 per cent in 2011, rising to 11.2 per cent in 2021.

As was noted in Caraher and Reuter (2019, p 202), the Family Resources Survey (FRS), recorded that median income fell by 22 per cent for the self-employed from 2008/9 to 2012/13 as opposed to employees who over the same period saw earnings drop by only 5 per cent (ONS, 2014). The ONS, presenting updated figures from the FRS, notes that the 'modal income category – the level of earnings which is most common – among the self-employed is lower than among employees. The distribution of self-employed income appears centred around £240 a week, much lower than that for employees, which is centred around £400 a week' (ONS, 2018, p 4).

Furthermore, it was also clear that

> the poorest 20 per cent of self-employed workers earn a quarter less than the poorest 20 per cent of employees ... 30 per cent of households with one self-employed worker (and no other earners) are in poverty, compared with 14 per cent of households with one employee (and no other earners). (Dellot and Read, 2016, p 12)

The Institute for Fiscal Studies (IFS) notes that there has been an 8 per cent increase in the lowest paid self-employed, rising from 15 to 23 per cent over the 20-year period from 1999 to 2019 (Giupponi and Machin, 2022).

There are then a range of challenges with respect to the self-employed, including marked differences in taxation that raise questions of fairness, inequitable access to social protection and the benefits of salary sacrifice schemes, and unequal levels of exposure to social risks due to the distinct demographics of solo self-employment.

Politics of tax reform

In light of the issues discussed in the previous section, it is worth asking why there have been no successful attempts at addressing them – or why, in other words, the taxation of earnings from employment has undergone only marginal changes in recent years.

To answer this question, we will proceed in three steps. First, we will argue that tax reform is generally a challenging undertaking, drawing on the work by Evans et al (2017) on the multiple levels of tax reform, with particular attention to the Mirrlees Review (2011) as the latest reform plan for a holistic change to the UK tax system. Second, focusing especially on the differences in taxation of employment and self-employment, we will summarise the reasons for the failure of the UK government's proposal in 2017 to increase NICs for the self-employed, following the analysis by Bennett (2019). Finally, we will conclude this section by highlighting some further reasons related to media scrutiny and the role of vested interests that help to explain the difficulties of reform.

The Mirrlees Review, launched by the IFS in 2006 to make proposals for a fundamental and holistic reform of the UK tax system to obtain efficient progressivity while ensuring neutrality with minimal exceptions, recommended among other changes a merger of income tax and NICs, a more straightforward schedule of tax rates and the alignment of taxation of income from employment and self-employment (Evans et al, 2017, pp 297–8). It represented a tax reform as 'an intermediate significant political event' (Evans et al, 2017, p 280), going further than tax changes arising out of normal processes of policy development while falling short of being a tax reform at constitutional level. However, no changes to the tax system followed from this proposed reform, and British governments continued to pursue smaller-scale changes, such as increases to the personal allowance, the removal of the NICs rebate for employees with an occupational pension in 2016, or the temporary increase in NICs to pay for health and social care in April 2022 – changes that left the basic architecture of the tax system intact.

Possible explanations until then were an unwillingness to commit government resources and political capital to such a complex undertaking of limited salience to voters, the dynamics of coalition government between 2010 and 2015, the focus on other policy challenges such as the aftermath of the global financial crisis of 2008, the Scottish independence referendum of 2014, the consequences of the UK's decision in 2016 to withdraw from the European Union, and most recently the fallout from the COVID-19 pandemic.

That the UK government adopted a relatively careful approach to tax reform may also be explicable by the experience of the failed attempt in March 2017 to abolish flat-rate Class 2 NICs for the self-employed while Class 4 NICs would be increased from 9 to 11 per cent, with better access to social protection as counterpoint. As highlighted by Bennett (2019), the proposals received widespread support from commentators with an interest in tax reform but were abandoned as a consequence of strong resistance from tabloid newspapers, from supporters of the governing Conservative Party who saw the tax increase as contradictory to the ideals of an entrepreneurial, low-tax economy and of poor communication by the government about the planned use of the additional revenue or the wider set of reforms regarding the labour market as outlined in the Taylor Review (Bennett, 2019, p 240). This example of a doubly failed tax reform, in other words, one that not only failed to meet its objectives but also harmed the government politically, illustrates well the risks attached to segmented and incremental as opposed to holistic and more radical reform packages, as summarised by Evans et al (2017, p 303).

Success in major tax reform is more likely to follow from a carefully crafted package than from an incremental approach. A package remedies defects more quickly; almost of necessity requires a statement of objectives that makes it easier to keep on course; offers substantial recognisable gains to taxpayers as well as losses; provides revenue scope for necessary or desirable measures of compensation; and, by attacking all vested interests together, enables reformers to stand on principle and present the lobby groups as the enemies of the public interest. But it carries dangers for its proponents and takes courage to embark on it. A package requires careful implementation: gains and losses must be seen to be interdependent; the government should give a clear lead; consultation and discussion should be extensive but conducted without undue delay; the forum of discussion must be appropriate, with the opportunity for views, both for and against, to be publicly presented and probed.

Overall, one of the main impediments to effective tax reform is the individualistic way in which tax issues are framed in the media and in the wider political discourse in the UK. With a focus on who stands to gain and lose, on who is asked to pay more, within a context of general reluctance to accept tax rises and incentives for government and opposition parties to present themselves as in favour of a generally low level of taxation (with caveats of course), vested interests find good conditions to defend their positions and argue against any detrimental changes to their taxation – while potentially being able to depict their actions as being in the wider public interest or at least to imply that higher taxes for them ought also to be of concern for other groups.

Moreover, tax reform is likely to run into difficulties if fragmented measures are taken without sufficient consideration of the wider interconnectedness of challenges. If, for example, changes are to be made to the taxation of different forms of income from work and the social protection offered as counterpart of tax and NI payments, then equity and consistency should be the aim across the labour market, in order to reduce anomalies in the current system.

The Self-Employment Income Support Scheme, launched in March 2020 to support self-employed individuals who lost income due to the COVID-19 pandemic, illustrates this well. This scheme was launched weeks after the equivalent support scheme, the Coronavirus Job Retention Scheme (CJRS), for employees who were put on furlough, with delays to the initial payouts, and a number of conditions imposed that resulted in the exclusion of some self-employed persons in need of support (for example, it excluded those who had only launched their business within the last 12 months). Instead of conceiving a comprehensive and linked-up safety net to respond to the extraordinary challenges of the pandemic, the government appeared to only address the needs of the self-employed as an afterthought, once pressure arose to tackle the gaps in the newly created system. However, despite these initial gaps and the time lag, the scheme was regarded as more generous to the self-employed than the CJRS was to employees, and it drew an interesting comment from the then Chancellor who suggested that 'it is now much harder to justify the inconsistent contributions between people of different employment statuses. If we all want to benefit equally from state support, we must all pay in equally in future' (Seely, 2022, p 28). This provides a clear statement of intent, but for the reasons outlined earlier, this is an objective that may not be easily achieved.

Conclusion: The difficulty of change

Understanding public finance decisions, including those related to the taxation of employment, as inherently political and in most cases incremental helps to comprehend the difficulties in achieving change – even if, as shown in this chapter, arguments in favour of change seem to abound. The combination of simplicity and complexity in the British tax system with respect to employment creates further challenges. The question of alignment between NICs and income tax rates illustrates this difficulty well.

The overall progressiveness of taxation of employment income is undermined by the reduced rate of NICs above the upper earnings limit or the upper profits limit. This flattened progressiveness can be deemed problematic for reasons of social justice and in light of the need for increased government revenue for the provision of essential public services and social benefits. Therefore, a merger of income tax and NICs, or at least an alignment of the latter with the former, appears as a reasonable and fairly simple solution.

However, the loss of disposable income for individuals earning above these upper limits would be considerable, rendering such a tax increase electorally unattractive for any political party. Moreover, as the number of persons affected by such a change has tripled over the last 30 years, due to increases to earning limits falling behind average wage increases, the political fallout of such a tax rise would be substantive. Further, depending on housing costs, childcare needs and other factors, earning above the upper limit is no longer a guarantee of a comfortable living standard, so that the imposition of higher NICs may not even be presentable as a fair measure without problematic implications for the wellbeing of households.

Therefore, raising NICs above the upper earnings limits to align with income tax is not as simple as it may appear. Such a decision would likely need to be accompanied by a range of other measures to alleviate its negative social and political consequences, such as the introduction of a larger number of income tax bands or a more fine grained system of tax allowances to reflect the financial circumstances of individual households (for example numbers of dependent children), as in Germany (IPPR, 2018). In other words, to manage a simple adjustment, more far-reaching changes would need to be considered in line with the argument by Evans et al (2017) on the benefits of holistic reform packages.

Another example of particular relevance to the question of social justice is the use of salary sacrifice schemes, particularly for workplace pensions. Initially promoted by tax consultants, these may provide substantial savings to income earners whose employers are able to offer them. Such schemes are not available universally, with the available data showing overall only a quarter of employees have salary sacrifice arrangements, and those in the private sector (30 per cent) are more likely to have such arrangements than public sector employees (9 per cent) (May, 2015; ONS 2020). Moreover, they are not progressive from a taxation perspective. They also raise the fundamental question of 'why the tax-paying public should ever entertain subsidising these transactions' (Sinfield, cited in Brunsdon and May, 2016, p 6), instead of providing relevant benefits via the social protection system.

If more far-reaching reforms are undertaken, with the investment of political capital and the risk of unintended consequences that come with any ambitious reform package, one could ask whether there are not richer pickings elsewhere in tax reforms that ensure income from employment or self-employment is treated more favourably than income derived from assets, such as wealth or land, reforms that would not only help to address shortcomings in government revenue and distributional problems but would also prioritise productive activity over the interests of rentiers. These, however, would be reforms of a truly radical nature, running counter to the decades-long trend of the British political economy towards rentier capitalism (Christophers, 2020). As public finance is an expression of conflictual politics (Wildavsky, 1964), for such a radical change to materialise, a major change in political conditions would be required.

Further reading
- Delestre et al (2022) – highlights the features of the tax system that create tax avoidance opportunities and reduce the tax take overall.
- Ruane et al (2020) – excellent discussion of why taxation is highly relevant to social policy.

- Whitworth and Carter (2022) – concise summary of key employment issues in the UK.

References

Bennett, F. (2019) 'Social protection for the self-employed in the UK: the disappearing contributions increase', *Poverty and Social Justice*, 27(2): 235–52.

Brunsdon, E. and May, M. (2016) 'W(h)ither salary sacrifice?', CHASM briefing paper, Available from: https://www.birmingham.ac.uk/Docume nts/college-social-sciences/social-policy/CHASM/briefing-papers/2016/ bp7-2016-whither-salary-sacrifice.pdf

Caraher, K. and Reuter, E. (2019) 'Mind the gaps: Universal Credit and self-employment in the United Kingdom', *Journal of Poverty and Social Justice*, 27(2): 199–217.

Caraher, K. and Reuter, E. (2020) 'Risk privatisation and social investment: self-employment in the United Kingdom', *Journal of Social Policy Research/Zeitschrift für Sozialreform*, 66(3): 261–84.

Christophers, B. (2020) *Rentier Capitalism: Who Owns the Economy, and Who Pays for It?*, London: Verso.

Collins, M.L., Ruane, S. and Sinfield, A. (2022), 'Taxation and social policy', in P. Alcock, T. Haux, V. Mcall and M. May (eds) *The Student's Companion to Social Policy* (6th edn), Oxford: Wiley Blackwell, pp 244–51.

Cribb, J., Miller, H. and Pope, T. (2019) 'Who are business owners and what are they doing?', London: IFS.

Deane, J. (2016) 'Self-employment review: an independent report', UK government, Available from: www.gov.uk/government/uploads/system/ uploads/attachment_data/file/529702/ind-16-2-self-employment-rev iew.pdf

Delestre, I, Kopczuk, W., Miller, H. and Smith, K. (2022) 'Top income inequality and tax policy', IFS Deaton Review, Available from: https:// ifs.org.uk/inequality/top-income-inequality-and-tax-policy

Dellot, B. and Read, H. (2016) 'Boosting the living standards of the self-employed', Royal Society of Arts, Manufacturing and Commerce, Available from: https://www.thersa.org/discover/publications-and-articles/reports/ boosting-the-living-standards-ofthe-self-employed

DWP (2022) 'Universal credit for the self-employed', Available from: https:// www.gov.uk/government/publications/universal-credit-and-self-emp loyment-quick-guide/universal-credit-and-self-employment-quick-guide#showing-that-you-are-gainfully-self-employed

Evans, C., Hasseldine, J., Lymer, A., Ricketts, R. and Sandford, C. (2017) 'Tax reform', in *Comparative Taxation: Why Tax Systems Differ*, Malvern: Fiscal Publications, pp 279–307.

Giupponi, G. and Machin, S. (2022) 'Labour market inequality', IFS Deaton Review of Inequalities, Available from: https://ifs.org.uk/inequality/labour-market-inequality

Giupponi, G. and Xu, X. (2020) 'What does the rise in self-employment tell us about the UK labour market?', Institute for Fiscal Studies, Available from: https://ifs.org.uk/sites/default/files/output_url_files/BN-What-does-the-rise-of-self-employment-tell-us-about-the-UK-labour-market-1.pdf

Hills, J. (2015) *Good Times, Bad Times: The Welfare Myth of Them and Us*, Bristol: Policy Press.

HM Revenue and Customs (2016) 'Employment status manual', Available from: https://www.gov.uk/hmrc-internal-manuals/employment-status-manual/esm0003

HM Revenue and Customs (2022) 'Rates and allowances: National Insurance contributions', Available from: https://www.gov.uk/government/publications/rates-and-allowances-national-insurance-contributions/rates-and-allowances-national-insurance-contributions#historical-and-future-rates

IFS (2020) 'Going solo: self-employment in today's labour market', Available from: https://ifs.org.uk/publications/15185

IPPR (2018) 'Prosperity and justice, a plan for the new economy', Institute for Public Policy Research, final report of the IPPR Commission on Economic Justice, Available from: https://www.ippr.org/files/2018-08/1535639099_prosperity-and-justice-ippr-2018.pdf

May, M. (2015) 'SMART (Save money and reduce tax) pensions in the UK: salary sacrifice and auto-enrolment', briefing paper BP2, CHASM: University of Birmingham, Available from: bp2-2015-smart-pensions-in-the-uk.pdf (https://www.birmingham.ac.uk/Documents/college-social-sciences/social-policy/CHASM/briefing-papers/2015/bp2-2015-smart-pensions-in-the-uk.pdf)

May, M. (2022) 'Occupational welfare', in P. Alcock, T. Haux, V. Mcall and M. May (eds) *The Student's Companion to Social Policy* (6th edn), Oxford: Wiley Blackwell, pp 258–65.

Miller, H., Pop, T. and Smith, K. (2021) 'Intertemporal income shifting and the taxation of business owner-managers', London: IFS.

Mirrlees, J., Adam, S., Besley, T., Blundell, R., Bond, S. and Chote, R. et al (2011) 'Tax by design', London: IFS.

O'Leary, D. (2014) 'Going it alone', DEMOS, Available from: www.demos.co.uk/files/DEMOS_GoingitAlone_web.pdf?1409503024

ONS (2014) 'Why has the number of self-employed increased?', Available from: http://webarchive.nationalarchives.gov.uk/20160105160709/http://www.ons.gov.uk/ons/rel/lmac/self-employed-workers-in-the-uk/2014/rep-self-employed-workers-in-the-uk-2014.html

ONS (2018) 'Trends in self-employment: analysing the characteristics, income and wealth of the self-employed', Available from: https://www.ons.gov.uk/employmentandlabourmarket/peopleinwork/employmentandemployeetypes/articles/trendsinselfemploymentintheuk/2018-02-07

ONS (2020) 'Coronavirus and self-employment in the UK: an overview of self-employment across the UK, looking at the industrial, occupational, geographic and demographic characteristics of those who are self-employed', Available from: https://www.ons.gov.uk/employmentandlabourmarket/peopleinwork/employmentandemployeetypes/articles/coronavirusandselfemploymentintheuk/2020-04-24

ONS (2022) 'Employment in the UK: February 2022', Available from: https://www.ons.gov.uk/employmentandlabourmarket/peopleinwork/employmentandemployeetypes/bulletins/employmentintheuk/latest#employment

Resolution Foundation (2019) 'The RF earnings outlook: Q1 2019', Available from: https://www.resolutionfoundation.org/app/uploads/2019/09/Earnings-Outlook-Q1-2019.pdf

Ruane, S., Collins, M.L. and Sinfield, A. (2020) 'The centrality of taxation to social policy', *Social Policy & Society*, 19(3): 437–53.

Sandford, C., Pond, C. and Walker, R. (eds) (1980) *Taxation and Social Policy*, London: Heinemann Educational Books.

Scottish Government (2022) 'Income tax rates and personal allowances', Available from: https://www.mygov.scot/income-tax-rates-and-personal-allowances

Seely, A. (2022) 'Coronavirus: Self-Employment Income Support Scheme', House of Commons Library, Available from: https://researchbriefings.files.parliament.uk/documents/CBP-8879/CBP-8879.pdf

Sefton, T. (2008) 'Distributive and redistributive policy', in M. Moran, M. Rein and R.E. Goodin (eds) *The Oxford Handbook of Public Policy*, Oxford: Oxford University Press, pp 607–23.

Tanzi, V. (2020) *The Economics of Government*, Oxford: Oxford University Press.

Taylor, M. (2017), 'Good work: the Taylor Review of modern working practices', Available from: https://assets.publishing.service.gov.uk/government/uploads/system/uploads/attachment_data/file/627671/good-work-taylor-review-modern-working-practices-rg.pdf

Toovey, J. (2020) 'The self-employed landscape in 2020', IPSE, Available from: https://www.ipse.co.uk/policy/research/the-self-employed-landscape/the-self-employed-landscape-report-2020.html

Toovey, J. (2021) 'The self-employed landscape in 2021', IPSE, Available from: https://www.ipse.co.uk/policy/research/the-self-employed-landscape/the-self-employed-landscape-report-2021.html

UK Government (2021) 'Ethnicity facts and figures: self-employment', Available from: https://www.ethnicity-facts-figures.service.gov.uk/work-pay-and-benefits/employment/self-employment/latest#data-sources

UK Government (2022) 'Income tax rates and personal allowances', Available from: https://www.gov.uk/income-tax-rates

Whitworth, A. and Carter, E. (2022) 'Employment', in P. Alcock, T. Haux, V. Mcall and M. May (eds) *The Student's Companion to Social Policy* (6th edn), Oxford: Wiley Blackwell, pp 324–30.

Wildavsky, A. (1964) *The Politics of the Budgetary Process*, Boston: Little, Brown and Company.

Woodcock, J. and Graham, M. (2020) *The Gig Economy: A Critical Introduction*, Hoboken: Wiley.

6

Pensions and taxation

Micheál L. Collins and Andy Lymer

Introduction

Pensions and pensions policy represent one of the major areas where taxation and social policy interact. Decisions impact on the current and future living standards of most individuals, involve substantial and growing state expenditure, raise questions of equity and efficiency, and grapple with the issue of the long-term sustainability of current approaches given demographic trends.

Pension provision has sat at the heart of the welfare state model of most countries since the emergence of these models in the late 1800s. States intervene to provide income to individuals once they reach an age where they are no longer required to work, via a state pension scheme in conjunction with a benefit system, pursuing a policy objective of preventing poverty in old age. States also adopt policies to encourage individuals (and/or their employers on their behalf) to save from current income during their working lives such that this income is available in retirement, pursuing a policy objective of income smoothing and in the process creating some degree of reduced reliance on state provision alone for the costs of retirement.

This chapter examines the linkages between pensions and the taxation system in the UK and traces their evolution over time. In particular, it focuses on the current suite of tax-based incentives for occupational and personal pension savings and highlights the very significant tax-advantaged position provided for this form of long-term savings over most other forms in which capital value can be accumulated to support living costs in retirement.

The chapter is structured as follows. The next section outlines the current UK pensions system. It is followed by an assessment of the pensions policy landscape, with some contextualising comparative comment on this landscape internationally. The fourth section then provides an overview of how pensions and taxation interconnect to motivate (and constrain) pension savings and to aid income adequacy objectives. The fifth section considers a series of key issues that arise from recent and possible future reforms of the pensions-taxation policy space and explores these in the context of the taxation and social policy choices that look set to arise in the years to come. The final section offers some concluding comments.

The UK pension system

The UK's pension system comprises three core components:[1]

1. A state-provided welfare pension – where the right to receive a pension is linked, in large part, to the payment of National Insurance contributions (NICs);
2. Occupational or workplace pensions – where pension income derives from contributions made by, and/or on behalf of, an individual during their working lifetime and where the value of the pension is either related to final pre-retirement salary (defined benefit or DB) or is based on the scale of pension savings built up (defined contribution or DC); and
3. Personal pensions – where individuals, often those who are partly or fully self-employed, pay into a group pension fund or their own pension savings product and subsequently draw a retirement income from this.

As these components of the pension system are not mutually exclusive, individuals, depending on their circumstances, may possess pension entitlements from anywhere from none to all three elements.

The taxation system plays an important role in the functioning of the system. NI-related state pensions are the main source of income for retired people in the bottom 60 per cent of the income distribution and, according to Office of National Statistics (ONS) data for 2020/21, represent one third of all pensioners' gross income in the UK.[2] These pensions are funded on a Pay-as-You-Go basis using the contributions of current NI contributors and taxpayers to finance the entitlements of current recipients. Entitlement is based on one or more of the following: age, past contributions, low income, widowhood and ill-health.

Taxation measures also play an important role in supporting occupational and private pension saving, in particular, with various features of the taxation system designed to encourage personal, long-term, saving into pension-related products, reward pension-fund accumulation and maximise the disposable income individuals have available to them in retirement.

The headline descriptive numbers underscore the scale of the UK's pensions industry and its significance in public and social policy. ONS data report that at the end of 2019 the market value of pension funds exceeded £2.2 trillion,[3] equivalent to 100 per cent of 2019 UK GDP. In that year, 40.7 million individuals were members of occupational pension schemes (61 per cent of the total UK population), slightly more than half (55 per cent) in defined contribution schemes. HMRC report that the total net cost of income tax relief granted in 2019/20 was £22.1 billion,[4] equivalent to 11 per cent of total income taxation that year; and a further £19.7 billion in NICs relief, equivalent to 14 per cent of total NICs for that year.

The pensions policy landscape

Before we explore more deeply how taxation plays an important role in the implementation of social policies around pensions, we initially consider its role in the context of the broader pensions policy landscape. Each issue outlined represents an area of social and public policy in and of itself, with implications beyond those that purely arise for pensions. However, collectively these provide the context for current and future decisions on pension policy and the role of taxation measures in pursuing pension policy objectives.

Demographics and public finances

Increases in life expectancy and a long-term fall in fertility rates have combined over recent decades to drive an ageing of the population in most developed world states (Eurostat, 2020, pp 8, 16). As a result, the proportion of the population aged above the traditional retirement age of 65 years has grown and is expected to continue to do so into the foreseeable future (Figure 6.1). In the UK, those over 65 years are projected to increase from one in five of the population in the early 2020s to one in four by 2050.

This reality carries important implications for pension systems and their design. Simply, with more people who are living longer, the role of pension systems in providing adequate retirement incomes continues to grow. Simultaneously, the number of individuals aged over 65 years compared to those of working age continues to increase (Table 6.1). As most state pensions, both social insurance and public-sector occupational, are financed on a Pay-as-You-Go basis, that is, from current NICs and taxation revenues (and therefore termed 'unfunded' in contrast to private pension provision that is based on an accumulated pension fund), there are growing public

Figure 6.1: Projected percentage of the population aged 65 years and above, 2020–60

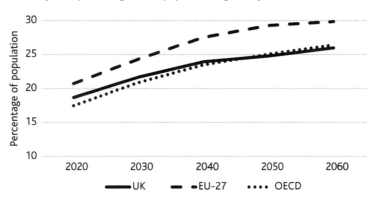

Source: OECD online database (https://stats.oecd.org/index.aspx?DataSetCode=POPPROJ#)

Table 6.1: Number of old-aged individuals per 100 of working age, 1950–2080 (selected countries)

	1950	1960	1990	2020	2050	2080
UK	17.9	20.2	26.9	32.0	47.1	55.1
EU-27	14.6	16.0	21.6	33.6	56.7	62.0
OECD	13.6	15.0	20.0	30.4	52.7	61.1
France	19.5	20.8	24.0	37.3	54.5	62.2
Germany	16.2	19.1	23.5	36.5	58.1	59.5
Ireland	20.9	22.8	21.6	25.0	50.6	60.0
Italy	14.3	16.4	24.3	39.5	74.4	79.6
USA	14.2	17.3	21.6	28.4	40.4	51.1

Notes: Data are historical outcomes and projected values. Old-aged are individuals aged 65 years and above; working aged are those aged 20–64 years.
Source: OECD (2021b: 173)

finance challenges associated with funding and sustaining expected future pension payments.

These population trends have driven various pension policy initiatives over recent years, including increases to the retirement age (taking effect after 2010), higher NICs alongside more rigorous qualification criteria, and initiatives to encourage current workers to save more of their own earnings so that they are less dependent on state support in retirement. Frequently, taxation measures, through tax-breaks on saving and on capital gains, have been used to encourage more pension savings, even though the associated taxation revenue forgone has also grown substantially (see Chapter 4).

Earnings and wealth inequality

Changes in the distribution of earnings over recent decades, most particularly the pronounced growth in high pay and the sustained gender pay gap, have brought greater attention to earnings divides and their implications (see Chapter 11). Given that retirement income is explicitly linked to working incomes, there has been a growing awareness of how these working-life earnings inequalities are replicated, if not magnified, in retirement. Among high earners, it is not unusual for pensions to be used as a form of renumeration, thereby increasing their use of taxation-supported savings incentives. Conversely, statistics highlighting that almost one in five UK workers are low paid underscores the presence of a large cohort of the working population who are unlikely to be able to afford private pension savings and will inevitably be dependent on support from the welfare state in retirement (OECD, 2021b, p 399). Gender pay divides and asymmetries in the distribution of care also imply that across their working lives females receive less earnings from which to save for their generally longer retirement, thereby ensuring they receive less pension taxation supports and lower retirement incomes (see also Chapter 11).

The emergence of new and recurring wealth data over recent years has propelled renewed focus on the topic of wealth inequalities and in particular the concentration of wealth among small proportions of the population (see discussion in Chapter 10). ONS data indicate that private pension assets represent the largest area of average family net wealth, standing at 38 per cent of total assets in 2016–18. The ONS also noted the concentration of this wealth among a small proportion of all households. Although there are challenges associated with accurately valuing pension assets, in particular defined benefit pensions (Daly et al, 2021), the ONS Wealth and Assets Survey data highlight the importance of pension savings, and pension entitlements, as a form of wealth and a component of wealth inequality. Consequently, reforms to pension savings and related taxation measures have important wealth inequality contexts.

The changing nature of work

Individuals' experience of paid work continues to change. It is becoming more common for individuals to experience multiple roles across their working life, retrain mid-career for alternative employment, experience periods of unemployment or work precarity, work in multiple countries, and have expectations of working beyond what would have been considered a 'normal' retirement age. Requirements to leave paid work to provide unpaid care, for both children and older family members, also continue to disrupt people's paid working lives, particularly for women and particularly in the context of the high cost of market-provided care.

Such work–life patterns contrast with the simplicity of traditional pension provision models, both private and state, where the accumulated contributions across a lifetime of work lead to a pension income that approximates some proportion of working or at-retirement earnings. Although pension reforms since the 1990s in particular, have attempted to accommodate some of these new patterns of working life, as detailed subsequently, most are still implicitly based on a full-time work for 40 years 'male breadwinner' model that does not universally fit with the profile of the modern labour market. Consequently, these more modern life and work patterns frame some of the policy challenges around reforming pension provision to better align with the reality of the current and future labour force.

Shifting risk on to individuals

A central feature of pensions policy initiatives across most states over at least the past two decades has been a shift towards an enhanced role for private pensions and away from employer and state provision (Pensions Commission, 2004; Ebbinghaus and Whiteside, 2012). Driven by the previously discussed demographic changes and fiscal pressures, DB pensions are being replaced almost entirely by DC pensions.

Similarly, many states are now pursuing policies to automatically enrol (auto-enrol) earners into private pension (occupational) schemes so that they save some of their own resources to provide retirement income. The UK has done likewise with auto-enrolment for those in work (although only those earning above £10,000 per annum) being rolled out between 2012 and 2017.

Qualification criteria have also been tightened for social insurance-funded pensions, such that individuals need longer records of continuous employment to receive a full state pension. In the UK, the state pension now requires at least ten years of NICs to create qualification, and full entitlement is only achieved after 35 years of such contributions (increased from 30 years in April 2016).

Collectively, these ongoing trends reflect a shift of risk on to individuals. Although the state continues to provide a minimum retirement income, via a means-tested welfare pension, beyond this, post-retirement income is being ever more aligned to the performance of pension savings investments with the consequences of under provision, or under performance, being borne by individuals. As part of this shift, taxation measures have played an increasing role through the incentivisation of savings and the favourable treatment of capital gains and pension income drawdown.

Political choices, political cycles, power and adequacy

Four further key issues are also important in understanding the current pension policy landscape and the context within which decisions around taxation issues are made. First, taxation is a controllable element among several other key, but much less controllable, elements in what makes up the pension landscape. These other elements include population mortality, occupational mortality, incomes, investment returns and inflation (Reddin, 1980, p 116). As such, the nature of how pensions develop for UK citizens is only partly a matter of political choice – namely how to apply taxation on pension fund contributions/inputs, earnings made by funds once invested or on payouts and outputs from this activity when pensions are drawn upon – as this is one of a limited set of levers a government can pull to affect these 'phases' (Reddin, 1980, p 119) of pension provision towards a desired outcome. However, political choices are at the heart of how this landscape is made up, and tax can have a significant influence on the overall nature of the landscape. Therefore, the changing ideology of those behind the prevailing pension choices made from time to time is key to the development of the landscape. This in turn drives outcomes, determines the nature and speed of reform and can create periods of inaction where other ideological positions may have resulted in action.

Second, pensions are an inherently long-term issue, associated with savings and entitlements that accumulate over decades, and this can contrast with the shorter-term political cycle. Consequently, pension policy reform can be treated with less urgency and therefore delayed or postponed, particularly if these reforms involve changes that are justified on the basis of the long-term sustainability of the pension system but that come with immediate alterations to pension structures, tax relief entitlements or the age of retirement. Similarly, these immediate objections can crowd out the longer-term reform objectives given the political cycle.

Third, desires to reform pension systems are frequently met with, or driven by, powerful and well-resourced lobby groups intent on protecting the status quo or augmenting it further in their favour. These include the businesses that make up the pensions industry (pension funds and pensions advisors), taxation and accountancy practitioners and, to some degree, trade unions representing workers with entitlements to defined benefit pensions in both the public and private sector. This group also includes employers and their associations (Confederation of British Industry, Institute of Directors and so on) who also have vested interests in pension costs not becoming any higher than they are at any given point (Sinfield, 2019). Their resources and established connections contrast with those arguing for reform on the basis of sustainability and fairness, the latter capturing those most closely associated with the realm of social policy and the role of taxation within social policy interventions.

Fourth, there appears to be ample evidence of political indifference to addressing the question of adequacy of pension provision. This may be motivated by political short-termism or more fundamentally the result of political or ideological positioning on the need for state provision for those who are unwilling to provide for their own longer-term income adequacy (for example, over short-term consumption desires). This fails, of course, to address the issue of adequacy of current income to enable both adequate current consumption to maintain reasonable living standards while leaving sufficient income to also save for future income needs (meaning many of the supposed 'unwilling' may in fact be 'unable' to save).

Pensions, policy and taxation

The use of the tax system to motivate pension savings has been a longstanding feature of many countries' pensions policies. Dilnot and Johnson (1993) suggest the following justifications for why pensions should get some support from the tax system:

- Paternalistic motivation – a government knows not everyone will adequately prepare for retirement needs, therefore tax incentives are justified to move decision-making in the direction a paternalistic government believes to be society's best interests;
- Reduce other forms of state expenditure – tax incentives to develop greater self-support in retirement will reduce the otherwise greater need for state provision of such support;
- Private pension provision is a superior form of investment for an economy – the long-term nature of such investments can cope with short-term fluctuations in value and the presence of significant pension fund investment can lead to longer-term views being more able to be taken to counter short-term savings behaviour; and
- Some form of reward to saving longer term is needed – in order to encourage setting aside shorter-term consumption desires.

However, the extent of the necessary incentives required to achieve these goals is hotly debated – particularly where the costs of such provision can be significant and can prove difficult to target to the areas where state support of pension provision may be most needed (see Chapter 4).

In broad terms, the interaction between taxation and pensions can be categorised into taxation measures associated with motivating (or constraining where deemed necessary) pension saving, and those associated with the pursuit of income adequacy objectives.

Taxation as a motivator or constraint on pensions

Governments pursue various tactics to encourage pension savings, ranging from behavioural change tactics to nudge savings, to more formal regulatory interventions requiring individuals and employers to contribute to pensions (de Clercq et al, 2019). Where policies are pursued to trigger behavioural change, these can take the form of taxation measures designed to provide a tax advantage to individuals making or accumulating pension savings or via non-tax incentives such as matching or subsidising pension saving contributions (OECD, 2021a, p 5). Therefore, many of the associations between taxation and pensions are designed based on the assumption that, in their absence, individuals would behave differently and use these resources in other ways.

There are three stages where taxation incentives may be applied to pension savings (Reddin, 1980, p 119):

1. On inputs – when making pension contributions;
2. On the earnings (or 'accruals') from pension investments via interest, dividends or capital gains; and
3. On outputs – related to pension withdrawals when the accrued pension funds return money to their contributor.

A decision to exempt (E) the taxation (T) that would otherwise be due at one or more of these stages is used as an incentive to encourage individuals to allocate funds to pensions. Consequently, governments incur a tax expenditure on the revenue forgone from these savings and gains, one that frequently amounts to one of the largest areas of recurring fiscal expenditure by states. In 2019/20, this totalled £41.8 billion in the UK (see Chapter 4).

Approaches to the provision of tax incentives for pension savings differ across countries – see Figure 6.2. There is no single consensus on the best way to use the tax system to support pensions. The UK adopts the approach that is the most commonly applied within the OECD, taken by 17 of 38 member states – the 'Exempt-Exempt-Taxed' (EET) tax regime, where:

- the funds input to pension savings are exempt (E) from income tax,
- the earnings within the pension fund are exempt (E) from any tax on dividends or interest received and on any capital gains tax when investments held within the fund are realised, but
- outputs from the fund are subject to income tax (T) as the pension savings and capital gains are drawn down.

Seven further OECD states also provide tax exemptions at two of the three stages; however, they charge taxation on the income used for pension contributions while again exempting the gains but also the withdrawals (a TEE approach).[5]

Eleven OECD countries exempt just one of the three stages, although they segment into groups that approach the provision of these tax incentives in different ways. Four countries exempt the income used for pension contributions but tax the investment gains and the withdrawals (ETT). Three countries do the opposite and only exempt the withdrawals (TTE), while four others exempt the internal gains but tax the income used for contributions and the income received from pension savings (TET). Among the 38 OECD states, only three provide tax incentives that exempt all stages of pension savings (EEE) and none tax all three (TTT).

Taxing pensions

In the UK in 2022, the funds used to make most pension contributions attract an income tax exemption at the saver's marginal rate of income taxation

Figure 6.2: Different approaches to taxing pension savings, OECD member states, 2021

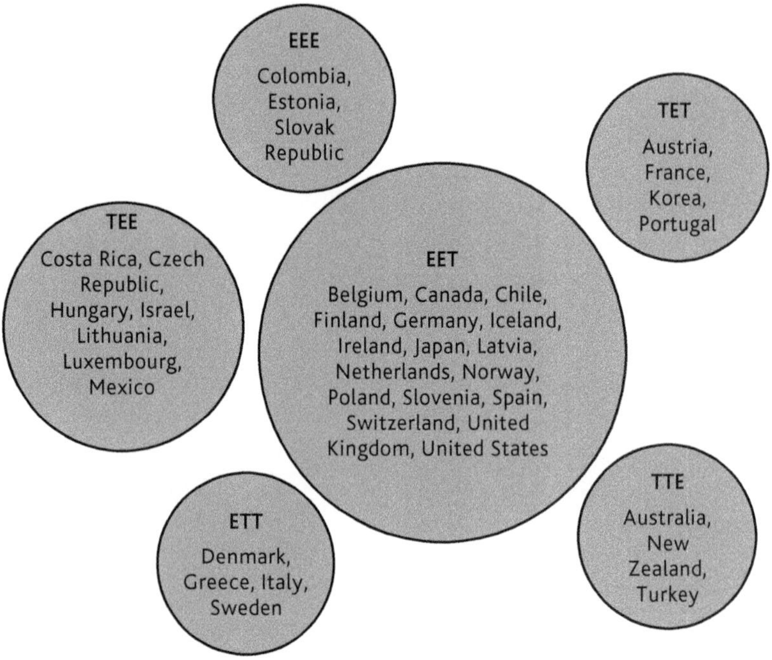

Note: Classification is for main pension plan in each country. 'E' stands for exempt and 'T' for taxed.
Source: OECD (2021a, p 5)

(the rate of taxation arising on the last £1 of income). This continues a longstanding feature of the system that commenced with the Finance Act 1921. Using the income tax rates and bands applicable in England, Wales and Northern Ireland in 2022, this means that earners with an income below £50,270, who pay a basic rate of 20 per cent of their income as income tax above a tax-free personal allowance, need to save 80p for every £1 they put into pension savings – the other 20p is provided via a relief on the income tax that they would otherwise have paid (this 20p is claimed on the saver's behalf by their pension provider). Earners with an income between £50,270 and £150,000 are subject to a higher marginal tax rate of income tax of 40 per cent and consequently need only to contribute 60p for every £1 they wish to put into pension savings – the other 40p is provided via the income tax relief. Earners above £150,000 (falling to £125,140 after April 2023) have a 45 per cent marginal income tax rate on all income above this threshold, and where these earnings are used for pension contributions, they only need to save 55p for every £1 they put into their pension savings.[6]

As increasing marginal tax rates tend to be a feature of progressive taxation systems, the provision of pension tax relief at the contributor's marginal rate gives rise to a regressive benefit on inputs to pensions where the initial disposable income loss associated with a given nominal pension contribution is less for those with a higher income than it is for those with lower incomes. Consequently, it could be argued that pension tax reliefs should be standard-rated and made available to all income taxpayers at one rate. Some may go further and suggest that those paying higher marginal rates should have a lower tax deductibility for pension savings. This could be argued on the basis that a tax incentive to save into a pension to those on likely larger disposable incomes is not needed. This could potentially enable some of the very significant cost (of foregone taxes) of this current provision to be redirected towards further support for those on lower incomes to enable them to save larger sums more quickly.

The exemption to taxation of the earnings of pension funds also represents an important tax incentive experienced by UK pension savers. In general, returns made on investments are subject to taxation when realised. This includes both profits paid out in the form of dividends or interest, and in the form of capital gains tax when investments are disposed of, and a profit is earned on the asset value gain over the time of ownership. (See Chapter 3 for details of applicable rates on dividends and capital gains.)

The exemption of taxation for any form of return to pension savings means that pension savers are rewarded with the full value of any investment profits their savings earn, an outcome that contrasts with that experienced by many other forms of saving. Further, as the value of this exemption rises with the level of income a taxpayer enjoys, the tax exempting of earnings from pension funds provides a regressive advantage that compounds that available to pension contributors on their inputs, as detailed earlier. These gains can therefore dwarf those received on inputs over the life of a pension as a long-term investment – at a very significant cost to the revenue purse and again befitting most those who save the most.

Unlike the treatment of inputs and earnings in the UK's pension system, outputs from drawing on a pension are subject to tax (the 'T' in the EET system). However, this could perhaps more accurately be described as a partial 't' rather than a full 'T' (Whitehouse, 2005). This is because some income tax relieving measures also exist even on the output process, which implies a lower rate of tax is likely to be charged than that which would apply to the equivalent sum received from other sources. In particular, the UK tax system allows pension savers to receive up to one quarter of their total pension savings pot as a tax-free lump sum (a feature of the UK pension system since 1925), meaning that only three quarters of the total accumulated pension pot is often taxable. Further, pension income can be paid out over a number of years, often at a level that maximises the use of income tax-free personal allowances and minimises the exposure of the income to higher marginal rates (Adam et al, 2012).

This further tax-free feature of private pensions stands in direct contrast to state pension provision on which no such lump-sum is available – tax free or otherwise. For those relying on state provision, this provides a further tax-related disadvantage compared to those who had disposal incomes that enabled pension provision to be acquired.

The UK system now allows lump-sums, and access to pension income drawing on the remaining capital, to be paid out from 55 years of age, although traditional retirement ages are in general a decade or more older than this (this is rising to 57 in 2028 alongside a corresponding rise in the state pension age maintaining, but not shortening, this ten-year bias for private pensions access). This is a further example of inequity that exists between those with and without private pension provision. This is particularly noteworthy as there is no invested time limit related to gaining the full tax advantage available on inputs and earnings – that is, a taxpayer can contribute to their private pension fund at age 54 years 364 days, receive full tax deductibility on these sums going into their pension fund and draw on it on their 55th birthday, including entitlement to 25 per cent of this pot tax free.

Taken together, the favourable tax treatment of pension inputs, earnings and (to a lesser degree) outputs in the UK pension system provides a very significant tax-advantaged position for pension savings. Barr (1992) summarised the redistributive nature of these policy initiatives as 'voluntary welfare', with their tax expenditures part of 'the hidden welfare state' (Greve, 1994 p 203). While the pension savings system could be considered to simply be a deferral of income, such that the tax relief experienced on contributions is deferred and paid in retirement, given the very favourable tax treatments available to these savings, the system is at best one of generous and only partial deferral.

Beyond personal income taxation relief related to pension savings, the tax system also provides support for employer contributions to pensions via employer NIC relief on these payments. In 2019/20, this represented £19.7 billion of the total net tax relief provided for private pensions.[7]

Constraining pension savings

Although much of the relationship between taxation and pensions is linked to motivating individuals to save, there are aspects of the system used to limit the level of tax-relieved pension saving an individual can avail themselves of. In the UK system, individuals are allowed to save into a private pension up to 100 per cent of their income each year. This is subject to a maximum limit of £40,000 per annum (made up of any contributions they and their employer may make) or £120,000 in total over any three consecutive years before tax benefits cease to be reclaimable (2022 values – this annual limit is set to rise to £60,000 a year from April 2023).

Prior to changes announced in Budget 2023, there was also a lifetime pension fund (savings plus any returns) cap of £1,073,100 (Lymer and Oats, 2022, p 159) before a tax charge started to be applied (on the excess over this cap). However, in Budget 2023 it was announced, somewhat surprisingly, that the fund size cap is to be removed from April 2024 so that there will no longer be a tax cost applied to very large pension pots.

While the (50 per cent larger) annual contribution cap will continue to apply, it brings into question where the government views that an individual needs no further incentives to save for their retirement. The annual contribution limit provides some cap to the tax expenditure exposure of the state to the tax management practices of individual taxpayers. However, this contrasts dramatically with the incomes and ability to save of most earners. The previous annual £40,000 threshold was already equivalent to 128 per cent of the gross median earnings of a full-time UK worker (£31,285) in 2021 (ONS, 2021). Similarly, the lifetime pension fund limit contrasted with ONS data showing the value of the median private pension fund of only £57,000 (£75,000 for males and £43,500 for females, giving a gender pensions gap of 42 per cent) in the period April 2018–March 2020.[8] These limits also reflect an approach to the design of a system primarily suited to those in consistent full-time employment over many decades, which is not necessarily the experience of all workers, especially women (see Chapter 11).

Taxation as an income adequacy measure

Decisions around the taxation of pension income can also reflect considerations of income adequacy, particularly given policy objectives related to minimising pensioner poverty. Contrasting perspectives are reflected in the design of these decisions, with one set of views arguing that lower taxation rates should be used to enhance the disposable income of pensioners, while another cites the principles of income deferral and tax neutrality to argue the merits of income being taxed in the same way irrespective of when it is received (Collins and Hughes, 2017). These views explain the presence of age-related income taxation credits and allowances in some countries, which reduce the average level of pensioner income taxation (for example, Canada and Ireland), and their absence in others (including the UK, where age-related allowances were withdrawn over a number of years up to 2016).

In general, pension recipients do face lower NICs, or social insurance, in most countries. In the UK, individuals cease paying on their earnings once they reach state pension age; prior to this, employees pay 12 per cent on earnings from £9,880 up to £50,270 and 2 per cent on income after this (rates applicable after 6 November 2022 for the tax year 2022/23). Such measures automatically increase the disposable income of pension recipients, although this contrasts with the broader objectives of progressivity in income taxation, and depend on views regarding the classification of NICs as a tax or an intergenerational risk-sharing insurance fund where only employers and working-age individuals contribute.

Key issues and potential for reform

Given the contemporary pensions policy landscape and the current structure of pension taxation measures, this section highlights a series of key issues, many interconnected, that arise for the current and future interaction between taxation and pensions.

Rising costs

As populations age, societies face additional and growing costs in health care, social care and pensions. These rising costs trigger pensions policy questions regarding the generosity and sustainability of current approaches. Government accounts show some £100 billion is being spent annually on benefits related to retirement, and the cost of tax and related reliefs for non-state pensions reduces revenue by another £42 billion (Collins et al, 2022). These substantial current costs, equivalent to around 20 per cent of total annual taxation revenue, will continue to increase in the future in the absence of policy change. They will inevitably trigger future policy debates and changes in the taxation and social policy pensions space. Who should pay what, and in what way, are key future social policy and taxation questions.

The data on the distribution of current private pension tax support highlights how these are skewed towards those at the top of the income and earnings distribution (Sinfield, 2018; Ruane et al, 2020). Governments face the challenge to both facilitate individuals to income smooth (so that they are encouraged and supported to use income from their working lives to help them to be as self-supporting in retirement as possible) with a policy desire to minimise deadweight (that is, to limit the use of state resources to support individuals to save resources for retirement that they would have saved in any event). However, the arbitrary nature of some pension savings thresholds, differences in the age when private and welfare pensions can be accessed, and the generosity of some of the tax breaks provided, suggests that deadweight is likely to be a feature of many of the current pension taxation supports.

Further, change is also likely to be resisted by current pension savers and providers, as it has been for many years to date. Understandably, groups will lobby to preserve their current favourable arrangements and will commit significant resources to achieve this. Regrettably, there are fewer voices highlighting the broader context of these issues and arguing for reforms centred on equity and efficiency objectives.

Automatic enrolment

Since the early 2000's, the UK has adopted policies to automatically enrol employees into private pension schemes. Early adopters of this approach to widening private pension provision include both Italy and New Zealand in 2007, with countries including the UK, Canada, Germany, Turkey and Poland adopting auto-enrolment policies in the period since that date (UK commencing in 2012).

Rather than exclusively using taxation measures to induce pension savings, these policies rely on inertia, with behavioural expectations that savers once enrolled in a pension saving scheme will be unlikely to stop saving. Countries have varied between mandatory participation for employees not already undertaking private pension saving (such as UK, Poland, Italy and New Zealand) to voluntary participation (as in the United States, Canada and Germany). In general, employers are also required to contribute a set proportion of earnings. Incentives to encourage individual pension saving have also been used, including partial matching of contributions by the state (New Zealand) or tax relief on these pension contributions (UK).

To date, 'auto-enrolment' has successfully increased pension participation, particularly in the private sector. ONS data from the Annual Survey of Hours and Earnings show that UK workplace pension participation increased between 2012 and 2020 from less than half to 78 per cent of employees. However, issues remain regarding the adequacy of contributions, their long-term effectiveness in providing an adequate post-retirement income beyond welfare pensions (where available) and the additional tax support costs these initiatives incur.[9]

Further, as the rules for auto-enrolment only apply to those earning more than £10,000 per annum, there is also a question of how such systems support those on the lowest incomes, which disproportionately include women, ethnic minorities, the self-employed and those in precarious employment. These will therefore likely remain on average more dependent on reducing state provision.

Finally, private pension coverage growth via auto-enrolment was primarily among those who were over the income threshold but not previously earning enough above this to be likely to already have a pension from part of their employment offering. As such, the tax incentives given towards motivating inputs into these funds may only be of a limited value, as they are only paid at the taxpayer's likely low marginal rates and not otherwise enhanced.

Pension freedoms

The freedom of individuals to control and use their accumulated pension funds, both pre- and post-retirement, highlights an important interface between broader societal objectives for pensions policy and more libertarian views on individual rights and behaviours. Those holding the latter views argue that individuals have an entitlement to do as they wish with their pension savings while those who attach more importance to the broader social objectives of pensions policy contend that these savings should be incentivised by the state such that they can be used across an individual's retirement to support their income on an ongoing basis. Any alternative use of these funds therefore runs the risk of detracting from the purpose for which these tax incentives were provided (at significant cost).

These contrasting views trigger a debate between individual rights to freely use pension savings versus state objectives to minimise poverty risk (De Clercq et al, 2019). From a taxation and social policy perspective, they highlight an issue regarding whether the provision of tax relief comes with implicit expectations and restrictions on the future use of these funds. Furthermore, it raises the issue of whether these expectations should be more explicit.

Pension freedoms in the UK have grown considerably since the major reform of private pensions on 6 April 2007, the so-called 'Pension A-Day' (Thurley, 2008). This included many of the key features of the current tax-incentivised pension system including the introduction of the lifetime cap on pension pot size, the provision to allow up to 100 per cent of annual earnings to be contributed to a pension fund (subject to a maximum annual cap), the provision of tax relief at the highest marginal rate of the taxpayer and relaxations on what pension funds could be invested in. These features all remain in place today, albeit with revised thresholds, as detailed earlier.

Further key freedoms were introduced in 2015 as part of several changes to the UK pension system from what became known as 'Pensions Freedom Day' (6 April of that year). These included the removal of the requirement to buy an annuity with the remaining funds in a pension pot after the tax-free lump sum was withdrawn. Previously, this 'guaranteed income for life' product was seen to be a key requirement to aid income adequacy, although the sums available from the purchase of annuities had fallen significantly in the years in the run up to this change, thus creating political pressure to make it.

A further key change introduced in 2015 was to allow defined contribution pension pots (i.e. most private pensions, although not all workplace pensions) that are unspent (not used to buy an annuity) to become inheritable assets. A pension pot can now be passed tax free in the UK to a beneficiary chosen by the pension holder if they die before the age of 75. If the pension holder dies after that age, the pot is subject to tax at the marginal rate of the beneficiary. Further, it is generally the case that these pension pots are not liable to inheritance tax. As state pensions are unfunded and there is no such pot to pass on, tax free or otherwise, the extra tax 'perk' of these arrangements further distances those who are reliant on state provision funded by their NICs from those with private pensions (Adam et al, 2022).

Gender, ethnicity and pensions

There are contrasting perspectives between private and public pension provision and taxation supports when considered by gender. For private pensions, the gender pay divides among working-age adults are replicated in retirement, with women in receipt of lower nominal taxation supports while accumulating pension savings and lower pension incomes in retirement (Collins, 2020). Social policy consequently focuses on the 'gender-pension gap', in both pension savings and outcomes, and explores debates around its origin, appropriateness and reversal (Foster, 2012). These gaps also arise when pensions are considered by ethnic group (Vlachantoni et al, 2015; ONS, 2020).

Lower female incomes also imply lower nominal contributions to NI; yet as women on average live longer, they are likely to receive more from this fund as a result.

Taken together, there is significant need for a more integrated assessment of the combined impact of pension receipts, taxation and NIC divides and the scale of their distributional consequences for the gender division of resources (see Chapter 11).

Alternative pension approaches

As Figure 6.2 illustrates, there are a number of possible approaches that countries can take to using taxation measures to support pension savings. From the perspective of tax neutrality, one can argue that it should not matter where the tax relief is provided (on inputs or on output) once the liability is eventually paid; however, this assumes that current systems simply displace tax liabilities that are not supported by current structures and their outcomes. In the UK, limited debate exists on the merits of changing the current EET (or EEt) tax-relief system to an alternative taxation support structure, say a TEE approach, although this was briefly presented as one policy option in 2016 before being abandoned. There are significant short-term Exchequer benefits to realising taxation revenues at the outset of pension saving, and these may be useful given the increase in pension provision costs the UK faces. However, the limited debate so far merits more engagement from the social policy community in exploring these alternative approaches and their possible outcomes.

The idea of an unconditional Universal Pension, akin to a Universal Basic Income for the retired, is also an area of pensions in need of greater exploration. Coupled with a policy to remove tax relief on pension savings, as New Zealand did in the late 1980s, this highlights questions regarding the overall use of current resources and the need for more comprehensive exploration of the alternative use of these resources (welfare expenditure and tax relief) given policy objectives.

Conclusion

Pensions and pension policy is a key social policy issue affecting all of the UK's population, including those drawing on the various forms of pension provision currently or those paying into them currently for their own future benefit or in support of those who are in receipt of state pension provision.

Huge sums of money are involved in this industry – both in terms of sums invested that support large parts of the UK economy and in terms of tax expenditures foregone to motivate long-term savings into these funds. As such, getting this policy area right, and keeping it working effectively, is key to the welfare of large parts of the UK and its economy.

The tax system is heavily used to influence pension fund development and the way in which pensions are drawn upon – at least for private pension provision. State pension provision receives no tax inducement to support it, and actions of recipients cannot directly and personally influence the nature or extent of their state provision (beyond ensuring they make minimum NI payments to make a given year count towards their state pension computation). This places those reliant on this source for their retirement income at considerably more risk than those on higher incomes during their working lives. They have been able to benefit from a heavily tax incentivised system that has enabled many to build up large sums. These sums are not taxed at input stage, as funds accruing value over long periods of investment, nor in part even when drawn upon. At this output stage, significant parts of the accumulated pot (up to 25 per cent to a maximum of just under £270,000) can be taken tax free. Only income drawn from the pension is taxed, and then at likely lower rates of tax than was exempted at the contributor's marginal rates when inputs were made, as when drawing on their pensions, a recipient's overall income is likely to be much smaller than it was when they made the contributions.

The development of auto-enrolment has started to make some inroads into the provision of private pension pots for those on lower incomes – those who may otherwise have been largely reliant on state provision previously. However, there remains significant concern that, despite the fact that these pots accrue with the same tax incentives that other private pension provision is entitled to, it receives no larger subsidy or support that could be made possible by an alternative system that supported more substantially those on lower incomes. This could be provided at the cost of those who may do so otherwise on higher incomes without needing the extra benefits that accrue to them under the current structure where tax relief is based on their highest marginal rates of tax.

Reform in this domain, via the lever of tax incentives or otherwise, is undoubtedly called for to create a more level playing field for all in terms of private pension provision. This will be particularly the case if state provision is to continue to deteriorate, as appears sadly likely, demographic changes continue to follow current trends and wealth inequality is allowed to continue to develop largely unchecked. However, with very strong lobbying against this from many quarters with vested interests in this large industry, and with the lack of clear ideological and political will to so do, significant change to a fairer system seems unlikely in the near future.

Notes

[1] Components 2 and 3 are often referred to collectively as 'private' pensions to distinguish them from publicly provided pensions per component 1.

[2] See https://www.ons.gov.uk/peoplepopulationandcommunity/personalandhouseholdfinances/incomeandwealth/datasets/householddisposableincomeandinequality

[3] Table 2 – https://www.ons.gov.uk/economy/investmentspensionsandtrusts/articles/ukpensionsurveys/redevelopmentand2019results

[4] https://www.gov.uk/government/statistics/main-tax-expenditures-and-structural-reliefs

[5] An economic analysis of the potential to change the UK to a TEE approach can be found in Armstrong et al (2015), a report produced in response to the UK consultation released in 2015 that called for evidence to review this possible change in the UK.

[6] The same approach applies in Scotland, although there are small differences in the various income tax rates and bands used.

[7] This sum of NIC relief includes employers not having to pay NIC on what was paid into employees' pensions as well as the savings to the employee, who otherwise would have to pay NIC on that same amount if it was included in their wages.

[8] Table 6.10 – https://www.ons.gov.uk/peoplepopulationandcommunity/personalandhouseholdfinances/incomeandwealth/datasets/pensionwealthwealthingreatbritain

[9] Particularly interesting work into how auto-enrolment pensions can be best used to support income adequacy in retirement in the UK is being done by NEST Insight, part of the National Employment and Savings Trust – the UK government-created pension scheme provider for auto-enrolled pensions and the largest provider in this market, with excess of 10 million members and approaching 1 million employer users.

Further reading

- HMRC (2022) – provides detailed UK pension statistics: https://www.gov.uk/government/statistics/personal-and-stakeholder-pensions-statistics/commentary-for-personal-and-stakeholder-pension-statistics-september-2021
- Institute for Fiscal Studies – produces regular research reports on pensions policy, pensions taxation and pension reform: https://ifs.org.uk
- NEST Insight – produces research and analysis on the development of effective auto-enrolled private pension provision in the UK: https://www.nestinsight.org.uk
- OECD – provides biennial 'Pensions at a Glance' reports providing comparative descriptive statistics and policy analysis for pension systems across OECD and G20 states: https://doi.org/10.1787/19991363
- OECD (2018) provides significant discussion on tax and pensions.
- ONS – produces regularly updated reports on occupational pensions in the UK: https://www.ons.gov.uk/economy/investmentspensionsandtrusts/articles/ukpensionsurveys/redevelopmentand2019results
- Pensions Policy Institute – produces research reports and briefing notes explaining structures, proposals and policy developments in the UK pension system: https://www.pensionspolicyinstitute.org.uk

References

Adam, S., Browne, J. and Johnson, P. (2012) 'Pensioners and the tax and benefit system', IFS briefing note BN130, London: Institute for Fiscal Studies.

Adam, S., Delestre, I., Emmerson. C. and Sturrock, D. (2022) 'Death and taxes and pensions', IFS Report R235, London: Institute for Fiscal Studies. Available from: https://ifs.org.uk/sites/default/files/2022-12/Death-and-taxes-and-pensions-Institue-for-Fiscal-Studies.pdf

Armstrong, A., Davies, P. and Ebell, M. (2015) 'An economic analysis of the existing taxation of pensions (EET) versus an alternative regime (TEE)', NIESR discussion paper no 455, London: National Institute of Economic and Social Research.

Barr, N. (1992) 'Economic theory and the welfare state: survey and interpretation', *Journal of Economic Literature*, 30(2): 741–803.

Collins, M.L. (2020) 'Private pensions and the gender distribution of fiscal welfare', *Social Policy and Society*, 19(3): 500–16.

Collins, M.L. and Hughes, G. (2017) 'Supporting pension contributions through the tax system: outcomes, costs and examining reform', *Economic and Social Review*, 48(4): 489–514.

Collins, M.L., Ruane, S. and Sinfield, A. (2022) 'Taxation and social policy' in P. Alcock, T. Haux, V. McCall and M. May (eds) *The Student's Companion to Social Policy* (6th edn), Oxford: Wiley Blackwell, pp 244–51.

Daly, S., Hughson, H. and Loutzenhiser, G. (2021) 'Valuation for the purposes of a wealth tax', *Fiscal Studies*, 42(3–4): 615–50.

De Clercq, B., Lymer, A. and Axelson, C. (2019) 'An analysis of the tax simplification initiatives for pension provision in the United Kingdom and South Africa', in C. Evans, R. Franzsen and L. Stack (eds) *Tax Simplification: An African Perspective*, Hatfield: Pretoria University Law Press.

Dilnot, A. and Johnson, P. (1993) 'The taxation of private pensions', London: Institute for Fiscal Studies.

Ebbinghaus, B. and Whiteside, N. (2012) 'Shifting responsibilities in Western European pension systems: what future for social models?', *Global Social Policy*, 12(3): 266–82.

Eurostat (2020) 'Ageing Europe: looking at the lives of older people in the EU', Luxembourg: Publications Office of the European Union.

Foster, L. (2012) 'Using a political economy and life course approach to understand gendered pension provision in the UK', *Sociology Compass*, 6(11): 883–96.

Greve, B. (1994) 'The hidden welfare state, tax expenditure and social policy: a comparative overview', *Scandinavian Journal of Social Welfare*, 3(4): 203–11.

HMRC (2022) 'Commentary for personal and stakeholder pension statistics: September 2021', Available from: https://www.gov.uk/governm ent/statistics/personal-and-stakeholder-pensions-statistics/commentary-for-personal-and-stakeholder-pension-statistics-september-2021

Lymer, A. and Oats, L. (2022) *Taxation: Policy and Practice, 2022/23* (29th edn), Malvern: Fiscal Publications.

OECD (Organisation for Economic Co-operation and Development) (2018) 'Financial incentives and retirement savings', Paris: OECD.

OECD (2021a) 'Financial incentives for funded private pension plans: OECD country profiles 2021', Paris: OECD.

OECD (2021b) 'Pensions at a glance 2021: OECD and G20 indicators', Paris: OECD.

Office of National Statistics (2020) 'Household wealth by ethnicity', Available from: https://www.ons.gov.uk/peoplepopulationandcommunity/personala ndhouseholdfinances/incomeandwealth/articles/householdwealthbyethnic itygreatbritain/april2016tomarch2018

Office of National Statistics (2021) 'Annual survey of hours and earnings, 2021', Available from: https://www.ons.gov.uk/employmentandlabou rmarket/peopleinwork/earningsandworkinghours/bulletins/annualsurve yofhoursandearnings/2021

Pensions Commission (2004) 'Pension: challenges and choices; the first report of the Pension Commission', London: HM Stationery Office.

Ramm, A. and Eames, C. (2020) 'The valuation of pension wealth for the purpose of a UK wealth tax', Wealth Tax Commission background paper, 142, London School of Economics and University of Warwick, UK. Available from: www.wealthandpolicy.com/wp/142.html

Reddin, M. (1980) 'Taxation and pensions', in C. Sandford, C. Pond and R. Walker (eds) *Taxation and Social Policy*. London: Heinemann, pp 115–34.

Ruane, S., Collins, M. and Sinfield, A. (2020) 'The centrality of taxation to social policy', *Social Policy and Society*, 19(3): 437–53.

Sinfield, A. (2018) 'Fiscal welfare and its contribution to inequality', in C. Needham, E. Heins and J. Rees (eds) *Social Policy Review 30*, Bristol: Policy Press, pp 91–110.

Sinfield, A. (2019) 'The benefits and inequalities of fiscal welfare', in M. Powell (ed) *Understanding the Mixed Economy of Welfare* (2nd edn), Bristol: Policy Press.

Thurley, D. (2008) 'Pension tax simplification', House of Commons standard note SN 2984, Available from: https://researchbriefings.parliament.uk/ ResearchBriefing/Summary/SN02984

Vlachantoni, A., Feng, Z., Evandrou, M. and Falkingham J. (2015) 'Ethnicity and occupational pension membership in the UK', *Social Policy and Administration*, 49(7): 801–23.

Whitehouse, E. (2005) 'Taxation: the tax treatment of funded pensions', World Bank Pension Reform Primer Series, Washington, DC: World Bank.

7

Tax, benefits and household income

Stephen McKay

Introduction

Household incomes depend primarily on rewards from the labour market and the ways in which the state intervenes to affect the link between gross earnings and final incomes and the prices of goods that may be consumed. This set of government interventions includes the direct tax system (principally income tax and National Insurance contributions [NICs] in the UK), indirect taxes such as value added tax (VAT) and specific duties on products like petrol, plus the system of welfare benefits paid to people, particularly the state retirement pension for those over the requisite age (currently 66, but rising for younger cohorts), Universal Credit as a means-tested benefit for those of working age and many other remaining contributory and other benefits. The existence of taxes and benefits may also affect people's incentives to work (or to generate income in other ways, such as through the return on savings) and the amount of time they work – although the links between taxes, benefits and behaviour has long been controversial (for example, see discussion in Deacon and Bradshaw, 1983 or indeed in Sandford et al, 1980).

For much of the post-war period, the design of benefits was based on the contributory system of Beveridge (1942), with money paid in via NI and paid out in times of interruptions to work. In more recent times, the emphasis has shifted towards means-tested benefits, and particularly for those of working age rather than those in retirement. This policy shift was seen in wage supplements, Family Income Supplement (introduced in 1970) and Family Credit (from 1986), before increasingly wide-scale tax credits were introduced under New Labour (in office 1997–2010). More recently, a new system known as Universal Credit has subsumed most of the income-replacement benefits for non-disabled people of working age, which previously were different for those in work compared to non-workers. However, the key concerns about means-testing have not gone away, including lower take-up (not all eligible people will claim them), and potential changes affecting the incentives for self-provision (for example, savings, or extra hours of work, or relying on family members for assistance). This chapter complements the analysis in the first two chapters of this collection.

The chapter will include a discussion of the methodological difficulties and main methods used to chart the distributional impacts of the tax/benefit system. It charts the changing scale of inequality in the UK over time and the associations with taxes and benefits – the significance of the erosion of NI benefits and the contributory principle, compared with means-tested approaches, and in particular the arrival of Universal Credit. I also consider the implications of changes in the tax system, including a move towards indirect taxes and away from direct taxes, and a longer-term shift towards NI and away from income taxation. The chapter concludes with reminders of policy difficulties and some potential routes forward.

Taxes and transfers

Key taxes

For the purposes of this chapter, we are interested in the larger taxes that most directly affect people's ability to achieve a particular standard of living. That is, the direct taxes on their incomes, and the key taxes on their spending. Other chapters in this text deal with housing (Chapter 9), wealth (Chapter 10) and so on. There is a much more detailed description of how incomes from employment and self-employment are taxed in Chapter 5. It should be acknowledged that in practice taxation is a complex matter, and these outline details barely scratch the surface about these different types of taxes and, in particular, their interactions and therefore behavioural impacts.

The biggest three sources of revenue in the UK are income tax, NICs and VAT – see Chapter 3 for more detailed descriptions and analysis. Income tax, the most widely recognised tax, accounts for about one quarter of all government revenue. Most personal income is subject to this tax, after a basic personal allowance that is free from tax for all but the highest incomes (those above £100,000 a year). The second largest source of revenue is then NICs. These are payable on most forms of employment, but not other sources of income such as private pensions, rents or interest from savings. Moreover, there is an 'upper earnings limit' and compared with income tax a lower starting point for when payment starts. Chapter 5 discusses other key differences between NICs and income tax, including debates about how far they could, and should, be more fully integrated (see also McKay, 2019).

Next there are taxes on people's spending, sometimes called consumption taxes. The most important of these is VAT, but there are also excise duties of various kinds, such as on petrol, tobacco and alcoholic drinks. VAT is paid at 20 per cent on most goods and services, though there are also lower rates of 5 per cent (for example, home energy) and 0 per cent (such as on most food and on children's clothes), while some goods/services are exempt. Since 2018, there has also been a 'Soft Drinks Industry Levy', more popularly known as the 'sugar tax', to reduce sugar levels in some soft drinks – as with other excise duties (for example, on tobacco), there is arguably a health benefit to having such a tax. However, it is also clear that consumption of some of these highly taxed products is not proportionately affected by price rises. They are price-inelastic, to use a technical term, or more plainly 'addictive' to use a common term, meaning that the higher price resulting from a higher level of tax does not have a large effect on consumption (at least in the shorter term).

A feature of consumption taxes is that they clearly only affect those who consume such products, and in practice this is often those on lower rather than higher incomes. This is most clear with tobacco and betting taxes (see analysis in Table 7.2). However, some such taxes (for example, on airplane travel) are more likely to have a larger effect on the better-off.

The three main taxes combined (income tax, NICs and VAT) account for around 22 per cent of national income and 58 per cent of tax revenue (Office for Budget Responsibility [OBR] Public Finances databank).[1] Figure 7.1 tracks trends in the tax take in the UK for these three main taxes covering from 1999/2000 until 2019/20 and then as forecast (by the OBR) until 2025/26. Income tax has long been the largest single source of government revenue, though slightly decreased from over 10 per cent of national income in 2007–8 to around 9 per cent in the last few years.

Since income tax is among the most progressive of taxes, the reduction in the emphasis on this tax will have tended to have increased rather than decreased inequality. The revenue raised each year from VAT and NICs is often quite comparable in money terms. VAT accounts for around 6 per cent of national income, with NICs a little higher. The move towards VAT and NICs, and away from income tax, is also likely to be of advantage to those with income from savings or from rents, as these are subject to income tax but not to the latter two taxes. The longer-term transition from income tax

Figure 7.1: Trends in the tax take in the UK (1999/2000–2025/26)

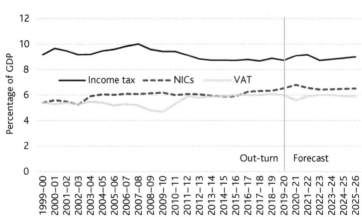

towards NICs is discussed by McKay (2019), who also notes the sizeable shift over a longer time period.

Social security benefits

Spending on social security benefits represents one of the largest elements of state spending in many countries, including the UK. In 2019/20, total spending on 'welfare benefits' was around £230 billion, representing 10.2 per cent of national income – see Figure 7.2. Measures taken during the COVID-19 pandemic added as much as 3.8 per cent to this total on the main furlough and self-employment support packages, in addition to specific increases in Universal Credit and in the numbers requiring such support. Most spending is on older people, rather than those of working age (Figure 7.2).

Different types of social security benefits

Social security benefits in the UK, and most advanced economies, cover a diverse range of schemes, too many and too complex to cover even briefly. A critical commentary and overview of the direction of policy is provided by Royston (2017). It is, however, customary to divide social security benefits into three groups according to the conditions of entitlement to them, namely: contributory benefits, means-tested benefits and other benefits sometimes called contingent or categorical benefits. In this context, it is worth pointing out that some benefits, including retirement pensions and

Figure 7.2: Trends in the size of social security spending (1997/98–2025/26), including pandemic-related additions

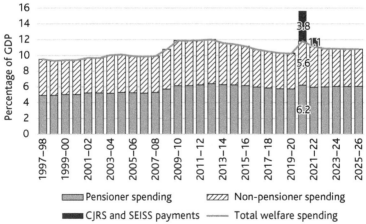

some benefits for the unemployed, are also subject to income tax. Others – including the newer Universal Credit – are not.

Contributory benefits – widely known as 'social insurance', and in some countries as 'social security' – rely on having a past record of monetary/ other contributions into the system, in the UK through sufficient NICs over time. Means-tested benefits (also known as 'social assistance' or, in the United States, simply as 'welfare' to distinguish them from 'social security') are those that depend on people's levels of income, typically being an anti-poverty policy (or, at least, a poverty relief policy). Contingent benefits tend to be defined by positions and categories, like health or having children or caring responsibilities.

It is worth emphasising that this division into three groups is something of a simplification of differences between benefits. Means-tested benefits do not just depend on financial resources; they tend to also rely on some combination of being in a particular situation or a particular family type. For example, unemployed people may only claim Universal Credit if they meet conditions relating to their job search, and some contributory benefits are reduced if a person receives a private pension. For housing-related benefits (Housing Benefit), rates of payment increasingly depend on the local market conditions and are capped, and with those of working age (but not pensioners) judged on the amount of space they need for their family. Over time, the extent of conditions appears more onerous and more interventionist. David Webster demonstrates that such sanctions have fewer opportunities to be contested than would be found in the criminal justice system, and noted that 'the number of financial penalties ("sanctions") imposed on benefit claimants by the Department of Work and Pensions now exceeds the number of fines imposed by the courts' (Webster, 2015).

In the UK, the main blueprint for the current social security system is generally regarded as the Beveridge Report published in the early 1940s (Beveridge, 1942). However, insurance-based and other benefits were introduced much earlier than this to begin the replacement of the poor laws with their even longer history; indeed, the report was originally envisaged as a means of tidying up what had become a complex web of protections and benefits. The core insight underpinning the contributory approach is the idea that people face a range of risks that might lead to severe reductions in living standards, and they need to be insured against – just as is the case for car drivers, or those taking out home insurance. The key 'social risks' to steady employment include unemployment, sickness and eventually retirement. Entitlement to social insurance benefits to cover those risks is based on having paid NICs and being in a risk covered by these benefits, such as unemployment or retirement. These benefits are individualised in that the earnings of a partner do not generally affect entitlement. The main benefit in this group is the state retirement pension. Other contribution-based benefits include parts of Jobseeker's Allowance and elements of Employment and Support Allowance.

Means-tested benefits ('social assistance') generally bring up a person's or household's level of resources if it is deemed too low. In practice, entitlement to means-tested benefits depends on both income and savings/assets. The main examples in the current British system are Universal Credit for those of working age and Pension Credit for those older than state pension age. There is also Council Tax Support determined at a local level by each Local Authority in England, with nationally determined but locally implemented Council Tax Reduction schemes in Northern Ireland, Scotland and Wales.

Before the phased introduction of Universal Credit, progressively rolled out nationwide since 2013, there was a stark split between out of work means-tested benefits, such as Income Support (IS), and certain tax credits paid for those in-work, such as Working Tax Credit (WTC). At 16 hours of paid work per week, one set of benefits (like IS) became largely replaced by the other (like WTC), with some benefits (like Housing Benefit) being available both for workers and non-workers (or those working fewer than 16 hours a week). Hence Universal Credit was designed to replace: IS, Housing Benefit, WTC, Child Tax Credit, and the non-contributory elements of both Jobseeker's Allowance and Employment and Support Allowance. It brought these together into a single system, removing some anomalies and inconsistencies of approach. Other associated changes – such as moving from previous patterns of weekly payments to monthly payments and including paying Housing Benefit direct to claimants instead of to landlords (Northern Ireland excepted) – have caused particular controversy, even if most have welcomed the overall simplification a move to Universal Credit provided (for a dissenting view on the overall concept, see Millar and Bennett, 2017).

Countries differ a great deal in the extent of their types of benefits, and particularly in the scope of social assistance. For example, in Australia and New Zealand almost all benefits include an element of 'means-testing'. In much of Northern Europe, social assistance plays a much smaller role, picking up those not covered by the main social insurance system. In addition, means-tested benefits are often administered locally, with local organisations having some discretion about the precise rules of entitlement. By contrast, the UK's benefit system is heavily centralised and based on rules rather than discretion.

There are also some benefits which are neither means-tested nor contributory, which are sometimes called contingent benefits as they depend on particular personal statuses, including health.. For these benefits, entitlement depends on the existence of certain circumstances (or contingencies) such as having a child (Child Benefit) or being disabled (Personal Independence Payment). In the British social security system, some benefits effectively recognise that certain groups of people face extra costs that the state will share. The clearest example is benefits for dependent children and Child Benefit. There is no test of contributions. However, entitlement to Child Benefit has been reduced where a parental income exceeds £50,000 per year, falling to zero at £60,000. In practice, these figures relate to taxable income, so that those contributing to pensions may be earning slightly more than these figures but not experiencing the reduction.

One feature that has been criticised is that these income thresholds only look at the higher income within a couple – so Child Benefit might be entirely lost if there is just one worker earning £65,000 but would be fully retained if both parents were working and each earned £49,000 for a total household income of £98,000. This is one instance where the tax system is based around individuals in their own right (see the discussion in Chapter 3), whereas the benefits system tends to look at family units. Hence there are apparent anomalies when, as with taxing away Child Benefit, the two come together (see also discussion in Chapter 11). Disability benefits provide another example where some elements are purely contingent and reflect neither means nor previous contributions.

Another benefit meeting specific costs is Housing Benefit (now incorporated into Universal Credit, for those of working age), which helps people pay their rent if they are on a low income. The OBR's welfare trends report in October 2014 tracked changes over time and showed an increase from 0.8 per cent of GDP in 1983/84 to 1.5 per cent in 2013/14. The cost of this benefit increased dramatically in the last three decades because there was a deliberate policy shift from subsidising 'bricks and mortar' (in terms of low council rents) to subsidising individuals (by raising rents and paying benefit to those on low incomes). While low-paid renters can receive help, those with mortgages are mostly denied assistance with their housing costs unless not working at all. This and other points are explored more fully in Chapter 9 on housing.

The scale of social security in the UK

The sheer scale of different social security benefits may be readily appreciated by the size of spending, with the value of selected benefits shown in Table 7.1. In 2019/20, the government spent almost £100 billion on the state retirement pension, plus around £65 billion on earnings-replacement for those of working age (mostly Universal Credit). In addition, £25 billion went on benefits relating directly to disability. By 2025/26, spending simply on the state retirement pension is forecast to be close to £130 billion each year.

Put another way, this represents around £7,500 each year for every family in the country. Around half of all UK families receive at least one social security benefit (FRS, 2021) and 15 per cent of families receive at least one means-tested benefit (FRS, 2021).

Table 7.1: Spending (£ billion) on selected benefits, current and projected

	2019–20 (actual)	2025–26 (forecast)
Older people		
State pension	98.8	129.1
Pensioner housing benefit	5.8	6.5
Pension credit	5.1	4.8
Working age		
Universal Credit	18.2	61.5
Personal Tax Credits	18.0	2.0
Incapacity benefits	14.0	8.2
Working-age housing benefit	12.1	4.7
Income Support (non-incapacity)	1.4	0.1
Jobseeker's Allowance	0.7	0.2
Disability		
Personal Independence Payment	13.0	23.4
Disability Living Allowance	7.2	5.4
Attendance Allowance	5.9	7.0
Other		
Northern Ireland social security	6.4	9.0
Carer's Allowance	3.2	4.7
Maternity and paternity pay	2.5	2.9
Total (including other benefits not shown)	228.0	286.5

Source: OBR Welfare Trends Report (database)

Governments have also used the benefit system to guide behaviour. Since April 2017, levels of benefits do not increase further for any children born beyond the first two – a policy memorably described by Bradshaw (2017) as being 'the worst social security policy ever … just morally odious'. There are also overall limits on the total level of benefits that may be received (the 'benefit cap') whatever the circumstances of the families who are affected (with exemptions for having disabled family members). Behavioural conditions are also set for those expected to seek work in the labour market, and these have been tightened in various ways in the last 40 years (see further the discussion in Chapter 5 on employment and taxation).

Devolution of powers to Scotland and Wales initially made little difference to benefits, as most powers were reserved to Westminster. However, over time the Scottish government has become more active, for example introducing the Scottish Child Payment in 2021 at £10 per child, then increased to £20 in April 2022, for low-income families with a child under six. In March 2022, it was announced that the payment would increase to £25 per week for all children under 16. Northern Ireland has long had powers to run separate benefits but has generally mirrored policy in the rest of the UK.

Benefits for older people remain the largest part of UK social security (Table 7.1). They also represent an area of the social security system that has been unusually well protected since 2010, despite a policy of austerity in public finances with significant reductions in spending on benefits for those of working age (McKay and Rowlingson, 2016). The benefit freezes and cuts affecting the working population have simply not been applied, in most cases, to those above state pension age – although the 'triple lock' (which mandates state pension increases by the highest of inflation, wage growth and 2.5 per cent) was suspended in light of the rapid wage increases following the COVID-19 lockdowns.

Universal Credit: fulfilling the vision for a negative income tax?

At various points, including during the 1970s, the idea of integrating taxes and benefits into a single system was discussed – a kind of negative income tax where pure means-testing would mean that people either paid tax or received benefits depending on their market incomes. At present, many people both receive benefits and pay taxes. Indeed, a new temporary benefit, Family Income Supplement, came out of that discussion. The overall idea may be traced to American liberal economist. Milton Friedman. Indeed the United States conducted negative income tax experiments based on such thinking (Moffitt, 2003). However, while certain elements of the benefits system may have such features (such as the US Earned Income Tax Credit), no system exclusively relies on such methods, and in particular pensions (for older people) remain largely based on contribution conditions.

However, tax-benefit integration runs into numerous conceptual and practical barriers that have tended to make it unviable, at least in the UK context, despite some strong claims about the advantages (see, for example, Dilnot et al, 1984). In particular, the current separation between income tax and NICs would need to be confronted, with any 'merger' of these schemes certain to generate large numbers of winners and losers. Moreover, taxes paid on an individual basis and benefits calculated for family units or for households clearly create further obstacles to consider (Mirrlees et al, 2011, chapter 5).

Universal Credit goes much less far towards a 'rational' or perhaps economics-led approach. It combines a series of benefits and is based purely on means-testing and not on any past contributions. Contribution-based benefits – outside of the state retirement pension – continue to be eroded over time, often raising reliance on the means-tested benefits available in their absence. The next section considers how these relate to levels of income inequality.

Inequality of incomes in the UK

Measuring incomes

Before considering inequality between people's incomes, we have to be clear what is going to be counted as income, and this is far from straightforward. Indeed, there are formidable issues in measuring people's incomes and using them to draw conclusions about inequality of incomes. Just to mention a few points, how might policy makers and analysts judge how incomes (for example, the earnings of one family member) are shared between their partners, members of their households and their wider families? Is it appropriate to assume that all members of the same household share the same standard of living, and, if not, what alternative approach to that may be made? In most cases, whatever set of units is included, typically a family unit of a single person or couple with any dependent children, people within those units are assumed to be at the same level of income, whatever the correctness of such an assumption (for example, Jenkins, 1991).

Another key question is how to treat families of different sizes and composition – or the concept of 'horizontal equity' (discussed by Lymer and Oats, 2021, pp 47–8, in the context of taxation). We expect that a single person on £25,000 is materially better-off than a couple with two children with the same income, but just how much better-off? In other words, what income for a couple with two children is equivalent to an income of (say) £25,000 for that single person? This issue is known as equivalisation, and there are some generally well-recognised (though not universally accepted) weightings that seek to put all family types on to the same footing for comparing incomes.

We also need some way to compare different incomes over time: as prices change, the same income will not buy the same amount of goods and services. Hence, a price index is generally used to make comparisons over time – again, there are choices about what index is best for such purposes. In 2022, as inflation reaches levels not seen for decades, such an issue becomes more pressing than in years of lower rates of price changes.

In the UK, two quite separate sets of data are used to generate statistics about income distribution. The Office for National Statistics (ONS), using the Household Finances Survey, looks at the full range of taxes (including indirect taxes) and benefits (including some in-kind benefits). This series is generally called 'The effects of taxes and benefits on household income', or ETB. Second, the Department for Work and Pensions (DWP), using data from the Family Resources Survey (and prior to 1994/95 the Family Expenditure Survey), uses data on incomes and direct taxes to generate the series known as 'Households Below Average Incomes' (HBAI), and more broadly known as the poverty figures (or, at least, counts of families on different levels of low income). The DWP figures invariably produce two sets of results, one quoted before housing costs (BHC) and the other taken after housing costs (AHC). Since older people tend to have lower housing costs than most other groups, having paid off mortgages for house purchases or a higher proportion being in social housing, the AHC/BHC split tends to matter for the composition of who is on a low income.

Incomes and government intervention

The ONS ETB methodology calculates a number of different types of incomes and allocates tax revenue across different households according to both income and spending. The latter point is important since many taxes apply to spending rather than being taken directly from household incomes. Some key summary results are shown in Table 7.2.

There is a very high degree of inequality of original incomes – with those in the top 20 per cent having an average 'original income' (that is, before government taxes and some transfers) that is some 12 times higher than those in the bottom 20 per cent. This is somewhat mitigated by the effects of direct taxes and benefits, and particularly of in-kind benefits (for example, NHS, education, social care). Note that from 2017 onwards the value of NHS services is adjusted according to local deprivation – those in poorer areas receive a poorer service – though this is not done when calculating the value of other benefits in kind. The total effect reduces the level of disparity to a 4:1 ratio between the top and bottom quintiles of income. However, benefits in kind are not something you can spend, and if we simply look at disposable incomes that are under people's direct control, then the richest fifth still have more than six times the spending power of those in the bottom fifth. It should also be acknowledged that there is considerable inequality within that top 20 per cent, with the very richest commanding much higher incomes than those just inside this grouping.

Looking in a little more detail, the lowest income fifth received £7,700 a year in direct cash benefits, against an overall average of £5,900. ONS also credits this group with receiving welfare state services worth £13,800 compared to an overall average of £11,300 (things like education, the NHS, social care). There is certainly redistribution taking place through benefits and the wider working of the welfare state, but this remains in a system still subject to very high levels of inequality.

Direct and indirect taxes

As noted, direct benefits, including those in kind, strongly reduce inequality, and direct taxes are also quite equalising. The richest fifth pay an average of

Table 7.2: What happens to incomes (£ annual figures), by quintiles of income

Incomes	1 (low)	2	3	4	5 (high)	All
Original income (total)	11,500	23,600	39,600	61,500	135,100	54,300
Original income (equivalised)	8,500	17,800	30,400	48,000	107,800	42,900
Final income (equivalised)	18,600	27,700	33,400	41,600	75,600	39,400
Disposable income (equivalised)	12,500	22,500	30,300	40,900	78,100	36,900
Direct cash benefits	7,700	9,000	6,500	3,900	2,500	5,900
Benefits in kind	13.800	12,800	11,900	9,900	8,300	11,300
Indirect taxes: total, of which:	4,800	5,700	7,300	8,500	10,800	7,500
VAT	2,100	2,600	3,500	4,100	5,300	3,500
Hydrocarbon oils	480	620	740	950	900	740
Tobacco	360	350	340	410	200	330
Direct taxes: total	3,300	4,700	7,800	13,600	41,000	14,100
Direct taxes/original income	28.7%	19.9%	19.7%	22.1%	30.3%	26.0%
Indirect taxes/disposable income	38.4%	25.3%	24.1%	20.8%	13.8%	20.3%
Indirect taxes/original income	41.7%	24.2%	18.4%	13.8%	8.0%	13.8%
Total taxes/original income	70.4%	44.1%	38.1%	35.9%	38.3%	39.8%

Source: Analysis of average incomes, taxes and benefits of all individuals, retired and non-retired by decile group. Released 28 May 2021, https://www.ons.gov.uk/peoplepopulationandcommunity/personalandhouseholdfinances/incomeandwealth/bulletins/theeffectsoftaxesandbenefitsonhouseholdincome/financialyearending2020

£41,000 a year in such taxes, compared with an overall average of £14,100 and some £3,300 in the bottom fifth of incomes. Of course, we may still question why those on the lowest incomes should be paying as much, and if the richest group might afford to pay more, but the effect is clearly progressive. The richest fifth paid 30 per cent of their 'original incomes' in direct taxes, compared with 22 per cent for the next richest fifth and 26 per cent across all incomes.

However, taxes on consumption do not have the same equalising effect and fall more heavily on those on lower incomes. There are several explanations for this. Even where taxes on spending appear equal (for example, the 20 per cent standard rate of VAT), the fact that those on higher incomes can save more of their incomes would mean that such taxes are a lower proportion of their total incomes, whereas those on lower incomes tend to spend all of their incomes (or, with increasing debt, more than that). Those on higher incomes are also able to take greater advantages of the fiscal welfare and tax expenditures (see the discussion in Chapter 4) that reduce their taxes. On the other hand, VAT has various exemptions (such as on more basic foodstuffs) on which poorer people tend to spend proportionately more money, which leads to a more proportional effect of this tax.

As we see in Table 7.2, the amounts paid in indirect taxes do not vary as much with incomes as do direct taxes. Indeed, the regressive nature of most indirect taxes is a key contributor to inequality. The ONS has in fact argued that '[i]ndirect taxes made the largest contribution (4.3 percentage points) to income inequality over the last 10 years'. See Chapter 14 for more detailed analysis.

Patterns in income inequality

Trends in Great Britain

The UK is well served with good sources of data on people's incomes, enabling us to look at how inequality has changed over time with a high level of confidence, although not total confidence, in the robustness of the results. A particular omission is that those on the very highest incomes tend not to be well represented in the relevant surveys. Although some adjustments are made for this, those living the most comfortable lives may rely on resources not well captured as incomes, such as by selling assets. However, leaving aside these caveats, overall trends in income inequality in Britain are shown in Figure 7.3, based on income calculations for the HBAI series.

There are various ways of measuring income inequality, each with different advantages and limitations. The 'Gini coefficient' is one of the most commonly calculated measures. In brief, it varies from 0 to 1, where 0 would mean everyone had the same level of income, and 1 would mean that just one person in the population had all the income. This is the measure shown in Figure 7.3.

While income inequality was decreasing during the late 1970s, the clearest change was the marked increase during the 1980s with a shallower one in the 1990s. After housing costs, the rise was even greater, with the Gini rising from 0.25 in 1978 to 0.37 in 1991. Fluctuations since 2000/1 look relatively minor in comparison.

For social policy and political analysts, it is natural to associate the steep rise in incomes inequality in the 1980s with the governments of Margaret Thatcher and some of their key policies, such as shifting the balance away from income tax and towards VAT, and reductions in certain elements of benefits such as earnings-related supplements. It is also true that this change in income equality took place in several other countries over this period, most notably in the United States under the administration of Ronald Reagan, which adopted similarly pro-market policies. However, elsewhere any such

Figure 7.3: Trends in income inequality in Great Britain (1961–2018/19)

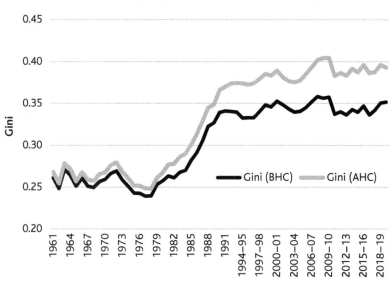

Note: Results for the UK, also including Northern Ireland, are only available in the latter part of this time period from 2002 to 2003.

increases in equality were rather more muted than in the UK (see Gottschalk and Smeeding, 1997, who look in particular at inequality of earnings).

There are a number of key causes of such a change, or at least possible causes. These include the rise in unemployment taking place in the early 1980s, the tax reductions on higher incomes, the drop in unionisation rates over this time and the reduction in manufacturing jobs during the 1980s (partly owing to an oil-inflated higher currency). Some of these causes relate directly to policy changes (for example, on taxes), while others may have happened without those specific policy changes (such as a higher currency linked to the role of oil in the UK economy).

The large increase in income inequality was due to higher unemployment in the early 1980s and to rising self-employment earnings inequality later in the 1980s, with increasingly greater inequality between occupations. In particular, the earnings of manual workers (even skilled) fell behind the wage growth rates of service workers (Brewer et al, 2009).

In the latter part of the 1980s (1984–88), the key factor in overall income equality was those with earnings moving away from the economically inactive. During this time, the uprating of the state pension had been moved to be in line with prices rather than earnings, so it was somewhat inevitable that pensioners (at least those mostly reliant on the state retirement pension) would fall behind those in the labour force – which they did. However, it was around this time that some pensioners started to become rather better-off, with strong effects from rising inequality of investment incomes as well as increasing numbers of better-off groups benefitting from occupational and personal pensions.

Another key contextual factor was the change in the mix of housing tenures. According to analysis by Brewer et al (2009, p 7), in the 1970s the incomes of social tenants were around 10 per cent below the national average. By the 2000s, tenants of local authorities and housing associations had incomes more than 30 per cent below the average.

ONS estimates tell a slightly different story, with more of an emphasis on rising inequality taking place during the 2010s, although HBAI figures seem to show a more gradual rise with more year-to-year variation. However, it is perhaps not surprising to see a further increase in income inequality resulting from austerity in public finance. This was the motivation behind placing a tight squeeze on the level of social security benefits (McKay and Rowlingson, 2016). ONS concluded that the 'rise in inequality of household income after taxes and benefits in the last decade is largely down to the diminishing effectiveness of cash benefits to redistribute income from the richest to the poorest, coinciding with the freezing of many cash benefits at their financial year ending (FYE) 2016 values' (ONS, 2021, online in section 1, no page numbers).

Inequality across countries

Countries differ in the extent of their redistributive efforts. The Organisation for Economic Co-operation and Development (OECD) looks at a wide range of countries and calculates inequality both from market income (wages, pensions) and after direct taxes and transfers. Results for 26 countries, all with data from 2017 or later, are illustrated in Figure 7.4, with the UK highlighted. The chart shows the Gini coefficient for people's original or market-based incomes and then the same after transfers and direct taxes (so not including taxes on spending in this case), and the difference in size between these two concepts. The countries are ordered from those with the smallest difference between pre- and post-transfer inequality (least redistribution by the state) to those with the largest difference between pre- and post-transfer inequality (in other words, with the most redistribution taking place).

Among these countries, the UK ranked sixth highest in terms of pre-transfer inequality but was second in terms of post-transfer inequality, with only the United States being more unequal after taxes and transfers. This is because the redistributive system in the UK did rather less than most countries to offset market-based inequalities – on the OECD figures, changing from a Gini coefficient of 0.51 pre-transfer to 0.37 post-transfer. Most other countries show a larger reduction in inequality occasioned by their system of taxes and transfers.

Figure 7.4: Inequality in comparative perspective (Gini coefficients for incomes before and after taxes and transfers)

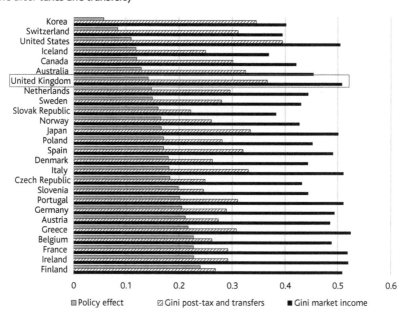

By way of comparison, both France and Ireland start with more inequality than the UK in terms of market-based incomes (each having a Gini coefficient above the UK at 0.52), but post-transfer were more equal with both having a post-transfer Gini coefficient of 0.292 – the kind of lower level of inequality not seen in the UK for some time, massively below the UK's current level of 0.37. Only the United States fails to correct the high level of market inequality to a lesser extent than the UK, with a reduction from 0.505 before taxes and transfers to 0.395 afterwards.

COVID-19, lockdowns and beyond

The COVID-19 pandemic led to considerable reductions in economic activity, as governments sought to promote working from home and reduced opportunities for in-person interactions. This disproportionately affected those in services occupations, with younger people the most likely to have been unable to continue work as normal. The benefits system may be seen as having responded positively to COVID-19 and the various lockdowns that it prompted. For those unable to remain in work, or not able to be part of the various furlough and job retention schemes (the Coronavirus Job Retention Scheme [CJRS]), or separate support for the self-employed (the Self-Employment Income Support Scheme), the numbers claiming Universal

Credit rose dramatically – the specific pandemic schemes representing close to 4 per cent of GDP (see Figure 7.1). The CJRS ('Furlough') supported 11.7 million employments from March 2020 to September 2021, and the number on Universal Credit doubled in a year, from 3 to 6 million (McKay and Rowlingson, 2021).

At the time, in what looks like an admission of the inadequacy of the system, the government increased the rates of Universal Credit by some £20 a week (on what was a temporary basis, from 2019 to 2021). Support for housing was also increased, undoing some previous freezing of levels of support for rent and returning to the point where benefit claimants may be able to afford up to the bottom 30 per cent of rent levels in their local area.

While it is too soon to deliver a final assessment of the various COVID-related policies, Brewer and Tasseva (2021, p 433) show that 'policies protected household incomes to a substantial degree'. However, after a long period of austerity in the benefits system, it is also true that the previous benefits system (they model the 2011 system) would have provided more effective income protection for many people affected during the COVID period. Looking more broadly, a study of five countries (France, Germany, Italy, Spain and Sweden) found that COVID, and the policy reaction to it, had reduced income inequality (Clark et al, 2021). The authors suggest that this resulted from greater income protection for poorer than for richer households.

Times of crisis may prompt change, such as the wartime Beveridge Report, but are hardly guaranteed to do so (for example, the 2008 global financial crisis). Certainly, UK governments do not seem minded to make radical nor generous reforms to social security, with a renewed emphasis on cutting taxes while also addressing widespread concerns about the costs of energy.

Conclusion

The UK has seen a large rise in inequality over time and remains one of the more unequal countries in the developed world. The high level of inequality of final incomes is not simply about market inequality, as several other countries are less equal before taxes and benefits, and more equal after them, compared to the UK. France and Ireland are two clear examples of this, and indeed only the United States (among major modern economies) has a system that does less than the UK's to reduce inequality.

In the UK, inequality rose sharply in the 1980s and has been on a slowly rising trend ever since. Some of the reasons for that are linked to taxes and benefits, with ONS attributing some of the increase in inequality to the strong reliance on indirect taxes (a major contributor to the inequality of final incomes), and the recent increase in inequality to the long-running benefits freeze imposed on benefit recipients under austerity provisions within government.

Reforms are certainly possible for both taxes and benefits if the timing is right. Indeed, during the COVID-19 pandemic the benefits system was able to react quite quickly – although, in terms of the key £20 a week increase in the main benefit for those of working age, only temporarily. Overall, systems of taxes and benefits play a large role in offsetting the kinds of inequality found among earnings and private sources of income. In the UK, this is done to a lesser extent, and to an extent that is reducing over time.

Looking to the future, the high level of income inequality remains an issue in the UK, alongside the inability of taxes of benefits to tackle inequalities, whilst retaining high levels of non-transparency. There are issues at the levels of particular taxes and benefits, and some relating to the overall structure. However, the benefits system was able to react to the COVID-19 pandemic measures and support many people who may have been unfamiliar with benefits before. It remains to be seen if the wider remit given to Universal Credit, covering the risks generated by the pandemic, proves to be a short-lived experiment or a platform for future generosity. At the time of writing, various elements (higher inflation, rising food prices, increasing NICs) are generating a cost-of-living crisis. Policies towards taxes and benefits could certainly address this crisis, given the right political will.

Note

[1] See https://obr.uk/data.

Further reading

Some further resources may be found at the following sites:
- DWP figures on HBAI: https://www.gov.uk/government/collections/households-below-average-income-hbai--2
- Living standards, poverty and inequality in the UK – collated figures from the Institute for Fiscal Studies (IFS): https://ifs.org.uk/tools_and_resources/incomes_in_uk
- The IFS also has a resource ('tax lab') explaining more about the functioning of taxation in the UK: https://ifs.org.uk/taxlab
- There are regular reports on welfare reform and on the levels of tax and government fiscal outlook from the OBR: https://obr.uk
- OECD supplies figures for a wide range of countries through its income distribution (and wealth distribution) databases – incomes data before and after transfers, and measures of inequality, are available at: https://stats.oecd.org/Index.aspx?DataSetCode=IDD
- ONS – figures on the effects of taxes and benefits on household incomes: https://www.ons.gov.uk/peoplepopulationandcommunity/personalandhouseholdfinances/incomeandwealth/bulletins/theeffectsoftaxesandbenefitsonhouseholdincome/financialyearending2020

References

Beveridge, W. (1942) 'Social insurance and allied services', London: HMSO, Cmd 6404.

Bradshaw, J. (2017) 'Why the two-child policy is the worst social security policy ever', Social Policy Association 50th Anniversary Blog Series, no 3, Available from: https://www.social-policy.org.uk/50-for-50/two-child-policy

Brewer, M. and Tasseva, I.V. (2021) 'Did the UK policy response to COVID-19 protect household incomes?', *Journal of Economic Inequality*, 19(3): 433–58.

Brewer, M., Muriel, A. and Wren-Lewis, L. (2009) 'Accounting for changes in inequality since 1968: decomposition analyses for Great Britain', London: Institute for Fiscal Studies Report for the National Equality Panel.

Clark, A., Ambrosio, C. and Lepinteur, A. (2021) 'The fall in income inequality during COVID-19 in five European countries', Available from: https://halshs.archives-ouvertes.fr/halshs-03185534/document

Deacon, A. and Bradshaw, J. (1983) *Reserved for the Poor: The Means Test in British Social Policy*, London: Blackwell and Robertson.

Dilnot, A.W., Kay, J.A. and Morris, C.N. (1984) *The Reform of Social Security*, Oxford: Clarendon Press.

FRS (2021) Family Resources Survey: financial year 2019 to 2020. Available from: https://www.gov.uk/government/statistics/family-resources-survey-financial-year-2019-to-2020/family-resources-survey-financial-year-2019-to-2020

Gottschalk, P. and Smeeding, T.M. (1997) 'Cross-national comparisons of earnings and income inequality', *Journal of Economic Literature*, 35(2): 633–87.

Jenkins, S.P. (1991) 'Poverty measurement and the within-household distribution: agenda for action', *Journal of Social Policy*, 20(4): 457–83.

Lymer, A. and Oats, L. (2021) *Taxation: Policy and Practice 2021/22*, Malvern: Fiscal Publications.

McKay, S. (2019) 'National insurance', in J. Bradshaw (ed) *Let's Talk about Tax: How the Tax System Works and How to Change It*, London: Child Poverty Action Group, pp 59–69.

McKay, S. and Rowlingson, K. (2016) 'Social security under the Coalition and Conservatives: shredding the system for people of working age; privileging pensioners', in H. Bochel and M. Powell (eds) *The Coalition Government and Social Policy: Restructuring the Welfare State*, Bristol: Policy Press, pp 179–200.

McKay, S. and Rowlingson, K. (2021) 'Financial inclusion: annual monitoring report 2021', University of Birmingham, Available from: https://www.birmingham.ac.uk/documents/college-social-sciences/social-policy/chasm/financial-inclusion/financial-inclusion-october-2021.pdf

Millar, J. and Bennett, F. (2017) 'Universal Credit: assumptions, contradictions and virtual reality', *Social Policy and Society*, 16(2), pp 169–82.

Mirrlees, J., Adam, S., Besley, T., Blundell, R., Bond, S. and Chote, R. et al (2011) 'Tax by design', London: IFS.

Moffitt, R.A. (2003) 'The negative income tax and the evolution of US welfare policy', *Journal of Economic Perspectives*, 17(3): 119–40.

ONS (2021) 'Effects of taxes and benefits on UK household income: financial year ending 2020', Available from: https://www.ons.gov.uk/peoplepop ulationandcommunity/personalandhouseholdfinances/incomeandwea lth/bulletins/theeffectsoftaxesandbenefitsonhouseholdincome/financia lyearending2020

Royston, S. (2017) *Broken Benefits: What's Gone Wrong with Welfare Reform*, Bristol: Policy Press.

Sandford, C., Pond, C. and Walker, R. (eds) (1980) *Taxation and Social Policy*, London: Heinemann.

Webster, D. (2015) 'Benefit sanctions: Britain's secret penal system', Comment, Centre for Crime and Justice Studies, Available from: https:// www.crimeandjustice.org.uk/resources/benefit-sanctions-britains-sec ret-penal-system

8

Taxation, health and social care

Sally Ruane

Introduction

While government expenditure dominates the funding of health care in the UK, with £180 billion spent by government on the National Health Service (NHS) in England alone, by far the largest portion of English social care is provided unpaid by family and friends – at an estimated value of £62–£103 billion (NAO, 2018; King's Fund, 2021a). This dramatic difference in approach is part of the contrasting stories of health and social care, related in this chapter. The chapter examines the taxation basis for the funding of the NHS and its durability over time and juxtaposes this with the persistent calls for change in the way social care – only partially funded through taxation – is financed. While these contrasts are UK-wide, variation in approaches to funding across the four UK territories will be noted.

The chapter also explores growing public support for raising taxes to increase funding for the NHS, the increased use of taxation to fund private health care providers and attempts by both private providers and NHS Trusts to reduce tax liabilities through appeals to 'charitable' status.

Finally, the chapter considers two key ways in which taxation is implicated in the need to reduce socio-economic inequalities in order to reduce health inequalities. The first concerns the role of taxation in achieving a redistribution of resources and the second the levying of taxes on health-harming behaviours at both industry and individual levels.

There are two notes of caution to sound at the outset. The first is that much of the discussion is framed in terms of the use of taxation to fund services. However, this 'common sense' perspective is increasingly challenged by many adherents of modern monetary theory, who hold that government spending precedes taxation and that taxation does not fund services but fulfils other macro-economic and social functions (for example, Murphy, 2015). Second, in selecting the focal points of this chapter, we have omitted other legitimate topics, such as the tax treatment of NHS employees and general practitioners, including tax treatment surrounding medical pensions, and a wide range of the more elaborate tax planning strategies adopted by private providers of health and social care.

The dominance of taxation in the funding of the NHS

The NHS of all four territories in the UK is funded almost entirely through general taxation and National Insurance (NI). Only a very small proportion of funding is derived from charitable donations or patient charges, this low level of cost-sharing making the UK unique in inter-country comparisons. Even when health-related long-term care is included in the measure of health spending, as it is with Organisation for Economic Co-operation and Development (OECD) data, only six out of 25 of the world's wealthier countries have a smaller proportion of spending derived from private contributions (ONS, 2019).

Some of the advantages of general taxation as a means of funding health care were identified by Aneurin Bevan, the chief architect of the new National Health Service in 1948, under an overarching 'collective principle' (Bevan, 1978): the apparatus of healing should be placed at the disposal of all, without charge, when it was needed, and treatment and care should be a communal responsibility. For Bevan, financial anxiety hindered recovery, and denial of access to health care on the grounds of means was uncivilised. The key significance, then, of taxation as the funding base is that the process of paying taxes is entirely divorced from a consultation for advice from a general practitioner or a referral to a hospital specialist. As a result, a scarce resource can be allocated directly on the basis of need, unmediated by the sick person's ability to pay. In Bevan's view, social or private insurance would have tied access to services to contribution record, producing a host of anomalies, anxiety and inequities arising from the individual's attempts to fund out-of-pocket payments when insurance coverage fails and an 'administrative jungle' (Bevan, 1978).

To these intrinsic benefits were added further advantages of general taxation as a means of funding the health system set out in Sir Derek Wanless's 2001 analysis, commissioned by then Chancellor of the Exchequer Gordon Brown. Wanless (2001) pointed to the resilience and sustainability general taxation enjoyed as a mode of funding the health system since the very wide base of general taxation includes the whole population and a broad range of revenue-raising activities such that, outside a recession, a dip in revenue from one is likely to be offset by stability in others. A second macro-economic consideration was that funding through general taxation provided for strong cost containment since, subject to the wishes of Parliament, a government could raise or reduce the overall amount and the proportion of public revenues spent on health. Funding health care through taxation also allows for the fact that both ability to pay and the need for health care vary across the life cycle. Moreover, general taxation permits the better-off to pay a higher proportion of their income towards the costs of health care, where the overall tax system is progressive. Finally, while socio-economic inequalities are often cumulative (for example, low income is often associated with poor housing or living in urban areas of high pollution, deepening the inequality), equality of access to tax-funded NHS care can offset other inequalities and avoid deepening them further.

Wanless's review of funding options for the NHS was not the first in its history. As early as the 1950s, the Guillebaud Report, established because of government concern about the cost of health care, surprised ministers by concluding that spending on the NHS represented good value for money, and when Harold Macmillan explored the case for a NI-based health system, he found he could not pursue the idea for electoral reasons (Baggott, 1998). The 1970s Royal Commission on the NHS (1979) reviewed options for raising finance from non-Exchequer sources and, like Wanless, concluded taxation-based funding remained the best option (Mohan, 1995, p 4). A secret, but leaked, review in 1982 by Thatcher's Central Policy Review Staff was charged with exploring alternatives to taxation. They considered the option of an insurance-based system, but hostile public reaction forced the prime minister reluctantly to reject the report (Mohan, 1995, p 56). A 1988 review also considered a state health insurance system and increasing private funding of health care, but these were considered politically unrealistic (Baggott, 1998).

Blocked by electoral riskiness, but being an individualist rather than a collectivist and keen to make a dent in the taxation basis of the service, Thatcher instead raised and extended charges to increase health care costs to patients at the point of use. However, prescription charges were abolished in post-devolution Scotland, Wales and Northern Ireland, and while receipts from charges accounted for about 2 per cent of the NHS budget in the 1970s, they accounted for 1.1 per cent of the Department of Health and Social Care budget in 2019–20 (Baggott, 1998; King's Fund, 2021b).

A small proportion of overall spending in the NHS is derived from charitable giving, encouraged by Thatcher and John Major through tax concessions to charities and payroll contribution schemes (Baggott, 1998). Charitable giving is boosted by a tax subsidy since donations from income taxpayers enjoy income tax relief. NHS Charities Together comprises around 240 member charities based in NHS Trusts around the UK and gives around £365 million annually to the NHS (NHS Charities Together, 2021), less than one quarter of 1 per cent of total funding on average (more in some Trusts, especially specialist Trusts) (Varley, 2019). As well as benefitting from gift aid on donations themselves, charities are not required to pay tax on most of their income from donations, their rental or investment income (estimated to be around 18 per cent of all NHS Charities Together income) or profits from trading or on profits when assets are disposed of (Varley, 2019; UK Government, 2021).

Because central government taxation is decided mainly by the UK chancellor, it is the UK government that determines revenues allocated to the governments across the UK. However, these governments can divide this revenue differently across public services and, in addition to this, the Scottish government has powers to set income tax rates in Scotland. Government choices have resulted in England having the lowest spending per head of population in the UK and Scotland having the highest (MacKinnon, 2019).

Public attitudes to raising taxes for health care

Funding through general taxation allows universal access based on need rather than a contributory record, and this intrinsic interconnection with access has helped to make alterations to the NHS funding system hitherto politically off-limits. This makes the level of funding for the NHS to some extent influenced by popular attitudes towards tax rates and beliefs about how well funded the service is. Data are regularly collected on public attitudes to tax rises for the purpose of increasing spending on public services, for example in the annual British Social Attitudes Survey. The proportion of those questioned supporting tax rises to increase NHS funding has risen over time – 40 per cent in 2014 and 61 per cent in 2017 (King's Fund, 2018). An Ipsos Mori survey commissioned by Deloitte and Reform (a right-leaning think-tank) found 62 per cent of those questioned supported higher taxes for more extensive public services and 79 per cent believed the NHS should be protected from cuts (Deloitte and Reform, 2018). More recently, surveys have shown public support for specific tax rises and not merely the principle of raising taxes (for example, Glover and Sleaford, 2020).

Surveys find that support for the additional public spending made possible by tax rises is often linked to preferences about where the money is spent (Hebden et al, 2020). The NHS is consistently seen as the priority for additional government spending, although the extent of the preference may depend on levels of spending at the time (Cream et al, 2018). However, the public have also voted against political parties running on tax-raising manifestos (for example, Labour lost the 1992 general election after campaigning on a tax-raising manifesto). In his Budget speech of 2002, Gordon Brown tackled this public ambivalence by explicitly connecting an additional penny in the pound on NI to an increase in NHS funding of £40 billion or 43 per cent over a five-year period (BBC News, 2002). This policy, accepted by the public, resulted in a noticeable increase in the NI proportion of NHS funding from 6.1 per cent in 1974 to 16.1 per cent in 1988 and 21.5 per cent in 2004 (after the specific NI increase). It is now around 19 per cent each year (Rahman, 2018a; King's Fund, 2021b). It should be stressed, however, that NI is used here as a tax and not as a set of premiums paid by individuals for specific entitlements by those individuals.

This is an example of 'soft hypothecation' since the additional revenues raised by the penny increase were all allocated to NHS funding, but this contributed only a limited proportion of total NHS funding.

There is little support for hard hypothecation in the UK where the NHS is concerned, although the idea of a specific health tax recurs from time to time and the Health and Social Care Levy, introduced for a few brief months in 2022, translated the idea into policy. Currently, there is some limited support among 'Centrists' for a NI health tax, with some arguing this as part of a vision of moving towards an NHS National Mutual where access to health care is based on residency and contributions (Field, 2015). Supporters argue that such a tax offers greater transparency in the use of tax revenues and raises awareness of the cost of the services paid for. In practice, however, governments have pursued a combination of policies governed by varying mixes of ideology and expediency, and most taxes paid go into an undifferentiated pot of tax revenues (Sussex, 2018).

Mixed economy in social care

In contrast to the NHS, the funding of social care has been disputed territory for several decades, and it is here that earmarked taxes are more central to the debate. Unlike other countries such as Germany, France and the Netherlands, there has historically been no mandatory insurance to cover the costs of social care in the UK. Social care is funded on a means-tested basis, and the cuts in funding in the decade after the 2008 financial crash resulted in tightened eligibility criteria: only those with substantial needs and few assets can access publicly funded social care. Local authority funding for this is derived from central government grants funded through general taxation and local property taxes (council tax and business rates), which are devolved and subject to different legislation in England, Wales and Scotland. Further funds from general taxation are secured from local NHS budgets: for example, in England from the Integrated Care Board budget via the Better Care Fund and via the NHS Continuing Health Care budget, which, if allocated for an eligible patient, covers social care as well as health care costs. In Northern Ireland, social care is integrated into health care and funded through taxation, again subject to means testing (Oung et al, 2020).

While 120,000 more people requested social care support between 2015–16 and 2019–20, around 14,000 fewer people received it (Bottery and Babalola, 2021). The National Audit Office (2018) found that for 2016–17 at least two thirds of social care was provided by friends and family unpaid, while publicly funded care amounted to £22 billion and self-funded care totalled around £11 billion. In response to criticism of funding cuts, central government provided some tax-funded temporary grants to local authorities and, from 2016–17, introduced the 'social care precept' in England allowing local authorities to increase council tax annually by 2 percentage points without holding a referendum. The additional revenues thus raised are ring-fenced for social care – another example of soft hypothecation. Local authority funding derived from council tax rose from 33 per cent in 2009–10 to around 50 per cent by 2018–19 (Atkins, 2020). Around half the additional monies available for social care between 2016–17 and 2019–20 were derived from the adult social care precept and the flexibility associated with this (LGA, nd).

The growing pressure on public budgets, the unpredictable nature of social care needs accompanied by the unpredictable risk of facing very high social care costs, along with the possibility of having to sell off assets accumulated over a lifetime to pay for care, have led to repeated calls over several decades to establish a better way of funding social care. However, if general taxation is the near consensus view on how to fund the NHS, this is certainly not the case in social care among those seeking change. Major policy proposals have included the 1999 Sutherland Commission (Royal Commission, 1999), which recommended taxation funding for narrowly defined personal care (implemented in Scotland only) with housing and living costs split between state and individual, and the 2011 Dilnot Commission (Dilnot, 2011), which proposed cost sharing between state and individual with a £35,000 cap on personal care costs (not implemented). Prime Ministers Gordon Brown in 2009–10 and Theresa May in 2017 both suffered electorally in their attempts to tackle the funding of social care by following proposals for a levy on estates, widely denounced as a 'death' and 'dementia' tax, respectively, and misrepresented as a variant of inheritance tax but in fact a payment for services already received.

In 2021, the Conservative government announced an increase of 1.25 per cent on dividend tax and a weakly hypothecated third tax on income: the Health and Social Care Levy (H&SCL), with revenues ring-fenced for the NHS and social care. The levy, commencing April 2022, would comprise 1.25 per cent on employee earnings, employer wage costs and self-employed income on that portion of income liable to NI. The levy would apply to pensioners' income from work unlike standard NI contributions. At the same time, a cap on personal care costs of £86,000 from October 2023 was announced, and the means test threshold was altered so that those with assets below £20,000 would not face asset-based charges for social care (although they might still be required to contribute from their income). Individuals with assets up to a maximum of £100,000 could be eligible for some local authority help with care costs, although individuals may still not qualify if their level of needs is considered too low.

With the government enjoying an 80 seat majority, the proposals comfortably passed a House of Commons vote but attracted widespread criticism. The decision to apply the levy to that proportion of income or profits for which NI is liable means that it added to the costs of labour and fell heavily upon low- and middle-income workers who pay a higher proportion of their incomes in NI than workers on the higher and additional rate tax bands. Like NI, the levy would not apply to unearned income or to rental income, which are more likely to be enjoyed by the better-off; the increased dividend tax offset this to a limited extent, but the combined effect on earnings was 2.5 per cent (employee and employer rates combined), while the tax on dividend income increased by only 1.25 per cent. Pensioners, who are more likely to need care than adults of working age, remained relatively protected since, like NI, the levy would not be applied to income from state, personal or occupational pensions or to the income from their savings, although it would apply to pensioners' income from work. The levy added a further complication to an already complex tax system whereas an equivalent increase in income tax would have spread liability more progressively and less unevenly across age groups. The policy reinforced a trend seen in previous years of shifting tax liabilities towards earnings and widened the gap between taxes paid on the incomes of the self-employed and those paid on the incomes of employees (IFS, 2021). Despite the additional 'pain', the gain for social care would be limited since the vast majority of the revenues raised were slated for the NHS.

Announced in September 2021 and implemented in April 2022, the levy was cancelled with effect from November 2022 by the subsequent Conservative government: the additional funds for health and social care were now to come from borrowing.

The use of taxation to fund the private health sector

Government tax interventions have shaped UK private health insurance take-up. In 1981, both employers and employees were given tax incentives to encourage health insurance as a fringe benefit, ostensibly to boost workplace health care and tackle working-age ill health and absenteeism. In 1989, tax relief was extended to private health insurance for those over 60 years of age (even if the payers of that insurance were under 60), although this was abolished by the 1997 Labour government (Baggott, 1998). Currently, private health insurance provided by an employer is seen as a business expense attracting tax relief for the company but also as a benefit in kind to the employee and therefore subject to tax. Insurance premiums may be seen as a valid business expense for the self-employed where insurance is in place to enable the individual to get back to work. There are other benefits that can be provided to employees free of tax, notably: welfare counselling, eye tests for employees working at screens and the costs of medical insurance when working abroad. Private health insurance premiums are now subject to insurance premium tax of 12 per cent, and although in recent years corporate health trusts have grown to avoid insurance premium tax, these are confined mainly to large employers, introducing another inequality. Unlike insurance premiums paid to an insurance company that funds employee health care costs and that can take profit, in corporate health trusts, payments are made to a trust that enables employers to self-fund health benefits and retains any surplus funds. The full value of all these tax reliefs to business is not publicly disclosed.

Since the 2000s, the use of tax revenues to expand the independent health care sector has grown. Until 2010, growth was fostered by market-making policies: Labour deliberately sought to pluralise the supply of NHS-funded care, arguing that additional providers would drive down waiting lists and that patients would benefit from choice. After 2010, Conservative/Coalition policies were founded upon the idea that the NHS should operate as a market with a 'level playing field' in which no a priori preference should be given to NHS providers. Policies to constrain NHS capacity have proved an additional driver to use tax revenues to support the private sector. For example, as NHS hospital beds continue to decline and elective care is squeezed in the winter when emergency admissions rise, tax-funded health care is commissioned from the private sector in preference to expanding the capacity of the NHS. Thus while the private acute hospital and clinic sector derived 5 per cent of its revenues from tax-funded NHS contracts in 2007, it had become dependent for revenues upon such tax-funded contracts to the tune of 32 per cent by 2018 (Barrett Evans et al, 2018). Some companies have benefitted from this tax funding while pursuing tax avoidance practices. For example, Virgin Care Ltd, which has secured well over £2 billion worth of NHS and local authority contracts in recent years, has been criticised for using 13 intermediate holding companies ostensibly to distance the firm's health care company from the parent company based in the British Virgin Isles. As it technically makes no profits in the UK, it pays no corporation tax (Molloy, 2015; Hiscott, 2020).

The role of the independent sector in the provision of tax-funded services has become more entrenched during the COVID-19 pandemic. Waiting times had grown even before the pandemic, adding to the backlog of health care needed. A £2.4 million per day contract was brokered between the Department of Health and Social Care and the Independent Healthcare Providers Network in March 2020 to provide elective and other care while NHS capacity was devoted to (largely COVID-19) emergency admissions; and a further £10 billion of tax funding was made available for the October 2020 Increasing Capacity Framework, which facilitates contracting with pre-approved private sector providers over a period of four years.

Tax treatment and strategies for reducing tax liabilities

As well as benefitting from tax funding, independent providers registered as charities also gain from lower business rates than those NHS organisations are required to pay (and see Chapter 12). Surgeries, clinics, health centres and hospitals must all pay business rates, which are taxes paid on non-residential properties and amount to around 50 per cent of the property's rateable value (Valuation Office Agency assessment of how much it would cost to rent). Changes in the rateable value of property, which came into effect in 2017, differentially affected public and independent sector health care organisations (Rahman, 2018b). The new valuation increased the value of NHS hospitals in England and Wales by about 19 per cent on average, leading to a 24 per cent increase in business rates by 2019–20 (Rahman, 2018b). However, private hospitals saw their rateable value rise by only around 9 per cent on average and thus faced much smaller increases in tax liability. The city centre locations of some NHS hospitals and the completion of a small number of new build NHS hospitals may have contributed to the differentiated impact of revaluation.

Moreover, many independent sector health providers, registered as charitable organisations on the basis they are 'advancing health or saving lives', are entitled to an 80 per cent discount on their business rates. This unequal treatment led, in 2016, to some 80 NHS Trusts submitting claims to local authorities seeking a discount in the business rates levied upon them plus a rebate for overpayment in the previous six years on the grounds that they should be considered charities and not public sector bodies (Ruddick, 2017). However, the High Court ruled that NHS Trusts could not be classed as charities (Neville, 2021). While there are no official estimates of the number of private health care organisations registered as charities, property consultants CVS estimated that slightly more than one quarter are (Rahman, 2018b), so this discount benefits a sizeable proportion of the private health care sector.

Another approach to reducing tax liability adopted by some NHS organisations has been the establishment by NHS Trusts of subsidiary companies (known as SubCos). These are private companies owned or controlled by another company or organisation (the parent company, in this case typically the NHS Trust). It is a separate legal business, and any losses it makes do not necessarily transfer to the parent company. Staff in the affected services (for example, estates management and property maintenance, catering and cleaning) are transferred to the new private subsidiary company. By 2019, 65 such SubCos had been set up (Patients4NHS, 2020). A range of reasons are given by NHS Trusts for setting them up, often to do with cost reduction: for instance, new staff can be employed on terms and conditions and rates of pay worse than those in the NHS.

One such cost reduction route concerns value added tax (VAT). Treasury rules were introduced in the 1980s to encourage the commissioning of goods and services from outside the NHS where this was cheaper. The in-scope services are listed in the Treasury's 'Contracting out Direction', which identifies where VAT payments can be reclaimed (Carding, 2020; Lowdown, 2020). This rule has been used to reduce the VAT liabilities of Trusts by purchasing estate management and other services from their wholly owned SubCos since the latter are private companies. It appears that for some Trusts this has been the main consideration in setting up a SubCo (Syal and Campbell, 2017), although both NHS Improvement and the Treasury have tried to clamp down on the establishment of SubCos primarily for tax avoidance purposes (Patients4NHS, 2020). In August 2020, the Treasury published proposals to simplify the rules governing how the public sector is refunded for VAT payments, and the simplification is expected to remove the incentive to set up SubCos (Carding, 2020), though at the time of writing these had not been implemented.

Taxation, inequality and the promotion of health

Access to good health and social care is only part of what is necessary in a society organised for the health and wellbeing of its members. As Bevan (1978) observed, particular kinds of social arrangements and patterns and practices of living on all levels are required if a society is to be conducive to good health. This is usually secured through collectivist interventions: for instance, via sanitation systems, food regulation, enforcement of health and safety at work, building standards and road safety laws. Taxation has a role to play here too.

The working group on inequalities in health established in 1977 by the then Labour government concluded that both mortality and access to some health services were influenced by class (Black et al, 1980). The most comprehensive recent approach to socio-economic inequalities and health inequalities is found in Professor Sir Michael Marmot's work (Marmot et al, 2010, 2020). The 2010 'Marmot Review' found that a complex interaction of many factors, including income, housing, education, disability and social isolation, gives rise to health inequalities and that all of these factors are strongly affected by economic and social status.

Addressing health inequalities, Marmot and colleagues concluded, unavoidably entails addressing inequalities across a broad range of factors: early child development and education, employment and working conditions, housing and neighbourhood conditions, standards of living and, more generally, the freedom to participate equally in the benefits of society (Marmot et al, 2010, p 10). The review asserted that economic growth by itself would not address health inequalities because of these intervening factors and that reducing relative inequality would be required, with income inequality particularly significant since it shapes the lives people are able to lead (Marmot et al, 2010, p 12).

Reducing wider inequalities in order to reduce health inequalities concerns taxation in two ways. First, the tax system can raise revenue in such a way as to contribute to a redistribution of resources that (a) reduces the social gradient in the standard of living; (b) reduces the severe income drop for those moving between wages and benefits; and (c) makes available vastly improved services in several critical areas, including support to 'give every child the best start in life'. The combined UK tax, benefits and welfare services system is a redistributive one: inequality between the better-off and less well-off households decreases after taxes have been taken and cash benefits and in-kind services have been allocated (ONS, 2021). However, the extent of its redistributive impact depends upon the precise design of the system. Reed (2020) has shown that changes in the taxation and benefits system between 2010 and 2017, ostensibly designed to reduce the deficit, had a regressive impact, with lower-income households losing more proportionately and in absolute cash terms than better-off households. The Office for National Statistics concluded in 2020 that there had been little change in household income inequality in the previous ten years on some measures and an increase on others (O'Neill, 2020).

Second, consumption taxes, such as VAT and excise taxes, represent a further way in which taxes can promote health. They operate by raising the price of a good or service to reduce demand and alter behaviour, often where costs or harms associated with the product are not reflected in its price. While originally introduced to raise money, excise taxes have increasingly been seen as a tool of social policy for altering behaviour to bring about social policy goals such as reducing the harms and associated health care and other costs arising from excessive consumption. For example, there is a strong evidence base for taxes on alcohol or the price of alcohol to be inversely related to indices of alcohol-related health outcomes (Elder et al, 2010); and for the impact of taxes on raising prices to reduce smoking and related harms (Whitehead et al, 2018).

Because the logic of the consumption tax intervention is to reduce demand (and therefore consumption) by raising prices, vigilance is needed in monitoring the responses of, in these examples, the alcohol and tobacco industries: for example, where they fail to pass tax rises on to consumers. This has certainly been the case in recent years with tobacco in the UK (Whitehead et al, 2018). This points to the limitations of consumption taxes when used as a sole intervention to alter behaviour through pricing and to the need for governments to find alternative or complementary price control strategies.

One of the disadvantages of consumption taxes is that they are typically regressive: they take on average a higher proportion of a poorer household's income than that of a better-off household (ONS, 2021). To combine the use of consumption taxes to alter specific behaviours with the reduction in inequalities called for by Marmot and others, it is thus necessary to review the design of the tax system as a whole. At present, the benefits of taxation as a means of achieving social policy goals such as the reduction of inequality are not fully realised, since, while the allocation of cash benefits and in-kind services reduces inequality, the operation of the tax system itself serves to increase the average gap between the poorest and best-off households (Byrne and Ruane, 2017). This is partly because the impact of regressive indirect (consumption) taxes outweighs that of progressive direct taxes such as income tax, and partly because of the operation of tax reliefs and allowances. Income tax reliefs generally benefit those with higher incomes more than those with lower incomes, yet the distributional impact of such means-enhancing tax rules is poorly understood and rarely investigated (for example, Chapter 4). The Institute of Alcohol Studies has argued that the regressive effects of consumption taxes can be offset by dedicating revenue raised to pro-poor policies such as tax cuts for low-income households or expenditure on public services. In a variant of the hypothecated tax debate, Gordon Brown announced in 1999 that the revenues from tobacco duty would be directed to the NHS (Beecham, 1999).

Following similar moves in other countries, the UK Soft Drinks Industry Levy was introduced in 2018 to reduce sugar intake as part of the government's childhood obesity strategy. Since it is levied on manufacturers rather than on customers at the point of sale, it provides only an indirect incentive for individuals to change their drinking habits. Manufacturers can decide whether to pass the levy on to their customers or they can opt to reformulate their beverages and reduce sugar content. Announced two years in advance, the levy had resulted in more than 50 per cent of manufacturers reformulating products and avoiding the new tax by the time of its introduction (Thornton, 2018). After one year, the volume of soft drinks purchased had not altered (in comparison with what had been expected prior to the announcement of the levy), but the quantity of sugar in drinks purchased had decreased by 10 per cent per household per week (Pell et al, 2021). Thus, without damaging the drinks industry, there appears to be a public health benefit, at least short term. More broadly, the evidence for the effectiveness of drinks taxes to alter harmful consumption is stronger than the evidence for the effectiveness of food taxes (Smith et al, 2018).

Conclusion

This chapter has examined key aspects of the role of taxation in the fields of health and social care. Although much public debate on taxation surrounds income tax, in the aspects of health and social care considered in this chapter the importance of taxation concerns general tax revenues for funding services and then, more specifically, NI, council tax, consumption taxes including VAT, and business rates. Soft hypothecation, in NI and consumption taxes (health care), council tax (social care) and, for a short period, the Health and Social Care Levy, appears as a (not always successful) strategy to raise revenues in politically palatable ways. Income tax is not completely absent from our picture, however, since, as the only major UK tax that is progressive through the income range, it makes a particular contribution to reducing income/economic inequality, considered essential for the reduction in health inequalities. Finding ways of offsetting the inequality-increasing effect of consumption taxes remains one of the principal challenges facing those who wish to alter health-harming behaviours while simultaneously reducing inequalities, echoing the inequality and taxation theme found throughout much of this book.

The use of tax funding shapes access to health and social care in particular ways. Social care has endured a long-criticised patchwork approach to funding that has impeded access, and it is a sign of the widespread diffusion of neoliberal ideas that in recent decades no political leader of any party has sought to or felt able to raise the additional funds needed for social care exclusively through general taxation. This was not significantly altered by the new Health and Social Care Levy, even before its abolition, since, as revenue was shared with the NHS, it was very unlikely to raise all the sums needed for social care, and the high cap for personal care costs points to the continuing and central role of individuals' assets and unpaid family labour.

The near total funding of the NHS through taxation is precisely the policy mechanism that confers universal access on the basis of need. It could be argued, therefore, that most of the population has a vested interest in retaining this policy, contributing to the durability of the NHS as a popular institution and to its status as the service most likely to receive public support for additional spending through tax rises. However, the albeit short-lived experience of the new levy may yet open the way to change: while challenges to the taxation basis of NHS funding have typically emerged from marginalised policy entrepreneurs, 'centrists' with an interest in linking access to health care to a contribution record may in the future introduce a revised levy, using levy 'contributions' as a marker of eligibility to NHS care. It is also possible to imagine a more subtle approach to change, with constraints on the overall funding of the NHS being used by so-minded governments to tip more patients into self-funded or insurance-funded health care as NHS waiting lists continue to grow, accelerating the recent trend in this direction (Health, 2021). This would effect a shift towards a higher proportion of health funding coming from private contributions and deepen heath inequalities.

Alternatively, governments could pursue approaches that are progressive and avoid introducing barriers to accessing health care, such as a net wealth tax, with the Wealth Tax Commission concluding that a one-off tax on wealth could raise up to £260 billion over five years (Advani et al, 2020).

Given Marmot's (2010) analysis of the role of inequality in ill-health, reluctance to increase the redistributive impact of taxation may not bode well for population health. Many measures that would increase the progressivity of the tax system are unpopular either with the public (such as increasing inheritance tax) or with politicians (such as increasing the higher or additional rates of income tax). While the Soft Drinks Industry Levy has been accepted, the role of taxes on food and drink more broadly remains contentious partly because of their regressive impact, partly because their mid- and long-term impact on reducing obesity and improving health remains unknown and partly because of an ideological preference by the food and drinks industry for voluntary self-regulation.

It is evident that matters of taxation are deeply implicated in health and social care services as well as in health and wellbeing itself. By the same token, a discussion of taxation in health and social care inevitably speaks to some of the dominant concerns of social policy, such as how to allocate resources and tackle inequality, how to shape behaviour and how to meet need and improve access to services.

Further reading
- Bottery and Ward (2021) – excellent overview of social care.
- Marmot et al (2020) – sets out policy proposals for reducing health inequalities and why this is necessary.
- Sussex et al (2019) – explores public deliberation on funding options.
- Whitehead et al (2018) – examines strengths and limitations of tobacco taxation and pricing strategies.

References

Advani, A., Chamberlain, C. and Summers, A. (2020) 'A wealth tax for the UK', Final Report of the Wealth Tax Commission, Available from: https://www.wealthandpolicy.com/wp/WealthTaxFinalReport.pdf

Atkins, G. (2020) 'Local government funding in England', Institute for Local Government, Available from: https://www.instituteforgovernment.org.uk/explainers/local-government-funding-england

Baggott, R. (1998) *Health and Health Care in Britain* (2nd edn), Basingstoke: Macmillan.

Barrett Evans, D., Blackburn, P., Laing, W., Risebrow, H. and Townsend, T. (2018) 'UK healthcare market review 30th edition', London: LaingBuisson.

BBC (2002) 'Tax bills rise to boost NHS', *BBC News*, 17 April, Available from: http://news.bbc.co.uk/1/hi/uk_politics/1934690.stm

Beecham, L. (1999) 'Tobacco tax to be ringfenced for NHS', *British Medical Journal*, 319(1322), 20 November.

Bevan, A. (1978) *In Place of Fear*, London: Quartet Books.

Black, D. et al (1980) 'Inequalities in health: report of a research working group', London: Department of Health and Social Services.

Bottery, S. and Ward, D. (2021) 'Social care 360', London: King's Fund.

Byrne, D. and Ruane, S. (2017) *Paying for the Welfare State in the 21st Century*, Bristol: Policy Press.

Carding, N. (2020) 'Bid to simplify outsourcing "could reduce need for subsidiary firms"', *Health Service Journal*, 17 September.

Cream, J., Maguire, D. and Robertson, R. (2018) 'How have public attitudes to the NHS changed over the past three decades?', King's Fund, 1 February.

Deloitte and Reform (2018) 'Government beyond Brexit: the state of the state, 2018/19', London: Deloitte and Reform.

Dilnot, A. (2011) 'Fairer care funding: the report of the Commission on Funding of Care and Support', vol 1, London: HMSO.

Elder, R., Lawrence, B., Ferguson, A., Naimi, T., Brewer, R. and Chattopadhyay, S. et al (2010) 'The effectiveness of tax policy interventions for reducing excessive alcohol consumption and related harms', *American Journal of Preventive Medicine*, 38(2): 217–29.

Field, F. (2015) 'A national health and social care service: proposals to close the funding gap', King's Fund Annual Conference, 19 November, Available from: https://www.kingsfund.org.uk/audio-video/frank-field-health-soc ial-care-funding

Glover, B. and Sleaford, C. (2020) 'A people's budget: how the public would raise taxes', London: Demos.

Heath, L. (2021) 'Private healthcare: self-pay UK market report' (3rd edn), London: Laing and Buisson.

Hebden, P., Palmer, R. and O'Hagan, E.M. (2020) 'Talking tax: how to win support for taxing wealth', London: Tax Justice UK.

Hiscott, G. (2020) 'Richard Branson's Virgin Healthcare has paid no tax on £2billion NHS deals', *The Mirror*, 26 January.

IFS (2021) 'An initial response to the Prime Minister's announcement on health, social care and National Insurance', Institute for Fiscal Studies, 7 September, Available from: https://ifs.org.uk/publications/15597

King's Fund (2018) 'Does the public see tax rises as the answer to NHS funding pressures?', London: King's Fund, 12 April, Available from: https://www.kingsfund.org.uk/publications/does-public-see-tax-rises-answer-nhs-funding-pressures

King's Fund (2021a) 'The NHS budget and how it has changed', Available from: https://www.kingsfund.org.uk/projects/nhs-in-a-nutshell/nhs-budget

King's Fund (2021b) 'How the NHS is funded', London King's Fund, 1 March, Available from: https://www.kingsfund.org.uk/projects/nhs-in-a-nutshell/how-nhs-funded

LGA (nd) 'Adult social care funding: FAQs', London: Local Government Association.

Lowdown (2020) 'The beginning of the end of Subcos that affect low paid NHS staff?', Lowdown, 22 November.

MacKinnon, S. (2019) 'Scotland's NHS outperforms the rest of the UK: here's why', Business for Scotland.

Marmot, M., Allen, J., Goldblatt, P., Boyce, T., McNeish, D. and Grady, M. (2010) 'Fair society, healthy lives: the Marmot Review', London: Institute of Health Equity.

Marmot, M., Allen, J., Boyce, T., Goldblatt, P. and Morrison, J. (2020) 'Health equity in England: the Marmot Review 10 years on', London: Institute of Health Equity.

Mohan, J. (1995) *A National Health Service?*, Basingstoke: Macmillan.

Molloy, C. (2015) 'Cameron's biggest broken promise on the NHS', Open Democracy, 26 March. Available from: https://www.opendemocracy.net/en/ournhs/camerons-biggest-broken-promise-on-nhs/

Murphy, R. (2015) *The Joy of Tax*, London: Transworld.

NAO (2018) 'Adult social care at a glance', National Audit Office, London: HMSO.

Neville, S. (2021) 'NHS trusts abandon appeal for hospitals to receive rates relief', *Evening Standard*, 29 March.

NHS Charities Together (2021) 'What do NHS charities do?', NHS Charities Together, Available from: https://www.nhscharitiestogether.co.uk/what-we-do-1

O'Neill, J. (2020) 'Household income inequality, UK: financial year ending 2020 (provisional)', Newport: Office for National Statistics.

ONS (2019) 'How does UK healthcare spending compare with other countries?', Newport: Office for National Statistics.

ONS (2021) 'Effects of taxes and benefits on UK household income: financial year ending 2020', Newport: Office for National Statistics.

Oung, C., Schlepper, L. and Curry, N. (2020) 'Who organises and funds social care?', in 'Adult social care in the four countries of the UK', Explainer Series, London: Nuffield Trust.

Patients4NHS (2020) 'NHS SubCos', Patients4NHS.

Pell, D., Mytton, O., Penney, T., Briggs, A., Cummins, S. and Penn-Jones, C. et al (2021) 'Changes in soft drinks purchased by British households associated with the UK Soft Drinks Industry Levy: controlled interrupted time series analysis', *British Medical Journal*, 372(254).

Rahman, G. (2018a) 'How is the NHS funded', Full Fact, 6 July, Available from: https://fullfact.org/health/how-nhs-funded

Rahman, G. (2018b) 'NHS and private hospitals: who pays business rates?', Full Fact, 24 October, Available from: https://fullfact.org/health/nhs-and-private-hospitals-who-pays-business-rates

Reed, H. (2020) 'The distributional impact of tax and social security reforms in the UK from 2010 to 2017', *Social Policy and Society*, 19(3): 470–86.

Royal Commission on Long Term Care for the Elderly (1999) 'With respect to old age: long term care; rights and responsibilities', Cm 4192-I (the 'Sutherland Report'), London: HMSO.

Royal Commission on the NHS (1979) 'Report of the Royal Commission on the NHS', Cmnd 7615, London: HMSO.

Ruddick, G. (2017) 'Cash-strapped hospitals ask for £1.5bn tax rebate', *The Guardian*, 29 November.

Smith, E., Scarborough, P., Rayner, M. and Briggs, A. (2018) 'Should we tax unhealthy food and drink?', *Proceedings of the Nutrition Society*, 77(3): 314–20.

Sussex, J. (2018) 'Tax funding of health and social care internationally: does hypothecation help?', Health Foundation blog, Available from: https://www.health.org.uk/blogs/tax-funding-of-health-and-social-care-internationally-does-hypothecation-help

Sussex, J., Burge, P., Lu, H., Exley, J., King, S. and RAND Europe (2019) 'Public acceptability of health and social care funding options', Working paper no 4, Health Foundation.

Syal, R. and Campbell, D. (2017) 'NHS trusts accused of backdoor privatisation over subsidiary firms', *The Guardian*, 30 October.

Thornton, J. (2018) 'The UK has introduced a sugar tax, but will it work?', London School of Hygiene and Tropical Medicine, Available from: https://www.lshtm.ac.uk/research/research-action/features/uk-sugar-tax-will-it-work

UK Government (2021) 'Charities and tax', Available from: https://www.gov.uk/charities-and-tax/tax-reliefs

Varley, J. (2019) 'Member charities financial comparison', Warwick: NHS Charities Together.

Wanless, D. (2001) 'Securing our future health: taking a long-term view', Interim report, London: HM Treasury.

Whitehead, R., Brown, L., Riches, E., Rennick, L., Armour G. and McAteer, J. et al (2018) 'Strengths and limitations of tobacco taxation and pricing strategies', Edinburgh: NHS Health Scotland.

9

Homes, housing and taxation

James Gregory, Andy Lymer and Carlene Wynter

Introduction

In 1980, housing policy in the UK was described as 'a dog's breakfast' that could not be rationalised either in terms of declared government housing objectives or the more general aims of the fiscal system (Whitehead, 1980, quoting Crosland, 1975). This chapter explores the extent to which this situation has changed in respect of the interaction between tax and housing policies in the 40 years since these remarks were made.

The provision of housing is a contentious issue for governments, as they seek to balance the scales between providing affordable but quality homes for a growing population, providing reasonable returns for 'investors' to support the development of the desired housing stock to supplement public investment, and enabling homeowners to develop a valuable asset that they can own, enjoy and (potentially) pass on to their heirs or use to support later life care costs.

In this chapter, we will focus on the taxation-related tools used by governments in creating the national housing supply. The use of general taxation is key to the provision of direct public revenue to support these housing objectives. However, governments also make use of varied tax interventions that are directly housing related, including providing a variety of tax reliefs and applying a mix of various taxes specifically on housing, including stamp duty, council tax (developed more fully in Chapter 12), capital gains tax (CGT), inheritance tax (IHT), income tax and value added tax (VAT). We will touch on how each of these are used in this chapter.

Housing-related taxation can be used to shape the overall structure of housing provision by directly influencing the attitudes and behaviour of households and individuals. Since 1980, for example, there has also been a growing emphasis on the home as an asset, rather than just a consumption good. As we shall see, the treatment of the home as an asset reflects a longstanding policy and fiscal bias that favours owner-occupation (Kemeny, 1981, Ronald, 2008), arguably leading to even more of a 'dog's breakfast' than the housing policy of the 1970s and '80s. The sums involved are also very considerable – for example, the total tax advantage provided by the

UK tax system to owner-occupiers over other tenures could be worth up to £40 billion (Bentley, 2018).

In this chapter, we focus on the key housing and taxation themes that are of most importance for the society, polity and UK economy as a whole:

- the decline of social housing as a proportion of all UK homes;
- a home-owning culture and the ideals of a 'property-owning democracy';
- the growth of the small landlord and the buy to let, private rental, sector;
- the tax treatment of owner-occupation as both a consumption good and an asset;
- IHT, CGT and the special treatment of primary residences; and
- taxes on housing development and renovation.

The chapter is concluded with some suggestions on 'Where next?' for housing, taxation and social policy.

Context: UK housing tenure mix and the development of a home-owning culture

The UK housing stock is made up primarily of three tenure types:

1. socially rented – either from a local authority as a 'secure' tenant or from a not-for-profit landlord such as a housing association or registered social landlord;
2. privately rented – usually in the form of an assured shorthold tenancy; and
3. owner-occupied – including where the owner holds the freehold of the building and land, but also leaseholders, where the land is rented for a specific period before reverting to the freeholder.

The UK has been experiencing a significant shift towards owner-occupation for many years now (Forrest et al, 2021). Figure 9.1 illustrates the rapidly rising owner-occupation trend since the early 1950s (when owner-occupied dwellings only amounted to 30 per cent of all stock), peaking in the early 2000s at around 70 per cent of stock, before dropping back slightly over the following 20 years to just over 60 per cent.

Correspondingly, rented stock dropped from 70 per cent in 1951 to around 30 per cent by 2000, with socially rented stock (the total of privately registered providers of social housing, local authority stock and other public sector stock) rising initially as a percentage of this part of the overall dwelling stock until the 1980s and then falling back over the following 20 years to around 20 per cent – a level that has been maintained fairly constantly over the last 20 years.

Figure 9.1: Dwelling stock: by tenure, Great Britain, historical series

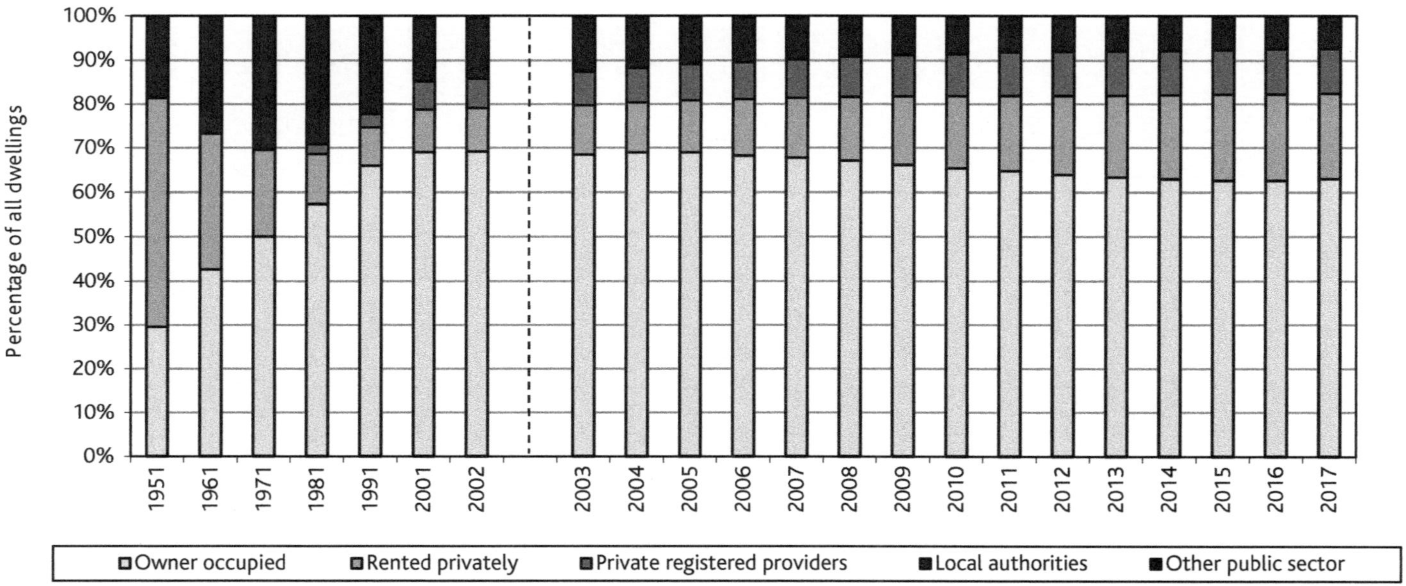

Source: https://www.gov.uk/government/statistical-data-sets/live-tables-on-dwelling-stock-including-vacants

In 1986 (the first year in which we have directly comparable data), 25.9 per cent of all homes in the UK were owned by a local authority, compared to 2.4 per cent owned by a housing association. By 2019, only 7.3 per cent of all homes in the UK were owned and let by local authorities, compared to 10 per cent owned by housing associations (Stephens et al, 2021, table 17).

This change in the mix of social to private tenanted property in the national dwelling stock can be attributed to the specific political and policy interventions of the early 1980s, the most significant of which was perhaps the introduction of the Right to Buy policy in 1980, which gave sitting council tenants the right to buy their home at a discount of up to 30 per cent on its open market value. Over the course of 35 years, some 2.7 million social homes were sold in this way (Murie, 2016) and, by one estimate, by 2010 the total cost of these discounts (and therefore the subsidy provided to owner-occupation) was between £150 billion and £200 billion (Hills, 2013, p 187). Additionally, this policy led to the removal of this stock from the social rental market, both reducing the stock subsequently available for use as well as the rental income that would have been received thereon that, in part, would have supported growth of further social housing.

Compared to the wider population, social tenants today are significantly more likely to experience a range of social disadvantages, such as a higher likelihood of unemployment and a greater risk of physical or mental illness (Feinstein et al, 2008). Taken together, these processes are often referred to as the 'residualisation' of social housing.

Much of the social policy literature addresses these issues through the lens of policy analysis and the impact of specific housing policies.

While housing policy itself is of course important, it has long been accepted that the bias towards ownership is embedded in broader institutional structures, central to which are the taxation and legal institutions of the UK (Murie and Williams, 2015). In contrast to many other European countries, the UK has historically offered limited tax incentives for the development of a strong and well-maintained private rental sector. The absence of sufficient choice and quality in the private rental sector can be regarded as a 'push' factor that has driven ownership trends. At the same time, there have been a range of 'pull' factors. These include not just the favourable tax treatment of owner-occupation but also the availability of relatively cheap mortgage debt, which was widely available as early as the 1930s (Malpass, 2005).

Earlier narratives of the superiority of owner-occupation over social housing stressed the value of virtuous independence from the welfare state. This narrative has since developed to embrace a wider range of households, bringing us all under the normative expectation that we will only seek housing support from the welfare state in extremis. There has therefore been a growing emphasis on the role of the home as a store of wealth that can be used for future welfare consumption (Doling and Ronald, 2010). However, as illustrated by the ongoing social care crisis, the expectation that the home can and should finance future welfare needs is very often not practical, either for individual owners or as a social policy strategy. In practice, the store of UK housing wealth is far more likely to be passed on to children and wider family rather than being drawn down to finance welfare consumption.

The trend of the last 70 years towards greater owner-occupation has more recently seen a shift in one crucial respect – a growing proportion of outright owners against a declining proportion of mortgaged owners (see Figure 9.2). At the same time, there has been a shift in the relationship between owner-occupation and the tax system that may be motivating this change in part. Where previously there was an explicit tax bias favouring mortgage debt (the tax deductibility of mortgage debt for many years until it ceased in 2000 in particular), today the bias is more evident in the favourable taxation of housing wealth. Of particular significance is the tax treatment of the home as an asset. While almost all other privately owned assets in the UK are subject to CGT, homeownership remains exempt. A person's primary residence is also, increasingly, protected from IHT.

In contrast to many other European countries, the UK has historically offered very little tax incentive for the development of a well-maintained private rental sector. Together with a favourable tax regime for owner-occupiers, ownership evolved as a preferred tenure in terms of both quality and cost (Lunde and Whitehead, 2021). Social housing was also an increasingly attractive and accessible housing option but, with a declining supply from the early 1980s onwards, preferences were increasingly channelled into ownership.

Figure 9.2: UK tenure trends since 2009/10

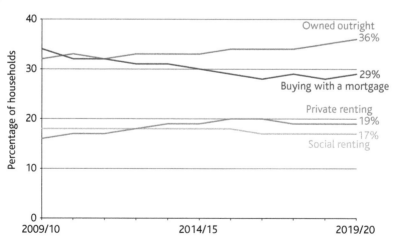

Source: https://www.gov.uk/government/statistics/family-resources-survey-financial-year-2019-to-2020/family-resources-survey-financial-year-2019-to-2020#tenure-1

Change in the make-up of the rental sector

A key recent trend in the UK's housing tenure mix has been the rise of the private rental sector – replacing some decreases in the last 20 years of levels of owner-occupation (see Figure 9.1). While this is likely to be related in large part to rising house costs, the tax system is also likely to have influenced this trend. Rental income from these properties is taxed at the same rate as the individual's (non-savings-related) income from other sources, and CGT and IHT is payable when the property is sold or disposed of on death respectively. Nevertheless, for many years, a landlord could claim generous tax relief on their mortgage payments for the property if financing costs were incurred in owning the property. This was available at the taxpayer's marginal rates of tax, that is, a deduction worth up to 45 per cent of the cost.[1] The longer-term effects of this incentive will continue to influence the UK housing market and so the distribution of property/wealth for many years to come in terms of artificially inflated house prices this created.

It is hard to offer a precise figure of the number of small landlords in the UK today. However, by one estimate there were just over 2 million private landlords in 2012 – a fourfold increase since 1991 (Ronald and Kadi, 2018). Analysis specifically of Buy to Let (BtL) properties (which are more likely to be owned by small landlords) suggests that by 2018 these properties represented around 6 per cent of all housing sales, down from a peak of 11 per cent in 2015 (UK Finance and Zoopla, 2019).

A related issue is the volume of former social homes that later came on to the market and were bought as investment property and let out at market rates for private profit, potentially with a proportion of the rent met by housing benefit. There are reports that as much as 40 per cent of former council homes are being used in this way (Barker, 2017).

Since 2009/10 annual expenditure on housing benefit and the housing element of the Universal Credit has exceeded £20 billion (Stephens et al, 2017, table 117). This provides important support for households across the UK, but it also, in part at least, feeds into private rental income for a large number of small landlords and brings with it a number of tax implications discussed subsequently. This housing benefit bill also presents a stark contrast to the £9.7 billion in direct capital support for the development of new social housing in England for the whole of the five-year period 2019/20 to 2023/24, and the £3.6 billion allocated in Scotland for the eight years from 2016/17 to 2020/21 (Stephens et al, 2017).

The growth and subsequent decline of BtL investment illustrates the power of tax incentives in relation to housing supply. When BtL mortgages first came to the market in 1996, one of the key tax incentives was generous mortgage interest relief. But rising concern that BtL investors were bolstering the private rental sector, and were thereby squeezing out first-time buyers, finally led to reduction of some more advantageous aspects of the tax regime. This started with an additional 3 per cent on stamp duty on BtL transactions and was extended by a reduction in higher-rate deductions of financing cost relief in 2021. This has led to a steep decline in new BtL mortgages, other than among cash buyers who were able to invest without borrowing. Research shows that in 2020, 12 per cent of homes bought in Great Britain were bought for investment purposes, down from 16 per cent of 2015, and just over half of these were bought with cash (Beveridge et al, 2021).

Tax as a supply-side housing subsidy

To examine the tax incentives on housing more directly, we will view the structure of housing taxation in the UK from two perspectives: supply-side and demand-side incentives. The first perspective focuses on the financial gains being made related to housing and targeted tax incentives for housing developers. The second examines the tax bias towards homeownership as a tenure of choice.

VAT and houses

Tax subsidies related to housing having a supply-side influence include exemption from VAT on building materials and supplies for new builds, and a reduced VAT rate for materials used in the conversion of houses into flats. Since housing may be thought of as a consumable durable, the presumption is that it would normally attract VAT on acquisition like other such goods. However, the UK is among only a handful of Organisation for Economic Co-operation and Development (OECD) countries that zero-rates the construction of new builds, and VAT is only applied in relation to repairs to existing housing (and as such can be considered to be a form of fiscal welfare – see Chapter 4). Within the EU, Denmark and Germany adopt a similar approach to the UK in exempting new construction but charge respectively 25 per cent, 19 per cent and 20 per cent on repairs.

Zero-rating of housing construction costs in this way implies that no VAT is charged to the consumer on purchase, but any VAT paid by those incurring costs of construction can be reclaimed. For construction work to be zero-rated in the UK in this way, it must qualify as a *genuinely* new, self-contained house or flat.

This approach provides a significant cost reimbursement to those in such businesses at the cost of the Exchequer and thereby provides a significant subsidy to house building in the UK. VAT zero-rating for the construction and sale of relevant properties amounted to £14.5 billion in 2020/21 (HMRC, 2021).

Although the standard VAT rate in the UK on repairs is 20 per cent, there are some activities that attract rates of 0 and 5 per cent. For example, repairs to meet a disabled person's needs are zero-rated, while installation of mobility aids for the elderly in domestic accommodation is subject to a reduced 5 per cent VAT. Conversion of non-residential properties into either single or communal residences is subject to VAT at a reduced 5 per cent rate.

As such, it is noteworthy that current VAT rules, viewed in the absence of any other adjustments to reduce this effect, can be said to work against motivating repairing and converting of existing property relative to incentivising new builds. This may have sustainability, circular economy and emissions implications that could also be affected adversely by such a policy (see Chapter 14 and Menteth, 2013).

Housing development and the need for land taxation

There is a long-running debate on the potential for taxation of land used for housing development. Leaving aside the intrinsic value of land for leisure activities and in support of wellbeing, without the right to use land to develop homes on (or property for commercial use), it has limited economic potential beyond its possible use for agriculture. Yet on gaining building permission, the same land can become very valuable. This can be especially the case where there is limited available supply but great demand for new housing. We see this clearly historically in popular urban areas across the UK, most notably in large cities, where the land is close to existing urban areas or near infrastructure that will enable those who will eventually be living in such areas to easily reach their places of work. However, more recently these areas have been somewhat displaced by changing demands for rural and more remote property in light of changing technology and work location patterns.

From a tax perspective, this is regarded by many economists as both inefficient and unfair (Adam et al, 2010, pp 370–7). Landowners may add no value to the economy in this process (for example, if the land is already suitable for development) yet benefit from the rising values of their land that come from the granting of these rights to changed use of their land. This process creates privately available value from a socially created process without a share of this reward coming to the wider society (at least directly) in this process if this change in value of the land is not taxed.

Given land in the UK is owned predominately by the wealthier sections of the UK population, this can provide significant wealth boosts to those already favoured by the economic system to the cost of the rest. However, despite widespread acknowledgement of this issue, attempts to tax this kind of unearned profit have proven to be hard to design and implement in practice (Jones et al, 2018).

An alternative strategy to control this form of economic rent-seeking is the use of the planning consent system. The precise structure of this system varies within the devolved nations of the UK, but the general process is similar to the operation in England under its '106 agreements' (so-called after Section 106 of the 1990 Town and Country Planning Act). As land value is dependent on building permission for local authorities, councils have been able to negotiate with private developers, granting construction or development permission only if they supply a proportion of affordable homes alongside private development.

The 106 system has various flaws – for example, it is used only at the discretion of local authorities, and only on developments of ten housing units or more – but many housing economists treat it as a de facto 'land tax' that has had significant success in at least generating more alternative housing tenure mixes in new developments than would otherwise have incurred – providing some value back to the wider society in the process.

The UK has not had a more general land tax in its modern history, although this is regularly proposed by reformers and is a feature of other countries' tax systems. However, some forms of tax linked to land development potential have featured periodically in the UK tax system (for example, the Betterment Levy [1967–70] and Development Land Tax [1976–85]). Crook et al (2016) calculate that the most revenue raised by a 'land tax' of this form in recent years was the £68 million raised in the year 1983–84 (using Development Land Tax), but this is a trivial sum compared to nearly £6 billion raised in the year 2016–17, based on combined cash and benefits in kind from 106 agreements.

Land and property transaction taxes

Transaction taxes are levied on consumers buying a house in the UK to live in or as an investment. In England, this tax is called Stamp Duty Land Tax (SDLT), in Scotland the Land and Buildings Transaction Tax and in Wales the Land Transaction Tax (Wynter et al, 2021).

The rules are applied slightly differently among the devolved nations, but they follow a very similar premise – tax is paid by a purchaser of land or property based on its transaction value. Above a minimum threshold, tax rates currently vary for residential property between 2 and 12 per cent (in the latter case for properties currently being sold for more than £1.5 million). This is supplemented in England by a further 3 per cent at all levels if the property will be a BtL property. In Scotland and Wales, a supplement of 4 per cent is added instead for such 'additional' (that is, additional to the owner's first/main home) dwellings. In Wales, the rate starts at 3.5 per cent and rises to 12 per cent. Some differences to the purchase price values at which different rates apply exist between the devolved nations, but these are broadly the same (for fuller details, see Lymer and Oats, 2021, pp 296–304).

Technically, these are transaction taxes – a means of taxing consumption activity in the housing market (to sit alongside council tax – see Chapter 12). As such, they can be regarded as an entry price for those joining this market. Some economists criticise transaction taxes such as these in this context, suggesting these taxes are an impediment to efficient markets and argue that they do not add to economic productivity or support commercial growth (Adam et al, 2010, pp 371–2). There has also been a tendency for short-term manipulation of SDLT as a form of fiscal support for the housing market in the face of broader economic downtowns. We have seen this in the last 15 years, with (for example) the first Stamp Duty payment 'Holiday' that operated from 3rd September 2008 to 31st December 2009 following the financial crisis of 2008, and the payment holidays linked to the response to the COVID-19 pandemic (two separate holidays operating from 8 July 2020 to 30 June 2021 and from 1 July to 30 September 2021).

The risk of the use of policies such as temporary tax payment holidays is that they tend to be inflationary in that those selling can artificially adjust their prices knowing this saving is temporarily available to buyers. This results in some locking out of the next cohort of buyers entering the market after the lapse of the tax 'holiday'.

We can also view the tendency to use these forms of property taxes as an economic tool from another perspective: the ease with which a tax holiday can be announced points to an attractive flexibility that can react relatively quickly to the negative social effects of other housing policies. For example, there is a strong argument for this when we view the use of higher stamp duty rates to dampen the market for second-homes, or to charge a higher market entry price for those seeking UK residential property simply as investment for capital growth (in essence using UK housing simply as a global asset class).

Despite these various concerns about the impact of transaction taxes in this market, housing transaction taxes have proved a rich source of tax revenue, providing £11.6 billion in 2019–20, so they appear likely to stay a feature of housing taxation in the UK for the foreseeable future.[2]

A tax bias towards owners? Demand-side incentives

In addition to supply-side tax effects on the housing market, demand-side tax incentives can also be used to influence and effect change in this market and therefore in the mix of tenures.

Mortgage Interest Relief and imputed rent

As the result of a growing political consensus presumption in favour of owner-occupation (Murie and Williams, 2015), for many years, homeowners were able to reclaim some of their mortgage costs by off-setting interest payments against their income tax liabilities. This process was originally introduced by the Labour government in 1969. It was initially operated as a direct relief claim made by property owners to the government. Latterly (following the Howe Budget of 1983) this was provided at source (and so was entitled 'Mortgage Interest Relief at Source' or MIRAS). Prior to 1969, there had been tax relief on all household debt, which included, but was not exclusive to, mortgage debt. The use of MIRAS became markedly more aggressive under the Conservative government in the early to mid-1980s. At its peak in 1990/91, MIRAS cost the Treasury over £7 billion a year in foregone tax (Murie, 2015).

MIRAS was gradually scaled back from 1988 onwards and its abolition (from April 2000) was announced in Budget 1999 by the then (Labour) Chancellor, Gordon Brown. Similar reliefs have been abolished in the great majority of countries with notable exceptions including Denmark, the Netherlands and the United States.

While some close to the government at the time suggested that the scrapping of MIRAS was primarily related to budgetary cost issues, there were two primary reasons publicly cited for the abolition of MIRAS. First, and most critically at the time, it was seen as regressive, favouring those with larger properties/larger mortgages. Secondly, the tax on which MIRAS was founded had historically been (somewhat at least) balanced by another tax to produce less of a specific tenure-favouring position. This tax was no longer applied, and as such this basis to favour owner-occupiers had been created. The so-called 'Schedule A' of the tax code contained a tax on 'imputed rent' for owner-occupiers. This had originally been introduced pre-1914 when most homes were owned by private landlords, who paid tax on their rental income. Under this system, an owner-occupier's overall tax contribution included tax on the notional financial benefits of living in (that is, consuming) their own home, which, had they not owned, they would have had to pay rent on (Bentley 2018).

In practice, however, this basis in favour of owner-occupiers had been longstanding, even when this imputed rent tax had applied. The rate of tax on imputed rent was at a far lower rate than the tax on rental incomes of landlords. When abolished in the UK (in 1963), the tax had fallen to almost negligible levels, having still been based on 1936 values (Lund, 2017, p 36). Imputed rents have been politically unpopular across countries that have used them, and no OECD country still taxes imputed rent except for the Netherlands (Lunde and Whitehead, 2021).

Inheritance Tax and the home

Two other forms of tax relief on owner-occupation are politically contentious and provoke deeper debates about distributive justice (Prabhakar et al, 2017). The first is tax relief on the primary residence in the UK's IHT system (see Chapter 10). There is no IHT due on transfers between spouses/civil partners on the death of the first partner. However, tax will arise potentially on the transfer of the family home to children (or anyone else) once both parents have died.

No inheritance tax is payable on the first £325,000 (in 2022/23 – unchanged since 2007) of a person's estate. Thereafter it is taxed at 40 per cent of its value. Also in 2007, the Chancellor agreed to allow transfer of any of a deceased spouse's unused tax-free allowance to their partner. That meant a maximum of £650,000 could be passed on free of IHT on the death of the second spouse, a move targeted at favouring those with greater wealth.

Until 2007, the primary residence was given no special treatment within the overall tax treatment of inheritances. However, the steady growth of house prices over the preceding decade fed into a highly charged political debate, creating a popular perception that more 'ordinary' people were being pushed into a tax system designed for the rich. This once-in-a-lifetime redistribution is a key element of the justification for IHT. In reality, however, the proportion of estates eligible for IHT was only 4 per cent in 2019/20 (Prabhakar et al, 2017) and has never exceeded 6 per cent (Seely, 2021). So this is largely a misnomer, underlining further the particular value of this extra relief to wealthier homeowners.

Since 2015, following Conservative promises to lift the IHT tax-free threshold to £1 million overall, there has also been an extra main residence 'family home' allowance of £175,000. This can be claimed above the general inheritance allowance if the property is passed to direct descendants. Intended to take a large chunk of the primary home's value out of estate, this allowance is also transferable to a spouse, potentially adding a further £350,000 tax exemption for residences available – raising the total amount of tax-free inheritance that can be passed on to £1 million (that is, [£325,000 x 2] + [£175,000 x 2]).

Decreasing the overall regressive nature of these policies a little, there is a cap on the value of estates that can claim this additional exemption. Estates over £2 million receive a less generous main residence exemption.

The total cost of the primary residence reliefs (direct and indirect) introduced in 2007 is estimated to have been around £3.1 billion in the year 2008–9 (Seely, 2021, p 19) but rose to £5.5 billion in 2020/21 (HMRC, 2021). However, this cost is dwarfed by the second home-ownership tax relief we cover next in this section.

Capital Gains Tax and housing

There are two issues to consider in respect of CGT on residential property: the treatment of CGT of investment property and the exempting of CGT on a taxpayer's main residence. Taken together, they provide an inconsistent application of capital taxation to UK housing.

CGT is designed to tax the increase in value of an individual's assets received while owning those assets (see Chapter 3). For the individual, this may include gains from the increased value of investment property owned. Currently, the sale of an investment property used for rental income attracts 18 per cent tax on the increased value of the property since purchase (above an annual exempt amount that for 2022/23 is £12,300, falling to £6,000 for 2023/24 and further to £3,000 from 2024/25), rising to 28 per cent for individuals in the higher bands of income tax. As investment properties are likely to be owned by those who are more than averagely wealthy, this provides a small counter to the largely regressive tax policies related to housing we have detailed so far. However, as income received in the same tax band would attract 40 per cent tax, this does offer a significantly lower tax cost per pound received.

However, unlike investment properties, in the UK (as in most countries around the world) no CGT is levied on a person's main residence when they sell it. This creates a very large sum of tax foregone in the UK. HMRC's own estimates put this tax expenditure at £30.2 billion for 2021/22 alone – rising in cost by 16 per cent since 2016/17 (HMRC, 2021). A number of countries do tax main residence-related capital gains, particularly when only briefly owned. For example, in Austria, Finland and Iceland CGT is payable if the property is sold less than two years after it was bought (Lunde and Whitehead, 2021).

Applying CGT to a main residence is controversial and attracts very polarised views (Corlett and Leslie, 2021). It can be argued that not applying CGT could be justified in terms of supporting housing's use as an asset to offset future demands on the state in retirement. Further, on the one hand it may feel counter-intuitive to treat a person's home in a way that resembles the taxation of activities undertaken with the aim of making profit. On the other, there has been a cultural and policy trend towards just such a view of housing – as an asset and opportunity to grow inheritable wealth – as well as being a 'home'.

We must also add the impact of luck in the generation of at least some of the gain from home ownership. Huge housing wealth has been built up for some who simply had the good fortune to buy their home in a different economic climate, or in a location with house price growth above the average for reasons beyond their own creating. One recent estimate is that capital growth from 2000 to 2020 has, after inflation, amounted to an unearned windfall of £3 trillion for homeowners across Great Britain (Corlett and Leslie, 2021). This arguably creates justification for payment of a tax of some form given individuals are able to profit personally from a growth in wealth largely driven by external circumstances.

One of the most pressing issues arising from this is the intergenerational inequalities we can see in the housing market and, within younger cohorts, the transmission of broader socio-economic inequalities that are amplified by housing wealth.

Asset or commodity: home or investment?

Although the owned home has always been a potential store of wealth, it is only since the 1980s that the home as an asset has taken on the policy significance that it has in the UK today. Prior to this, it was viewed primarily as a consumption good, albeit one that derived much of its utility from the expectation of significantly reduced housing costs later in life.

Where previously the owned home came with the personal or household expectation of reduced housing costs – and a better standard of living – later in life, government policy was increasingly based on the tacit assumption that the home would be used as a store of wealth to replace rather than augment the income maintenance function of the welfare state (Gregory et al, 2022). This has been described as a process of 'financialisation' in the social policy literature (Finlayson, 2009) and as 'housing asset-based welfare' in housing studies (Watson, 2009; Doling and Ronald, 2010).

In some respects, the label of 'welfare' in the housing case is somewhat misleading. For the most part, there has been little direct subsidy for owners, and therefore little support from the state to underpin an expectation that individuals are to build up their own private safety net by accruing housing wealth.[3]

As we have seen, however, there has been significant indirect support for owners through the tax system. To some degree, this support is based on a similar policy rationale to the favourable tax treatment of pension savings (see Chapter 6): if the expectation is that private households are to rely less on the state in later life, some commentators and policy makers argue that the indirect support of the state earlier in life is more of a rebalancing of the welfare state rather than a withdrawal of the safety net (Dol and Hoekstra, 2018).

However, even if it is argued that home ownership is not part of an implicit welfare strategy, there is a broad consensus that ownership rates influence broader attitudes to the welfare state. The issue has been summed up by Kemeny (2005) as the 'big trade-off': if households feel pressure to finance home ownership early in life, the financial pressures that come with this are likely to lead to greater tax aversion. The expectation that individuals build up their own safety net through housing wealth may offer support to the widening of welfare provision based on general taxation (see also Castles, 2005). This leads to a potential push–pull cycle: if people are encouraged to own through the tax system, they may also be less supportive of the general taxation that underpins a strong welfare state and, over time, a weakened welfare state may increase the perceived desirability of ownership still further.

Conclusion: Social policy challenges and opportunities for change

Housing wealth is a driver of social cleavage, both between and within generations. Baby-boomers who bought their homes in an era of lower housing prices and greater financial security experienced greater choice and opportunity than more recent generations are likely to secure for themselves. Those who can afford to own today often draw on an intergenerational transfer of private wealth that others cannot rely upon. More than ever, there is a need for a national conversation about the ways in which we may reform our taxation system in light of these social cleavages.

The taxation of housing in the UK lacks a clear overall policy framework. Forty years on from Whitehead (1980), it still very much has the feeling of the 'dog's breakfast'. Those most in need of support in their reasonable housing consumption desires still receive the least help, at least via tax policy. In conclusion, we suggest what steps could be taken in tax policy development to better aid housing policy towards fairer support for all tenures.

The relationship between the tax system and housing is a complex one and clearly not one that is neutral in its impact and effect. Owner-occupation is given significant tax advantages over other forms of tenure, and there is limited political appetite to reverse or even slow down this trend.

Several key changes to UK tax policy could be beneficial. First, housing needs to be considered as both a consumption good and as an asset, and taxed as such, with a key objective of making the system more financially neutral than currently.

We agree with Adam (2021), who proposed that VAT should be charged on new housing and on annual usage based on updated rental values to reflect the fact that 'housing' is an asset being personally consumed and to replace both the current council tax and SDLT. He also argued for a 'usage' annual charge to be applied to owners on updated property housing values to provide an allowance for a normal 'rate-of-return' to the investment made in housing.

While these changes could create a more financially neutral system for housing generally, helping to reduce the current levels of housing asset inequality, they would do little to motivate growth in availability of social rent property. This sector has very little by way of specific tax favour currently (beyond general construction VAT zero-rating) and yet remains a key aspect of the UK housing tenure landscape. Given the importance of this tenure option for many UK citizens, it is vitally important to provide more support for this tenure group – a key aspect of provision for creating a balanced range of housing tenures that market-led development seems very unlikely to provide sufficiently to meet.

The current UK tax system also does little to support housing construction generally of all forms of tenure, despite the significant housing shortage. Land is not taxed directly, and as such there is little incentive to put land to effective use beyond an economic imperative to do so. Other countries use land tax for this purpose.

Development taxation has been attempted on more than one occasion in the UK to seek to return socially provided asset value gains back to the wider society. It remains unclear why such a social return cannot be achieved in practice, and further effort should be put into developing a tax on this base.

Taxation of housing gains once in a lifetime, via inheritance tax, has also been significantly curtailed recently since the new nil rate band on main residences was introduced in 2015. This significantly reduces housing wealth redistribution and instead contributes to wealth concentration. The argument for maintaining this special treatment, along with continued CGT exemption, is difficult to support albeit a highly politically charged issue.

Tax policy should not, of itself, be the only tool used to deliver better housing policy, and other areas of policy management (in particular planning policy) may be better positioned to make the key changes needed in the UK housing market to develop a better balance to the available tenure mix. However, tax policy can play a key part in this process if used effectively with clear policy motivations, and therefore this chapter argues that a significant rethink of the current impacts of tax policy on housing is very much past due.

In all of this, it must be remembered that housing is more than just an asset – either to be acquired to support current and future consumption, or as a form of investment. All of us need and deserve a home, not just a house, as a place in which we feel safe and secure and from which we can live our desired lives to the fullest. Tax policy, and the wider social responsibility associated with housing policy generally, must keep at its heart this motivation that all deserve to have a home. The desire to achieve that for all should be what drives housing policy.

Notes

[1] This relief is now restricted back to only basic-rate deductions (20 per cent currently) since April 2021.

[2] https://www.gov.uk/government/statistics/uk-stamp-tax-statistics

[3] A notable exception is the introduction of a Help to Buy ISA in 2015. This allowed tax-free savings for individuals for the dedicated purpose of saving for a housing deposit.

Take up for this savings scheme was low, however, and the scheme has now closed for new accounts.

Further reading

- Adam (2021) – for a fuller discussion of the links between taxation and housing.
- Corlett and Leslie (2021) – for a review of the possibilities for changed application of CGT to UK private housing.
- Jones et al (2018) – for a review of attempts to apply land taxes in the UK.
- Lunde and Whitehead (2021) – for an overview of how housing-related taxation is applied across European countries.
- Seely (2021) – for a comprehensive review of the operation of IHT in the UK.

References

Adam, S. (2021) 'Taxation and housing: how do we get the relationship right?', Presentation to Tax Research Network Conference, 9 September 2021, Available from: https://ifs.org.uk/publications/15760

Adam, S., Besley, T., Blundell, R., Bond, S., Chote, R. and Gammie, M. et al (2010) *Dimensions of Tax Design: The Mirrlees Review*, Oxford: Oxford University Press.

Barker, N. (2017) 'Revealed: the scale of ex-RTB home conversions to private rent'. Inside Housing 7/12/17. Available from: https://www.inside housing.co.uk/insight/insight/revealed-the-scale-of-ex-rtb-home-conversi ons-to-private-rent-53525

Bentley, D. (2018) 'Imputed rents: forgotten but not gone', Civitas, Available from: https://www.civitas.org.uk/2018/11/23/imputed-rents-forgot ten-but-not-gone

Beveridge, A., Fell, D. and Blease, A. (2017), 'Has the door closed on buy-to-let?', Hamptons Report. Available from: https://mr1.homeflow.co.uk/ files/site_asset/image/4541/0317/buy-to-let-reports.pdf

Castles, F.G. (2005) 'The Kemeny thesis revisited', *Housing, Theory and Society*, 22(2): 84–6.

Corlett, A. and Leslie, J. (2021) 'Home county: options for taxing main residence capital gains', London: Resolution Foundation.

Crook A., Henneberry, J. and Whitehead, C. (2016) *Planning Gain: Providing Infrastructure and Affordable Housing*, Oxford: Wiley Blackwell.

Crosland, A. (1975) 'Speech to the Housing Centre Trust, June 18, 1975', Partly published in *Housing Review* (September/October).

Dol, K. and Hoekstra, J. (2018) 'Using the owner-occupied home as a pension: attitudes towards housing equity release in 6 European countries', Conference papers of the European Network for Housing Research.

Doling, J. and Ronald, R. (2010) 'Home ownership and asset-based welfare', *Journal of Housing and the Built Environment*, 25(2): 165–73.

Feinstein, L., Lupton, R., Hammond, C., Mujtaba, T., Salter, E. and Sorhaindo, A. (2008) 'The public value of social housing: a longitudinal analysis of the relationship of housing and life chances', Centre for Research on the Wider Benefits of Learning, Institute of Education, University of London.

Finlayson, A. (2009) 'Financialisation, financial literacy and asset-based welfare', *British Journal of Politics and International Relations*, 11(3): 400–21.

Forrest, R., Murie, A. and Williams, P. (2021) *Home Ownership: Differentiation and Fragmentation*, London: Routledge.

Gregory, J., Lymer, A. and Rowlingson, K. (2022) 'Personal savings for those on lower incomes: towards a new framework for assessing the role of the state in relation to savings schemes', *Social Policy and Society*, 21(3): 336–51.

Hills, J., Bastagli, F., Cowell, F., Glennerster, H., Karagiannaki, E. and McKnight, A. (2013) *Wealth in the UK: Distribution, Accumulation, and Policy*, Oxford: Oxford University Press.

HMRC (2021) 'Estimated cost of non-structural reliefs', Available from: https://www.gov.uk/government/statistics/main-tax-expenditures-and-structural-reliefs

Jones, C., Morgan, J. and Stephens, M. (2018) 'An assessment of historic attempts to capture land value uplift in the UK', Inverness: Scottish Land Commission.

Kemeny, J. (1981) *The Myth of Home-Ownership: Private versus Public Choices in Housing Tenure*, Abingdon: Routledge.

Kemeny, J. (2005) '"The really big trade-off" between home ownership and welfare: Castles' evaluation of the 1980 thesis, and a reformulation 25 years on', *Housing, Theory and Society*, 22(2): 59–75.

Lund, B. (2017) *Understanding Housing Policy*, Bristol: Policy Press.

Lunde, J. and Whitehead, C. (2021) 'How taxation varies between owner-occupation, private renting and other housing tenures in European countries: an overview', Glasgow: UK Collaborative Centre for Housing Research.

Lymer, A. and Oats, L. (2021) *Taxation: Policy and Practice 2021/22* (28th edn), Malvern: Fiscal Publications.

Malpass, P. (2005) *Housing and the Welfare State: The Development of Housing Policy in Britain*, Basingstoke: Palgrave Macmillan.

Menteth, W. (2013) 'Incentivising design quality and sustainability', RIBA report, Available from: https://pure.port.ac.uk/ws/portalfiles/portal/7975024/13_03_15_RIBA_VAT_Proposals.pdf

Murie, A. (2016) *The Right to Buy? Selling Off Public and Social Housing*, Bristol: Policy Press.

Murie, A. and Williams, P. (2015) 'A presumption in favour of home ownership? Reconsidering housing tenure strategies', *Housing Studies*, 30(5): 656–76.

Prabhakar, R., Lymer, A. and Rowlingson, K. (2017) 'Does information about wealth inequality and inheritance tax raise public support for wealth taxes? Evidence from a UK survey', in B. Peeters, H. Gribnau and J. Badisco (eds), *Building Trust in Taxation*, Cambridge: Intersentia, pp 335–54.

Ronald, R. (2008) *The Ideology of Home Ownership: Homeowner Societies and the Role of Housing*, New York: Springer.

Ronald, R. and Kadi, J. (2018) 'The revival of private landlords in Britain's post-homeownership society', *New Political Economy*, 23(6): 786–803.

Seely, A. (2021) 'Inheritance tax', Research briefing, House of Commons Library, Available from: https://commonslibrary.parliament.uk/research-briefings/sn00093

Stephens, M., Perry, J., Williams, P., Young, G. and Fitzpatrick, S. (2021) 'UK housing review', Chartered Institute of Housing. Available from: https://www.ukhousingreview.org.uk/ukhr21

UK Finance and Zoopla (2019) 'The changing shape of the UK mortgage market', Available from: https://www.ukfinance.org.uk/system/files/The-changing-shape-of-the-UK-mortgage-market-FINAL-ONLINE-Jan-2020.pdf

Watson, M. (2009) 'Planning for a future of asset-based welfare? New Labour, financialized economic agency and the housing market', *Planning, Practice & Research*, 24(1): 41–56.

Whitehead, C. (1980) 'Fiscal aspects of housing', in C. Sandford, C. Pond and R. Walker (eds) *Taxation and Social Policy*, London: Heinemann, pp 84–114.

Wynter, C., Manochin, M., Hidayah, N. and Lauwo, S. (2021) 'Property tax management and its impact on social housing and governance: a case of the stamp duty land tax exemption for social registered landlords', London: Chartered Institute of Taxation.

10

Wealth taxation: the case for reform

Karen Rowlingson

Introduction

This chapter argues that wealth taxation in the UK is over-ripe for reform. The chapter starts by reviewing the current system in the UK, pointing out that it is barely 'a system' at all. Indeed, there is not even a clear or agreed definition of what wealth taxation is or why it exists in different forms. Nevertheless, some taxes are clearly linked to wealth in different ways, and the chapter reviews these along with data on how much revenue is raised from them in the UK.

The chapter then sets out the case for reform of wealth taxation, which it argues can help reduce wealth inequality, increase equality of opportunity, raise much-needed revenue for public investment, simplify the system and increase tax equity and efficiency in the use made of wealth. The case is powerful, but there are also barriers to reform that help explain the lack of reform over the last few decades in the UK. These barriers include concern about low revenues raised by wealth taxes in contrast to high administrative costs (linked partly to issues of disclosure and valuation); high levels of avoidance and evasion; the risk that investors or entrepreneurs will move (their capital) elsewhere and/ or people will be discouraged from saving and investing; and opposition from both wealthy, powerful groups and the wider general public. These barriers may seem insurmountable, but they are not as great as sometimes claimed. A common thread emerges here in that the dominance of certain ideas about wealth, inequality and taxation serve to maintain the current approach to the benefit of the wealthy. The chapter concludes by suggesting a way forward to challenge these ideas and achieve reform.

The UK's current 'system' of wealth taxation

The current UK wealth tax system is complex and lacks a clear set of objectives (Rowlingson and McKay, 2011; Summers, 2021). Indeed, there are different views about what 'wealth taxes' are. One way of defining and categorising wealth taxes is to focus on taxes that affect different kinds of assets. For example, in the Wealth and Assets Survey,[1] household wealth is divided into five asset classes as follows:

- Net property wealth includes physical property and land owned by the household, net of any loans or mortgages secured on the property.
- Physical wealth includes household contents, including antiques, artwork and vehicles.
- Private pension wealth is the value of all occupational and personal pensions.
- Financial wealth includes the value of formal investments such as bank or building society current or savings accounts, individual savings accounts (ISAs), endowments, stocks and shares, informal savings, and children's assets, less financial liabilities.
- Business assets include the value of assets used within a business in which the wealth-owner is self-employed or is a director or partner.

Taxes can, and indeed are, applied to each of these different asset types, but we can also look at wealth taxation in terms of the different ways that these assets can be taxed with various examples, as follows (see also Evans et al, 2017):

- taxing the *income used to accumulate* wealth;
- taxing the *returns/interest from accumulating* wealth;
- taxing money when *assets are withdrawn*;
- taxes on *wealth transfers* including lifetime gifts and inheritance;
- taxes on *wealth ownership*; and
- taxes on *consumption of wealth*.

For example, when people make contributions to their pensions, these contributions are made from income that is exempt from income tax, and this means that higher-rate income taxpayers are subsidised more, by the state, than basic-rate taxpayers who, in turn, are subsidised more than non-income-taxpayers (see Chapter 6). Tax can also be levied on the returns/interest from accumulating wealth. For example, interest from ordinary savings accounts is taxed at the same rate of income tax that the saver pays (although there is now – since 2015 – a personal savings allowance of £1,000 on the amount of interest earned for basic-rate taxpayers, £500 for higher-rate taxpayers and £0 for additional-rate taxpayers). Finally, assets can be taxed when money is withdrawn from them. For example, pension income is subject to tax.

These different ways of categorising wealth taxes help to illustrate the complexity of the very concept of wealth. For example, is a tax on the income from savings a wealth tax or an income tax or both? Only the very wealthiest people will pay this tax given the current thresholds, so it might be considered an income tax on the very wealthy. Is council tax a tax on wealth? It is linked to the value of property wealth but levied on the *resident* of a property who is not necessarily the owner so this is not straightforward.

Value added tax (VAT) is a consumption tax that therefore covers both spending of income and spending of wealth. This leads to an even more fundamental question about the difference between income and wealth. Income is normally considered a flow of money whereas wealth is a stock, but income can be turned into wealth and wealth into income, so the two are very closely connected (Rowlingson and McKay, 2011).

So it is not easy, conceptually, to define wealth taxes. We can look empirically, however, at the current UK taxes that are specifically related to wealth and compare these with other taxes as in Table 10.1. As mentioned, income tax and VAT might be considered, in some ways, as taxing wealth, but they are generally seen differently, as taxes on income and consumption respectively. The main current UK 'wealth' taxes are therefore considered to be council tax (albeit with the caveats mentioned earlier), capital gains tax, stamp duty and inheritance tax. It is clear from Table 10.1 that these wealth taxes provided relatively little tax revenue in 2020/21 compared with income tax, National Insurance contributions and VAT. The 'big three' income/consumption taxes provided more than half of all tax revenue in 2020/21. By contrast, council tax raised 5 per cent and other 'capital taxes' raised just under 4 per cent altogether. Of these 'capital taxes', capital gains tax raised the most (1.4 per cent of total tax revenue), then Stamp Duty Land Tax (SDLT) (1.2 per cent), inheritance tax (0.7 per cent) and stamp duty on shares (0.5 per cent) (see also Chapter 3).

The main capital taxes listed in Table 10.1 are therefore capital gains tax, inheritance tax and stamp duty, with council tax[2] not listed under capital taxes

Table 10.1: UK public sector current receipts from April 2020 to March 2021

	Amount raised (£793 billion total)	Percentage of total 100%
Income tax	196	25
National insurance contributions	144	18
VAT	117	15
Corporation tax	54	7
Council tax	38	5
Capital taxes, of which:[10]	30	4
capital gains tax	11	1.4
inheritance tax	5.3	0.7
stamp duty land tax	9.5	1.2
stamp duty on shares	3.7	0.5
Tobacco and alcohol duties	21	3
Fuel duty	21	3
Business rates	17	2
Other receipts	87	11
Other taxes	68	9

Source: Keep (2021)

but raising more than all the others combined. Council tax was introduced in 1993 as a successor to the highly political 'poll tax'/community charge, which, in turn, had replaced domestic rates. However, council tax is levied on residents rather than owners of properties. Some residents may be eligible for council tax reductions if they are on a low income or receive social security benefits, but this system has become much less generous since 2013 with the abolition of a national system of council tax benefit in England, which has led to increased council tax debt for millions (McKay and Rowlingson, 2021). Scotland, Wales and Northern Ireland have national council tax reduction schemes.

The next largest wealth tax in terms of revenue is capital gains tax, which was introduced in 1965 as a tax on the profit made when someone sells (or disposes of) an 'asset' that has increased in value – though tax allowances apply (£12,300 in 2020/21) and so limit the amount of tax paid. For capital gains tax purposes, assets include the following: most personal possessions worth £6,000 or more (apart from a car); property (but not the main home unless it has been rented out, used for business or is very large); shares that are not in an ISA or personal equity plan; and business assets. Capital gains tax rates are levied differently on residential property from other assets. Disposing of an asset includes selling it, giving it away or transferring it to someone else, swapping it for something else, or getting compensation for it – like an insurance payout if it has been lost or destroyed. The rates also vary depending on the taxpayer's income.

Stamp duty comprises two distinct types of tax – SDLT, introduced in 2003 though dating back, in various ways, to the 17th century, is paid when land or a property is bought over a certain price in England and Northern Ireland. Scotland has a Land and Buildings Transaction Tax, and Wales has a Land Transaction Tax. There is also stamp duty on shares. The current SDLT threshold (as of September 2022) for residential properties is £250,000. The threshold for non-residential land and properties is £150,000, although there have been various reliefs/discounts in recent years, and the precise rates depend on a range of factors. Stamp duty on shares is usually paid at a rate of 0.5 per cent on transactions if bought electronically (Stamp Duty Reserve Tax, dating to 1986); if bought using a stock transfer form, it is paid on transactions over £1,000.

Inheritance tax[3] is a tax on the estate – the property, money and possessions — of someone who has died. It was introduced in its current form in 1986, but taxes on probate/estates go back to at least the 18th century. As of December 2021, there is normally no inheritance tax on a single (deceased) person if the value of the estate is below the £325,000 threshold. But rules introduced in 2015 effectively raised the threshold to £1 million for couples when the family home is included (see Chapter 9). The standard rate is a fixed 40 per cent and only charged on that part of the estate above the threshold. Contrary to general belief, very few estates pay any inheritance tax at all. According to HMRC statistics, the tax was paid on 23,000 estates at death in 2019/20, representing around 3.8 per cent of all deaths, raising just over £5 billion (Seely, 2021a). Summers (2019a) had previously estimated that inheritance tax raised about 4 per cent of the £120 billion left in estates in 2015/16.

These taxes clearly raise a relatively small percentage of overall tax revenue at present. As we shall see, this is not because there is little wealth to tax but due to the way the taxes are designed in terms of thresholds, reliefs and exemptions (see Chapter 4). The taxes are generally very complex as a result and therefore open to tax avoidance. Despite all of this, capital taxes still contributed £30 billion to the public purse in 2020/21 (with council tax contributing another £38 billion) and so played an important part in the tax system – see table 10.1. Evans et al (2017) note the decline since 1964 in revenue from wealth taxes from 2.62 per cent of total tax revenue to 0.66 per cent by 2014 (defined here only as annual personal net wealth taxes and death/gift taxes). This decline was not unique to the UK, with similar declines of wealth tax revenue across the Organisation for Economic Co-operation and Development (OECD) both as a percentage of tax revenue and of GDP.

Comparison with other OECD countries also shows that 22 of the 35 OECD countries surveyed by Evans et al (2017) had a 'transfer tax at death', with the vast majority being levied on the recipient of the bequest and only three levied on the estate (the UK, the United States and in some parts of Switzerland). All those countries with a tax levied on the recipient of any bequests also taxed lifetime gifts. Taxation of capital gains was almost non-existent prior to the 20th century, but by 2017 it was near universal (with the sole exception of New Zealand). However, the nature of capital gains tax in different countries varied considerably. Only four countries had an annual net wealth tax in 2017 (France, Norway, Spain and Switzerland).

This comparison with other countries reminds us that taxation 'systems' can vary between countries as well as over time. The question remains, however, of whether these taxes are playing an appropriate role in the UK now and whether or not they should be reformed for the future.

The case for reforming and increasing wealth taxation

There are many arguments for reforming wealth taxation in the UK. For example, reform of wealth taxation can:

- help redistribute wealth and so help to reduce high levels of harmful and unjust wealth inequality;
- increase equality of opportunity;

- raise much-needed revenue for public investment;
- simplify what has become a very complex system; and
- increase tax equity and efficiency.

The first two arguments are linked and relate to increasing levels of wealth and wealth inequality. Personal wealth has been growing both in absolute terms and in comparison to income. The total net wealth of private households in Great Britain was £14.6 trillion in 2016–18,[4] and the total amount of wealth was four times national income by the mid-2000s compared with 'only' twice in the 1960s and 1970s (Hills et al, 2013).

Wealth is also very unequally distributed, much more so than income, and increasingly so. For example, in 2016/18, the median family in the poorest 10 per cent of families had negative net wealth (that is, their debts exceed their assets), while the median family in the distribution overall has over £100,000 in net wealth per adult. The median family in the top 1 per cent, however, had almost £5 million in net wealth per adult. Wealthier families (those in the top 1 per cent) held a higher share of wealth in 2016/18 than a decade ago, while those in the middle held a smaller share (Advani et al, 2021a). This change has been driven by rising financial wealth relative to property wealth. So the major driver of rising wealth inequality has been the fact that people who were already wealthy have simply owned a greater share of higher-yielding assets (financial wealth) than others rather than having worked any harder or because of increased saving.

But even those holding slightly less 'profitable' kinds of wealth such as property have seen massive increases in property prices in the UK, which have risen at a faster rate in 2021 than in any year since 2004, according to the Halifax.[5] Indeed, prices increased by 9.8 per cent in 2021, with the average UK property price increasing by £24,000 to hit a new record high of £276,091 in December 2021. This increase alone is very similar to the annual median gross wage,[6] showing that people with property 'earnt' roughly the same in a year as the average worker. House prices flattened off from the middle of 2022, however, and fell near the end of the year but, despite this, average property prices in November 2022 reached £285,579, a rise of £12,801 on the previous November[7]. The distribution of wealth is therefore at least partly the result of the wealthy growing richer simply because they already own (the right kinds of) wealth rather than through any particular hard work or merit (Rowlingson and Connor, 2011). And much of this increase in wealth will be completely untaxed capital gains on main residences. The key question here is whether unearned wealth should be taxed at similar if not higher rates than earned income.

Increasing levels of wealth inequality also severely limit equal opportunities to succeed in life because those born into wealthy families can receive far more financial support relating to housing, education and training than others. A growing body of evidence shows inequality directly leading to higher levels of poverty, lower levels of social mobility and further inequality, thus creating a vicious cycle (Atkinson, 2015; Hills et al, 2019).

There is also growing evidence that income and wealth inequality have negative impacts on a range of health, social, economic, political and environmental outcomes. Wilkinson and Pickett's seminal work placed a spotlight on the links between economic inequality and poor health and social outcomes (Wilkinson and Pickett, 2009). Further studies have shown how the rich and super rich exert their power and influence in ways to ensure that governments act in their interests rather than the voters or citizens more generally. This severely compromises the democratic principle that every vote should have equal weight (Hacker and Pierson, 2010; Robeyns, 2019). Concerns about the impact on the economy have led major international organisations such as the IMF and OECD to raise concerns (OECD, 2008, 2015; IMF, 2014, 2017). As the then Managing Director of the IMF, Christine Lagarde, explained to the World Economic Forum at Davos:

> Excessive inequality is corrosive to growth; it is corrosive to society ... the economics profession and the policy community have downplayed inequality for too long. Now all of us – including the IMF – have a better understanding that a more equal distribution of income allows for more economic stability, more sustained economic growth, and healthier societies with stronger bonds of cohesion and trust. (Lagarde quoted in Weldon, 2013)

More recent research reveals the impact of wealth inequality on the environment, with Gough (2017) for example arguing that the consumption and related carbon footprint of the rich has an excessively detrimental effect on the environment, with evidence that the top 10 per cent by income in the UK in 2006 emitted 5.7 tonnes more carbon emissions than the next highest decile.

The problems of wealth inequality can, however, be tackled in various ways, not least through reform of wealth taxes. Indeed, the increase in wealth inequality in the late 20th and early 21st centuries is at least partly the result of taxes on the incomes and wealth of the richest being reduced (Rubolino and Waldenström, 2020). For example, the income tax treatment of savings changed significantly over the last 30 years due to the 1980s tax reforms reducing the top marginal rate on savings income from 98 to 40 per cent (Adam et al, 2010). This, as well as other tax cuts, allowed high earners to invest more and more often in higher-return assets (Fagereng et al, 2020) given their higher propensity to save (Bozio et al, 2017). At the same time, the growth of owner-occupation has stalled, and defined benefit pensions have all but disappeared to new workers, leaving those in the middle to fall behind relative to the wealthiest (Hills et al, 2013; Alvaredo et al, 2018; Perret, 2021). There is a clear case for wealth taxation to be reformed and increased to reverse this process.

In the United States, levels of wealth inequality are also high and linked to changes in taxation over time. As Saez and Zucman (2019, p 503) have powerfully argued: 'The greatest injustice of the U.S. tax system today is its regressivity at the very top: billionaires in the top four hundred pay less (relative to their true economic incomes) than the middle class.' The pressure for wealth tax reform is likely to be even greater in a post-COVID-19 context given that the pandemic has exacerbated existing inequalities and hit the poorest hardest while also increasing levels of public debt (OECD, 2020). The more recent 'living cost crisis', particularly in the UK, may also provide further arguments for redistribution through the tax and social security systems. The scope to tax incomes or consumption, however, may be limited, and this may lead to increased, and more progressive, wealth taxation, as has been the case after major wars or previous fiscal crises (for example, Scheve and Stasavage, 2016). Wealth taxes certainly have the potential to raise substantial revenue. Advani et al (2020) estimated that, after accounting for non-compliance and administration costs, a one-off wealth tax payable on all individual wealth above £500,000 and charged at 1 per cent a year for five years would raise £260 billion; at a threshold of £2 million, it would raise £80 billion. This would be paid by individuals whose total wealth after mortgages and other debts, and after splitting the value of shared assets such as a jointly owned family home, exceeded the tax threshold, and only on the value of wealth above that threshold. Alternative tax rises that could also raise £250 billion over five years include:

- basic rate of income tax to rise by 9 per cent (20 to 29 per cent);
- all income tax rates to rise by more than 6 per cent;
- all VAT rates to rise by 6 per cent (taking main rate from 20 to 26 per cent); and
- corporation tax to rise by 5 per cent and VAT to rise by 4 per cent.

These comparative examples help illustrate the point about the potential for wealth taxation to raise considerable revenue in the UK.

The lack of coherence to the wealth tax 'system', and the tax system more broadly, also suggests that it is ripe for reform, and greater attention to tax equity and efficiency here would be helpful. James Meade (1978) pointed out in the 1970s that wealth provided people with opportunity, security, social power, influence and independence. He therefore argued that wealth should be taxed alongside income and consumption for reasons of equity. More recently, Leslie (2020) has also argued that

[t]here is a clear case for reforming wealth taxes in the UK. We have previously highlighted the inequities in the design of capital gains taxes and the inefficiency in differences in the rates of taxes on income from wealth and labour. The analysis presented here suggests that the case for wealth taxes are magnified by the rising scale of wealth, and that these gains have largely materialised from passive changes in asset prices.

Barriers to reforming and increasing wealth taxes

The case for reforming wealth taxes may seem powerful, but, as mentioned earlier, various barriers have actually led many countries to *reduce* rather than increase their wealth taxes in recent years. Focusing specifically on annual net wealth taxes, Perret (2021) shows that most of the twelve OECD countries that levied individual net wealth taxes in 1990, all in Europe, had repealed these taxes in the 1990s and 2000s (including Austria, Denmark, Germany, the Netherlands, Finland, Iceland, Luxembourg and Sweden). By 2020, Norway, Spain and Switzerland were the only OECD countries that still levied individual net wealth taxes. The main barriers highlighted in that study and other literature (Evans et al, 2017; Perret, 2021) include:

- low revenues raised in contrast to high administrative costs (related largely to issues of disclosure and valuation);
- high levels of avoidance and evasion;
- the risk that investors or entrepreneurs will move (their capital) elsewhere and/or people will save and invest less; and
- opposition from wealthy, powerful groups and the wider general public.

These barriers are often interlinked. For example, the cost of administering wealth taxation is partly a result of the complexity of the system, which then makes tax avoidance/evasion easier. This leads some to question whether wealth taxation is worth the effort to collect relatively small amounts of revenue. However, wealth taxation has certainly raised more revenue in the past, so the current low levels are not necessarily inevitable. Administrative costs can also be reduced by simplifying the system in ways that retain or even increase tax equity and efficiency. Nevertheless, the collection of wealth taxes involves challenges relating to the valuation of wealth and finding ways to ensure that people disclose their wealth (Evans et al, 2017).

Another concern about wealth taxes relates to fears of capital migration, reduced savings/investment and avoidance/evasion (Perret, 2021). But these concerns are not necessarily justified by actual evidence. Advani and Tarrant (2021), for example, point to very few studies on the impact of wealth taxation on capital migration. There does, however, appear to be significant evidence to support concerns about widespread avoidance and evasion. But, as mentioned earlier, this may be partly due to the design of wealth taxes, with their bases having been narrowed by tax exemptions and reliefs that are then used by wealthy taxpayers to minimise their wealth tax burden. By simplifying the system and reducing the exemptions and reliefs, it may be possible to also reduce tax avoidance and evasion. Perret (2021) suggests considerable progress on international tax transparency in recent years has enhanced countries' ability to tax wealth and reduce avoidance/evasion.

It is helpful to understand the reason for any 'design flaws' in wealth taxation in order to identify some of the underlying barriers to reform, as these flaws are, themselves, often the result of powerful lobbying by vested interests to obtain special exemptions. Similarly, threats, or even simply concerns, that people or capital will leave the country can therefore affect policy outcomes regardless of whether or not this would actually happen (Hacker and Pierson, 2010). Clarke et al (2020), for example, point to concrete examples of the wealthy directly wielding their power to reduce wealth taxes, including that of Stefan Persson, former CEO of H&M, who used high-profile media appearances to threaten to leave Sweden in the 1990s, contributing to the repeal of the wealth tax. This is a reminder of the capacity of elites to exercise direct (instrumental) influence over policy outcomes.

As well as (real and assumed) opposition from powerful, wealthy people, another barrier to reforming wealth taxation is the concern that such taxes are unpopular among the general public. This leaves politicians wary of proposing increases in wealth (or indeed any) taxes. There is certainly some evidence that the public dislike certain wealth taxes, not least inheritance tax, which half the population in the UK consistently say that they wish to see abolished entirely (Rowlingson, 2016). Prabhakar (2021) identifies the 'tyranny of the status quo' in relation to tax reform, whereby direct 'losers' will be particularly unhappy, whereas the 'winners' may not appreciate their position or feel proportionately happy since people generally feel losses more than equivalent gains. As a result, policy makers may prefer to maintain the status quo.

However, much of the research on attitudes to taxation asks people for their views on individual taxes without any context, and so it is easy for people to call for abolition of taxes if there are no consequences to such a change. However, when the public are given real choices to make, we see a different response. For example, a UK study on public attitudes in the summer of 2020 found people more likely to say that they would be personally prepared to pay more in taxes than see cuts to public services (Rowlingson et al, 2021). The same survey found much higher support for increasing wealth taxes rather than income or consumption taxes and a clear preference among the public for those who had most wealth to pay most tax. The public thought the most compelling argument for a new wealth tax was high levels of wealth inequality. This was perhaps surprising given that the study was carried out at the height of the COVID-19 pandemic, when the British government had just borrowed billions to support the economy and health service. In terms of arguments against a new wealth tax, there was some concern about possible unfairness or discouragement of saving, but the main public concern was that the wealthy would find ways to avoid paying it.

The Rowlingson et al (2021) study suggests that the general public in the UK may be much more supportive of increased wealth taxation than is often thought. However, even where the public have concerns about increased taxation, these views do not necessarily affect voting behaviour, which is based on a complex range of factors. For example, Clark et al (2021) found that (concerns about) public views were not a contributing factor in any of the contemporary or post hoc rationalisations of wealth tax abolition that they reviewed. Rather than voter preferences driving wealth tax reforms, their conclusion was that 'structural power' was the most compelling force influencing policy outcomes, with this being primarily exercised through policy makers' perceptions of powerful groups' potential behavioural responses. As discussed earlier, these perceptions were not necessarily based on any clear evidence nor on any explicit lobbying. These perceptions were part of a broader dominant discourse about wealth inequality and taxation that Clarke et al (2020) suggest the media played a key role in propagating.

This dominant discourse is related to the rise of neoliberal ideologies in the 1970s and 1980s (Campbell, 1998; Carstensen and Schmidt, 2016; Hopkin and Shaw, 2016). The abolition of the Royal Commission on the Distribution of Income and Wealth in 1979 was one of the earliest and clearest indications that the Thatcher government was pursuing a 'strategy of inequality'. These different ways of framing issues have considerable impact on policy outcomes (Prabhakar, 2021).

The barriers to wealth tax reform are real in the sense that they have encouraged/enabled some governments to reduce wealth taxation and deterred others from proposing and implementing reforms, but the arguments put forward against wealth taxes are much weaker than may at first appear to be the case. There is relatively little evidence that entrepreneurs or wealthy people will leave a particular country if wealth taxes increase, and there appears to be much less public opposition to wealth taxes than is sometimes argued. Wealth taxes may yield relatively little currently and are complex with high levels of avoidance, but these issues can be fixed through design changes. The underlying and most significant barrier appears to be the dominant discourse against wealth taxes, which is linked to the broader neoliberal discourse against taxation. This frames taxation as taking money away from one group of people to give to another. Those who are taxed are framed as people who have worked and saved hard for it and so deserve to keep it, spend it or give it to their family as they prefer. Those who are the recipients of taxed money are framed as less deserving. This powerful discourse has influenced political parties of all kinds to either reduce wealth taxes or avoid proposing increases. The next section of this chapter suggests a more positive discourse and framing of wealth taxation along with some ideas for particular reforms of wealth taxes.

A way forward for wealth tax reform in the UK

As argued in the previous section, one of the main barriers to wealth tax reform in the UK is a dominant negative discourse around taxation, which is seen as a burden and a transfer from the deserving to the undeserving. A much more positive discourse exists and needs to be promoted further. This presents taxation as a positive contribution made by everyone to the benefit of all. As will be clear from this volume, tax is paid by almost everyone in our society given that it is levied on consumption as well as income and wealth. Everyone contributes, with some contributing more because they have greater capacity to do so. And everyone benefits, with those in the middle and at the 'top' of society benefitting just as much, in different ways, as those at the bottom (Hills, 2015). The case for wealth taxes in particular can be made by contrasting the relatively low level of tax currently levied against (unearned) wealth with that levied against (earned) income. The lack of progressivity in the tax system could also be highlighted more. In general, we need much more public education about the nature of the tax system and the level of inequality (which the public consistently underestimate).

However, while a more positive discourse and framing of taxation should be further developed and widely promulgated, there are signs that the public are already more supportive of wealth taxation to tackle wealth inequality than they are often given credit for (Rowlingson et al, 2021). This suggests that politicians could respond to this and not give in to their fears about the possible risks of proposing reform. The tide now seems to be turning in many countries, as some have introduced new wealth taxes with improved designs (Perret, 2021). The COVID-19 pandemic has further strengthened the case for wealth taxes, with the UN Secretary-General in April 2021 urging governments to consider introducing a new 'solidarity or wealth tax' in response to a $5 trillion increase in the wealth of the world's richest individuals during the pandemic.[8] The IMF has also recommended that countries consider taxes on high wealth, emphasising the 'symbolic impact of this type of contribution' in the context of recovery from the COVID-19 crisis.[9]

Having set out the broad case for wealth taxation, the question remains of which particular reforms to pursue. There are many suggestions for reform to choose from, not least revisiting the Mirrlees Review (2010), which took a holistic view of tax reform in the UK, setting out a wide array of proposals for taxes on savings, pensions and bequests. On the last, it recommended introducing a lifetime transfer tax to include gifts as well as the receipt of inheritances (rather than taxing the estate as currently occurs). This approach has also been supported by others such as the Resolution Foundation, which suggested replacing council tax and inheritance tax with a genuine property tax and a 'Lifetime Receipts Tax' (Corlett, 2018; Corlett and Gardiner, 2018).

In 2019, the Resolution Foundation also proposed five more limited reforms (Bell and Corlett, 2019) that would limit entrepreneurs' tax relief from £10 million to £1 million; make council tax more progressive in England, in line with the reforms in Scotland in 2017; reform inheritance tax, for example to reduce tax reliefs; cap the tax-free pension lump sum at £40,000; and remove various expensive wealth subsidies such as the Lifetime and Help to Buy ISAs. These reforms were estimated to have the potential to raise £7 billion a year by 2022–23. Leslie (2020) and Bangham et al (2020) also suggested a range of reforms of existing wealth taxes, including freezing the threshold for inheritance tax, simplifying and reducing income tax-free allowances, reducing the maximum pension tax-free lump sum and a Council Tax Supplement for homes worth over £2 million. A further report suggested ways to make main residences subject to capital gains tax (Corlett and Leslie, 2021).

In terms of a broader framework for reform, Summers (2019b) has set out a clear agenda for change in the short, medium and long term, with key objectives as follows: to make wealth taxes more progressive, to raise more from wealth taxes as a percentage of all taxes and to reduce inefficiencies in the system that distort people's investment decisions and/or allow scope for tax planning to avoid paying wealth taxes. In the short term, reform should focus on reforming and increasing the taxation of returns to wealth (particularly capital gains) before then reforming and increasing the taxation of wealth transfers. And Tax Justice UK (2019) have also set out their own manifesto for tax reform, proposing 33 areas in need of reform including: tax inequality (for example, inequalities in how income and wealth are taxed by increasing wealth taxes as well as making wealth taxes more progressive), avoidance and evasion, and tax administration.

Other reviews have been more focused on exploring the potential for new taxes rather than reforming existing ones. There has been considerable interest in new net wealth taxes since Piketty (2014) suggested introducing a progressive global capital tax on the highest levels of wealth and income. In the United States, a new wealth tax proposed by Saez and Zucman (2019) received much interest from politicians including Elizabeth Warren, who proposed a tax on wealth above $50 million. In the UK, the Wealth Tax Commission (Advani et al, 2021b) explored the potential for a new net wealth tax, with the commissioners concluding that a one-off net wealth tax could help pay for the measures taken in response to the COVID-19 pandemic. They noted that such a tax would be based on wealth at a past point in time and so would not distort behaviour.

The idea of a land value tax has also attracted much interest, particularly in Scotland, where the Scottish Land Commission (2018) outlined numerous strong arguments in favour of such a tax: the taxation of land does not reduce the amount of it, it is hard to avoid and can help to incentivise landowners to put land to productive use. The Mirrlees Review (2010) had previously also concluded that there was a strong case for replacing business rates with a land value tax, and for reform of council tax.

While this chapter has focused on the UK, there is some variation between the devolved nations and further variation possible given some devolved powers over taxation. For example, Fawcett and Gunson (2019) have argued that Scotland has the legislative power to introduce a new local inheritance tax provided any revenue raised goes to fund local government expenditure. Drawing on international examples of sub-state inheritance or estate taxes, they calculate that a flat 10 per cent marginal tax rate above a threshold of £36,000 could provide up to £200 million additional revenue per year.

It is clear from this very brief review that there is no shortage of ideas for reform of wealth taxation, whether that involves an overhaul of the whole 'system', reforms of current taxes or the introduction of new ones. In fact, the existence of so many different proposals may in itself be a barrier to change as 'experts' spend time trying to work out the perfect system or reform rather than focus on challenging the discourse on tax.

Conclusion

This chapter has set out a case for reform of wealth taxes in the UK, pointing out that the current 'system' lacks coherence and clear purpose. It taxes wealth much less than income or consumption and much less than it did in the past. This has allowed wealth inequality to increase. Growing wealth and income inequality causes a range of social, political, economic and environmental problems while reducing equality of opportunity. The main source of increased wealth is now simply holding particular kinds of wealth rather than working and saving from earnings. This seems particularly unjust at a time when poverty is increasing and revenue is needed for collective forms of welfare such as health and education. Wealth taxes can help tackle wealth inequality and raise revenue for public investment. The arguments against wealth taxes are not as strong as is often claimed, and many can be addressed through careful design of wealth taxes to reduce opportunities for avoidance and evasion. But the main barrier is the discourse that suggests that wealth taxes are unfair and will lead to negative outcomes. This discourse can be challenged with a more positive narrative, which the public already support to some extent. It is now for governments and opposition parties to reflect this and set out their proposals for changes to wealth taxes. They have a large selection to choose from. There will be opposition to such reforms from powerful groups, but reform is nevertheless necessary, possible and desirable. And there is a very strong risk that if it does not happen soon then current levels of inequality will simply increase to the point at which our economic and political systems collapse entirely.

Notes

[1] https://www.ons.gov.uk/releases/totalwealthingreatbritainapril2018tomarch2020
[2] https://www.gov.uk/council-tax
[3] https://www.gov.uk/inheritance-tax
[4] https://www.ons.gov.uk/peoplepopulationandcommunity/personalandhouseholdfinances/incomeandwealth/bulletins/totalwealthingreatbritain/april2016tomarch2018
[5] https://www.propertynotify.co.uk/news/halifax-house-price-index-average-uk-house-price-rise-of-24500-in-2021
[6] https://www.ons.gov.uk/employmentandlabourmarket/peopleinwork/earningsandworkinghours/bulletins/earningsandemploymentfrompayasyouearnrealtimeinformationuk/latest
[7] https://www.lloydsbankinggroup.com/media/press-releases/2022/halifax/halifax-uk-housing-market-review-and-outlook-for-2023.html
[8] 'U.N. chief pushes tax on rich who profited during pandemic', Reuters, https://www.reuters.com/article/us-health-coronavirus-un-idUSKBN2BZ281.
[9] https://www.bbc.co.uk/news/business-56665505
[10] https://www.ons.gov.uk/economy/governmentpublicsectorandtaxes/publicsectorfinance/datasets/appendixdpublicsectorcurrentreceipts

Further reading

- Advani et al (2020) summarise the conclusions of their Wealth Tax Commission.
- Bell and Corlett 2019, Corlett 2018; Corlett and Gardiner 2018; and Corlett and Leslie 2021 discuss various proposals for reforming wealth taxes more generally.
- Evans et al (2017) the chapter 'Capital or Wealth Taxes' places the UK in a helpful comparative context.
- Summers (2019b) provides a clear overview of wealth taxes in the UK.
- Resolution Foundation reports: Bell and Corlett (2019), Corlett (2018), Corlett and Gardiner (2018) and Corlett and Leslie (2021) discuss various proposals for reforming wealth taxes more generally

References
Adam, S., Browne, J. and Heady, C. (2010) 'Taxation in the UK in "Dimensions of tax design: the Mirrlees Review"', London: IFS.

Advani, A. and Tarrant, H. (2021) 'Behavioural responses to a wealth tax', *Fiscal Studies*, 42(3–4): 509–38.

Advani, A., Chamberlain, E. and Summers, A. (2020) 'A wealth tax for the UK', Final report, London: Wealth Tax Commission.

Advani, A., Bangham, G. and Leslie, J. (2021a) 'The UK's wealth distribution and characteristics of high-wealth households', *Fiscal Studies*, 42(3–4): 397–430.

Advani, A., Miller, H. and Summers, A. (2021b) 'Taxes on wealth: time for another look?' Introduction to special issue, *Fiscal Studies*, 42(3–4): 389–95.

Alvaredo, F., Atkinson, A.B. and Morelli, S. (2018) 'Top wealth shares in the UK over more than a century', *Journal of Public Economics*, 162: 26–47.

Atkinson, A. (2015) *Inequality: What Can Be Done?* Cambridge, MA: Harvard University Press.

Bangham, G., Corlett, A., Leslie, J., Pacitti, C. and Smith, J. (2020) 'Unhealthy finances: how to support the economy today and repair the public finances tomorrow', London: Resolution Foundation, November.

Bell, T. and Corlett, A. (2019) 'How wealth taxes can raise billions more without scaring any horses', London: Resolution Foundation.

Bozio, A., Emmerson, C., O'Dea, C. and Tetlow, G. (2017) 'Do the rich save more? Evidence from linked survey and administrative data', *Oxford Economic Papers*, 69(4): 1101–19.

Campbell, J. (1998) 'Institutional analysis and the role of ideas in political economy', *Theory and Society*, 27(3): 377–409.

Carstensen, M. and Schmidt, V. (2016) 'Power through, over and in ideas: conceptualizing ideational power in discursive institutionalism', *Journal of European Public Policy*, 23(3): 318–37.

Clark, E., Gronwald, V., Guerrero Fernandez, R. and Ramírez Casillas, E. (2020) 'The political economy of the abolition of wealth taxes in the OECD', London: Wealth Tax Commission.

Corlett, A. (2018) 'Passing on: options for reforming inheritance taxation', London: Resolution Foundation.

Corlett, A. and Gardiner, L. (2018) 'Home affairs: options for reforming property taxation', London: Resolution Foundation.

Corlett, A. and Leslie, J. (2021) 'Home county: options for taxing main residence capital gains', London: Resolution Foundation.

Evans, C., Hasseldine, J., Lymer, A., Ricketts, R. and Sandford, C. (2017) *Comparative Taxation: Why Tax Systems Differ*, Cheltenham: Fiscal Publications.

Fagereng, A., Guiso, L., Malacrino, D. and Pistaferri, L. (2020) 'Heterogeneity and persistence in returns to wealth', *Econometrica*, 88(1): 115–70.

Fawcett, J. and Gunson, R. (2019) 'Thinking bigger on tax in Scotland: using Scotland's local tax powers to their full potential', Edinburgh, paper for the Institute for Public Policy Research Thought, Available from: https://www.ippr.org/research/publications/thinking-bigger-on-tax-in-scotland

Gough, I. (2017) *Heat, Greed and Human Need*, Cheltenham: Edward Elgar.

Hacker, J. and Pierson, P. (2010) 'Winner-take-all politics: public policy, political organization, and the precipitous rise of top incomes in the United States', *Politics & Society*, 38(2): 152–204.

Hills, J. (2015) *Good Times, Bad Times: The Welfare Myth of Them and Us*, Bristol: Policy Press.

Hills, J., Bastagli, F., Cowell, F., Glennerster, H., Karagiannaki, E. and McKnight, A. (2013) *Wealth in the UK: Distribution, Accumulation and Policy*, Oxford: Oxford University Press.

Hills J., McKnight, A., Bucelli, I., Karagiannaki, E., Vizard, P. and Yang, L. et al (2019) 'Understanding the relationship between poverty and inequality: overview report', CASE report 119, LIP paper, London: LSE, 10 January.

Hopkin, J. and Shaw, K. (2016). 'Organized combat or structural advantage? The politics of inequality and the winner-take-all economy in the United Kingdom', *Politics and Society*, 44(3): 345–71.

IMF (2014) 'Fiscal policy and income inequality', IMF policy paper, Washington, DC: IMF.

IMF (2017) 'Tackling inequality', Fiscal Monitor: discussion note, Washington, DC: IMF, October.

Keep, M. (2021) 'Tax statistics, an overview', House of Commons library, Available from: https://researchbriefings.files.parliament.uk/documents/CBP-8513/CBP-8513.pdf

Lesley, J. (2020) 'The missing billions', London: Resolution Foundation.

McKay, S. and Rowlingson, K. (2021) 'Financial inclusion monitor 2021', Birmingham: University of Birmingham.

Meade, J. (1978) 'The structure and reform of direct taxation', London: IFS.

Mirrlees, J., Adam, S., Besley, T., Blundell, R., Bond, S. and Chote, R. et al (eds) (2010) *Reforming the Tax System for the 21st Century*, Oxford: Oxford University Press.

OECD (2008) 'Growing unequal? Income distribution and poverty in OECD countries', Paris: OECD.

OECD (2015) *In It Together: Why Less Inequality Benefits All*, Paris: OECD.

OECD (2020) *OECD Employment Outlook 2020: Worker Security and the COVID-19 Crisis*, Paris: OECD.

Perret, S. (2021) 'Why did other wealth taxes fail and is this time different?', London: Wealth Tax Commission.

Piketty, T. (2014) *Capital in the 21st Century*, Cambridge, MA: Harvard University Press.

Prabhakar, R. (2021) 'What are the barriers to taxing wealth? The case of a wealth tax proposal in the UK', *Journal of Social Policy, 1-18*. https://www.cambridge.org/core/journals/journal-of-social-policy/article/abs/what-are-the-barriers-to-taxing-wealth-the-case-of-a-wealth-tax-proposal-in-the-uk/2109AF0B1296BA5740AAEBE8E5E39EC0

Robeyns, I. (2019) 'What if anything is wrong with extreme wealth', *Journal of Human Development and Capabilities*, 20: 251–66.

Rowlingson, K. (2016) '"You can't take it with you when you die": wealth, intestacy rules and inheritance tax', in K. Woodthorpe and L. Foster (eds) *Death and Social Policy in Challenging Times*, London: Palgrave Macmillan.

Rowlingson, K. and Connor, S. (2011) 'The "deserving" rich? Inequality, morality and social policy', *Journal of Social Policy*, 40(3): 437–52.

Rowlingson, K. and McKay, S. (2011) *Wealth and the Wealthy: Exploring and Tackling Inequalities between Rich and Poor*, Bristol: Policy Press.

Rowlingson, K., Sood, A. and Tu, T. (2021) 'Public attitudes to a wealth tax: the importance of "capacity to pay"', *Fiscal Studies*, 42(3–4): 431–55.

Rubolino, E. and Waldenström, D. (2020), 'Tax progressivity and top incomes evidence from tax reforms', *Journal of Economic Inequality*, 18: 261–89.

Saez, E. and Zucman, G. (2019) 'Progressive wealth taxation', Brookings Papers on Economic Activity, Fall, pp 437–533.

Scheve, K. and Stasavage, D. (2016) *Taxing the Rich: A History of Fiscal Fairness in the United States and Europe,* Princeton, NJ: Princeton University Press.

Scottish Land Commission (2018) 'Investigation of potential land value tax policy: options for Scotland', Edinburgh: Scottish Land Commission.

Seely, A. (2021) 'Inheritance tax', House of Commons briefing paper, no 93, April.

Summers, A. (2019a) 'Taxes on inheritances and gifts', in J. Bradshaw (ed) *Let's Talk about Tax: How the Tax System Works and How to Change It*, London: Child Poverty Action Group, pp 123–34.

Summers, A. (2019b) 'Taxing wealth: an overview', in J. Bradshaw (ed) *Let's Talk about Tax: How the Tax System Works and How to Change It*, London: Child Poverty Action Group, pp 115–22.

Summers, A. (2021) 'Ways of taxing wealth: alternatives and interactions', *Fiscal Studies*, 42(3–4): 485–507.

Tax Justice UK (2019) 'A manifesto for tax equality', London: Tax Justice UK.

Weldon, D. (2013) 'Miliband, Obama and Lagarde on reforming capitalism', Touchstone Economics, 19 February. https://touchstoneblog.org.uk/2013/02/miliband-obama-and-lagarde-on-reforming-capitalism/

Wilkinson, R. and Pickett, K. (2009) *The Spirit Level: Why More Equal Societies Almost Always Do Better*, London: Allen Lane.

11

Gender and taxation

Susan Himmelweit

Introduction

That social policies have gender-differentiated impacts has long been commented on. But recognition that the same was true of taxation came only in the late 1980s with the beginnings of the Gender Responsive Budgeting (GRB) movement. This chapter will outline how since then attention has moved from challenging gender inequality within taxation itself to examining how the tax system works to increase or decrease gender inequalities in society. After a brief look at independent taxation, the defining gender issue when *Taxation and Social Policy* was published in 1980, the next two sections introduce GRB, first as an international movement, and then as manifested in the UK. GRB's main principles are then outlined, before being applied successively to the societal functions of tax and some specific taxes.

Independent taxation

UK social policy has long been criticised for erroneously assuming and thus reinforcing a male breadwinner model of the family in which women were primarily treated as dependants. That same assumption lay behind the joint taxation of married couples, whereby the income of a married woman was added to the income of her husband and taxed as if it was his, with all tax allowances given to him. By the 1980s, that system was beginning to creak: it was recognised that many married women were earning, but the Wife's Earned Income Allowance still went to the husband. Campaigns such as 'Why be a wife?' and for the 'Legal and financial independence of all women' fought for independent, that is, individual, taxation.

Independent taxation was finally enacted in 1990, though some hangovers such as the Married Couple's Allowance still remain for older couples, and two recent changes have undermined its principle. Since 2015–16, a lower or non-earning spouse or civil partner has been allowed to transfer some of their personal allowance to their basic-rate taxpaying spouse or civil partner. This has small similar effects to joint taxation: discouraging the lower-earner's employment while reducing the tax paid by the higher earner.

The High Income Child Benefit Charge levied on higher-rate taxpayers claws back some or all of any Child Benefit received in their family. Here it is one person being taxed for income possibly received by their partner that directly contravenes independent taxation.

Since the mid-1980s, industrialised countries have mostly moved to individual taxation, though like in the UK often with features that undermine the general principle (OECD, 2022). In 2016, only five of the then 28 EU member states still mandated joint taxation, but of the rest only two, Sweden and Finland, had a strictly individualised income tax system (Meulders, 2016).

The objections to joint taxation were threefold, all raising gender equality issues that remain key to contemporary debates about taxation:

- Distributional: for women to be taxed at a marginal rate dependent on their husbands' generally higher income is unjust. Further, women should receive their own tax allowances, with any for children split between parents.
- Behavioural: that taxing married women at a higher marginal rate discourages them from taking employment, reinforcing rather than challenging traditional gender roles.
- Rights-based: that married women were denied the right to keep their financial affairs private from their husband, while no such disclosure was required from husbands to wives.

Gender Responsive Budgeting

Campaigns and discussions about the gender effects of taxation have continued under the umbrella of GRB, an international movement advocating that budgets and all fiscal policy should be gender responsive, that is, their impact on gender inequalities should be analysed and taken into account in formulating policy. The movement's aim is to ensure that policies bring about greater equality between women and men through acting on such analysis of gender equality impacts (O'Hagan and Klatzer, 2018).

Budgets need to be gender responsive because gender is structural, that is, economies depend on the different roles that men and women play; these different gendered roles, across paid and unpaid work for example, are part of how the economy and society runs. Women and men face different constraints, assume different socially determined responsibilities and consequently tend to make different decisions and behave differently. There are therefore gender differences in the impact of all policies including budgetary policies, differences that are not chance but reflect how men and women are structurally positioned in society.

The case for GRB is based on both equity and efficiency: equity in ensuring that inequalities are recognised and policy designed to reduce them; efficiency in that considering gender differences in likely impacts and behavioural responses is vital in ensuring that policy meets its goals in an efficient manner. This efficiency case applies to all policy, whatever its goals, and has tended to be accepted more readily by policy makers than the equity case.

Gender Equality Impact Assessment (GEIA) is the analysis used in GRB. It uses a variety of techniques to examine the gendered impacts of tax and other fiscal policies, focusing particularly on whether policies increase or reduce gender inequalities. As the example of independent taxation showed, there are a number of different types of inequalities on which policy can impact. Effective GEIA should cover as many salient ones as possible.

But GRB requires more than just analysis: it also requires that analysis should influence policy. While GEIA can be used to monitor the effects of already implemented policies, it should ideally be used prospectively to influence policy development. Where there are policies that reduce inequalities, these should be chosen over other ways of meeting the same policy objectives. And policy proposals that worsen inequalities should not be adopted, or if certain goals cannot be met without intensifying inequalities, other mitigating measures should be enacted to counteract that increase in inequality.

This chapter will concentrate on GRB, but similar arguments have been made for budgeting that is responsive to other 'protected characteristics' such as race, ethnicity and age.[1] Many of the methods of GEIA can be applied to other equality impact assessments, and analysis has been extended to the intersections of different inequalities (Women's Budget Group and the Runnymede Trust, 2017). However, each protected characteristic has its own history and causes, so that some issues discussed subsequently are specific to gender.

Although GRB was initiated in Australia in 1984, developing countries have adopted GRB methods more readily than more developed countries (Sharp and Broomhill, 2002). The Organisation for Economic Co-operation and Development (OECD), IMF and World Bank all now recognise GRB's potential. But, although legislation, both in the UK and the EU, requires the equality impact of government policies to be considered in formulating policy, there is little evidence of it having been considered in any major macroeconomic announcements, including those in response to the financial crisis or initial stages of the COVID-19 pandemic.

For most countries, the focus of GRB has tended to be on expenditure, on whether government spending reinforces or challenges exiting gender inequalities. Of 43 countries surveyed by the OECD, 19 governments practise some form of gender budgeting, but just five countries have a specific requirement for gender analysis of tax policy (OECD, 2022).

The focus of Gender Responsive Budgeting in the UK

In the UK, although GRB has not officially been adopted, there has been more focus on taxation than elsewhere in the world. Unlike in other countries, 'Budget Day' in the UK is mostly about revenue raising, with expenditure laid out in a spending review at a quite different time of the year, and there is generally far more media and political interest in the former. As a result, many of the techniques of GEIA for taxation, and for the closely related system of benefits/transfer payments, were developed in the UK, adapting existing tax–benefit models to incorporate gender.

In the absence of any government commitment to gender budgeting, the UK Women's Budget Group (WBG), an NGO advocating GRB established in 1989, regularly analyses the gender impacts of UK fiscal policy. The WBG has made the running both in UK and within the international gender budgeting movement in insisting that the revenue side of budgets and fiscal policy, including new taxes, changes in existing taxes and tax allowances, as well as the expenditure side, has to be an integral part of GRB.

Although the UK government has not adopted GRB procedures, there is legislation that compels it to pay some attention to the gender impacts of its policies. The Equality Act, passed by the Labour government just before it lost the 2010 election, contained the Public Sector Equality Duty, which requires all public authorities, including government departments, to have 'due regard' to the need to eliminate unlawful discrimination, advance equality of opportunity and foster good relations between those who have a characteristic protected under the Act and those who do not. Theresa May, as Equalities Minister in the incoming Coalition government, had to remind her Treasury colleagues that they would be legally required to pay due attention to the effects of the 2010 'Emergency' Budget on equality. The Coalition and successive Conservative governments watered down its content since then, including by insisting that GEIAs are not required: Prime Minister David Cameron called them "bureaucratic nonsense" (BBC, 2012).

Nevertheless, the Equality Act remains on the statute book and provided the basis for an application by the Fawcett Society (assisted by the WBG) for a judicial review of the Coalition's apparent failure to honour its legal duty to give 'due regard' to the impact on women in its 2010 Budget. The Equality and Human Rights Commission (EHRC) carried out an assessment of the Comprehensive Spending Review later that year on similar grounds. The former led to a rebuke to the government and the latter to a promise from the Treasury to work with the EHRC to improve its procedures for making fair financial decisions.

The Labour Shadow Equalities Minister regularly asked the House of Commons Library for a gender analysis of each Budget, showing the proportion of the net tax and benefit changes paid for by men and women (House of Commons Library, 2017). These analyses estimated that by 2020 women would have paid for 86 per cent of the net changes since 2010; while benefit cuts and freezes impacted particularly on women, simultaneous tax cuts, which were substantial despite austerity, went disproportionately to men. While this was partly due to gender-specific benefits such as those for maternity being cut, more of the differential was due to structural gender differences, explored subsequently, that result in women receiving more of their income in benefits and men paying more of theirs in tax.

This significant gender bias did not take account of cuts in public services, which also impacted disproportionately on women, particularly those provided by local authorities, whose funding from central government fell by over 56 per cent over the same period (WBG, 2019). Later analysis by the WBG incorporated the gendered distributional impact of public services (WBG and the Runnymede Trust, 2017).

Gender responsive versus gender blind?

The tax literature discusses horizontal and vertical equity, where the former requires those on the same income to pay the same amount in tax, while the latter means that people on higher incomes make a bigger contribution through tax. Both are talked about as desirable characteristics of tax systems.

But the ideas of horizontal and vertical equity are insufficient to capture the fundamental idea behind GRB, which is less about equality *within the tax system* and more about whether the tax system works to create greater equality *in society*. GRB requires being *responsive* to gender difference, and framing policy around it, not *blind* to it and imposing equal treatment as though gender inequality did not exist.

The proposal that men and women should pay different rates of income tax, put forward by Alesina and Ichino (2007), provides an example of the difference between the two approaches (see also Alesina et al, 2011). The proposal was made on the grounds that women already effectively pay a 'reproductive tax' on their earnings, the cost of replacing their unpaid caring work in order to be able to earn at all, for example, when they pay childcare fees. It would therefore be gender responsive and promote gender equality to tax women's earnings at a lower rate than men's, even though that goes against the gender-blind notion of horizontal equity of taxing incomes of the same level equally. Although GRB advocates have not in general adopted this proposal, rejecting the notion that all women are carers and all men are not, it is a good illustration of the difference between being gender responsive and gender blind. Gender responsiveness entails, as this example illustrates, being sensitive to a range of inequalities, including unequal gender roles, not just those directly taxed. Some commentators refer to impacts on those other inequalities as tax policy's 'implicit biases' (OECD, 2022).

Principles of gender budgeting

In taking account of fiscal impacts, some general principles have wide applicability.

Examine effects on a range on inequalities

'Inequality' is often taken to mean income or consumption inequality, but tax can impact on many other inequalities too. As we saw in the example of joint versus individual taxation, the way tax is filed can create gender inequalities with respect to rights, in that case to privacy and one's own tax allowances. Individual income matters because it enables not just greater consumption but also the power to make one's own decisions. Even if income is spent collectively for the household, how much each individual contributes affects their influence on household spending and their own autonomy (Bennett, 2013).

In particular, the impact on gender roles and relationships matters. Tax changes can influence behaviour, notably how worthwhile it is for the second earner in a household, usually the woman, to take employment. There are gender gaps in employment, earnings and pay, all to women's disadvantage, that changes in tax can influence through changing their gains from employment, how worthwhile it is for an employer to employ them and how much pay they actually receive.

This shows how gender impact analysis is not just a technical exercise but requires gender expertise in knowing about the full range of existing inequalities in order to assess whether measures will increase or decrease them. For example, knowing that men are more likely than women to own cars, drive to work and drive longer distances when they do so are all relevant, but in different ways, to the GEIA of taxes on motorists, on fuel, on company cars and expenditure on public transport.

Include effects on unpaid work as well as paid employment

Standard accounting categories exclude an important element of everyone's living standards, the contribution of unpaid domestic labour. That women take more responsibility for unpaid care work than men is arguably the key gender inequality that explains all others and is in turn reinforced by them (WBG, 2020a).

Tax policy can influence the amount and nature of unpaid work and its gender division. A controversial issue is whether there should be tax allowances for childcare, as a necessary employment expense for many mothers, like there are for other employment expenses more likely to be used by men. This is not a solution that has been favoured by many feminists, preferring direct provision of childcare or subsidies for its purchase. Nevertheless, the impact of tax policies on gender inequalities in unpaid labour, as well as in paid employment, should be considered and acted upon.

Consider effects on different types of households

Much policy assessment, including the tax–benefit microsimulation models that are used to examine the effect of tax and benefit changes, concentrates on household incomes, often divided into income deciles or household types.

By applying a tax–benefit model at the household level, the New Economics Foundation has shown that the disposable incomes of single parents and single pensioner households fell relative to those of other types of households in the first two years since the 2019 General Election in the UK (NEF, 2021). Since in both of these types of households the majority of adults are women, this is a rise in inter-household gender inequality.

The WBG often breaks households down into nine types, by whether the adults in them are men, women or a couple and then by whether they are pensioners or if, of working age, they have children. But other divisions are possible, for example dividing households by the number and gender of their earners. WBG analysed the differential impact of the package of tax–benefit measures leading up to and in the 2021 autumn Budget across household types. Those that lost the most were two-earner households, hit disproportionately by higher National Insurance contributions and the freezing of the income tax threshold, and no-earner households, for whom the package did not include any measures to mitigate the removal of the £20 uplift in Universal Credit (WBG, 2021a).

Consider effects on individuals as well as households

There is also the impact on individuals to consider. Tax policy can impact on inequalities between individuals across society and on intra-household inequalities as the example of joint versus individual taxation showed. Resources are not necessarily shared equally within households, nor do all household members have the same interests in how they are used (Bennett, 2013). Compared with most other European countries, taxes and benefits in the UK are relatively effective in reducing intra-household inequality in disposable incomes (Figari et al, 2011).

Look at effects over the life course

People do not live in one household all their lives. It is therefore important to analyse policy impacts, where possible, not only on how people are currently faring but also on their long-term prospects within and beyond their current household.

Women's lives tend to be more varied than men's. At various stages, women may give up employment opportunities and/or earn less because they are caring for others. This means that not only women's current earnings, but their long-term employment prospects and pay, tend to be lower than men's, and their lifetime earnings much lower. This has been analysed primarily in relation to living standards after divorce and pensions.

Look intersectionally wherever relevant

Gender is not the only inequality. Women and men are also of various ethnic groups, sexuality, immigrant status, class and so on. Each inequality has its own structural causes, and the way they interact is not always simply additive, so intersectional analysis should be carried out wherever possible. For example, in the poorest third of UK households, Asian women were projected to lose on average 19 per cent, Black women 14 per cent and White women just over 10 per cent of their income due to changes in taxes and benefits in the ten years to 2020 (WBG and Runnymede Trust, 2017).

Consider effects on the provision and receipt of care

Tax policy can also influence people's access to and quality of care. Not only do women provide far more care than men, but they are also more likely to require care from the state in old age and experience any shortfalls in the quantity and quality of that provision (with younger users equally likely to be men or women).

Social care is generally recognised to be in crisis, with major expenditure needed on it in coming years. The Johnson government claimed to have solved that crisis in 2021 by a rise in National Insurance to be called the 'Health and Social Care Levy', even though their proposals for spending the revenue were not so much on reforming how social care is provided as on compensating some people for some of the cost of their care. Both the rise in National Insurance and the funding proposals have since been rescinded and social care is in even deeper crisis.

The National Insurance rise, although regressive, would have slightly reduced gender inequality in disposable income, because men would have paid for more of it (WBG, 2021a). But any money spent on improving conditions in social care will disproportionately benefit women as the majority of its users as well of those providing paid and unpaid care.

Look at interrelated policies together

Tax policies' impacts interrelate with those of other policies. It therefore makes sense to examine gender impacts of interrelated social and economic policies together. For example, to consider the full effects of tax policies on people's standard of living, the impact on benefits received, on the use of public services and the contribution of unpaid domestic labour need to be considered.

A full GEIA assessment should, where possible, examine all these impacts, by including different households' use of unpaid labour and public services as part of their standard of living. There are models that allow such estimates of public service use to be made – indeed, the Treasury sometimes publishes figures showing the distributional impact of budgets that include the use of public services. As the EHRC recommended, it would be better if this were done on a regular basis, and not just by household income decile or quintile but also by protected characteristics including gender (EHRC, 2015).

The societal functions of tax

Tax policy does not only have distributional and behavioural effects; it has wider purposes too. Whatever its purpose, considering the potential gender impact of policy allows it to be more effectively designed. Legislation, both in the UK and the EU, requires the equality impact of government policies to be considered in formulating policy. However, there is little evidence of it having been considered in any major macroeconomic announcements of either jurisdiction, including those in response to the financial crisis or the initial stages of the COVID-19 pandemic.

Macroeconomic management

Tax can be used as a tool of macroeconomic policy to stimulate or dampen the economy. Generally, increasing taxes to spend more on public services stimulates an economy, because spending on directly employing workers has the stronger effect on overall employment. Spending on jobs that employ many women tends to be relatively good at stimulating the economy, because women typically work in more labour-intensive sectors. Thus feminists argued for a care-led recovery from COVID-19, arguing that spending on care would stimulate employment better and at lower net cost than more conventional stimulus spending on construction (De Henau and Himmelweit, 2021). Further modelling has shown that this macroeconomic stimulus is larger and sustained for longer if it is funded by wealth taxation, rather than a tax on earnings such as National Insurance (Oyvat and Onaran, 2021).

Because they are more concentrated on the lower rungs of the labour market, women are relatively empowered in a full employment economy and lose bargaining power in a recession. This is one reason why gender inequality in the labour market tends to be reduced by the effective economic stimulus of higher spending, even if accompanied by higher rates of tax. However, these macroeconomic effects depend on which particular taxes are raised. Taxes on wealth or on very high incomes that reduce inequalities, including gender inequalities, are also the taxes least likely to reduce aggregate demand because the wealthy spend a smaller proportion of their incomes than the poor.

Funding public spending

Views differ on whether increases in public expenditure directly require funding by increased taxation, with borrowing or 'printing' money seen as alternatives in the short or longer run. But, in practice if policy makers or the general public hold the view that increased spending has to be balanced by increased revenue, it may be difficult to argue effectively for increased spending without increasing taxation.

Most public spending tends to reduce gender inequalities. Indeed, women particularly benefit from public spending: directly as the majority of both public sector employees and the users of public services; indirectly through services, such as child and adult care, provided to family members reducing their unpaid labour; and financially as the majority of benefit recipients. And men as the better-off half of the population tend to pay more tax. This is another reason why increasing tax to fund expenditure generally reduces gender inequalities. But it matters what the expenditure is on: unless specifically focused on doing so, spending on the military will not reduce gender inequalities in employment but widen them.

Societal cohesion

Finally, taxes also have the function of binding citizens together, by enabling them to contribute to society and have a claim to be represented in decisions about the public finances. In recent years, politicians of all parties have represented taxation as a bad thing, an evil to be avoided wherever possible, and tended to include tax giveaways in budgets to court popularity. Since many policies that promote gender equality directly or indirectly require increased taxation, this is unfortunate. Ever since Labour's failure to win the 1992 election was attributed to the shadow Chancellor, John Smith, being too explicit about his tax policies, politicians have been scared of talking about taxes in any positive light. Given taxation's important role in enabling gender equality, this rhetoric needs challenging, and taxation recast as the positive contribution to a more equal society that it can be.

Specific taxes and tax allowances

Beyond such general principles, specific taxes and tax allowances raise their own gender equality issues.

Taxing income

The most significant tax in terms of revenue raised, personal income tax, making up 27 per cent of the UK's total tax receipts in 2021–22 (IFS, 2021), is also the UK's most redistributive tax.

Just a few personal income taxation systems are explicitly gendered. For example, in 2008, Argentina, despite having individual taxation of earnings, counted all non-labour income of a couple as the man's; in India, the income tax threshold was higher for women than for men (Grown and Valodia, 2010). Such explicit biases were common in many tax systems until the 1990s but have now largely been abolished. However, that does not mean that income tax's effects on men and women are equal.

Women tend to have lower individual incomes than men. So long as it is individually based, progressive income tax lowers gender inequality, making disposable incomes less unequally distributed than gross incomes.[2] However, in a taxation system based on a couple's joint income, the lower earner faces a higher marginal rate of tax, paying more tax and rendering employment less worthwhile. Since women tend systematically to be the lower earner, these are gender effects.

Like earning income through employment, unpaid domestic labour is a contribution to a household's standard of living, its *full income*. But personal income tax systems do not explicitly account for the contribution of unpaid labour. The proposal discussed earlier of taxing women less highly than men does recognise the value of the unpaid labour that is lost when women take employment. Compare two couple households with the same total earned income: one where both partners are employed and the other where only the man is employed, and the women contributes unpaid work. The second household has higher full income. Under progressive individual income tax, the second household will be taxed more highly, while under joint taxation the two households will be taxed equally. Debates about which is the fairer system can be interpreted as about recognising unpaid labour: is it fairer to have a system in which equal household earnings are taxed equally or one that takes account of the potential effects on a household's full income of having a full-time home maker?

Recognising the greater unpaid labour of women also makes clear why raising the threshold at which income tax starts being paid, which rose by 46 per cent between 2010 and 2020, increases gender inequality in disposable income (even more so for rises in higher-rate thresholds).

Raising the income tax threshold benefits only those who already pay income tax, with the full benefit experienced only by those earning at or above the increased threshold. The Treasury liked to boast that each successive rise took more women 'out of tax' than men, failing to recognise that those no longer paying income tax generally gained less than other taxpayers and that the vast majority of those who did not benefit at all from raising the tax threshold were women unable to earn more because of the unpaid labour they were doing (HMRC, 2015). Even those supposedly taken 'out of tax' in this way, of course, still pay many other taxes, particularly the more regressive ones, such as value added tax (VAT) and council tax.

Taxing wealth and property

Wealth is even more unequally distributed than income, with women controlling an even smaller share of it. If transfers between spouses are tax exempt, as in the UK, it may be 'tax efficient' to transfer the nominal ownership of wealth from husbands to wives, but if its management does not change, women may not gain much real control.

Wealth is not taxed directly in the UK, and income from wealth, for example dividends or interest, and capital gains are taxed at a lower rate than earnings, an anomaly that increases inequality, including gender inequality, since men are more likely to have income from wealth and make capital gains. Such anomalies also lead to scope for tax avoidance, incentivising people to claim what are really earnings as capital gains or as company dividends. These forms of tax avoidance are more available to those who can pay for tax advice, again favouring higher-paid men.

There are also taxes on the transfer of wealth, such as inheritance tax. By reducing the amount of inherited wealth, inheritance tax reduces gender and other inequalities in wealth. Although estates are now more likely to be divided equally among children, a gender bias still exists favouring sons in inheriting businesses. Replacing inheritance tax with a receipts tax, a progressive tax on all gifts received during a lifetime, would reduce inequalities in wealth more effectively. It would incentivise those leaving bequests to spread them more equally among recipients, reducing gender inequalities.

Property and land are immovable and easier to tax than financial wealth. Council tax is in urgent need of reform. It is regressive and levied on the occupants of housing rather than their owners. Elderly widows often live alone on low incomes, with high council tax bills. Helping them find more sensibly sized housing in the same neighbourhood makes more sense than taxing them highly. A land tax levied on owners and/or a local income tax would be ways to fund local government with more gender equalising effects. This is an issue of vital concern to women since, as noted, many of the public services they use are provided locally (WBG, 2020b).

Taxing companies

Corporation tax has been a live issue in the UK, with previous Conservative-led governments lowering its level from 26% in 2011/12 to 19% by 2019, in order to attract investment and prevent companies relocating. In 2022, the short-lived Truss government intended to go back to this policy. However, on becoming prime minister, Rishi Sunak reverted to his own 2021 policy as chancellor of the exchequer of raising corporation tax for the largest companies to 25 per cent from 2023/24 after granting them a 'super-deduction' of more than 100 per cent tax relief for investing in physical plant and equipment in the intervening two years (HM Treasury, 2021, see also Chapter 13).

Restricting the super-deduction in this way was always likely to widen the gender employment gap, since sectors that can benefit from investment in physical plant employ more men. It misses the equally urgent need for non-physical investment, for example in training and promoting equality. Although many small businesses are owned by women, men are much more likely to be owners of larger, more profitable firms that can benefit from the super-deduction.

Cuts in corporation tax rates, and giving such exemptions and special allowances, are part of a global race to the bottom in order to attract increasingly mobile capital. The business owners who benefit from such moves are disproportionately men (Cribb et al, 2019, p 13, table 2.1). Governments are deprived of revenue and their citizens of much-needed public spending that such revenue could finance. Recognising this, President Joe Biden attempted to set a global minimum tax rate that businesses could not avoid by moving to a lower tax jurisdiction. A global minimum tax rate of 15 per cent for large companies was agreed, but with significant loopholes and at a much lower rate than the 21 per cent originally proposed. The impacts on women and gender equality in poorer countries of any race to the bottom in corporate taxation are particularly severe, rendering governments unable to raise the revenue to fund even the most basic of health and social services or bring in even minimal employment protections.

Taxing expenditure

Indirect taxes are generally regressive because those with lower incomes tend to spend more of their income. The worldwide tendency since the 1980s to reduce the progressivity of income taxes and replace them with expenditure taxes has made tax systems overall much less progressive.

This is particularly true of universal expenditure taxes such as VAT. However, zero or lower rates of VAT and exemptions on certain goods can make a big difference to a VAT system's gender equality impacts. Lower rates on basic foodstuffs and other 'inferior' goods can reduce their impact on poor households. Lower rates on children's goods can reduce their impact on households with children. In both these types of households, women predominate, so lowering these rates tends to increase gender equality in post-tax incomes. The UK's VAT system zero rates most food, children's clothing and, after much campaigning, sanitary products, rendering it less gender unequal than many.

Excise duties are levied additionally to VAT on particular goods, typically those considered undesirable to discourage their consumption. Governments often find themselves in a dilemma if they rely too much on their revenue, which will fall if the tax is successful in discouraging consumption. Goods whose demand does not depend too much on price, in particular those that are addictive, such as alcohol, tobacco and gambling, provide a better source of revenue. Duties are also levied on goods with undesirable environmental impacts such as fuel and carbon more generally, with a similar dilemma for government. These revenues must fall if environmental targets are to be reached.

All such taxes are usually regressive in that poorer households spend more of their incomes on the 'sins' on which they are charged. However, this is not true of the biggest revenue raiser, fuel duties, on which rich and poor households spend about the same fraction of their income. This is partly because poorer households are less likely to own a car. Among car-owning households, low-income households spend more of their income on fuel (Adam and Stroud, 2019). However, with respect to gender equality the situation is simpler: women tend to consume less of all such goods than men, so that excise taxes tend to reduce gender inequality.

The frequent budget sweetener of a freeze in such duties, or even reducing them, goes against gender equality. Indeed, fuel duties have now been frozen every year since 2010, and reductions in alcohol duties frequently favour beer and spirits over wine, showing that the typical punter that chancellors try to please looks very like a man.

Tax reliefs

Women and gender equality generally do badly from tax systems with many reliefs. The current UK system of poorly designed tax reliefs, allowances and exemptions undermines the integrity of the tax system as a whole by creating opportunities for tax avoidance that go far beyond the original intentions of their design. Reliefs are often designed around the components of men's lifestyles, such as car ownership. But even when they are equally available to men and women, they are worth more to those with high marginal tax rates – more likely to be men. There does not seem to be any published analysis of uptake of tax reliefs by gender.

Instead of tax allowances to cover specific types of expenditure, for example for childcare, it is usually better for gender equality to have direct service provision or subsidies that are worth the same amount to all who are eligible for them. An important example is private pension contributions, which up to certain limits can be made out of pre-tax income. This concession is available only to those in employment and worth far more to higher earners. Unequal earnings from employment cumulate over time to a huge gender difference in lifetime earnings, so that women have barely a quarter of the private pension savings of men, an inequality exacerbated by pension tax relief. Gender equality would be much better served if the £41.3 billion spent on pension tax relief was instead spent on raising the state pension by up to 40 per cent (House of Commons Library, 2022; WBG, 2021b).

Such tax reliefs lead to large reductions in tax revenue, particularly from those who can pay for advice on how to make most profitable use of them. They also give official endorsement to the view that the payment of tax is an undesirable burden that can legitimately be avoided by clever schemes, rather than being a necessary and desirable contribution to a well-run society.

Like rich individuals, large businesses are much more adept at making creative use of tax allowances and other forms of legal tax avoidance or illegal tax evasion. Women are less likely to be the owners of such businesses. There is also some evidence that large firms with more women on their boards are less likely to engage in aggressive tax avoidance (Jarboui, 2020).

Men are not only more likely to gain from tax avoidance but are also more likely to be employed and to be better paid within the financial services sector, much of which specialises in advising firms on 'tax efficiency' and where some of the most spectacular gender discrimination has been demonstrated by court cases in recent years. Well under 20 per cent of the principals at the five largest accountancy firms in the UK are women (Financial Reporting Council, 2015).

Conclusion

This excursion into the gender equality impacts of taxation has shown how those impacts cannot be considered in isolation.

First, considering the effects of a tax change within that tax itself is not enough. For example, raising the income tax threshold is the most progressive change possible within income tax. But since it reduces the proportion of revenue raised by income tax, one of the most progressive taxes we have, it makes the tax system as a whole less progressive, as well as less able to fund other progressive policies. Similarly for gender effects, many ways of reducing the income tax paid by women will harm gender equality overall, especially if it results in either increases in indirect taxes or cuts in benefits or public spending.

Second, assessing the effects of tax changes without considering changes in benefits and other parts of the 'social wage' gives a distorted picture. Because of their caring roles, women are more likely to be eligible for benefits and make use of public services. Therefore, the gender equality impact of tax changes tends to be underestimated if effects on such other policies are ignored. For example, taking account of the impact of public services on living standards makes the gender effects of austerity measures much more severe than considering the effects on post-tax income alone (Reed and Portes, 2018).

The particular ways policies are targeted matters too. In general, gender inequalities are reduced by less means-testing of benefits and social provision. Not only do women use benefits and public services more but the means-testing of these produces traps that reduce further the gains to employment for low earners. On the other hand, progressive income tax targets better-off men and can be used to fund universal social provision without adverse gender equality effects.

Finally, we saw the impact of policies differing for different gender inequalities. Tax policies may reduce inequalities in one dimension while increasing them in another. In particular, effects on income and wealth inequalities and on gender roles with respect to paid and unpaid work do not always go together. For example, raising the threshold at which people start paying income tax makes it worthwhile for more women to take employment, reducing the gender employment gap. Nevertheless, most of the distributional benefit of raising the personal allowance will still go to men, and those who earn below the current threshold, far more likely to be women, gain nothing.

In general, using the tax system to incentivise women to do more of what men do now will inevitably reward those who are already doing it, and thus men more than women. This is an inherent dilemma in using the tax system for such purposes.

An alternative but little used strategy is to use the tax system to incentivise men to do more of what women are doing already, so that behavioural and distributional impacts both work to reduce inequalities. Examples of such policies include tax breaks for those doing caring jobs, provided the incentives are sufficient for men to consider taking jobs usually done by women and do not simply reinforce traditional gender roles by encouraging even more women to go into them.

This is one direction in which tax's wide-reaching behavioural, distributional and macroeconomic implications could be used to promote gender equality. But the example of the international effects of the race to the bottom in corporate taxation shows how interconnected tax systems are. As the gender budgeting movement notes, it is not enough to focus on one tax system's own explicit or implicit gender biases, what really matters is using it to create greater equality in society as a whole, and not just in one country but internationally.

Notes

[1] These protected characteristics are: age, disability, gender reassignment, marriage and civil partnership, pregnancy and maternity, race, religion or belief, sex and sexual orientation. The Equality Act applies to Great Britain, but legislation on the specific duties required of public bodies to carry out the Public Sector Equality Duty are devolved, with duties required in Wales and Scotland being somewhat more rigorous than in England.

[2] Conversely, making an income tax system less progressive increases gender inequality. Thus, 80 per cent of those gaining from Chancellor Kwarteng's removal of the top 45 per cent rate of income tax, from April 2023, would have been men (WBG, 2022), had it not been scrapped.

Further reading

- Bennett and Himmelweit (2019) – Overview policy paper on tax for the Commission on a Gender-Equal Economy,: https://wbg.org.uk/wp-content/uploads/2020/03/tax-and-social-security-overview.pdf
- O'Hagan and Klatzer (2018) – an introduction to gender budgeting.
- OECD (2022) – Recent survey of tax policies and their gender implications across a number of OECD countries.
- Use tax as a search term on the WBG website: https://www.wbg.org
- Resource for NGOs on how to do gender budgeting: https://womencount.wbg.org.uk

References

Adam, S. and Stroud, R. (2019) 'Revenue from fuel duties down by nearly 1% of national income (£19bn) since 2000: £28bn still to be lost if we don't act soon', IFS press release, 4 October, Available from: https://ifs.org.uk/publications/14409

Alesina, A. and Ichino, A. (2007) 'Why women should pay less tax', *Financial Times*, 17 April.

Alesina, A., Ichino A. and Karabarbounis L. (2011) 'Gender-based taxation and the division of family chores', *American Economic Journal: Economic Policy*, 3(2): 1–40.

BBC News (2012) 'Cameron "calls time" on Labour's equality impact assessments', 19 November, Available from: https://www.bbc.co.uk/news/uk-politics-20400747

Bennett, F. (2013) 'Researching within-household distribution: overview, developments, debates, and methodological challenges', *Journal of Marriage and Family*, 75(3): 582–97.

Cribb, J., Miller, H. and Pope, T. (2019) 'Who are business owners and what are they doing?', London: IFS, Available from: https://ifs.org.uk/publications/who-are-business-owners-and-what-are-they-doing

De Henau, J. and Himmelweit, S. (2021) 'A care-led recovery from Covid-19: investing in high-quality care to stimulate and rebalance the economy', *Feminist Economics*, 27(1–2): 453–69.

EHRC (2015) 'Future fair financial decision-making report', Available from: https://www.equalityhumanrights.com/en/publication-download/future-fair-financial-decision-making-report

Figari, F., Immervoll, H., Levy, H. and Sutherland, H. (2011) 'Inequalities within couples in Europe: market incomes and the role of taxes and benefits', *Eastern Economic Journal*, 37(3): 344–66.

Financial Reporting Council (2015) 'Key facts and trends in the accounting profession', Available from: https://www.frc.org.uk/getattachment/eb28d049-3daa-4245-ab88-d248309d4565/KFAT-2015.pdf

Grown, C. and Valodia, I. (eds) (2010) *Taxation and Gender Equity: A Comparative Analysis of Direct and Indirect Taxes in Developing and Developed Countries*, IDRC and London: Routledge.

Himmelweit, S., Santos, C., Sevilla, A. and Sofer, C. 'Sharing of resources within the family and the economics of household decision making', *Journal of Marriage and Family*, 75(3): 625–39.

HM Treasury (2021) 'Budget 2021', Available from: https://www.gov.uk/government/publications/budget-2021-documents/budget-2021-html

HMRC (2015) 'Income tax: personal allowance and basic rate limit for 2016 to 2017', Tax information and impact note, Available from: https://www.gov.uk/government/publications/income-tax-personal-allowance-and-basic-rate-limit-for-2016-to-2017

House of Commons Library (2017) 'Estimating the gender impact of tax and benefits changes', Briefing paper SN06758, 18 December, Available from: https://researchbriefings.files.parliament.uk/documents/SN06758/SN06758.pdf

House of Commons Library (2022) 'Reform of pension tax relief', Briefing paper CBP-7505, Available from: https://researchbriefings.files.parliament.uk/documents/CBP-7505/CBP-7505.pdf

IFS TaxLab (2021) 'Where does the government get its money?', Available from: https://ifs.org.uk/taxlab/taxlab-key-questions/where-does-government-get-its-money

Jarboui, A., Kachouri Ben Saad, M. and Riguen, R. (2020) 'Tax avoidance: do board gender diversity and sustainability performance make a difference?', *Journal of Financial Crime*, 27(4): 1389–408.

Meulders, D. (2016) 'Taxation des revenues et employ des femmes en Europe', TMTEESS, Ministère du Travail, de l'Emploi et de l'Économie sociale et solidaire. Imposition individuelle et emploi. Luxembourg: Éditions d'Letzebuerger Land.

New Economics Foundation (NEF) (2021) 'Half of UK families are £110 worse off a year since 2019 general election', Available from: https://neweconomics.org/2021/12/two-years-on-britain-has-been-torn-apart-not-levelled-up

O'Hagan, A. and Klatzer, E. (eds) (2018) *Gender Budgeting in Europe: Developments and Challenges*, New York: Springer.

OECD (2022) *Tax Policy and Gender Equality: A Stocktake of Country Approaches*, Paris: OECD, Available from: https://doi.org/10.1787/b8177aea-en

Oyvat, C. and Onaran, O. (2021) 'Tax wealth and profit income to fund social care and healthcare', blog posted 20 October, Available from: https://wbg.org.uk/blog/tax-wealth-and-profit-income-to-fund-social-care-and-healthcare

Reed, H. and Portes, J. (2018) 'The cumulative impact on living standards of public spending changes', EHRC research report, 120.

Sharp, R. and Broomhill, R. (2002) 'Budgeting for equality: the Australian experience', *Feminist Economics*, 8(1): 25–47.

WBG (2019) 'Triple whammy: the impact of local government cuts on women', Available from: https://wbg.org.uk/analysis/reports/triple-whammy-the-impact-of-local-government-cuts-on-women

WBG (2020a) 'Spirals of inequality', video, Available from: https://wbg.org.uk/analysis/spirals-of-inequality

WBG (2020b) 'Submission to HCLG Committee on the Spending Review and local government finance', Available from: https://wbg.org.uk/analysis/consultation-responses/submission-to-hclg-committee-on-the-spending-review-and-local-government-finance

WBG (2021a) 'Gender analysis of the cumulative distributional impact of 2022: tax and benefit changes and inflation', UK Budget Assessment, Available from: https://wbg.org.uk/analysis/uk-budget-assessments/gender-analysis-of-the-cumulative-distributional-impact-of-2022-tax-and-benefit-changes-and-inflation

WBG (2021b) 'Pensions and gender', Autumn Budget 2021: pre-budget briefing, Available from: https://wbg.org.uk/analysis/autumn-budget-2021-pensions-and-gender

WBG (2022) 'Response to the mini-budget announcement on 23 September 2022', Available from: https://wbg.org.uk/media/press-releases/wbgs-response-to-the-mini-budget-announcement-on-23-september-2022

WBG and the Runnymede Trust (2017) 'Intersecting Inequalities: the Impact of Austerity on BME Women in the UK', Available from: https://www.runnymedetrust.org/publications/intersecting-inequalities-the-impact-of-austerity-on-bme-women-in-the-uk

12

Taxation and local taxes

Michael Orton

Introduction

Understanding local taxation requires consideration of considerable technical and even obscure detail, but it is a subject with significant ramifications.[1] Local taxation, in the form of the poll tax in the 1990s, was the cause of the downfall of a politician of the stature of Margaret Thatcher amid widespread protest, an extensive campaign of non-payment and violence between police and protestors. Earlier in the 20th century, a revolt in the London borough of Poplar against the failure of local taxation to balance between richer and poorer areas led to the imprisonment of councillors including the future leader of the Labour Party, George Lansbury. More recently, 2022 saw part of the government's highly publicised Energy Bills Rebate scheme in response to the contemporary cost-of-living crisis delivered as a local tax rebate. In Wales, also in 2022, changes to local tax were announced as a means of tackling problems created by large numbers of second homes.

For individuals and households, local taxation has a double impact. The amount of tax that has to be paid directly affects people's disposable income, and changes in local tax have immediate consequences for household budgets. The second impact is on the provision of local services. The Local Government Association (a membership organisation of councils in England and Wales) describes local authority functions as affecting everybody every day. It is the breadth of services provided by councils that touches on quality of life from the day to day to the far more profound. Examples range from street lighting to social care, and libraries to child protection. The level of local tax contributes to the extent of services provided. A broken streetlight may not seem of great consequence, but a darkened pavement or road can turn a safe environment into a more dangerous one. The consequences of lack of funding for services such as home care for older people or safeguarding of children can be life threatening.

The focus of this chapter is on England, Scotland and Wales. This is because there is a separate system of local tax in Northern Ireland (see McCluskey et al, 2007). To explain, in England, Scotland and Wales local taxation for most of the 20th century was general rates, briefly replaced by the poll tax and then since 1993, council tax. However, in Northern Ireland there have been no such changes. As McCluskey et al (2007) note, the domestic rating system in Northern Ireland has remained virtually unchanged since its statutory inception in 1852. While some modifications to general rates have been made,[2] the local tax system in Northern Ireland has not undergone the major changes experienced in the rest of the UK.

A theme of this chapter is the increasing divergence even between England, Scotland and Wales, albeit within the common framework of council tax. Looking more widely, Britain is notable in relying exclusively on a single sub-national form of taxation (Evans et al, 2017, chapter 3). Other Organisation for Economic Co-operation and Development (OECD) countries all have two or more sub-national taxes, the only exceptions being Britain and the Republic of Ireland. Evans et al (2017) found a key determinant of the overall share of total taxation taken by sub-national tiers of government is whether the country in question is a unitary or federal state (the UK is the former and Australia is an example of the latter). In federal states, the share of total taxation taken by sub-national tiers (predominantly state, not local government) is almost double that in unitary states. However, even among unitary states there are differences, with Denmark, Japan and Sweden all having a sub-national share of local taxation similar to federal states. That is certainly not the case for Britain, which is at the lower end of the spectrum in terms of share of total tax accounted for at sub-national level.

From a comparative perspective, local taxation in Britain may have a lesser role than in federal states and even some unitary ones, but council tax is of interest as a specific tax instrument – it is Britain's primary property tax but also a somewhat idiosyncratic hybrid scheme – and also of relevance to a number of social policy issues. In particular, the structure of council tax means it is highly regressive, and the proportion of household income taken is highest among those with the lowest incomes. At the other end of the economic spectrum, the local tax demand on those with the highest levels of income has a strict ceiling, thereby protecting the wealth of the richest. The examination of council tax illustrates how a tax instrument is not solely about raising revenue but impacts on topics of interest to social policy such as poverty, economic inequality and quality of life as already noted.

The chapter begins with an overview of the history of local taxation in Britain. Particular attention is given to the shifts in the late 1980s/early 1990s from general rates to poll tax to council tax. Council tax as a tax instrument is then examined, including its hybrid nature and differences in approaches that have developed in Scotland and Wales. Next, council tax and social policy issues are discussed with a focus on regressivity and its impacts. Attention then turns to local tax in relation to businesses rather than households in the form of the national non-domestic rates/business rates scheme and its obscure system of reliefs. This is followed by examination of options for reform of local taxation. The chapter concludes by reflecting on the interrelationship of taxation and social policy as demonstrated by local taxes.

Local taxation in the UK

Local taxation in the UK began with the establishment of locally determined rates to fund individual projects such as bridge building (Cannan, 1912). By the early 19th century, a series of separate rates were being levied for purposes ranging from highways to building workhouses (McConnell, 1999). A long process of merging these numerous individual rates began in the 1830s and was largely (though not fully) completed in the 1920s, leading to the establishment of the general rates system.

General rates was a property tax, based on the individual value of a dwelling. There was some concern that the tax was regressive. The incidence of general rates was distributed unevenly across the population, and a higher proportion of the income of the poor was spent on the tax than was the case for the middle class (Offer, 1981). However, it was not until the Allen Committee Report of 1965 that clear evidence of the regressivity of general rates was established. This led to the introduction of a means-tested rebate system, and, by the time of their abolition in 1989/90, general rates were no longer regressive and were broadly neutral in their impact (Wilson, 1991).

Poll tax (or to use its proper name, the Community Charge) replaced general rates in 1989/90, covering England, Scotland and Wales but not Northern Ireland. Poll tax was a flat-rate tax on individuals. This meant that if poll tax in a local authority area was say £1,000, that was the amount paid by everyone irrespective of income, wealth or property value. A billionaire living in a multi-million-pound mansion paid exactly the same amount as someone on a low wage in a one-bedroom flat, as did everyone else. Being levied on individuals rather than a property meant that every adult within a household was liable to pay poll tax. In the hypothetical £1,000 example, a person living alone paid that amount, but a household with two adults had to pay £2,000, irrespective of income.

The structure of the poll tax was highly regressive. Its impact was dramatic in benefiting those with higher incomes over people on lower incomes. The change from general rates to poll tax led to households with a net weekly income of under £100 losing £1.30 a week; households with a net weekly income of £200 to £250 lost even more (£3.85 a week) because rebates ran out at that stage (Oppenheim, 1993). In contrast, households with a weekly net income of £600 to £1,000 gained £4.04 a week, while the greatest benefit went to those on the highest incomes – households that had a weekly income of over £1,000 gained £6.50 a week. As noted earlier, poll tax saw widespread protest and an extensive campaign of non-payment, leading to its rapid demise. In 1993, the poll tax was replaced by council tax.

Table 12.1: Council tax bands: England, Scotland and Wales

Band	Property value	
	England and Scotland (1991 prices)	**Wales (2003 prices)**
A	Up to and including £27,000	Up to and including £44,000
B	£27,001 to £35,000	£44,001 to £65,000
C	£35,001 to £45,000	£65,001 to £91,000
D	£45,001 to £58,000	£91,001 to £123,000
E	£58,001 to £80,000	£123,001 to £162,000
F	£80,001 to £106,000	£162,001 to £223,000
G	£106,001 to £212,000	£223,001 to £324,000
H	£212,001 and over	£324,001 to £424,000
I	Not applicable	£424,001 and above

Council tax

Council tax is primarily, though not wholly, a property tax. Its introduction involved domestic properties being valued and then placed in one of eight valuation bands, A to H (with H being the highest band). The valuation bands were based on 1991 prices. A different amount of tax is payable for each valuation band, with the liability for a band H property originally set at three times that of a band A property – a ratio of 3:1. Thus, the value of an individual property determines the council tax band in which it is placed, but council tax liability depends on the council tax band, not the actual property value. Councils set the local council tax rate – which therefore differs between local areas – but the framework of the tax is pre-determined, including some central government control over local tax rates through setting thresholds for tax rises and accompanying measures (see Sandford et al, 2021).

Since 1991, the scheme has remained unaltered in England, but changes have been made in Scotland and Wales. In the latter, a revaluation of properties was undertaken in 2003 and an additional band (I) was added – see Table 12.1. In Scotland, a revaluation has never been undertaken, but in 2017/18 the 3:1 ratio was changed with liability for properties in bands E to H increased and the ratio between a band H property and a band A property raised from 3:1 to 3.6:1 – see Table 12.2. As noted, in Wales changes to council tax are being used to tackle large scale ownership of second homes. As of April 2023, Welsh local authorities will be able to increase council tax premiums on second homes by up to 300 per cent.

No regular property revaluations means council tax now has a very weak link to real property values. Corlett and Gardiner (2018) provide

Table 12.2: Revised council tax ratios: Scotland only

Band	Council tax as percentage of band D charge (before 1 April 2017)	Council tax as percentage of band D charge (from 1 April 2017)
A	67	67
B	78	78
C	89	89
D	100	100
E	122	131
F	144	163
G	167	196
H	200	245

Source: https://www.gov.scot/counciltax

examples of this including a search of property comparison websites, which showed a three-bedroom flat for sale for £2.1 million in south London with a council tax bill of £700 per year while just one mile away another three-bedroom flat for sale at £400,000 had a council tax liability of £1,160 per year. Being based on outdated valuations means the relationship between council tax and property value is increasingly tenuous.

Council tax, however, is not a pure property tax, as liability also depends on additional criteria. In particular, council tax includes a system of discounts. For example, single householders receive an automatic 25 per cent reduction (the single-occupier discount). Other discounts, dependent on meeting certain criteria, can be applied for by people including apprentices, carers and students. Discounts are part of the structure of the council tax scheme and separate to the means-tested council tax benefit, which operated from 1993 but was abolished in 2013. Subsequent arrangements serve as another example of divergence. In Scotland and Wales, nationwide council tax reduction schemes were introduced. However, in England each local authority is responsible for designing its own scheme. In practice, both council tax benefit and council tax reduction are rebates, reducing the amount of council tax that a person has to pay.

The hybrid nature of council tax is idiosyncratic. While property taxes are used in many different countries (for example, see McCluskey et al, 2013), only Jamaica has used the system of valuation bands (Davis et al, 2004). As has also been seen, the relationship between council tax and property values is in reality weak.

Local taxation and social policy

It is important to note that analysis of local taxation focuses on impacts on households at different points in the economic distribution but is marked by lack of attention to other dimensions, whether racialised groups, disabled people and so on. The charity StepChange (2015) says its clients coming for advice about local tax debts are more likely to be families with children, women and single parents. The greater vulnerability of some groups to being on a low income means the impact of local tax will particularly affect those groups, but new research is needed to give detail to this gap in our knowledge.

Central to illustrating council tax's relevance to social policy is the tax's highly regressive nature. There are other elements of council tax that link with social policy concerns, for example council tax benefit/council tax reduction, council tax as a cause of debt and imprisonment for non-payment. However, it is the very structure of council tax and its built-in regressivity that is critical and shapes problems. This is demonstrated in Table 12.3, which shows the percentage of household income accounted for by local taxation (net of discounts and rebates). The proportion of household income accounted for by local taxation falls with each income quintile. For example, in the latest year for which data are available (2019/20) local taxation accounts for 6.1 per cent of gross household income for those in the lowest quintile of the economic distribution but only 1.3 per cent for those in the top quintile. Comparing this with 2003/4, the first year for which these data are available in the present form, it can be seen that the regressive impact has intensified. While the proportion of household income accounted for by local taxation for the top two quintiles has fallen, it has increased for the other 60 per cent of households and, in particular, for the bottom quintile.

A little over a decade after the introduction of council tax, the New Policy Institute (2005) found there were a quarter of a million households whose

Table 12.3: Local tax in the UK as a percentage of gross household income, net of discounts and rebates, 2003/4 and 2019/20

	Bottom quintile	Second quintile	Third quintile	Fourth quintile	Top quintile
2003/04	4.9	3.6	3.0	2.5	1.7
2019/20	6.1	3.8	3.1	2.4	1.3

Note: Council tax (England, Scotland and Wales), Northern Ireland rates after deducting discounts, council tax benefit/reduction and rate rebates.

Source: Compiled from Office for National Statistics dataset, 'Effects of taxes and benefits on household income', https://www.ons.gov.uk/peoplepopulationandcommunity/personalandhouseh oldfinances/incomeandwealth/datasets/theeffectsoftaxesandbenefitsonhouseholdincomefinancia lyearending2014

Table 12.4: Estimated average council tax bill with different ratios, 2007 figures (England only)

Band	Estimated average bill – £			Change – £ and %			
	Ratio 3:1	5:1	10:1	5:1 – £	5:1 – %	10:1 – £	10:1 – %
A	846	764	555	-82	-9.7	-291	-34.4
B	987	955	833	-32	-3.2	-154	-15.6
C	1,128	1,050	1,111	-78	-6.9	-17	-1.5
D	1,269	1,367	1,388	98	7.7	119	9.4
E	1,551	1,623	1,666	72	4.6	115	7.4
F	1,833	1,910	2,221	77	4.2	388	21.2
G	2,115	2,483	3,054	368	17.4	939	44.4
H	2,538	3,820	5,553	1,282	50.5	3,015	118.8

Source: Lyons Inquiry into Local Government (2007), annexes, table C3, http://webarchive.natio nalarchives.gov.uk/20130802123120/http://www.official-documents.gov.uk/document/other/ 9780119898583/9780119898583.asp

income fell below the poverty line by an amount less than they paid in council tax, meaning council tax tipped them from being above the poverty line to being in poverty. Given the increased amount of household income for those in the bottom quintile accounted for by council tax, a similar analysis today would no doubt find the quarter of a million figure to be even higher.

The key cause of this regressivity is the ratio between council tax bands and the relationship between the bands and the amount of tax that has to be paid. The importance of the ratio between council tax bands is demonstrated in Table 12.4, which is from the 2007 Lyons Inquiry into Local Government in England. The table shows the impact of three different ratios: the actual 3:1 ratio and hypothetical ratios of 5:1 and 10:1. The results are dramatic. For example, a 10:1 ratio would reduce liability in band A by 34 per cent and increase it for band H by over 100 per cent.

The wealth of the richest is protected by the strict ceiling on the top of the banding system. A percentage tax on income means the more income a person has the more tax they have to pay, but this is not the case with council tax. The highest council tax liability is on a band H property in England and Scotland or band I in Wales. The amount of tax to be paid for each band is set annually and serves as an absolute limit on liability, irrespective of how high an income a person has, the true value of their property or the total extent of their wealth.

That the protection offered to the rich is a clearly implied aim of the council tax scheme should not be doubted. The rich did lose something in the change from poll tax to council tax. Overall, the number of families who gained and lost was exactly the same, with the 'losers' being in the top 30 per cent of the income distribution (Hills and Sutherland, 1991). The impact of council tax could, however, have been very different. It was noted earlier that a bill for a band H property is three times higher than for a property in band A. If the rise in bills between bands was doubled, the number of gainers would have clearly outnumbered losers, with 10 per cent not 5 per cent losing more than £5 per week, most being in the top half of the income distribution.

Business rates

So far, this chapter has considered local taxation as relevant to domestic householders, but local tax is also levied on businesses. The formal title of this local tax is national non-domestic rates, but it is commonly referred to as 'business rates', so that is the term used in this chapter. Business rates are devolved to Scotland, Wales and Northern Ireland, but their essentials are the same across the UK, so this section, unlike that on council tax, is largely relevant to the UK as a whole.

A very helpful introduction to business rates is provided by Sandford (2021a) and is drawn on in this section. In short, business rates are a property tax paid on non-domestic properties. The rateable value for each liable property is set by the Valuation Office Agency in England and Wales, Assessors in Scotland, and Land and Property Services in Northern Ireland. The second element of business rates is the 'multiplier', which is expressed in pence per pound of rateable value. In England, the multiplier is set by the UK government, and the Scottish and Welsh governments set their own. In Northern Ireland, the Northern Ireland Executive and district councils set separate rating multipliers, with the full-rate liability collected by Land and Property Services.

The business rates bill for a property is determined by multiplying the rateable value by the multiplier. For example, if a property has a rateable value of £100,000 and the multiplier is 51.2 pence in the pound, the annual business rates would be £51,200. Table 12.5 shows the multipliers across the UK. Wales has a single multiplier; England has a standard multiplier and a lower multiplier for small businesses; Scotland has standard, intermediate and higher multipliers; and Northern Ireland has a standard multiplier to which is added district council multipliers containing some variance.

Business rates are collected by local authorities. In England, the revenue is partly pooled at central government level and redistributed, and part is retained locally. In Scotland and Wales, revenue collected is pooled at the devolved level and redistributed to local authorities via a needs-based formula. Formulae used for this are highly complex (Arnold et al, 2019).

Table 12.5: Business rate multipliers 2021–22

	Standard multiplier	Other multipliers
England	51.2p	49.9p (small businesses: £51,000 and under)
Scotland	49p	50.3p (intermediate: rateable value £51,001 to £95,000) 51.6p (higher: rateable value £95,000 and above)
Wales	53.5	
Northern Ireland	27.9	District council multipliers ranging from 22.12p to 31.13p, thus a cumulative multiplier of 50.02p to 59.03p

Source: Sandford (2021a, p 8)

Another element of the business rates scheme are reliefs that reduce the amount that has to be paid. These are explained in Sandford (2021b). Some reliefs are mandatory and some discretionary, the latter meaning local authorities only implement the relief if they wish to do so. Examples of mandatory reliefs include the following:

- Small business rate relief – different schemes in England, Northern Ireland, Scotland and Wales.
- Charitable rate relief – properties in England, Scotland and Wales that are occupied by charities and wholly or mainly used for charitable purposes are entitled to a mandatory reduction of 80 per cent in business rates, as are community amateur sports clubs. Local authorities have the discretion to increase this to 100 per cent, which is the relief in Northern Ireland for properties used for charitable purposes, with Northern Ireland's definition of charitable purposes extending to non-profit organisations and buildings occupied for community purposes.
- Rural rate relief – there are different schemes in England, Northern Ireland, Scotland and Wales.
- Scotland has an additional business growth accelerator relief.

Some business rates reliefs are introduced on a temporary basis, again with a mix of mandatory and discretionary. Sandford (2021b) lists examples of temporary reliefs from the late 2010s and early 2020s. These include telecommunications relief, enterprise zones and freeports relief, local newspaper relief and Welsh high streets rate relief. In response to the economic effects of the COVID-19 pandemic, further reliefs were made available to a number of sectors in the 2020–21 financial year. These included retail, leisure, hospitality, nurseries and pubs.

Business rates are rarely the subject of public or academic attention. A theme of 'are business rates killing the high street?' – linked to the issue of online retailers avoiding payment – sometimes appears in the media, and the

2021 announcement by the Labour Party of its intention to abolish business rates stimulated some debate. But discussion of the business rates scheme tends to be highly technical. For example, in examining the introduction of business rates, Denny and Ridge (1992) based their analysis on distinguishing between the impacts of revaluation versus the introduction of a uniform business rate and the importance of marginal equalisation models – hardly the stuff of everyday discourse or social policy analysis. The same can be said of a review undertaken in Scotland focusing on possible ways to reform business rates in which the focus was again largely on technical matters (Scottish Government, 2017).

So why is this of interest to social policy? The key point to emphasise is how this rarely considered form of taxation with its opaque system of reliefs and technical detail is built on myriad decisions that may appear to be administratively based but are in reality highly political with multiple impacts. Denny and Ridge (1992) discuss different models that could be adopted for local business rates, each with different consequences for businesses, local authorities and – ultimately – the lives of people living in these local communities. Collectively, decisions on rateable values, multipliers, reliefs and so on incentivise and reward particular economic behaviours, affecting business profitability from the smallest to the largest companies and consequent wealth accumulation. Similarly, each of these decisions affects the revenue available to local authorities for provision of services to their communities.

Options for reform of local taxation

Attention now returns to local taxation in relation to domestic households and options for reform. Reform of local taxation has been examined periodically during the 21st century, with separate, country-specific reviews in England, Scotland and Wales. Of particular note are: the 2007 Lyons Inquiry in England; in Scotland, the Burt Committee (2006) and Scottish Commission on Local Tax Reform (2015); and the Welsh government review of local government finance (Welsh Government, 2021). Each review has considered different approaches but with four recurring options: a reformed version of council tax, a local income tax (LIT), a land value tax (LVT) and a new property tax.

Reform of council tax

It has been seen that some reforms of council tax have been undertaken, with an extra valuation band added in Wales and ratios revised in Scotland. Each of the reviews have considered ways council tax could be reformed. In the most recent, the Welsh government review of local government finance (Welsh Government, 2021), the Institute for Fiscal Studies produced a report on how council tax might be reformed (Adam et al, 2020). Four options were identified:

1. Pure revaluation, meaning properties are revalued using current market value then placed into one of the existing council tax bands.
2. Revaluation with proportional bands. This is the same as option 1 except the relative tax rates assigned to each tax band would be proportional to the median property value in each band, rather than regressive with respect to property values as currently.
3. Revaluation with extra and proportional bands. This develops option 2 by adding two extra bands at the bottom and one extra band at the top of the value distribution.
4. Revaluation with extra and less regressive bands.

Table 12.4 showed how changes to ratios would alter the impact of council tax, and these options make clear the tax could be made less regressive; however, such changes would not address problems inherent to the fundamental structure of the tax. To emphasise, regressivity is inherent to the council tax scheme. Changes to bands, ratios and valuations may offer some amelioration, but they are treating symptoms not the cause of the regressivity problem. A recurring question is therefore not just about reform of council tax, but its abolition and replacement. Three ideas appear across different reviews: LIT, LVT and a new property tax.

Local income tax

Taxes based on income are commonly applied across the world at national level, for example the UK's income tax, but they can also be applied at sub-national levels. Eighteen out of 38 OECD countries use some form of LIT, and LIT provides more than 90 per cent of local revenues in Finland and Sweden (Bunt, 2020).

LIT has been considered periodically in the UK. The Royal Commission on Local Taxation of 1901 and Kempe Committee of 1914 both rejected the notion. But the 1976 Layfield Committee concluded that a LIT was the only feasible major new source of income for councils (Bunt, 2020).

On the face of it, LIT offers a simple alternative to council tax, or any other form of property tax. Being linked directly to a person's income means a clearer relationship with ability to pay and a more progressive impact. The Lyons Inquiry (Lyons, 2007) modelled two options based on additions to the basic rate of UK-level income tax, and in both options a progressive impact was evident. Lyons advocated income taxes as fairer than property taxes, more closely reflecting ability to pay, but also noted that LIT would impact more on those of working age than those who had accumulated wealth in property.

The Burt Review in Scotland (Burt Committee, 2006) considered the idea of a LIT but concluded it should not be pursued. Concerns included: the impact on incentives to work; income taxes already being a relatively large share of total UK tax revenues; yield from a LIT would be unpredictable; and a LIT would be fair only if it was levied on all income, but that would be extremely complex, especially if responsibility for collection rested with local councils.

The practical difficulties of introducing a LIT were also considered in the 2021 Welsh government review. While LIT modelling tends to be based on additions to UK income tax and the Pay-as-You-Earn system, the aim in Wales would be to implement a Welsh LIT independent of the rest of the UK. To do that would require a new administrative infrastructure for collecting income information (Bunt, 2020). With the exception of some US cities, Bunt's research found no current international examples of a LIT assessed and collected at the local level. Issues include the need for universal self-assessment tax returns, equalisation between areas with higher- and lower-income levels and using a LIT to replace business rates would add further complications.

A LIT is therefore not as straightforward as might first appear, and its practical introduction across the UK or within individual nations would need to overcome a series of complex practical issues.

Land value tax

The basic idea behind an LVT is that pieces of land get their value from their location and surrounding infrastructure rather than the quality of the development on them (Arnold et al, 2019). For example, land tends to be more valuable in the centre of a city with high footfall, or areas with good transport links, schools, hospitals and so on. This infrastructure has not been paid for by the landowner but by generations of taxpayers. Therefore, in economic theory, LVT is seen as an attempt to capture value that has nothing to do with the owner's efforts, and to reimburse society (Arnold et al, 2019). LVTs exist in Denmark, New Zealand and parts of Australia and the United States.

Proponents of LVT argue it has several advantages over other types of tax. Ap Gwilym et al (2020) note the following:

- more efficient use of land as a natural asset;
- capturing, and therefore taxing, the uplift in value gained by landowners as a result of decisions made by wider society;
- fairer and more progressive distribution of tax liability among taxpayers;

- economically efficient with less disincentive effects on investment;
- increasing diversity in the ownership of land and unlocking areas of 'land banking' for the sole purpose of asset appreciation.

Of particular interest to this chapter is the Welsh government's (2021) review of local government finance in Wales, which included consideration of LVT as a replacement for council tax. As part of the review, research on LVT was undertaken by ap Gwilym et al (2020). Key findings from the research include the following:

- A local LVT in Wales could raise sufficient revenues to replace the current local taxes, based on modelled land value estimates and a uniform national tax rate of 1.41 per cent on residential land and a uniform national rate of 3.9 per cent on non-residential land (although with caution urged about accuracy of land value estimates).
- Changing to LVT would have a significant impact on the distribution of household and business liabilities – it would be significantly more progressive than council tax.
- Data requirements for implementing an LVT are not currently met. Information on property characteristics, property transactions and precise mapping are needed.

The latter point links to practical issues that would need to be addressed such as gathering evidence on agricultural land ownership, modelling different rates of taxation and identifying legislative requirements. The Welsh government (2021) concluded that an LVT has the potential to raise revenues for local services in a more progressive way and possibly offers a number of opportunities and wider benefits but noted that '[i]t is less clear how we could definitively evidence whether a local LVT is overall a better regime than the existing local taxes, and whether the benefits justify the vast resource required [to implement an LVT]' (Welsh Government, 2021, p 27). So while an LVT has many positive features, the practicalities of implementing it are daunting.

A new local property tax

The final option to consider is that of a new local property tax. Detailed proposals for this have been made in reports by the Resolution Foundation (Corlett and Gardiner, 2018) and the Institute for Public Policy Research (IPPR) (Roberts et al, 2018).

The Resolution Foundation report models five options for a possible new property tax. The first two are:

- a proportional tax of 0.5 per cent of capital value of domestic properties (boosting annual yield by £1.6 billion compared to council tax);
- a slightly higher proportional tax of 0.7 per cent (boosting annual yield by £12.7 billion).

Other options add elements such as exempting properties under £100,000 but with a 1 per cent tax rate above that, and regionally specific tax-free allowances.

The IPPR report adopts the first of these options – a proportional tax of 0.5 per cent of capital value of domestic properties. It argues that this would be far more progressive than council tax and would capture increases in house prices, which the current system fails to do. This means the proposed new tax would act as both a property tax and a tax on consumption. The vast majority (80 per cent) of households would benefit from the change, and for those in the bottom half of the income distribution disposable income would rise.

The Resolution Foundation and IPPR reports both contain considerable further detail. This includes consideration of a mechanism to help the cash-poor but asset-rich,[3] scope for local discretion, use of new technologies to enable regular revaluations and developing the new tax to replace not only council tax but stamp duty as well. Interestingly, however, the new property tax is not suggested as a replacement for business rates. Rather, the proposal is that business rates are abolished and an LVT introduced.

It is again important to recognise differences within the UK. Separate reviews in Scotland and Wales have been drawn on and reflect expressed commitment to exploring more progressive options, tied in the case of the Scottish government to broader interest in using its devolved powers on taxation (for example, see Fawcett and Gunson, 2019). The significance of changes made to council tax thus far in Scotland and Wales are of importance but at the same time should not be over-stated – in terms of the overall council tax scheme, differences remain relatively modest. In England, consideration of reform is notable mainly by its absence.

Irrespective of territorial dimensions, the options for replacement of council tax cover a significant breadth of approaches, but it is a new property tax that perhaps offers the most feasible way forward. While a new local property tax would not constitute a shift to an entirely new basis of taxation as would be the case with LIT or LVT, it would be a major break from the council tax system, (re-)establish an authentic link between property value and tax liability and end the current regressive impact of local tax. It would also avoid the operational challenges and difficulties of other options, hence suggesting it as the most practicable approach. This still leaves the question of business rates, for which an LVT might be more realisable.

Conclusion

The UK policy and political context is dominated by economic uncertainty, the consequences of the COVID-19 pandemic and Brexit, Russia's invasion of Ukraine and much more besides, but issues relating to local taxation retain a rather timeless feel. Concern, and even crises, arise periodically, but issues remain remarkably the same in terms of forms of taxation, options for reform, and so on.

From a comparative perspective, local taxation in Britain plays a lesser role than in federal states and even some unitary ones. If the UK were ever to become a federal state, the likelihood is that sub-national taxation would grow in importance. In that scenario, or if one or more of the home nations became independent, there would be scope for different local tax schemes to be adopted, but the available choices, policy decisions and administrative and technical issues would not alter.

To focus specifically on council tax, the scheme is based on hopelessly out of date valuations, the banding system is idiosyncratic, liability between properties and locations is highly tenuous and the regressive impact of the tax increases over time. Consideration of options for reform focus on four recurring points: reform of the council tax scheme, an LIT, an LVT or a new local property tax. Each has merit, but in terms of practicality of implementation it is a new property tax that is potentially most realistically achievable. For business rates, however, an LVT offers a potential way forward.

From a social policy perspective, it is the issue of regressivity that is most important in relation to council tax, with direct consequences for the disposable income of those on middle and lower incomes. The introduction of council tax is best seen in the context of changes to other forms of taxation in the 1980s and 1990s that protected the wealth of the very richest. Regressivity means a growing demand on those with the lowest incomes and a lighter liability for those with the highest incomes. So while council tax has many apparent flaws, if its aim is seen in terms of limiting liability irrespective of how high an income a person has or the extent of their wealth, then on that point it is not flawed but has undoubtedly succeeded.

More broadly, local tax in Britain illustrates both the need and the opportunity for greater examination of the impact of taxation on social, political and economic life. Consideration of council tax bands and ratios, or business rates rateable values, multipliers and reliefs, may seem far removed from issues of excess wealth and poverty, or child protection and library services. But the opposite is the case.

Notes
[1]   Some of the introductory sections of this chapter draw on Orton (2019).
[2]   Source: https://www.finance-ni.gov.uk/articles/latest-developments-rating-policy

³ Concern with the cash-poor but asset-rich is common in debates about any form of property tax and is often used as an argument against increased taxation of higher-value properties. But it has been found that there are very few such households, so specific protection for them is entirely feasible (see Davies et al, 2007; Orton and Davies, 2009).

Further reading

- Corlett and Gardiner (2018) – provides discussion of different perspectives on local tax reform.
- Hills and Sutherland (1991) – illustrates the impact of different measures.
- McConnell (1999) – sets out the history of local taxation.
- Sandford (2021a) – examines the business rates system.
- Scottish Commission on Local Tax Reform (2015) and Welsh Government (2021) – provides details of reforms in Scotland and Wales respectively.

References

Adam, S., Hodge, L., Phillips, D. and Xu, X. (2020) 'Revaluation and reform of council tax in Wales: impacts on different councils and household types', London: Institute for Fiscal Studies.

Ap Gwilym, R., Jones, E. and Rogers, H. (2020) 'A technical assessment of the potential for a local land value tax in Wales', GSR report no 17/2020, Cardiff: Welsh Government.

Arnold, S., Krebel, L. and Stirling, A. (2019) 'Funding local government with a land value tax', London: New Economics Foundation.

Bunt, J. (2020) 'An assessment of the feasibility of a local income tax to replace council tax in Wales', GSR report no 74/2020, Cardiff: Welsh Government.

Burt Committee (2006) 'A fairer way: report on local taxation of the local government Finance Review Committee', Edinburgh: Local Government Finance Review Committee.

Cannan, E. (1912) *The History of Local Rates in England* (2nd edn), London: P.S. King and Son.

Corlett, A. and Gardiner, L. (2018) 'Home affairs: options for reforming property taxation', London: Resolution Foundation.

Davies, R., Orton, M. and Bosworth, D. (2007) 'Local taxation and the relationship between incomes and property values', *Environment and Planning C: Government and Policy*, 25(5): 756–72.

Davis, P., McCluskey, W.J. and Lim, L. (2004) 'Residential property taxation: a capital value banding approach?', Paper presented at the Regional Science Association: British and Irish Section 34th Annual Conference, University College Cork, 18–20 August.

Denny, K. and Ridge, M. (1992) 'The implications of a switch to locally varying business rates', *Fiscal Studies*, 13(1): 22–37.

Evans, C., Hasseldine, J., Lymer, A., Ricketts, R. and Sandford, C. (2017) *Comparative Taxation: Why Tax Systems Differ*, Cheltenham: Fiscal Publications.

Fawcett, J. and Gunson, R. (2019) 'Thinking bigger on tax in Scotland: using Scotland's local tax powers to their full potential', Edinburgh: IPPR Scotland.

Hills, J. and Sutherland, H. (1991) 'Banding, tilting, gearing, gaining and losing: an anatomy of the proposed council tax', London: Suntory-Toyota International Centre for Economics and Related Disciplines.

Lyons, M. (2007) 'Lyons Inquiry into Local Government', London: Stationery Office.

McCluskey, W.J., Davis, P. and Lim, L.C. (2007) 'Residential property tax reform in Northern Ireland: impact analysis and spatial redistribution', *Journal of Property Tax Assessment and Administration*, 4(3): 59–70.

McCluskey, W.J., Cornia, G.C. and Walters, L.C. (eds) (2013) *A Primer on Property Tax: Administration and Policy*, Chichester: John Wiley & Sons.

McConnell, A. (1999) *The Politics and Policy of Local Taxation in Britain*, Bromborough, Wirral: Tudor Publishing.

New Policy Institute (2005) 'Council tax benefit for working age households: a review of the problems and some options for reform', London: New Policy Institute.

Offer, A. (1981) *Property and Politics 1870–1914*, Cambridge: Cambridge University Press.

Oppenheim, C. (1993) *Poverty: The Facts*, London: Child Poverty Action Group.

Orton, M. (2019) 'Council tax', in J. Bradshaw (ed) *Let's Talk about Tax: How the Tax System Works and How to Change It*, London: Child Poverty Action Group, pp 180–8.

Orton, M. and Davies, R. (2009) 'Exploring neglected dimensions of social policy: the SDW, fiscal welfare and the exemplar of local taxation in England', *Social Policy & Administration*, 43(1): 35–53.

Roberts, C., Blakeley, G. and Murphy, L. (2018) 'A wealth of difference: reforming the taxation of wealth', London: IPPR.

Sandford, M. (2021a) 'Business rates', London: House of Commons Library.

Sandford, M. (2021b) 'Business rates: reliefs and grants', London: House of Commons Library.

Sandford, M., Keep, M. and Brien, P. (2021) 'Council tax increases 2020–2021', London: House of Commons Library.

Scottish Commission on Local Tax Reform (2015) 'Just change: a new approach to local taxation', Edinburgh: APS Group.

Scottish Government (2017) 'Report of the Barclay Review of non-domestic rates', Edinburgh: Scottish Government.

StepChange (2015) 'Council tax debts', London: StepChange.

Welsh Government (2021) 'Reforming local government finance in Wales', Cardiff: Welsh Government.

Wilson, T. (1991) 'The poll tax: origin, errors and remedies', *The Economic Journal*, 101: 577–84.

13

Corporate tax and corporate welfare

Kevin Farnsworth

Introduction

Governments use their tax systems in various ways to incentivise and disincentivise certain types of behaviour, reward or penalise particular individuals or groups, as part of broader macro-economic policy and to fund social and public policies. Taxation is not simply about raising revenues; it can also be about distributing favours and picking winners. Decisions on taxation rates, incidence and exemptions are taken in the round, alongside spending decisions and after taking into account benefits such as grants, subsidies and state services. What has become increasingly clear is that many of the rewards of the tax system over the past few decades have been distributed disproportionately to big business, coinciding with increases in other types of corporate welfare (government policies that are designed to meet the needs and/or demands of private businesses, Farnsworth, 2012).

Despite its importance, corporation tax is rarely examined as a social policy issue. It tends to be viewed in legalistic and accountancy terms. Yet, questions of where, when and how corporations pay tax are important if we are to address broader questions of economic inequality. Various tax benefits are also important – distributing resources to recipients through the tax system. Tax decisions also influence prevailing business and investment models, which, in turn, have huge implications for the direction and redistribution of public resources and the positive or negative impact of business activities on employees, communities and consumers. This chapter focuses on the issue of corporate taxation, but it also looks at how tax shares and tax benefits are distributed unevenly, not just between citizens and corporations but also between different types of business. It examines how governments have used the tax system to incentivise predatory corporate behaviour and it looks at the implications of the corporate tax environment on the future shape of the welfare state.

Corporate taxes are complex and contested

Compared with other taxes, those levied on businesses tend to be more complex, more contested and more unique. To begin with, corporate taxes have not been around as long as land, expenditure and other income taxes. The UK introduced corporation tax (corporate income tax) only in the 1960s, primarily to tax what was, in effect, incomes for the wealthiest. Indeed, the real beneficiaries of corporate tax policies are senior business executives and, secondarily, shareholders. They were therefore levied at the same rate as other income taxes. Secondly, corporate taxes are more controversial, not only because they are levied on powerful interests who have louder voices in opposing them but also because these same powerful interests can, more easily, offload corporate taxes on to workers (in lower wages) or consumers (in higher prices). Households have no such options. Thirdly, corporate taxation is often discussed and treated as if it is a blanket tax that falls on to one uniform constituency. Not only do corporations effectively pay a different mix of taxes within nations depending on their profits and employment practices but these different forms have varying impact on different types of businesses. Moreover, while it may be the case that 'businesses may be more successful in persuading governments of their "needs"' vis-à-vis applicable taxation rates and tax benefits (Sinfield, 2012), big business is also more successful than smaller businesses in achieving such ends.

Corporate power and corporate taxation

Power and political struggle are important in all areas of policy but especially so in the area of taxation. The drivers of change in corporation taxes include both direct political pressure – lobbying and other forms of direct political engagement – as well as structural power exercised by virtue of the fact that governments depend on businesses to invest within their jurisdictions and must, through the tax system and other methods, induce them to do so. Because governments, and citizens for that matter, depend on corporations to invest for tax revenues and livelihoods, they tend to favour business preferences on key areas that are important determinants of investment (including taxation). We will return to this point in the section on the global economy.

Corporate taxation is considered in three ways here in order to provide an indication of comparative incidence: headline rates, tax incidence as a percentage of gross domestic product (GDP) and the relative tax 'burden' on corporations. Countries are selected from different welfare regime types.

An examination of headline rates (Figure 13.1) confirms steep reductions since the 1980s (Figure 13.2). It also highlights the relatively low headline rates in the UK compared with its major competitors. This did mean that the UK government also felt it had some wriggle-room to increase taxes faced, as it was, by a tightening fiscal position, and the Chancellor of the Exchequer announced that corporation tax would be increased from 19 to

Figure 13.1: Headline rates of corporation tax (central and local government combined rates)

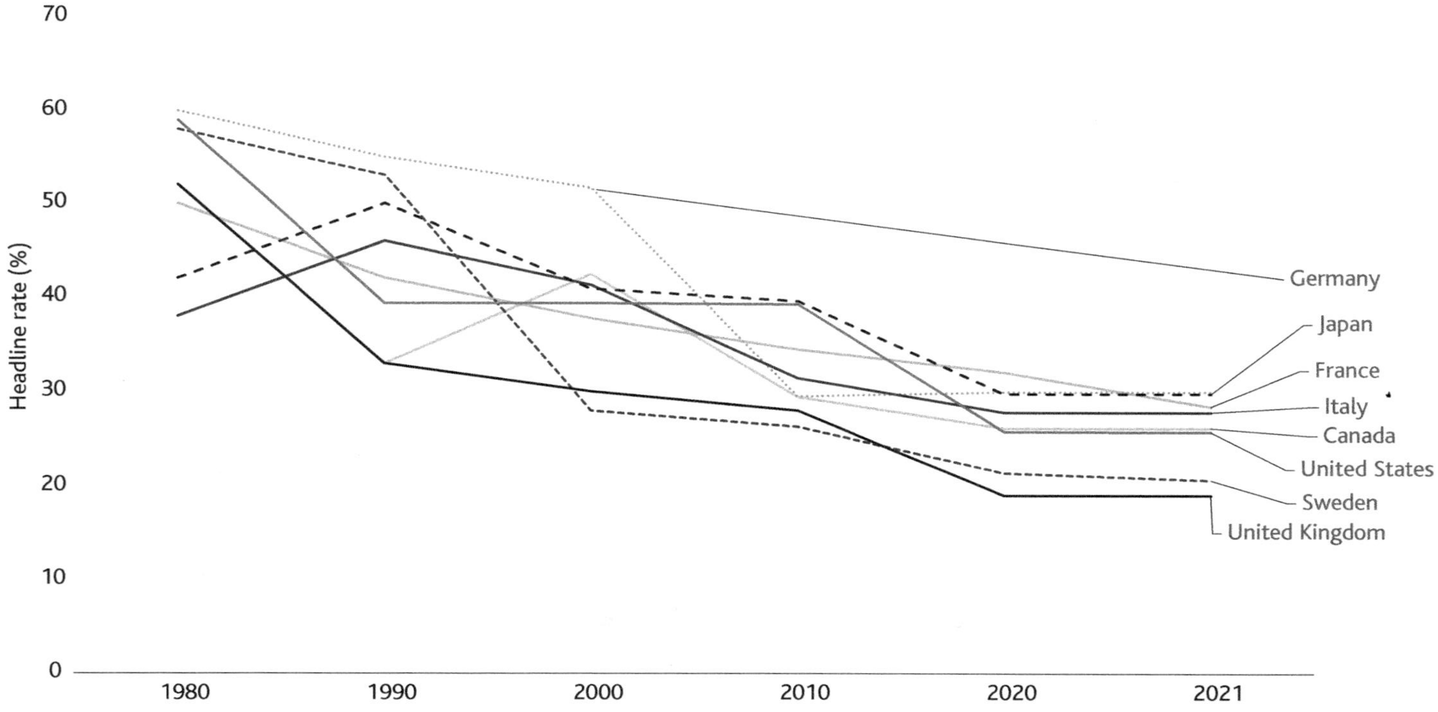

Figure 13.2: Taxes on incomes, profits and capital gains of corporate plus employer Social Security Contributions, 1970–2015

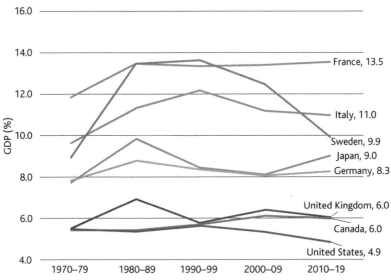

Source: Author's calculations based on data at www.stats.oecd.org

25 per cent from 2023. A change of prime minister in the UK in September 2022, however, meant that the 25 per cent increase was abandoned, with corporation tax rates held at 19 per cent. The government argued that retaining the 19 per cent rate was essential to boost growth on the grounds that financial incentives to businesses will help to induce investment. It stated that this will ultimately benefit everyone by 'creating the conditions for businesses to thrive, which will create jobs and increase investment in the UK' (HM Treasury, 2022).

Figure 13.2 reveals that corporation tax plus capital taxes paid by corporations together with employers' National Insurance contributions (NICs) across Organisation for Economic Co-operation and Development (OECD) countries was around 4.2 per cent of GDP between 2010 and 2015. The differences across nations are clear: France is a relatively high corporate-taxing economy, the UK and the United States appear to be low corporate-taxing economies. This figure does illustrate well the historical and contemporary differences between states. The problem with taking GDP as a measure of tax take, however, is that fluctuations in the denominator (GDP) cause apparent fluctuations in the numerator (the amount of tax paid). This is especially problematic when GDP contracts sharply, as happened during the period of the post-2008 financial crisis. For these reasons, it is useful to consider, alongside GDP, the relative tax shares borne by different groups.

Figure 13.3 looks at the main business taxes as a percentage of overall taxes. Although social policy discourse tends to focus on the income of the poorest, we also need to consider the proportion of income that states extract across the whole society and the impact of the ways they do this on different groups, areas and the wider society. Since the largest taxes are either linked with business activities or with earned income, it is important to compare the relative tax burden on businesses compared with workers. The relative tax share paid over time provides some sense of how businesses have been treated in the tax system compared with other actors.

Looking at Figure 13.3, the tax share paid by corporations ranged from between 8.5 per cent and 19 per cent of total taxation in the G7 plus Sweden in the 1970s. Since then, taxation levied on corporations has fallen, most markedly in higher-taxing nations. Sweden, selected here because it is a relatively high-tax and high-spending nation, increased the amount it levied on corporations during the 1970s but has since shifted taxes on business closer towards the prevailing rates of other nations, indicating the effects of international corporate-tax competition between states. The UK, an enthusiastic driver of such competition, raises least from corporations among this set of comparators.

What these figures do not reveal is that different types of corporate tax have a different impact on different businesses. Small businesses generally pay less in corporation taxes than larger ones since they tend to be based on

Figure 13.3: Corporate taxation as a percentage of overall taxes

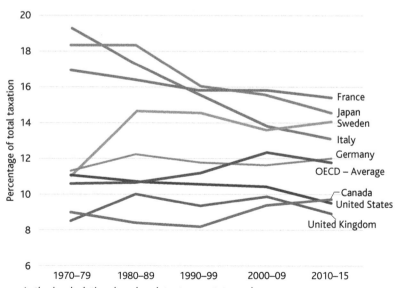

Source: Author's calculations based on data at www.stats.oecd.org

size and/or levels of profitability. Compared with medium-sized businesses, the largest corporations may pay more corporation tax as a percentage of the total revenues raised, but they also tend to be better at avoiding tax so that the amount paid tends to be much lower as a percentage of turnover than medium-sized businesses. But here there are important sectoral differences that matter. Financial companies, with fewer employees than manufacturing firms, are likely to pay less in NICs, and, as the most mobile forms of capital, they also tend to find it easier to avoid taxation. Less mobile companies – those that are tied to particular nations either because they depend on a customer base or fixed-assets – find it harder to avoid corporate income tax (although some have found new ways to do so, as discussed subsequently) and employers' NICs. Those that sell on the high-street also face high business rates charges unlike large online stores such as Amazon.

Corporate tax systems are leaky

According to the National Audit Office (NAO), 220 of the 700 largest firms in the UK paid no UK corporation tax at all in 2005/6, the period immediately preceding the 2008 global economic crisis (National Audit Office, 2007:10). A similar number paid no tax in 2012–13, four years after the crisis, suggesting that this is a reasonably established pattern (NAO, 2014). Later estimates by HMRC suggest that the corporation tax gap is some £5 billion each year (HMRC, 2022). Analysis conducted by MSCI, a global transnational corporation, estimated that, in total, transnational corporations (TNCs) avoided at least $82 billion of tax each year through tax havens (Johnson and Marriage, 2015). Interestingly, many of the largest tax havens include Jersey and Guernsey and other British protectorates (Shaxson, 2011).

One way in which companies avoid taxation is to remain on top of what is and what is not possible and permissible within the tax rules. It is common practice, for instance, for large accountancy firms to second staff to the Treasury to provide advice and glean intelligence on tax matters so that when they return to their firms, they have inside knowledge of how to identify tax loopholes (PAC, 2013).

Accountants can also use other legal methods of tax avoidance. In 2009, the four major accountancy firms alone earned £2 billion in the UK and as much as US$25 billion globally from their tax work; an estimated 50 per cent of their fees came from 'commercial tax planning' and 'artificial avoidance schemes' (HMRC, 2022, 2009). The substantial imbalance of resources between the private tax avoidance industry and tax authorities caused by this rapid development in professional expertise was highlighted as being significant by the Public Accounts Committee (PAC), which reported around four times as many staff working for the accountancy firms on transfer pricing alone as staff working for HMRC (PAC, 2013). As a result, the PAC stated that

> HM Revenue & Customs (HMRC) appears to be fighting a battle it cannot win in tackling tax avoidance. Companies can devote considerable resource to ensure that they minimise their tax liability. There is a large market for advising companies on how to take advantage of international tax law, and on the tax implications of different global structures. (PAC, 2013, p 3)

Even when companies are accused of having paid less tax than HMRC calculate is legally due, the outcome is more likely to be a negotiated settlement than legal action. Companies can devote considerable resources to minimising their tax liabilities and challenging tax authorities. A legal challenge brought against HMRC into the circumstances leading to one of these settlements with the US investment bank Goldman Sachs provides a rare insight into the extra-legal levers that TNCs can use to exploit their positions. Goldman Sachs was accused in 2011 of privately negotiating a reduction of £10 million on a total interest payment bill of £40 million. The interest charges were due on its outstanding tax liabilities, which arose because the company was found to have engaged in illegal tax avoidance practices in the 1990s. In negotiations over its tax liabilities with HMRC, Goldman Sachs 'threatened to withdraw' from a banking code of practice, which would, according to the Permanent Secretary for Tax at HMRC at the time, have been highly embarrassing for the Chancellor of the Exchequer and HMRC. Exacerbating the risks of such special deals between major corporations and the government is that investigations are conducted in private. The former head of HMRC came under attack for having 'an unduly cosy relationship with large companies it is trying to settle tax disputes with' and of having 'had a significant number of lunches and dinners with companies, tax lawyers and tax advisers – as many as 107 in two years' (PAC, 2011, p 16).

The relationship between tax collectors and corporate taxpayers is, therefore, at variance to citizen-taxpayers. Such is the power imbalance between government and corporations that governments have to negotiate with, implore and even embarrass corporations to comply with tax laws. In a swipe at Starbucks, David Cameron used his speech at Davos in January 2013 to warn companies to "wake up and smell the coffee". The consequence, he explained, would not be tougher regulations or the full force of the law, but unhappy consumers. There was no need for such tax avoidance, the then Prime Minister told businesses, because they were getting such a good tax deal already. It is difficult to imagine this kind of language being used to induce any other citizen to pay their taxes:

I think we're offering actually a fair deal to businesses. We're saying, 'Look we're going to have a really low rate of corporation tax' but I want to make damn sure that those companies pay it … Because some people say to me, 'Well, it's all within the law; you're obeying the law, it's okay.' Well, actually there are lots of things that are within the law but we don't do because actually we have some moral scruples about them and I think we need this debate about tax too. (Cameron, 2013)

Perhaps surprisingly, Margaret Hodge, Chair of the PAC at the time, made a very similar moral defence of corporate taxation as if corporations are driven by ethics rather than economics: 'We consider that paying an appropriate amount of tax in the country in which profits are made is not only a matter of basic economics. It is also a matter of morality. The UK should be taking the lead in making this point' (PAC, 2012).

What drives corporations more than morality, however, is profit, and some have sought to emphasise their tax compliance in order to boost their market positions. Starbucks, after being embarrassed by the PAC and facing a consumer backlash, vowed to pay 'above that which is currently required by law' in corporation tax over the subsequent next two years (Neville and Treanor, 2012). And other major corporations that are more nationally constrained and find it difficult to engage in tax avoidance sought to draw attention to their plight and to laud their tax credentials over some of their badly behaved competitors. Justin King, CEO of Sainsbury's, stated in an interview with Channel 4 News that

[w]e are entirely domestic, we pay our tax in the UK … Corporation tax for international corporations is an elective tax. They can choose quite legally to organise their affairs and choose to pay tax pretty much wherever they wish … I think it is now time for consumers to ask tough questions of the businesses … about where they choose to pay their corporation tax. Corporation tax is a way in which we invest back in the community and the country of which we are part. I think that companies that wish to trade here, enjoy the benefits of our consumers and of the investments in our infrastructure, our safety and so on, should answer themselves about whether they are contributing properly to our society. (King, 2013)

There is a difference here between different types of businesses: those who operate within more competitive markets and are more sensitive to customer opinion, for instance, as opposed to those who are able to focus more on profitability and returns to shareholders.

Ultimately, the fact that corporation tax systems are so leaky, and that policy makers resort to imploring TNCs to pay the corporation tax owing, captures the unequal power dynamic at play and the fact that legislators are unwilling or unable to tax corporations effectively.

Tax avoidance in a global economy

The general relaxation of capital and exchange controls that has characterised globalisation since the 1980s has increased capital mobility internationally so that even companies that have fixed plants within particular jurisdictions can shift their tax liabilities from high-taxing jurisdictions to more favourable tax regimes. Thus, globalisation adds to the volatility of corporate taxes, especially on those forms of taxation that apply to the largest, and most mobile, corporations. Unlike most citizens and immobile businesses (especially smaller businesses), big business has far greater choice about where and how it pays taxes.

Such conditions have placed increasing pressure on governments to compete aggressively in corporate taxation, and the reasons for this go beyond raising revenues. Governments can use the tax system to compete with other nations for private corporate investment. This can be seen in the figures on headline rates of tax, which act as important 'signalling devices' according to Swank (1998). Recall that the UK's corporation tax rates used to be in line with income taxes. Thus, the lowest corporation tax rate would not have fallen below 20 per cent in the UK if the two tax rates had continued to be pegged together. In reality, corporation taxes have been cut more dramatically, resulting in a fiscally compromising game of beggar thy neighbour (Rincke and Overesch, 2011), with the biggest impact on headline rates as revealed earlier.

Despite falling tax rates, corporations continually scramble for ever more sophisticated ways of avoiding paying even these reduced rates. One such method is to pay taxation within lower tax regimes either by re-siting head office operations or through transfer pricing mechanisms. In both instances, corporations are bound only by weak international agreements that state that taxation should be levied at the site of economic activity, and these are rarely enforced.

Transfer pricing describes tax-avoidance measures whereby one part of a company located in a lower-tax regime secures and 'sells' goods at inflated prices to other parts of the same company in higher-tax regimes, with the result that tax liabilities are shifted from the latter to the former. One widely cited estimate of the misuse of transfer pricing suggests that, in 2004, between 45 and 60 per cent of all international transactions related to the sale of goods and services involved manipulated prices at huge costs to the public finances (Baker, 2005). Inaccurate pricing in these transactions was calculated to account for 10–11 per cent of their value, indicating that transfer pricing alone accounted for 5–7 per cent of world trade (Baker, 2005).

In order to target such practice, the OECD has proposed international rules to ensure that profits are taxed where genuine economic activity is undertaken, as part of their base erosion and profit-shifting initiative (OECD, 2013). However, what constitutes a genuine site of economic activity is often difficult to determine, especially where companies divorce the distribution and sale of goods from the 'brand' and/or intellectual property that resides in the product. Starbucks claims, for instance, that a large part of its economic activity associated with the sale of its coffee stems from its research and development (R&D) activities in the United States, alongside its coffee-processing enterprise in Switzerland, where it buys raw beans, and the Netherlands, where its roasting plant is located. It then sells the coffee beans out of low-tax Netherlands to British retailers who are also liable to further royalty charges relating to the brand (PAC, 2012).

Similarly, Google claims that its services depend on its R&D activities in California, while Amazon claims that the technology, infrastructure and organisation residing in Luxembourg is what matters in the delivery of its products, rather than the warehouses in the UK that are argued to function primarily as distribution centres (PAC, 2012).

In response to such tax arrangements, Starbucks, Google and Amazon were accused of employing aggressive tax avoidance measures by the British Parliament in 2012. The PAC pointed out that Amazon employed just 134 staff in Luxembourg compared with 2,266 in the UK, generating an estimated £122.8 million profit in the UK in 2010 compared with just £2.2 million in Luxembourg. Despite this, it chose to pay its liabilities in low-tax Luxembourg and paid very little UK tax (PAC, 2012). Similarly, Starbucks managed to claim accounting losses in the UK while declaring huge profits in the United States. The PAC found that the company had paid no corporation tax at all in 14 of the 15 years the company had been trading in the UK. Similar data has been compiled by Rankin et al (2013), who argued that Amazon in 2013 earned £6 billion in sales in the UK yet paid only £517,000 in corporation tax, while in that same year, Google paid £11.6 million in UK corporation tax on UK revenues of £3.4 billion: £770 million less than it would have paid if it had paid tax at the full rate of 23 per cent in 2013.

As already noted, Starbucks responded by promising to contribute more in corporation tax. Operating as an oligopoly, Google felt no such pressure. In an interview for *The Guardian* newspaper, Eric Schmidt, then CEO of Google, responded to criticisms of Google's record on tax: 'I am very proud of the structure that we set up. We did it based on the incentives that the governments offered us to operate ... It's called capitalism. We are proudly capitalistic. I'm not confused about this' (Syal and Bowers, 2013). Similarly, in responding to the findings of the PAC, Matt Brittin, International Head of Business and Operations for Google, denied that Google had done anything wrong:

> [W]e make choices about where we locate and how we set up our structure, in order to ensure we can operate successfully and to minimise the costs and do the efficient things to run our business. That is what we are required to do by shareholders and by law, and that is what we do: play by the rules and manage our business efficiently. (PAC, 2012, question 578)

What Brittin is essentially saying here is that tax policies that ostensibly favour 'corporations' in fact favour people. This is an obvious point, but it is often lost in the discourse about 'corporations' or 'businesses'. The ultimate recipients of tax benefits extracted by businesses are rich and powerful businesspeople. While in the past, governments would seek to protect tax revenues by reducing corporate mobility through protectionist measures, international investment rules have shut such options down (Farnsworth, 2012). This has resulted in growing pressure on governments to exploit opportunities for tax competition to their own advantage by seeking to use corporate tax as a lure for new investors. In the case of Ireland, it has secured investment from the likes of Google by introducing the lowest rate of corporation tax in the OECD.

The OECD has responded to such pressures by establishing country-by-country tax reporting (which is designed to force corporations to disclose income, profits and taxation paid) and by laying down a minimum corporation tax rate of 15 per cent, which is designed to act as a floor to reduce the pressure of tax competition. While on the face of it such initiatives should prevent corporations from dodging tax and nations from competing aggressively with each other on corporation tax, both proposals are likely to prove to be less successful than many hope. To begin with, the treatment of subsidiaries remains a disputed area, thus failing to crack down on transfer pricing, and the floor, at 15 per cent, is actually lower than most corporation tax rates within developed economies (only Ireland falls below this). Second, governments will be able to compete in other ways, for instance by broadening the tax base. Tax allowances can be increased, taking more activities outside tax, as can tax expenditures, and international agreements will do nothing to reduce self-imposed pressures to compete vigorously with other governments over taxation policy. Not all countries compete in the same way, of course, and fewer countries have gone further than the UK in exploiting such mechanisms to induce corporate investment within its shores. Such issues are discussed in the following two sections.

From corporate tax to corporate welfare

Such pressures have meant that domestic corporate tax systems have become part of the corporate welfare system – where governments use taxation and tax-benefits to divert resources to private businesses (see Farnsworth, 2012). Two key ways in which governments use corporate welfare to induce investment are captured in the previous section: redistribution of the tax share away from businesses, and complicity in tax avoidance. This section deals with a third strategy, which is to target tax benefits on businesses.

Tax benefits – made up of various tax allowances and tax expenditures – increase the opportunities for tax avoidance and help to expand the gap between statutory and effective tax rates. As already noted, business is a powerful advocate of its own interests on taxation, and larger businesses are likely to extract greater benefits than smaller businesses. In a process that Hacker (2011, p 2) refers to as 'pre-distribution', such mechanisms not only ensure that the relative tax 'burden' is distributed unevenly but government revenues upon which public and social policies are built are lost before decisions on expenditure and priorities are made (Sinfield, 2012). Moreover, it also undermines the ability of citizens within democracies to mandate social change, redistribution and the expansion of collectively financed public goods (Sikka and Willmott, 2013).

The tax benefits offered to businesses in the late 2000s were annually worth around 1.5 per cent of GDP in the UK and around 4.5 per cent in the United States (OECD, 2010). The schemes offered by governments can contribute massively to profits. Companies can write off capital investment against tax and make use of 'accelerated depreciation' schemes, which typically allow the company to write off their entire investment in the first few years, much more quickly than the actual time taken for the asset to wear out (McIntyre and Gardner, 2014). The scope of tax breaks also tends to be widely drawn. Thus, while governments compete on headline rates of corporate taxation, an elaborate system of tax breaks when combined with tax avoidance results in tax rates that are far lower than statutory rates. In the UK, a Trade Union Congress-commissioned report in 2008 found that the 700 largest corporations in the UK had an effective tax rate of 7.5 per cent, a fraction of the statutory rate of 30 per cent at the time (Murphy, 2008).

Investigations by the NAO in 2020 document clearly how corporate tax benefits have dramatically increased in value, and that estimates of tax benefits (primarily in tax forsaken) tend to underestimate their true cost. Perhaps most surprisingly, when set against the backdrop of austerity, the NAO noted that the cost of tax benefits was 'poorly understood' by HMRC, and auditing measures were inadequate (NAO, 2020, p 36). Notwithstanding this, tax expenditures – where the government opts not to collect tax in the pursuit of social or economic goals – were estimated to be worth around £155 billion per year by the NAO. This is more than the total budget of the National Health Service. Moreover, many of the tax expenditures featured in the NAO report, which were also some of the most costly, were targeted at businesses. A number of examples illustrate both the high costs of certain forms of tax provision and raise serious questions of their wider benefits to society as a whole. Entrepreneurs' Relief, for instance, is paid to a relatively small number of business owners who can dispose of businesses to avoid capital gains tax. The annual cost of this form of tax relief has expanded much faster than expected. By 2017, such relief was worth £4.2 billion, falling back to £2.2 billion by 2018–19 (NAO, 2020, p 34). R&D tax credits, meanwhile, are considered to represent 'dead-weight' costs in that they make little or no difference to the level of R&D expenditure within firms. Questions have been raised about the value of such reliefs for taxpayers. The IPPR estimated that 80 per cent of the costs of R&D tax credits, or £3 billion in 2017, are dead-weight costs (Cox and Schmuecker, 2010). According to the NAO, if we ignore evidence of the systematic abuse of tax allowances by businesses and the well-off (NAO, 2014), savings from ending R&D tax credits and Entrepreneurs' Relief could more than pay for unemployment benefits. Considered another way, if the UK government raised the equivalent amount from corporation tax, employers' NICs and payroll taxes as France, it would be worth the equivalent of 6 per cent of GDP, or some £90 billion (though the exact amount would vary according to other intended and unintended behavioural effects).

Meanwhile, Film Tax Relief, widely abused as a tax avoidance vehicle (PAC, 2013), cost over £550 million in 2020; reliefs for patents, targeted primarily at TNCs was worth £1.15 billion; and R&D reliefs aimed at small businesses (and provided in addition to R&D tax credits that are primarily claimed by larger businesses) were worth some £2.3 billion (NAO, 2020, p 34). On top of all this are tax policies and initiatives that incentivise corporations and their staff to undermine the public good. As Adair Turner points out, the tax system and the various loopholes within it incentivised 'socially' and 'economically useless' trades that led to the economic crisis of 2008 (cited in Sinfield, 2012). These billions that are aimed at private businesses stack up considerably, especially when compared with benefits that are targeted at the much maligned unemployed. The cost of the main UK unemployment benefits (jobseekers' allowance, income support and universal credit) in 2017–18, for instance, was £7.5 billion (OBR, 2017).

Competing for capital through the tax system

The tax system that has emerged in the UK did not do so by accident. It is corporate-focused. The evidence for this can be found in the data, but it can also be located in its core principles and design, expressed in the way that government seeks to sell their tax systems to TNCs. Most governments pursue TNCs with inducements to invest within their borders.

The UK was one of the pioneers of aggressively pursuing international capital through tax inducements offered over the past 30 years or so. In the early 1990s, for instance, the UK government placed an ad in the German industrial press to persuade companies to divest from high-cost Germany to low-cost Britain. By 2004, the UK was proudly advertising its generous tax allowances alongside 'the lowest main corporation tax rate of any major industrialised country' with 'no additional local taxes on profits'. Ten years later, it was actively selling itself as an attractive environment for company headquarters or holding companies. This is exactly the kind of national strategy that was being so heavily criticised by the OECD at the time because it encouraged TNCs to declare taxes in low-taxing regimes. Undeterred, the UK stated that its 'competitive tax regime' and 'business-friendly environment' made it 'the ideal location for your European Headquarters project'. The UK government stated in 2013 that

> [t]he country is now a highly attractive location for a headquarters or holding company. It offers an attractive corporation tax rate, combined with dividend and capital gains exemptions. The UK is unusual in not having an outbound dividend withholding tax and, under the country's wide treaty network, withholding taxes on interest and royalties are often reduced to zero. HM Revenue & Customs (HMRC) can support taxpayers in agreeing Advance Pricing Agreements (APAs) with other fiscal authorities for complex transfer pricing issues, or in agreeing them unilaterally with HMRC. (UKTI, 2013, p 12)

A major problem with this strategy is that it not only sets countries up in a race-to-the-bottom on corporation taxes that apply to TNCs but it also risks locking nations into a particular set of tax policies and programmes that they cannot escape. When low taxes for TNCs are a fundamental part of a nation's investment strategy, it is very difficult to reverse.

Further evidence of how the selling of a nation's low-tax credentials to transnational corporations is illustrated in the UK's 2014 'Invest in the UK: Your Springboard for Global Growth' brochures:

> We are committed to creating the most competitive tax regime in the G20. The UK's corporation tax rate will be 20 per cent in 2015 – the

lowest in the G7 and joint lowest in the G20 ... Our overall tax burden is well below countries such as Germany, France, the Netherlands, Belgium, Sweden, Denmark and Italy, as well as below the average for the EU as a whole (Eurostat, 2011). Employers pay less social security contributions in the UK than in most other European countries. (UKTI, 2014, p 2)

Even for companies that pay no tax, the UK also offers generous tax benefits to support R&D:

For large companies, the existing 'super-deduction' regime provides an overall 130 per cent tax deduction for qualifying R&D expenditure ... UK-based companies [also] benefit from a reduced 10 per cent corporation tax rate on patented inventions: one of the strongest offers of its kind in Europe. The regime is flexible and generous and makes the UK a great place to invest in innovation. (UKTI, 2013, p 13)

Brexit (the UK withdrawal from the European Union) presented a challenge to the UK's method of competing for capital since it robbed the country of one of its major 'benefits' to investors: free and unhindered access to EU markets at relatively low cost to businesses. The UK's post-Brexit pitch continues to emphasise the fact that the UK offers 'one of the lowest corporation tax rates in the G20'. In the context of discussions of the ambiguity surrounding tax benefits, the promise of 'a range of tax reliefs to give flexibility to domestic and international companies' looks like it is pushing the UK still harder in the direction of lowest-common-denominator competition. The decision taken in 2020 to expand freeports (Webb and Jozepa, 2022) and provide an even greater range of tax reliefs gives a clearer glimpse into a post-Brexit tax regime that is likely to continue to favour business if for no other reason than to compensate TNCs for the loss of access to EU markets. Ultimately, of course, the UK will continue to depend on private investment, and low taxation is likely to play an important part of government strategies to induce businesses to invest in future. This is likely to further accelerate the UK towards a corporate welfare state, where corporations become more dependent on low taxation and high benefits. Even if corporate taxes increase, corporations have been induced to invest in the UK by promises of low-cost production, which is unlikely to contribute much to the welfare and wellbeing of citizens, especially as the strongest signal is for austerity to prevail into the 2020s. The alternative would be to transform the basis of UK competition policy by investing in policies designed to boost productivity, innovation and move towards more sustainable growth.

Tax avoidance and tax evasion

The discussion in the previous sections illustrates that businesses constantly challenge the clear intention of tax law, if not the letter of tax law. Tax loopholes and tax avoidance measures are not necessarily illegal, although they are anathema to collective welfare and can be incredibly expensive and harmful. Unlike avoidance, evasion is illegal, although the distinction between the two is often unclear. As already noted, the major accountancy firms use various measures to test tax law and, even when they cross the line, can often negotiate away their transgressions. However, the gains from testing tax laws are so lucrative that a whole 'tax avoidance' industry has sprung up. The rewards are so great that it makes the risks, including fines and prison sentences, worthwhile (Sikka and Willmott, 2013). Reports such as the Panama and Paradise Papers have revealed the lengths to which corporations and other political and financial elites hide their vast fortunes, often using complex and bogus ownership structures within tax havens, paying no tax at all and costing governments (and ordinary citizens) billions of dollars in lost revenues (International Consortium of Investigative Journalists, 2019).

Conclusion

This chapter has illustrated how power plays out within capitalist systems to encourage governments to use the tax system to favour corporate interests. The picture that emerges is one where powerful corporations, and the senior executives that run them, set up a unique relationship between taxpayer and tax-collector. Lobbying activities undoubtedly play a part in driving down headline rates of taxation, but even without this, the government goes out of its way to parade its tax-friendly investment environment in order to attract new investors to their shores. Once here, corporations enjoy various tax breaks, used partially to encourage 'positive' corporate behaviour but also to meet the 'needs' of businesses as defined by powerful business interests themselves. Even this is not enough, because the tax avoidance industry constantly challenges tax rules through ever more complex vehicles in order to maximise returns.

Governments and international governmental organisations such as the OECD are aware of the problems, but official inquiries and high-profile leaks continue to expose the limitations in practice and the paucity of available data relating to the cost of tax avoidance and even on the value of tax benefits provided to businesses. This has important implications for social policy since reducing the tax shares imposed on businesses means increasing the taxes on citizens, and lower-income citizens at that. Governments that compete aggressively on corporate taxes are also likely to compete in related ways on regulations or pay. The risk is that such policies create difficult-to-reverse competition regimes that incentivise predatory corporate behaviour and undermine progressive social policies. The risk is greater still in the UK in the face of its post-Brexit environment. The UK has failed to break with its policy of seeking new investment based on its low-tax, low-cost policy promise to TNCs and has instead sought to go even further down this route with its policy to set up freeports with reduced regulations and targeted tax breaks. The fiscal environment, coupled with pro-corporate public policies, is likely to continue to favour and empower the rich and wealthy while undermining the welfare and wellbeing of non-business citizens. Lost revenues, hidden wealth and growing inequality are products of the current tax system, and the effects on welfare states have been, and continue to be, devastating.

Further reading
- HC 716. Oral evidence. London: HMRC.
- PAC (2012) – this report provides a rare glance at corporate tax avoidance with evidence from three of the largest transnational corporations and how it is undertaken.
- Public Accounts Committee, Session 2012–2013. Minutes of Evidence.
- Shaxson (2011) – good insights into the operation of tax havens.
- Swank (1998) – a really useful theoretical understanding of the way in which TNCs influence corporate tax systems.

References
Baker, R.W. (2005) *Capitalism's Achilles Heel*, Hoboken, NJ: John Wiley.

Cameron, D. (2013) '£80 million start-up loans for new businesses', London: Prime Minister's Office.

Cox, E. and Schmuecker, K. (2010) 'Well north of fair: the implications of the Spending Review for the North of England', London: IPPR.

Farnsworth, K. (2012) *Social versus Corporate Welfare: Competing Needs and Interests within the Welfare State*, London: Palgrave.

Hacker, J.S. (2011) 'The institutional foundations of middle-class democracy', Policy Network, pp 33–7.

HM Treasury (2022) 'Corporation tax rise cancellation: factsheet', London: HM Treasury.

HMRC (2009) 'Measuring tax gaps', London: HMRC.

HMRC (2022) 'Measuring tax gaps 2021 edition: tax gap estimates for 2019 to 2020', Updated 8 February 2022, London: HMRC.

International Consortium of Investigative Journalists (2019) 'Offshore leaks database', https://offshoreleaks.icij.org

Johnson, S. and Marriage, M. (2015) 'The $82bn listed-company tax gap', *Financial Times*, 12 April.

King, J. (2013) 'Speech', in R. Murphy (ed), 'Tax-research blog', Available from: http://www.taxresearch.org.uk/Blog/2013/01/10/sainsburys-boss-says-its-time-to-take-action-on-tax-avoidance

McIntyre, R.S., Gardner, M. and Phillips, R. (2014) 'The sorry state of corporate taxes: What Fortune 500 firms pay (or don't pay) in the USA and what they pay abroad – 2008 to 2012'. https://www.ctj.org/wp-content/uploads/2017/11/sorrystateofcorptaxes.pdf

Murphy, R. (2008) 'The missing billions: the UK tax gap', London: TUC.

NAO (2007) 'Management of large business Corporation Tax', Report by the Comptroller and Auditor General. 614, Session 2006–2007, London: House of Commons.

NAO (2014) 'Tax avoidance: tackling marketed avoidance schemes', 29th report of session 2012–13, London: House of Commons.

NAO (2020) 'The management of tax expenditures', London: National Audit Office.

Neville, S. and Treanor, J. (2012) 'Starbucks to pay £20m in tax over next two years after customer revolt', *The Guardian*, 6 December.

OBR (2017) *Universal Credit and the Legacy Benefits in 2017–18*, London: Office for Budgetary Responsibility

OECD (2010) *Tax Expenditures in OECD Countries*, Paris: OECD.

OECD (2013) 'Addressing base erosion and profit shifting', Paris: OECD.

PAC (2011) 'HM Revenue & Customs 2010–11 accounts: tax disputes', PAC, 61st report, London: HMRC.

PAC (2012) 'Press release at the launch of the 2011–12 Public Accounts Committee investigation into tax avoidance', HM Revenue & Customs: Annual Report and Accounts 2011–12, 19th report of session 2012–13, London: HMRC.

PAC (2013) 'Tax avoidance: the role of large accountancy firms', 44th report, 15 April, London: House of Commons.

Public Accounts Committee, Session 2012–2013 investigation into corporate tax avoidance. Minutes of Evidence. HC 716. Oral evidence.

Rankin, J., O'Carroll, L. and Monaghan, A. (2013) 'Google paid £11.6m in UK corporation tax last year', *The Guardian*, 30 September.

Rincke, J. and Overesch, M. (2011) 'What drives corporate tax rates down? A reassessment of globalization, tax competition, and dynamic adjustment to shocks', *Scandinavian Journal of Economics*, 113(3): 579–602.

Shaxson, N. (2011) *Treasure Islands: Tax Havens and the Men Who Stole the World*, London: Vintage.

Sikka, P. and Willmott, H. (2013) 'The tax avoidance industry: accountancy firms on the make', Essex: Centre for Global Accountability, University of Essex.

Sinfield, A. (2011) 'Credit crunch, inequality and social policy', in K. Farnsworth and Z. Irving (eds) *Social Policy in Challenging Times*, Bristol: Policy Press.

Sinfield, A. (2012) 'On "Bringing corporate welfare in": a reply to Farnsworth', *Journal of Social Policy*, 42(1): 31–8.

Swank, D. (1998) 'Funding the welfare state: globalization and the taxation of business in advanced market economies', *Political Studies*, 46(4): 671–92.

Syal, R. and Bowers, S. (2013) 'Cameron refuses to say if he will quiz Google boss Eric Schmidt over tax', *The Guardian*, 20 May.

UKTI (2013) 'A guide to UK taxation', London: UK Trade and Investment, HMRC.

UKTI (2014) 'Invest in the UK: your springboard for global growth', London: UK Trade and Investment.

Webb, D. and Jozepa, I. (2022) 'Government policy on freeports', London: House of Commons Library.

14

The climate crisis and taxation

Paul Bridgen and Milena Büchs

Introduction

In 2019, the UK government became the first major economy to implement a legally binding net zero target. By 2050, any greenhouse gas (GHG) emissions produced within the UK must be reduced as far as possible or offset (HM Government, 2021). Yet few believe the policy framework in place for meeting this ambitious target is sufficient. The Climate Change Committee, the UK government's formal independent advice panel, has called, for example, for stronger, faster action, highlighting a potentially increased role for taxation (CCC, 2019; see also NAO, 2021). The Johnson government's 'Net Zero Strategy' (HM Government, 2021) was non-committal.

There is a strong economic case for carbon or energy taxation as a means to reduce GHG emissions: environmental degradation is a negative externality justifying corrective fiscal actions by the state (Pigou, 1932), particularly if focused on the greatest polluters and/or those whose adaption costs are lowest (IFS, 2011). From a social policy perspective, however, because carbon taxes generally increase prices, they raise concerns about distributive implications whether levied on businesses or consumers. Most research suggests that where carbon taxation has been introduced, it is highly regressive (for example, Wier et al, 2005; Feng et al, 2010), and modelling generally reaches the same conclusion (for example, Timilsinas, 2018). This is generally because such taxes are flat rate and levied on goods/services with a low- or negative-income elasticity of demand, such as household staples, like domestic energy. The consumption of these staples does not change substantially as income falls, so they make up a larger proportion of household expenditure for poorer compared to richer households.

The UK does not currently have a specific carbon tax but has introduced incrementally over a long period a range of fiscal instruments on individuals and businesses that affect the cost/price of GHG emissions. Most were not established specifically to address environmental objectives, but their impact on price signals mean they affect the market for carbon with behavioural and distributive implications.

Very little is known about these implications, individually or as a whole. This chapter will focus on their distributive impact (on the taxes' environmental impact and the optimality of these taxes, see, for example, NAO, 2021). Such knowledge is crucial for two main reasons. First, knowledge about the distributive impact of actually existing environment-related taxation and associated mitigating benefits provides a crucial context for assessing the distributive impact of a more generalised carbon tax. Viewed in isolation, as has been seen, the latter has been adjudged clearly regressive. But might the continuing incremental development of the existing system over coming years be a more regressive option than a more general reform? Secondly, if as seems likely the UK takes an incremental path towards greater carbon taxation, it is crucial from a social policy perspective to understand which parts of existing arrangements are most progressive and where greater mitigating efforts are required most. For reasons of space, this chapter cannot consider these matters in depth, but it does provide evidence about existing arrangements on which such a venture can proceed.

To do this, the chapter begins by briefly detailing the incremental and halting rise of UK environment-related taxation, outlining the design, stated purpose and rationale of the various fiscal instruments introduced. The distributive impact of these instruments, individually and overall, is then assessed, with most shown as clearly regressive. The chapter finishes by discussing the implications of this assessment for current policy debates.

The development of UK environment-related taxation

The consideration by UK government of taxes with an explicit environmental purpose only began from the mid-1990s, much later than in many EU countries (Jordan et al, 2013). Before this date, while taxes were charged on some goods that had an environmental impact, particularly cars through fuel duty and the vehicle excise licence, they were primarily revenue-raising devices. Air passenger duty, introduced in 1993, and value added tax (VAT) on domestic fuel, introduced in 1994, fulfilled a similar purpose. Developments throughout have been characterised by a 'subterranean' (Hacker, 2002), opaque and reactive incrementalism, with little or no systematic or coordinated analysis of the broader environmental or distributive impact or purpose of these taxes (Hayes, 2006; Jordan, 2013).

Concerted consideration of taxes specifically designed to fulfil environmental objectives mainly began under New Labour. The preceding Conservative governments had briefly seemed ready to move taxation in an environmental direction. Following the 1989 publication of the influential Pearce Report, which made the case for tax rather than regulation to fulfil environmental objectives, Thatcher accepted the main arguments for climate change in a Royal Society speech in 1988 (Carter, 2006) and a Department of Environment white paper supported environmental taxation (Dresner et al, 2006). But enthusiasm proved transitory. A tax on leaded petrol and a landfill tax were introduced, but both were small scale, and the first was short-lived. New Labour's interest was stimulated by the rising international interest in climate change after the agreement of the Kyoto Protocol. In power, a wide-ranging review of the potential of environmental taxation targeting household and business environmental behaviour was undertaken by the Treasury (Sorrell, 1999).

However, ultimately, these deliberations resulted only in a Climate Change Levy (CCL), introduced in 2001, and an Aggregates Levy, introduced in 2002. In the same year, the UK set up an Emissions Trading System (ETS) as a prelude to joining the European Union ETS in 2005 (Dresner et al, 2006), and the Renewables Obligation Certificates (ROC) scheme was established to encourage the production of renewable energy. But the scope and scale of these initiatives were severely restricted. The incidence of the new taxes fell entirely on businesses, although not all were affected, with no new direct taxation on households. Instead, increased costs on households occurred indirectly, as businesses passed on at least some of their tax liabilities in prices. This was also the case for other initiatives that had an environmental purpose, such as Energy Saving Obligations (ESOs) introduced in 1992. In terms of new revenue raised, the new initiatives were tiny, amounting by 2019 to about 1.5 per cent of total UK taxes and social contributions (ONS, 2021a – the figure for 2019 is used over 2020 because of the distorting impact of the COVID-19 pandemic on the tax take during the latter year).

Labour's caution was due in part to the strong political reaction against the Conservatives' introduction of VAT on domestic fuel in 1994, which it had pegged at 5 per cent once in power. An even bigger backlash followed in 2000, when massive fuel protests by haulage companies forced the Blair government to abandon a fuel duty 'escalator', first introduced by the Conservatives in 1993.

Thus by 2021 taxation designed specifically to address environmental concerns was still very limited. Only four taxes could be so characterised (Table 14.1). In addition, two taxes – motor fuel duty and air passenger duty – came under the Office for National Statistics' (ONS) more inclusive definition of environmental taxation in that they imposed a duty on goods or services with an environmental impact (NAO, 2021). VAT on motor and domestic fuel and vehicle excise duty were similar in this respect but were not included in the ONS definition. Of these taxes, fuel duty was by far the largest in terms of revenue, providing more than 54 per cent of total revenue collected in environment-related taxation. In 2019, the revenue delivered by fuel duty amounted to 1.25 per cent of UK GDP, whereas no more than 0.3 per cent was collected from any of the other taxes. In the next section, fuller details are provided of the structure and design of these taxes.

Table 14.1: Explicit and implicit environment-related taxes in the UK: introduction date, incidence, administration and revenue implications, 2021

	Year of introduction	Administration	Government revenue, 2020, £ millions	Government revenue, 2020, as % of GDP
Explicit environmental taxes (business)				
Landfill tax	1996	HMRC	711	0.03
Climate Change Levy including Carbon Price Floor	2001	HMRC	2,091[1]	0.09
Aggregates Levy	2002	HMRC	363	0.02
Renewables obligation	2002	BEIS	6,251	0.28
Contracts for difference	2017	BEIS	2,042	0.09
UK ETS	2002	BEIS	1,356	0.06
Total			*8,705*	*0.39*
Implicit environmental taxes				
Fuel duty (households)	1928	HMRC	14,485[1]	0.65
Fuel duty (business)	1928	HMRC	13,310[1]	0.60
Vehicle excise duty (households)	1919	HM Treasury	5,026	0.23
Vehicle excise duty (business)	1919	HM Treasury	1,999	0.09
Vehicle registration tax (households and business)	1919	Driver and Vehicle Licensing Agency	157	0.01
VAT on vehicle fuel (households)	1972	HMRC	6,438[2]	0.29
VAT on vehicle fuel (business)	1972	HMRC	1,931[2]	0.09
VAT on domestic heating fuel	1994	HMRC	1,768[2]	0.08
VAT on business heating fuel	1994	HMRC	2,021[2]	0.09
Air passenger duty (households and business)	1994	HMRC	3,810[1]	0.17
Total			*50,945*	*2.30*

Note: [1] 2019 figures used due to distorting impact of the COVID-19 pandemic; [2] author's calculations.
Source: ONS environmental taxes in the United Kingdom 2021 for all other than VAT on domestic fuel and ESOs

UK environment-related taxation

Explicit environmental taxes

The Climate Change Levy

This tax was introduced in 2001 after close consultations with business by the then New Labour government, overseen by Lord Marshall (chairman of

British Airways) (Dresner et al, 2006). It is levied on business and public sector energy consumption and collected by energy suppliers, who are exempt. In 2019, it raised just over £2 billion for the UK Exchequer (Table 14.1). It is less a tax on carbon than a general price-based incentive for business to be more energy efficient (NAO, 2021). Electricity use, for example, is taxed at the same rate regardless of the mix of generation methods providers use (for example, gas, coal, nuclear power, renewable energy technologies), despite their very different carbon emissions.[1] Lower rates are charged on direct use of gas, solid fuel or liquefied petroleum gas (Seeley and Ares, 2016).

The CCL operates in conjunction with a system of negotiated Climate Change Agreements designed to protect the most intensive energy-users against any adverse effects of the levy on their competitiveness. In return for binding commitments to improve energy efficiency (Martin et al, 2009), these businesses can secure 80 per cent reductions in the levy. The impact of the CCL on business costs when it was introduced was also mitigated by a 0.3 per cent reduction on business National Insurance contributions (NICs). In addition, uprating decisions since this time have not always maintained the real value of the levy (IFS, 2011).

The ETS and Carbon Price Floor

The UK's carbon 'cap and trade' system opened in 2002 (Dresner et al, 2006). It was subsumed into the new EU ETS in 2005 (IFS, 2011) and then 're-nationalised' after Brexit in 2021. Throughout, the scheme has operated in fundamentally the same way. It has been targeted at energy suppliers and the most energy-intensive companies, often those with climate change agreements, with aviation included from 2012. These companies are subject to carbon emission caps, often initially based on historic emissions (Hirst and Keep, 2018). Allowances to emit up to this cap were in the first instance provided without charge, but increasingly they have been auctioned by government. This process raised just under £1.4 billion for the UK Exchequer in 2020 (Table 14.1). Companies can also secure allowances through trading on the carbon market (Hirst and Keep, 2018).

The aim of the scheme is to reduce emissions by imposing a price on carbon and gradually reducing emission caps. However, in most years the EU scheme has had excess allowances, meaning prices dropped to very low levels (IFS, 2011). The solution to low prices in the UK was the introduction of a Carbon Price Floor (CPF) in 2013 (Hirst and Keep, 2018). While the UK was under the EU ETS, this operated by topping up the EU-designated allowance prices to the CPF target. This was meant to rise annually but was frozen in 2014 and remained so to 2021. With the introduction of a post-Brexit scheme, an Auction Clearing Price on allowances has replaced the CPF (BEIS, 2022).

The Renewables Obligation Certificate and contracts for difference

The RO was introduced in 2002 and operated up to 2017. It made it compulsory for electricity suppliers to source an increasing proportion of their supply from renewables (Toke 2010). Suppliers proved they were doing so by purchasing ROCs from accredited generators. This supplemented the income generators received from the general sale of renewable electricity. Government revenue was generated by buy-out clauses that electricity suppliers could use if they did not meet their renewable target. This raised more than £6.2 billion in 2020. The money from these buy-outs was redistributed among those suppliers that did meet their target (Garton et al, 2016).

Since 2017, the scheme has been wound down, replaced by contracts for difference. This scheme provides eligible renewable generators with a guaranteed price for the electricity they sell, that is, they receive a top-up from the government if the market price falls below the guaranteed level but pay back the difference to the government if market prices are above the guaranteed level (BEIS, 2020b). The top-up and costs of operating the scheme are funded by a statutory levy on all UK-based licensed electricity suppliers (Supplier Obligation and Operational Costs Levy). This raised just over £2 billion for the UK Exchequer in 2020 (Table 14.1).

Other taxes

There are also two other, smaller-scale explicit environment-related taxes, the Landfill Tax and Aggregates Levy. The first was introduced in 1996 based on tonnage of waste (Dresner et al, 2006; CCC, 2019). The Aggregates Levy was introduced in 2002 based on tonnage of aggregates extracted (Seeley, 2016). Both taxes involve compensation to the employers affected using reductions in NICs. Combined, the two taxes contributed just over £1 billion to government revenue in 2020 (Table 14.1).

Implicit environmental taxes

Motor taxes

Tax on hydrocarbon oils, commonly known as fuel duty, is applied to all sales of hydrocarbon-based fuels such as petrol, diesel, biodiesel, biogas and liquefied petroleum gas. It is collected by fuel suppliers mainly before sale of fuel to vehicle owners.[2] There are different rates for different types of fuel.

Fuel duty was established at the start of the last century mainly as a revenue-raising device, and this remains its central purpose (NAO, 2021). Duty rises became more regular after the Conservatives' 1993 Budget, which increased duty by 10 per cent and introduced a 'fuel duty escalator' under which duty would rise annually by 3 per cent above inflation. By 1997, this had increased to 6 per cent above inflation. The impact of these increases went largely unnoticed up to 1999 because oil prices were falling, but when they started to rise in 2000, massive fuel protests, with large public and media support, meant government was reluctant to increase duty even in line with inflation up to 2008–9 (Dresner et al, 2006). Under the Conservative/Liberal Democrat Coalition in 2012, the fuel duty escalator was officially abolished. Duty has been frozen ever since up to 2022 (HMT, 2021). Nevertheless, it raised almost £28 billion for the UK Exchequer in 2019, more than £14 billion paid by households (Table 14.1). This dwarfed the amount raised by the other environment-related taxes.

Indeed, vehicle taxes in the UK are comparatively high, particularly compared with Europe (Zahedi and Cremades, 2012). Combined with the current 20 per cent rate of VAT, added to fuel costs since 1973, taxes overall account for around 72 per cent of motorists' fuel costs (ONS, 2016). Partly for this reason, tax reliefs have been introduced to reduce the cost of fuel for some users, particularly in business. Most significantly, these have applied to so-called 'red diesel', that is, diesel fuel used in off-road vehicles such as in construction, which amounted to £2.4 billion tax foregone in 2019 (OECD, 2022). This figure will decline from 2022 as the scope of the relief is reduced (HMRC, 2021a).

In addition, most vehicle owners pay vehicle excise duty. Introduced as a revenue-raising device in the 19th century, it was a flat rate levy up to 2001. It was then banded in relation to CO_2 emissions. In 2022, this banding operates using a progressively higher first-year charge for vehicles emitting more, with a standard flat rate levy thereafter. Non-emitting, electric cars are not taxed (HMRC, 2015) but this will end in 2025 (Nanji 2022). There are separate bands for heavy goods vehicles based on their size (gov.uk, 2021).

VAT on domestic fuel

There is no explicit UK tax on the consumption of domestic energy, and until 1994 it was excluded from VAT. In 1993, the then Conservative government's desire to levy the latter tax at the same 17.5 per cent rate applied at the time to most other purchases was strongly opposed (Dresner et al, 2006).[3] This focused on the tax's regressive impact and thus its implications for fuel poverty (Laurance and Myers, 1993). Government was forced to limit the tax to 8 per cent and increase compensatory support for poorer households (Waterhouse and Schoon, 1993). Labour reduced the tax to 5 per cent when elected in 1997. It has stayed at this rate ever since, though in the context of spiralling fuel prices in 2022 serious consideration has been given to a zero rating (for example, Cameron-Chileshe and Parker, 2022). In 2020, it raised nearly £1.8 billion in government revenue (Table 14.1).

Air passenger duty

Air passenger duty is the only UK tax on flying, although since 2012 aviation has been part of the ETS (Hirst and Keep, 2018). VAT is not levied. The duty only applies to flights that depart from UK airports (and hence not on return legs on flights from abroad). It operates on a per-person-per-flight basis and is banded in relation to the distance of the destination and the class of seat. Those travelling up to 2,000 miles from London pay less than those travelling more. Rates for higher grade tickets are greater, with those travelling in smaller aircraft, with fewer than 19 passengers, paying the most. In 2019, it raised just over £3.8 billion for the UK Exchequer (Table 14.1).

The tax was not introduced for environmental purposes but primarily to raise revenue, particularly given the zero VAT rating for UK flying (IFS, 2011; NAO, 2021). Governments have argued international action is more cost-effective for addressing aviation emissions, hence support for incorporating it in the ETS (HMT, 2005). Based on this argument, intermittent freezes in rates and consideration of cuts, particularly to domestic duty on domestic flights, have been justified, notwithstanding criticism from environmental lobby groups (BBC News, 2021).

Quasi-taxes

Energy Savings Obligations

ESOs are regulatory devices that involve an indirect state role and no direct, explicit increase in taxation, with costs met by private actors in market exchange (Rosenow, 2012). However, because they increase consumer bills they have been considered quasi-taxes (Owen, 2006). The obligations set time-specified regulator/government-directed targets on energy producers for the provision of 'energy benefits' (that is, improvements in domestic energy efficiency such as wall insulation). Energy producers meet installation costs but can and do pass them on in prices.

ESOs were initially small scale when first introduced in the early 1990s, never implying much more than a £1 per customer per year increase in bills (Owen, 2006). By the mid-noughties, however, re-packaged as Carbon Emission Reduction Targets, ESOs implied a fivefold increase in energy bills to £51 per customer per year (DEFRA, 2007; Rosenow, 2012). Protection for low-income ESO consumers has increasingly become more systematic, with energy companies obliged to target 'priority groups' for efficiency improvements (Powells, 2009). Under the Coalition and majority Conservative governments up to 2021, ESOs continued but in reduced form and targeted only on lower and vulnerable groups.

Tax relief

Operating alongside these environment-related taxes is a highly complex set of tax reliefs that also affect the cost/price of GHG emissions. Some of these reliefs, such as the CCL and fuel duty rebates mentioned earlier, are directly linked to environment-related taxation, but many others are not. Some are designed to encourage behaviour that will reduce emissions, such as capital allowances on the purchase of electric cars (NAO, 2021), but much more significant in terms of revenue foregone are tax reliefs likely to result in higher emissions. The most important are granted to fossil fuel producers, particularly the oil and gas industry. These amounted to almost £3 billion of tax foregone in 2019, 59 per cent of which was granted for capital expenditure to aid exploration and development of new fields (authors' calculations based on OECD, 2022). VAT exemptions also are not clearly aligned with the objective of reducing emissions. For example, the more resource-intensive process of building new houses is not liable to VAT, whereas less intensive house renovation is liable to 5 per cent (UK Government, 2020). The tax foregone in relation to the former was £14 billion in 2020–21 (HMRC, 2021b, section 7.25).

The distributive impact of UK environment-related taxation: data and methods

The main consequence of this incremental and unsystematic introduction of environmental-related taxes in the UK is that little concerted consideration has been given to their impact, particularly their distributive consequences. It is on this issue that the rest of this chapter will focus. In what follows, we assess the distributive impact on households of the taxes. We assess each tax individually, determining whether they are progressive, proportional or regressive, and then consider the overall impact of all UK environment-related taxes. Using ONS and UK Living Costs and Food (LCF) Survey data (ONS/DEFRA, 2020), we calculate the average rate of tax for each decile group. We focus on the impact of these taxes as a proportion of *disposable* equivalised household income. Where the average tax incidence relative to income is higher for those on higher incomes, the tax is progressive; where it is lower, the tax is regressive; where it is constant, the tax is proportional.

Our assessment of the impact of air passenger duty, fuel duty (households) and vehicle excise duty is based on ONS data. These data are derived from the LCF and the UK Survey on Living Conditions and provide information on the average amount paid by households by equivalised decile group and also the average disposable incomes by equivalised decile group. From this information, we calculated the average tax paid in relation to the average disposable income of each decile. Disposable income is the most suitable income variable[4] for our purpose because it details the money available to households (after income tax has been paid and state benefits received) for purchasing the goods and services, the prices of which are affected either directly or indirectly by the taxes discussed in this chapter. It thus also includes some benefits (for example, cold weather payments) that directly compensate to a certain extent lower-income households for the costs incurred from purchasing some of the affected good/services (for example, heating).

On VAT, the ONS only provides information on the total amount paid by households, not broken down in relation to the good and/or services on which it is levied. For this reason, we used LCF data directly to calculate this, using rates equivalent to 20 per cent of untaxed expenditure on motor fuel and 5 per cent on domestic electricity and gas. The LCF Survey is a voluntary, representative UK household survey designed to provide information on household income and expenditure representative of the UK population. Data are collected on income (including cash benefits received from the state), income and indirect tax payments, with imputations also included for the impact on household income of public services. Households are ranked by their equivalised disposable income and then broken down into decile groups. Income is equivalised to adjust for differences in household size using the modified-Organisation for Economic Co-operation and Development scale.

Information on the impact on households of quasi-taxes and environment-related taxation on businesses is more difficult to access. On the former, the amount paid by households varies annually depending on the cost of the schemes (for example, ESOs, the ROC, and contracts for difference, and so on) with no single or separate rate specified explicitly. We thus rely on the National Audit Office's estimation of the cost of climate-change policies on domestic fuel bills (2016; see also Owen and Barrett, 2020).[5] It calculated this to be 13 per cent of average household bills in 2016, although this also includes the cost of initiatives not considered in this chapter (for example, feed-in tariffs; NAO, 2016, p 16).[6] We used this figure to calculate distributive impact using LCF data, meaning our calculations slightly over-state the impact of the quasi-taxes covered in this chapter. On the impact of environment-related business taxes on households, even less information is available, meaning our calculations while plausible should be regarded as illustrative. We assumed, like the ONS (2021b), that the whole cost of these taxes is passed on in prices. Based on this assumption, we calculated the impact of total environment-related business taxes (Table 14.1) as a percentage of total household expenditure using ONS family spending data (2021). This gave us a figure of 3 per cent, which we applied to the LCF and ONS data to determine the distributive impact of the taxes.

As part of our analysis, we consider how the distributive impact of taxes relates to the income elasticity of demand for the good on which it is levied. As mentioned earlier, this concept refers to how demand changes as income rises or falls. For most goods/services, as income falls demand for a good also falls. However, for more necessary staple goods/services, demand can remain closer to constant. Since income elasticities for necessities tend to be lower, particularly for lower-income groups, and because lower-income groups spend a higher proportion of their income on necessities, the impact of flat-rate taxes on such goods is generally regressive.

We first consider the distributive impact on households of each environment-related tax. We then compare the distributive impact of each tax before considering their overall impact.

The distributive impact of explicit and implicit environment-related taxation on households

Table 14.2 summarises the results of our analysis of the distributive impact of UK environment-related taxes on households. We can see that most taxes are clearly regressive and all of them impact disproportionately on the income of the bottom decile group. The only exception with regard to regressivity is air passenger duty. The following sections consider each tax in more detail.

Motoring-related taxes

Figure 14.1 details the regressive impact for households in 2019/20 of the two main taxes on motoring – fuel duty and vehicle excise duty – and VAT on motor fuel. As a percentage of equivalised disposable income, the average paid in fuel duty and vehicle excise duty declined consistently from 4.73 per cent and 1.78 per cent respectively for the bottom decile groups to 0.82 per cent and 0.28 per cent for the top groups. Given these results, it is not surprising that VAT on motor fuel, another flat tax, is similarly regressive, with the average amount paid as a percentage of equivalised disposable income also declining consistently from 2.35 for the bottom decile group to 0.42 for the top group.

The significant and uniformly regressive impact of taxes on motoring in 2019/20 is despite data suggesting car ownership is income elastic. Thus ONS data for 2018 (the most recent year available) show that, while only 35 per cent of households in the bottom decile owned a vehicle, in the top four deciles more than 90 per cent owned cars, with 26 per cent of the top decile households owning three (ONS, 2019). Lower-income groups thus have less access to private transportation and emit less as a consequence but nevertheless pay more in motor taxes as a proportion of their income than richer groups.

Table 14.2: The distributive impact of explicit and implicit environment-related taxation on households by equivalised decile groups as percentage of equivalised disposable income, 2019–20

Equivalised decile group	Fuel duty	Vehicle excise duty	VAT motor fuel	VAT gas	VAT electricity	Air passenger duty	Quasi-taxes	Environment-related business tax	Total
1	4.73	1.78	2.35	0.46	0.48	0.46	2.40	0.13	12.80
2	3.34	0.93	1.40	0.25	0.27	0.31	1.31	0.09	7.88
3	2.90	0.88	1.17	0.21	0.22	0.28	1.08	0.08	6.82
4	2.59	0.87	1.02	0.18	0.18	0.19	0.92	0.07	6.04
5	2.42	0.73	0.93	0.15	0.16	0.29	0.78	0.07	5.53
6	2.45	0.71	0.87	0.13	0.14	0.23	0.68	0.07	5.28
7	2.35	0.61	0.79	0.12	0.12	0.28	0.61	0.07	4.94
8	2.30	0.61	0.75	0.10	0.10	0.25	0.52	0.06	4.69
9	1.78	0.48	0.69	0.09	0.09	0.30	0.45	0.06	3.94
10	0.82	0.28	0.42	0.07	0.06	0.23	0.33	0.05	2.27

Source: Our calculations using LCF and ONS data

Figure 14.1: Average motoring-related taxes paid by equivalised income deciles as a percentage of equivalised disposable income, 2019/20

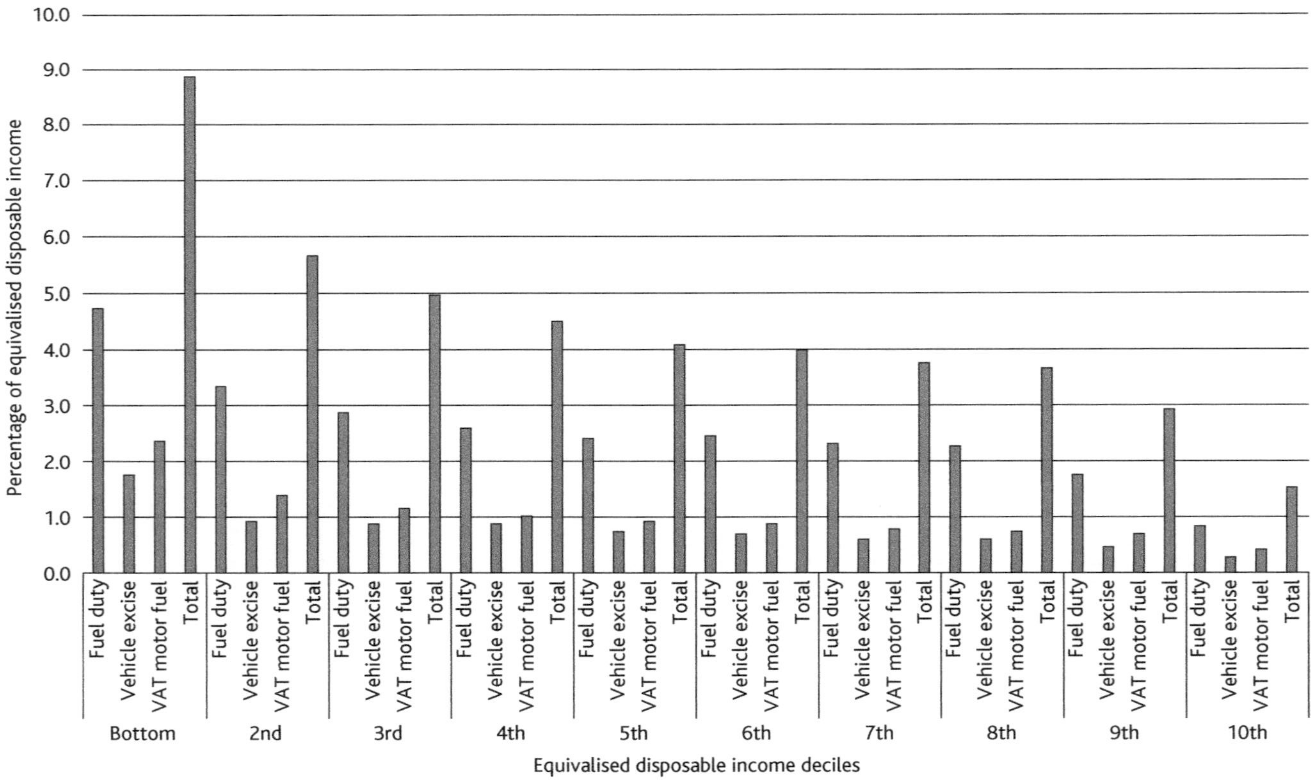

Source: Our calculations using ONS, 2021a and ONS/DEFRA, 2020

Results from previous research indicate distributional impacts are also likely to vary by gender. Men are more likely to own a car and drive than women and hence have significantly higher carbon emissions for motor fuels than women (Büchs et al, 2013, 2018). Men therefore bear higher burdens of motoring taxes than women (Büchs et al, 2021).

Domestic energy taxes

The overall impact on household income of VAT on domestic energy is lower than motor taxes for all income deciles, not rising in total to 1 per cent of equivalised disposable income for any decile groups (Figure 14.2). It would be higher if it operated at the same level of 20 per cent as other goods and services rather than the 5 per cent level set in 1997.

Nevertheless, the tax is clearly regressive. For both gas and electricity, the average amount paid as a percentage of equivalised disposable income declines consistently from close to 0.5 for both fuel types for the bottom decile to 0.07 and 0.06 respectively for the top income decile.

The regressive impact of VAT on domestic fuel is the product of levying a flat purchase tax on a good that has low-income inelasticity, particularly for lower-income groups. Thus, as can been seen in Figure 14.3, the most recent data suggest the amount of domestic fuel used and the amount spent on it varies very little across the income deciles, particularly between the first and eighth decile groups. As a consequence, lower-income groups spend a much higher proportion of their household income on this good.

Requirements for domestic energy also differ by gender. Previous research has shown that female-headed households (especially older single female households) use significantly more electricity and gas in the home than male-headed households (Büchs et al, 2013, 2018). Taxes on home energy therefore put significantly higher burdens on female-headed households than on male-headed households (Büchs et al, 2021).

Air passenger duty

Of the taxes paid directly by households, air passenger duty is the one that impacts least on household income, never rising above 0.5 per cent of equivalised disposable income for any decile group (Figure 14.4). It is also the least regressive. A significant gap is still evident between the bottom and top decile, and the bottom decile again pays markedly more than any other decile. But unlike the other taxes paid directly by households, the top decile group is not the one paying proportionately the least air passenger duty; both the fourth and sixth decile pay less.

The main reason the overall impact of air passenger duty on households is fairly proportional is that flying is highly income elastic, particularly towards

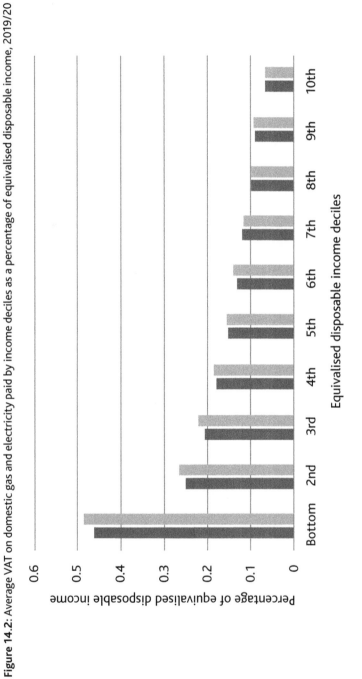

Figure 14.2: Average VAT on domestic gas and electricity paid by income deciles as a percentage of equivalised disposable income, 2019/20

Source: Our calculations using ONS/DEFRA, 2020

Figure 14.3: Gas and electricity expenditure and usage by equivalised income decile, 2019–20

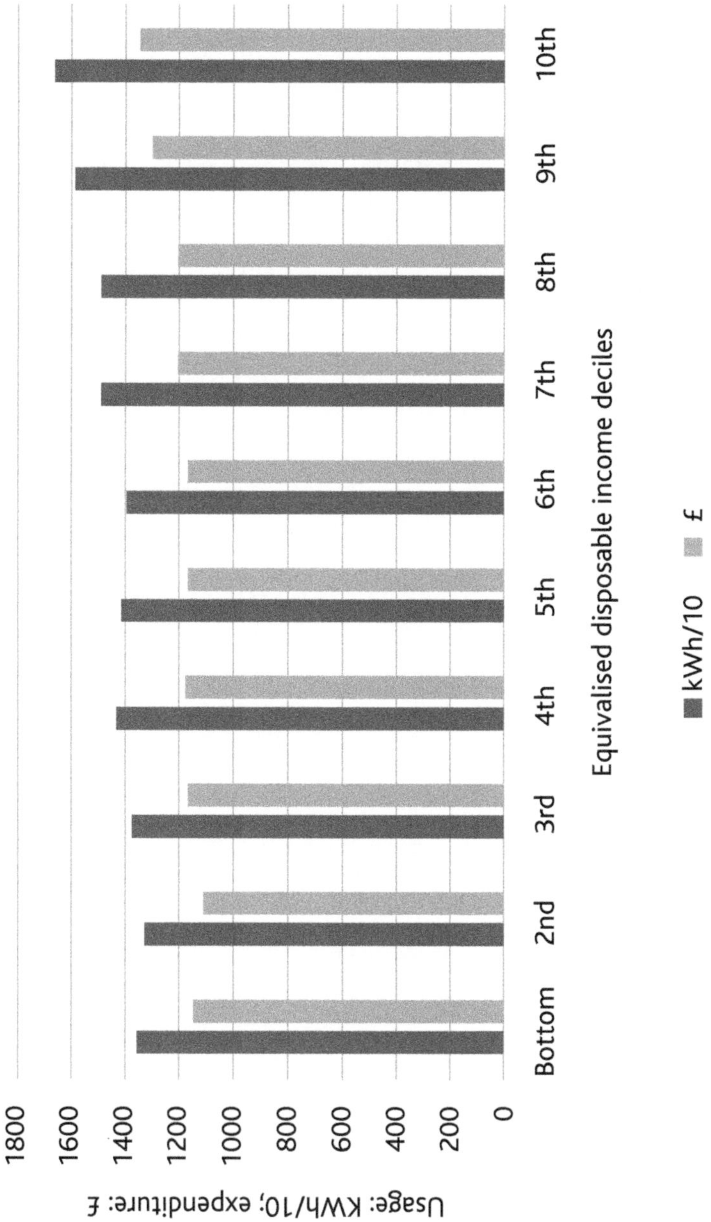

Source: Our calculations using ONS/DEFRA, 2020

Figure 14.4: Average air passenger duty paid by equivalised income decile as a percentage of equivalised disposable income, 2019/20

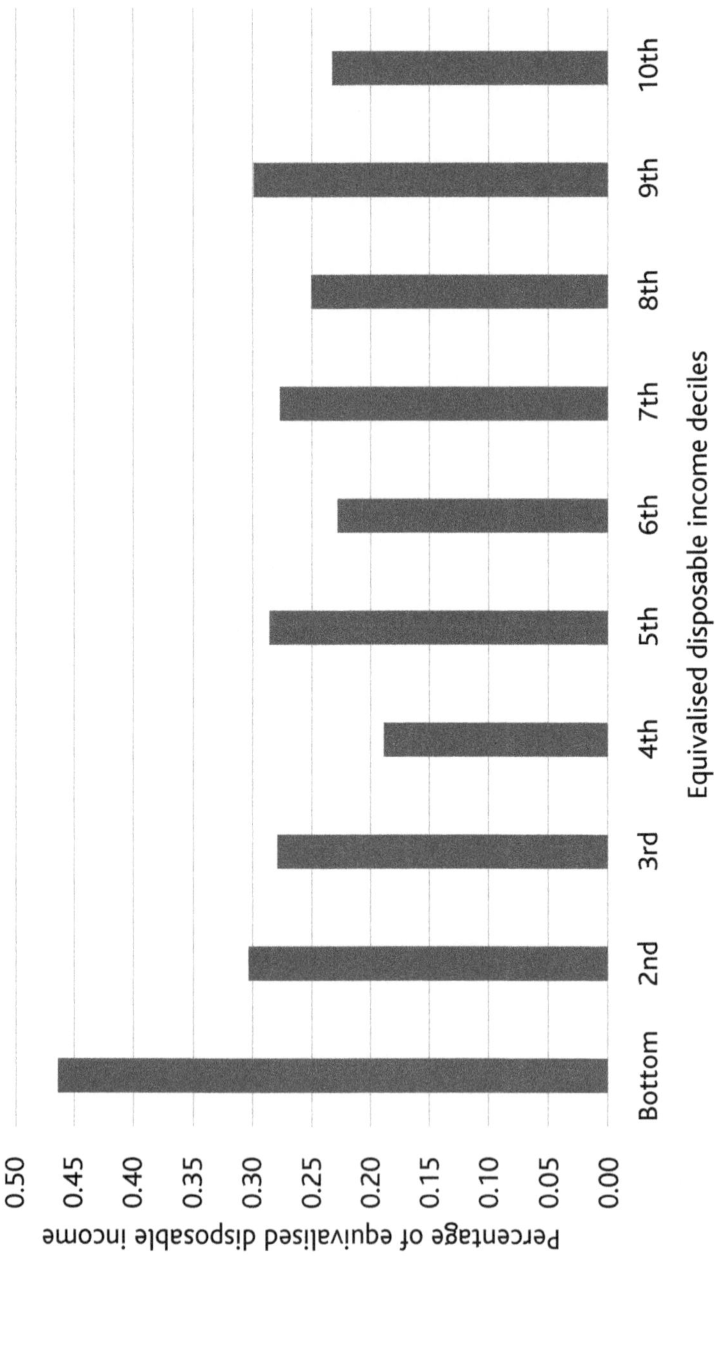

Source: Our calculations using ONS, 2021a

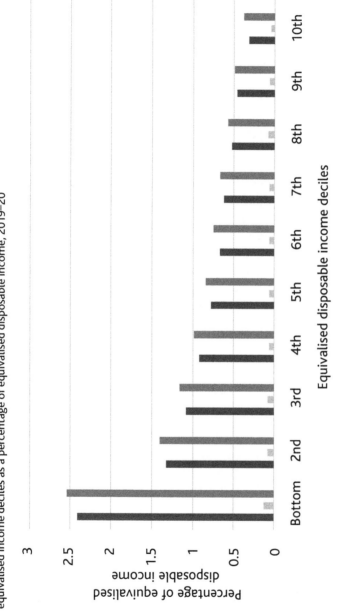

Figure 14.5: Impact of low-carbon energy policy quasi-taxes and environment-related business taxes on households by equivalised income deciles as a percentage of equivalised disposable income, 2019–20

Source: Our calculations using ONS/DEFRA, 2020

the top end of the income distribution (Büchs and Mattioli, 2021). Over time, the percentage of those in the lower-income groups participating in flying has increased significantly (from 15 per cent in 2001–3 to 23 per cent in 2016–18), such that in relative terms they have contributed more to the general increase in flying. However, in absolute terms increased air travel by the higher-income groups is the main reason for the overall increase in flying during this period. The impacts of taxes on air travel also vary by gender. Women are less likely to fly, and take part in fewer flights, than men (Büchs and Mattioli, 2021). Men therefore bear higher burdens from taxes on air travel than women.

Quasi-taxes and impact of environment-related business taxes on households

The overall impact on household income of quasi-taxation, the cost of low carbon policies paid through energy bills, is greater than the impact of VAT on these bills (see Figure 14.5). Thus, whereas the combined average impact of VAT on electricity and gas bills never amounts to more than 0.93 per cent of household income (that is, for the lowest decile), the equivalent figure for the average impact of low carbon policies is 2.4 per cent, also for the lowest decile. The average amount paid as a percentage of equivalised disposable income declines consistently from the 2.4 per cent paid by the bottom decile to 0.33 per cent paid by the top income decile. This quasi-taxation is thus clearly regressive.

Figure 14.5 also shows the result of our illustrative calculation of the impact of environment-related business taxes (for example, the CCL, the ETS and so on) on households. This shows this impact is much smaller than quasi-taxes, given the relatively small amounts collected in these taxes as a proportion of government revenue (see Table 14.1). The large majority of households do not pay more than 0.1 per cent of their income to cover these business-related taxes, assuming their cost is directly passed on in prices. Nevertheless, their impact is clearly regressive.

Overall distributive impact of UK environment-related taxes on households

In this section, we compare the distributive impact of the different environment-related taxes on UK households and assess the aggregate effect of these taxes. In Figure 14.6, the distributive impact of the taxes is compared. For each tax, the tax incidence for the lowest-income decile is expressed as a multiple of the tax incidence for the highest decile. The higher this figure, the more regressive the tax. It is clear the most regressive taxes are those on domestic power, with VAT on electricity slightly more

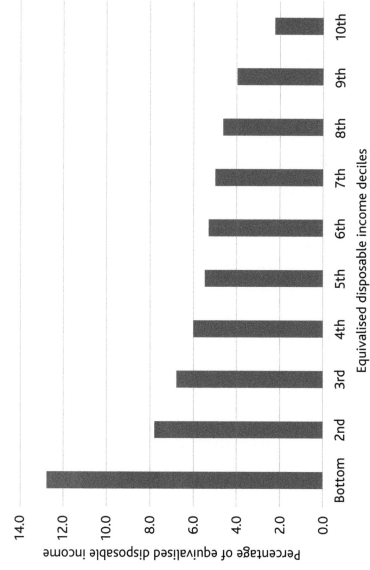

Figure 14.6: Overall distributive impact of environment-related taxation on households by equivalised deciles group as a percentage of equivalised disposable income, 2019–20

Equivalised disposable income deciles

Percentage of equivalised disposable income

Source: Our calculations based on ONS, 2021a and ONS/DEFRA, 2020

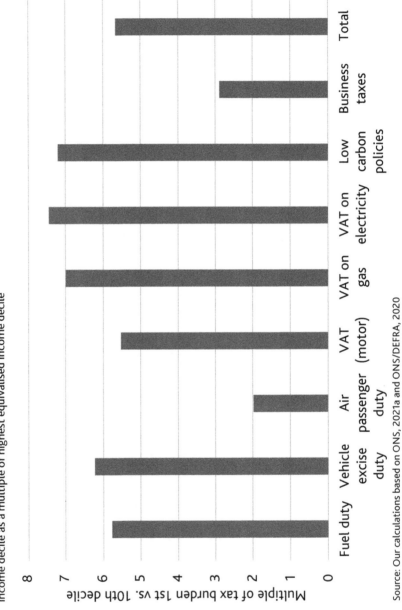

Figure 14.7: The incidence of environment-related taxation on the disposable equivalised income of the lowest equivalised income decile as a multiple of highest equivalised income decile

Source: Our calculations based on ONS, 2021a and ONS/DEFRA, 2020

regressive than VAT on gas. Motoring taxes are slightly less regressive, with air passenger duty the least regressive tax.

This figure also shows that in total the lowest decile households pay in excess of five times more in environment-related taxes as a proportion of their income than the highest decile. Figure 14.7 emphasises the particular incidence of environment-related taxes on the lowest decile. It shows that the gap between the lowest decile household and the next decile group is the highest between any neighbouring deciles. Thus, while environment-related taxation is clearly regressive at every point along the income scale, the burden on the poorest is disproportionately the greatest. In absolute terms, motoring taxes bear most heavily on this group. These account in total for more than 9 per cent (see Figure 14.1) of the equivalised disposable income of the bottom decile compared to domestic fuel taxes, which account for less than 1 per cent (see Figure 14.3).

Conclusion

Debates about the future development of environment-related taxes in the UK, particularly possible moves towards increased carbon taxation, have focused on the regressive impact of a carbon tax, generally considered in isolation. What this chapter emphasises is that carbon taxation already exists in the UK, but that its development has been characterised by the worst aspects of incrementalism: it has emerged unplanned and uncoordinated with very little concerted analysis of its distributive impact or the adequacy of benefit payments that mitigate to a limited extent its impact.

The chapter has shown the existing UK approach to be clearly regressive. This is particularly the case for VAT on domestic fuel, a situation exacerbated by the strongly regressive impact of quasi-taxation for climate change policies paid for by increases in energy prices. Taxes on domestic energy also disproportionally burden single-female households, older people and people with disabilities or long-term health issues due to their higher energy requirements. Motoring taxes are also strongly regressive but slightly less so. Only tax on aviation is close to proportional. Taxes on travel tend to have higher impacts on men than on women, younger people and people in employment. The main reason for these differences in regressivity is the varying income inelasticities of demand for the goods on which the tax is levied. Efforts to mitigate this regressive impact have developed in an entirely haphazard fashion and, as the results in this chapter suggest, are wholly insufficient particularly with respect to the lowest-income decile households.

In such circumstances, in the face of a climate emergency, the question from a social policy perspective is less whether there should be carbon taxation than which is the best way of making it as progressive as possible. A continuation of the uncoordinated incrementalism that generated existing arrangements is in our view likely to make them even more regressive. On domestic fuel, for example, political sensitivities make it highly unlikely that VAT will be charged at the standard rate, notwithstanding repeated calls from some influential quarters (IFS, 2011; Preston et al, 2013). Indeed, as has been seen, in light of dramatically rising fuel prices in 2022, there have been calls for VAT to be lowered further (Cameron-Chileshe and Parker, 2022). These have been rejected in favour of short-term, one-off compensatory payments (Xu, 2022). This resistance to increasing VAT on fuel can be viewed as positive, given such a change, introduced by itself, would be highly regressive. However, a better option might be a fuller re-consideration of domestic energy taxation encompassing the development of fully worked through compensatory mechanisms to make it less regressive (see, for example, Büchs et al, 2021). At the least, such a process would involve a more transparent consideration of the funding and distributive issues underlying the government's Net Zero Strategy. At present, it is generally left to Conservative neoliberals to articulate such concerns, mainly it seems to resist *any* state-led action to mitigate climate change (Taylor and Horton, 2022).

A more encompassing approach would also create space for the consideration of more innovative, transformative means for protecting those on lower incomes. The provision of free green electricity at the level of basic needs, for example, has been shown to have greater potential for reducing fuel poverty than current arrangements because it reduces people's expenditure on necessities (Büchs et al, 2021). Other in-kind measures to support low-income households to save energy, for instance free home insulation, energy-efficient boilers or even solar panels and heat pumps, can also assist in cushioning regressive impacts of environmental taxes on necessities. They are also likely to have greater potential for emission reductions than recycling the revenue through equal per capita cash rebates because in-kind measures trigger greater demand for public and private investment in renewable energy (Büchs et al, 2021).

On motoring, policy makers are equally reluctant to confront head-on the fiscal implications of reducing GHG emissions. The current government's focus is on tax-supported electrification, which is largely uncontroversial. However, in the short to medium term this development will also increase the regressivity of environment-related taxation. This is because lower-income households generally hold on to older vehicles for longer and, when they do replace them, are put off purchasing tax-favoured electric cars by their greater cost (Tovar Reanos and Sommerfield, 2017; Hull, 2018). Increasingly, it will be these households who will be paying the bulk of motoring tax. This situation is particularly problematic given it is on motoring taxes, particularly fuel duty, that the lowest decile groups pay by far the most overall in environment-related taxation. This is an issue that is barely mentioned in public debates, and policy makers seem equally determined to avoid discussion of alternatives to existing road levies (for example, road pricing), required as electrification reduces revenues (HM Government, 2021). In this policy area too, therefore, a more encompassing evaluation of tax options might create space for consideration of a broader range of compensatory mechanisms, for example the provision of free public transport to the level of basic needs (Büchs et al, 2021).

Finally, lack of public awareness about the more proportional distributive consequences of aviation taxation assists those resistant to its extension. Discourses on the negative impact of higher aviation taxes on 'hard-working families' (Büchs and Mattioli, 2021) are frequently referred to by those resistant to such changes, leaving the highly unequal distribution of air travel emissions across income groups unchallenged. Meanwhile, the segregated and opaque nature of the UK's patchwork of environment-related taxation makes the progressive consequences of such a move harder to see. Yet, analysis shows that a range of approaches such as a flat-rate tax per tonne of CO2, frequent flyer levies or combinations of these approaches, all have progressive distributional impacts, especially if the first return flight is excluded (Büchs and Mattioli, 2021). Indeed, higher taxes on flying could be introduced as part of a more general shift involving increased levies on 'luxuries' to fund lower levies on necessities. Such an approach would have great potential to create a fairer environmental tax system and thus also increase public acceptance of such taxes.

In short, consideration of current environment-related taxes and their likely development over coming years provides a crucial and neglected context within which to assess the case for the role of taxation in the UK's Net Zero Strategy. Policy makers have hitherto largely avoided scrutiny of environment-related fiscal policy. A more broad-ranging and encompassing consideration of taxation's role would at least make more likely a fuller assessment of its distributive consequences, and the variety of possible mechanisms for mitigating regressive effects, as part of a more general strategic reform.

Notes

[1] Technically, each kWh of electricity consumed from the grid has the same carbon footprint regardless of provider because it is drawn from the current electricity mix in the grid, but it could be argued that customers of providers that only feed renewable electricity into the grid should be rewarded with a lower-tax rate.

[2] Fuel oil burned in a furnace or used for heating is also subject to the tax.

[3] It was also in line with EU policy.

[4] The others available are original, gross, post-tax and final income.

[5] We are very grateful to Anne Owen for her assistance with this calculation.

[6] In response to the 2022 energy crisis, the government decided to cover some of the cost of these 'green levies' for two years, meaning the impact of 'quasi-taxes' on households will likely be lower during this period (HM Treasury, 2022).

Further reading

- Büchs and Mattioli (2021) – develops the case for taxes on air travel as the most progressive reform option as part of a broader, strategic approach.
- Büchs et al (2021) – provides the most recent confirmation of the regressive distributional impacts of carbon taxes on home energy and motor fuels, considering 27 European countries.
- Preston et al (2013) – the most fully developed case for a fairer system of carbon taxation, though this is now rather dated.

References

BBC News (2020) 'Climate change campaigners attack aviation fuel duty proposal', 15 January, Available from: https://www.bbc.co.uk/news/business-51121455

BEIS (2022) 'UK Emissions Trading Scheme markets'. https://www.gov.uk/government/publications/uk-emissions-trading-scheme-markets/uk-emissions-trading-scheme-markets

Büchs, M. and Mattioli, G. (2021) 'Trends in air travel inequality in the UK: from the few to the many?', *Travel Behaviour and Society*, 25: 92–101.

Büchs, M. and Schnepf, S.V. (2013) 'Who emits most? Associations between socio-economic factors and UK households' home energy, transport, indirect and total CO2 emissions', *Ecological Economics*, 90: 114–23.

Büchs, M., Bahaj, A., Blunden, L., Bourikas, L., Falkingham, J. and James, P. et al (2018) 'Sick and stuck at home: how poor health increases electricity consumption and reduces opportunities for environmentally-friendly travel in the United Kingdom', *Energy Research and Social Science*, 44 : 250–9.

Büchs, M., Ivanova, D. and Schnepf, S.V. (2021) 'Fairness, effectiveness, and needs satisfaction: new options for designing climate policies', *Environmental Research Letters*, 16(12): 124026.

Cameron-Chileshe, J. and Parker, G. (2022) 'Sunak pledges to scrap CAT on household energy bills', *Financial Times*, 26 July.

Carter, N. (2006) 'Party politicization of the environment in Britain', *Party Politics*, 12(6): 747–67.

Committee on Climate Change (2019) 'Net zero: the UK's contribution to stopping global warming', London: Committee on Climate Change.

DEFRA (2007) 'Carbon emissions reduction target April 2008 to March 2011', Consultation proposals, London: DEFRA.

Department for Business, Energy and Industrial Strategy (2019) 'UK becomes first major economy to pass net zero emissions law', Available from: https://www.gov.uk/government/news/uk-becomes-first-major-economy-to-pass-net-zero-emissions-law

Department for Business, Energy and Industrial Strategy (2020a) 'The future of UK carbon pricing: impact assessment', Available from: https://assets.publishing.service.gov.uk/government/uploads/system/uploads/attachment_data/file/889038/The_future_of_UK_carbon_pricing_impact_assessment.pdf

Department for Business, Energy and Industrial Strategy (2020b) 'Powering our net zero future', London: OGL.

Dresner, S., Jackson, T. and Gilbert, N. (2006) 'History and social responses to environmental tax reform in the United Kingdom', *Energy Policy*, 34: 930–9.

Feng, K., Hubacek, K., Guan, D., Contestabile, M., Minx, J. and Barrett, J. (2010) 'Distributional effects of climate change taxation: the case of the UK', *Environmental Science and Technology*, 44(10): 3670–6.

Garton Grimwood, G. and Ares, E. (2016) 'Energy: the renewables obligation', House of Commons briefing paper 05870, Available from: https://researchbriefings.files.parliament.uk/documents/SN05870/SN05870.pdf

gov.uk (2021) 'Vehicle registration', Available from: https://www.gov.uk/vehicle-registration/new-registrations-fee

Hacker, J. (2002) *The Divided Welfare State: The Battle over Public and Private Benefits in the United States*, Cambridge: Cambridge University Press.

Hayes, M. (2006) *Incrementalism and Public Policy Making* (2nd edn), Lanham, MD: University Press of America.

Hirst, D. and Keep, M. (2018) 'Carbon price floor (CPF) and the price support mechanism', House of Commons briefing paper 05927, Available from: https://researchbriefings.files.parliament.uk/documents/SN05927/SN05927.pdf

HM Government (2021) 'Net zero strategy: build back greener', London: OGL.

HM Treasury (2005) 'Budget 2005: investing for our future; fairness and opportunity for Britain's hard-working families', London: HMSO.

HM Treasury (2021) 'Budget 2021: protecting the jobs and livelihoods of the British people', London: OGL.

HM Treasury (2022) 'The growth plan 2022', London: OGL.

HMRC (2015) 'Vehicle excise duty', Available from: https://www.gov.uk/government/publications/vehicle-excise-duty/vehicle-excise-duty

HMRC (2021a) 'Reform of red diesel and other rebated fuels entitlement', Available from: https://www.gov.uk/government/publications/reform-of-red-diesel-entitlements/reform-of-red-diesel-and-other-rebated-fuels-entitlement

HMRC (2021b) 'Tax reliefs statistics (December 2021)', Available from: https://www.gov.uk/government/statistics/main-tax-expenditures-and-structural-reliefs/estimated-cost-of-tax-reliefs-statistics

Hull, R. (2018) 'Around 16m Britons can't afford electric cars', thisismoney.co.uk, Available from: https://www.thisismoney.co.uk/money/cars/article-6392669/Around-16-million-UK-motorists-say-afford-buy-electric-car.html

Institute of Fiscal Studies (IFS) (2011) 'Tax by design: the Mirrlees Review', London: IFS, Available from: https://ifs.org.uk/publications/5353

Jordan, A. Rüdiger, K.W.W. and Zito, A.R. (2013) 'Still the century of "new" environmental policy instruments? Exploring patterns of innovation and continuity', *Environmental Politics*, 22(1): 155–73. doi: 10.1080/09644016.2013.755839

Laurance, B. and Myers, P. (1993) 'VAT: domestic heating increase draws angry response', *The Guardian*, 17 March.

Martin, R.B., de Preux, L. and Wagner, U.J. (2009) 'The impacts of the Climate Change Levy on business: evidence from microdata', Grantham Research Institute on Climate Change and the Environment, working paper no 6, Available from: https://www.lse.ac.uk/granthaminstitute/wp-content/uploads/2014/02/WorkingPaper6.pdf

Nanji, N. (2022) 'Electric car drivers must pay tax from 2025', BBC News, 17 November. https://www.bbc.co.uk/news/business-63660321

NAO (National Audit Office) (2016) 'Controlling the consumer-funded costs of energy policies: the Levy Control Framework', London: NAO.

NAO (2021) 'Environmental tax measures: HM Treasury and HM Revenue and Customs', London: NAO.

OECD (2022) *OECD Inventory of Support Measures for Fossil Fuels: Country Notes; United Kingdom*, Paris: OECD, Available from: https://www.oecd.org/publications/oecd-companion-to-the-inventory-of-support-measures-for-fossil-fuels-country-notes-5a3efe65-en.htm

ONS (2016) 'Fuel prices explained: a breakdown of the cost of petrol and diesel', Available from: https://www.ons.gov.uk/economy/inflationandpriceindices/articles/fuelpricesexplainedabreakdownofthecostofpetrolanddiesel/2016-01-22

ONS (2019) 'Percentage of households with cars by income group, tenure and household composition: table A47', Available from: https://www.ons.gov.uk/peoplepopulationandcommunity/personalandhouseholdfinances/expenditure/datasets/percentageofhouseholdswithcarsbyincomegrouptenureandhouseholdcompositionuktablea47

ONS (2021a) 'Family spending in the UK: April 2019 to March 2020', Available from: https://www.ons.gov.uk/peoplepopulationandcommunity/personalandhouseholdfinances/expenditure/bulletins/familyspendingintheuk/april2019tomarch2020

ONS (2021b) 'Taxes and revenue: the effects of taxes and benefits on UK households' income', Available from: https://www.ons.gov.uk/economy/governmentpublicsectorandtaxes/taxesandrevenue

ONS and DEFRA (2020) 'Living Costs and Food Survey, 2019–2020, [data collection]' (2nd edn), Office for National Statistics, Department for Environment, Food and Rural Affairs; UK Data Service. SN: 8803. doi: 10.5255/UKDA-SN-8803-2.

Owen, G. (2006) 'Sustainable development duties: new roles for UK economic regulators', *Utilities Policy*, 14(3): 208–17.

Owen, A. and Barrett, J. (2020) 'Reducing inequality resulting from UK low carbon Policy', *Climate Policy*, 20(10): 1193–208. doi: 10.1080/14693062.2020.1773754

Pearce, D., Markandya, A. and Barbier, E. (1989) *Blueprint for a Green Economy*, London: Earthscan.

Pigou, A.C. (1932) *The Economics of Welfare* (4th edn), London: Macmillan.

Powells, G.D. (2009) 'Complexity, entanglement, and overflow in the new carbon economy: the case of the UK's Energy Efficiency Commitment', *Environment and Planning A, Economy and Space*, 41(10): 2342–56.

Preston, I., White, V., Browne, J., Dresner, S., Ekins, P. and Hamilton, I. (2013) 'Designing carbon taxation to protect low-income households', York: Joseph Rowntree Foundation, Available from: http://www.jrf.org.uk/sites/files/jrf/carbon-taxation-income-full.pdf

Rosenow, J. (2012) 'Energy savings obligations in the UK: a history of change', *Energy Policy*, 49: 373–82.

Seeley, A. and Ares, E. (2016) 'Climate change levy: renewable energy and the carbon reduction commitment', House of Commons briefing paper no 07283, 20 April, Available from: https://commonslibrary.parliament.uk/research-briefings/cbp-7283

Sorrell, S. (1999) 'Why sulphur trading failed in the UK', in S. Sorrell and J. Skea (eds) *Pollution for Sale*, Cheltenham: Edward Elgar.

Taylor, M. and Horton, H. (2022) 'Tories fighting net zero plans are dragging climate into new culture war, experts say', *The Guardian*, 8 February.

Timilsinas, G.R. (2018) 'Where is the carbon tax after thirty years of research?', World Bank Policy Research working paper 8493, Available from: https://openknowledge.worldbank.org/handle/10986/29946

Toke, D. (2010) 'Politics by heuristics: policy networks with a focus on actor resources, as illustrated by the case of RE policy under New Labour', *Public Administration*, 88(3): 764–81.

Tovar Reanos, M.A. and Sommerfield, K. (2017) 'Fuel for inequality: distributional effects of environmental reforms on private transport', Centre for European Economic Research (ZEW) discussion paper no 16-090, Available from: http://ftp.zew.de/pub/zew-docs/dp/dp16090.pdf

UK Government (2020) 'VAT rates on different goods and services', Available from: https://www.gov.uk/guidance/rates-of-vat-on-different-goods-and-services#building-and-construction-land-and-property

Waterhouse, R. and Schoon, N. (1993) 'All pensioners to get extra payments; VAT on fuel', *The Independent*, 1 December.

Wier, M., Birr, K., Pedersen, H., Klinge, J. and Klok, J. (2005) 'Are CO2 taxes regressive? Evidence from the Danish experience', *Ecological Economics*, 52(2): 239–51, Available from: https://www.sciencedirect.com/science/article/pii/S0921800904003672?casa_token=n7K0UhM3g8kAAAAA:WxAxRhHRHkUhT4icPT4b9yK43AcsxFDe3JzpFFahi-M17GtdzWzX4wernkxOvmHl6nRyFAxPDy_u

Xu, X. (2022) 'Support for households and living standards', Autumn Statement Analysis: IFS. https://ifs.org.uk/events/autumn-statement-2022-ifs-analysis

Zahedi, S. and Cremades, L.V. (2012) 'Vehicle taxes in EU countries: how fair is their calculation?', XVI Congreso Internacional de Ingeniería de Proyectos Valencia, 11–13 July, Available from: https://upcommons.upc.edu/bitstream/handle/2117/18150/vehicles.pdf

15

Conclusions: Taxation in a social policy context

Andy Lymer, Margaret May and Adrian Sinfield

In creating this book, we set out to fill a major gap in social policy and taxation studies by examining the tax–social policy nexus in the UK and its frequently overlooked effects, building on the identically titled volume of 1980 (Sandford et al, 1980). In doing so, we have deliberately taken account of a wider range of taxes and policy domains than the editors and authors of the 1980 text focused on. We examine their interaction with and impact on society, politics and the economy as well as continuing to pursue many of the questions the 1980 book raised and reviewing how these discussions have evolved in the more than 40 years since then. In summing up, we also reflect on how the intertwining of taxation and social policy could be better examined to encourage further research and improve the situation we find ourselves in, particularly that of those most in need of support.

The multiple interactions of tax and social policy

What comes across strongly in all the chapters of this book are the myriad ways in which taxation operates as an instrument of social policy and the value of examining the two in tandem. In this, we echo Sandford et al (1980, p 228), whose first conclusion, one that emerged 'with almost overwhelming force', was the sheer 'extent and complexity of the inter-relationship between taxation and social policy'. In the 40 years since, this remains as true as ever. Indeed, if anything it has become an even more 'complex and constantly changing environment', as Lymer demonstrates in Chapter 3.

To cite just two from the many examples in this book, Lymer, Gregory and Wynter's assessment of taxation's impact on homes and housing (Chapter 9) reveals the long-term, pervasive role of fiscal policies in supporting owner-occupation at the expense of other tenures – a bias maintained often long after direct subsidies had been reduced or ended and paralleled by the lack of measures to support alternatives. As they and Rowlingson (Chapter 10) also highlight, the structuring of inheritance tax for passing on the family home reinforces this differentiation and the many inequities and inequalities flowing from it.

A second example can be seen when scrutinising the relationship of taxation to health and social care services and population health (Chapter 8). Here Ruane traces the extraordinarily varied and intricate ways in which both public and private bodies have employed elements of taxation that favour the latter bodies to support their services. Together with the pressures of an austerity regime, this has pushed public bodies into creative use of tax reliefs as they responded to situations where private but not public services could take advantage of pre-existing fiscal subsidies. Receipt of these of course imposed constraints on the development of their services.

The policy-making significance of structural inequalities

A second, overlapping theme that can be seen as a thread throughout the book are the consequences of not examining social policy and tax arrangements in synchrony and the inequalities regularly disregarded in public debate that stem from a disconnected approach. Indeed, what has come through even more strongly than the editors expected is the extent to which successive authors draw attention to the policy making, or policy-averting, significance of the overall distribution of resources and the multiple ways in which taxation can shape and reinforce socio-economic differentials.

There has been a marked rise in economic inequalities since the 1980 book, as the authors emphasise. The biggest increase occurred during the subsequent Thatcher years, a period notable for just how much analysis of issues of inequity, even within the academic world, was dampened, if not smothered (Atkinson, 1983; Piketty, 2022). But, as they make clear, inequalities in income and especially in wealth have widened since, particularly over the last decade, sustaining gender, ethnic and generational disparities, amplifying health, care, pensions, housing and regional variances and increasing poverty levels.

McKay for instance details the extent to which, with household incomes in the richest quintile rising and falling in the poorest, the 'UK has seen a large rise in inequality over time and remains one of the more unequal countries in the developed world' (Chapter 7). This high level of inequality, moreover, is closely linked to an escalation in poverty, particularly since 2010, which is likely to increase even further if present policies persist.

McKay's assessment is reinforced by Rowlingson's analysis of wealth taxation and the difficulties of researching it (Chapter 10). The extremely limited evidence on the scale and impact of the considerable tax reliefs on wealth, capital and property is not only remarkable but indicates successive governments' unwillingness to tackle the hidden wiring that advantages the better-off. Like other contributors in documenting this, she draws much-needed attention to the rhetoric that has helped maintain resistance to change in the interests of those benefitting from existing arrangements and the failure to engage with the significant harms generated by stubbornly persistent and even increasing inequalities.

Likewise, in tracing the ways in which taxation is implicated in health and social care and health promotion (Chapter 8), Ruane delineates the related issue of the UK's health gap and the inequalities underlying it. As she points out, the likelihood of poorer health and shorter lives increases steadily down the socio-economic ladder and not just at the very bottom. The COVID-19 pandemic, which disproportionately impacted lower-income and ethnic minority groups, has exacerbated these risks.

Similarly highlighting the need to consider taxation and social policy in the round, the same overarching theme emerges from Bridgen and Büchs' own research (Chapter 14), which maps the clearly regressive overall impact of the taxes directly and indirectly affecting carbon emissions. These uncoordinated measures to tackle individual problems with individual compensatory mechanisms clearly do not bring the benefits that interventions as part of a broader taxing of 'luxuries' might have. This also leads them to another central social policy concern, the ways in which the haphazard picking up of social costs falls particularly on low-income and vulnerable groups. In effect, as Titmuss (1968, p 133) stressed, rather than support being recognised as compensations for the costs of social and economic change, the costs are too often allowed to lie where they fall.

What stands out from a social policy-based analysis is a clear depiction of the extent to which taxation plays a significant role in structuring social provisions and shaping the relationships between the state and society and groups within it. Even more starkly, it also reveals the subterranean ways in which the tax regime serves to maintain and even strengthen income and wealth inequalities.

The political context of taxation and social policy

Running throughout this second core theme of the policy-making significance of structural inequalities are two related strands: the variability and often paucity of publicly available data, and the factors that can inhibit debate. The constraints on distributional analyses posed by the former have necessitated both a re-analysis and interrogation of existing sources and new research, particularly by Bridgen and Büchs (Chapter 14). The shortage of data has also highlighted the difficulties of exploring the role of taxation in sustaining or mitigating gender and ethnic inequalities and its societal functions more broadly.

This applies particularly to the regressive, upside-down pre-distribution of direct tax reliefs (more commonly termed, tax expenditures) that leave their better-off recipients more protected, reinforced if not strengthened in their privileges (Chapter 4). A major element in hidden fiscal wiring, these tax expenditures are beginning to receive more attention, including from the Office for Budget Responsibility (OBR), National Audit Office (NAO) and various select committees. But their reinforcement and even strengthening of the existing patterns of inequality still remain largely undiscussed, let alone subjected to detailed focus by policy makers. What is more, as many contributors make clear, this neglect is by no means confined to tax expenditures but can be found in many other elements of taxation.

The limited attention paid to these and their interaction with social policy can in part be attributed to the UK's budgeting process and the continuing dominance of the political theatre surrounding the annual Budget.

Tax policy making has been described as not fit for purpose in a report by the Institute for Government, the Chartered Institute of Taxation and the Institute for Fiscal Studies (Rutter et al, 2017; Davis, 2022). Most fiscal changes emerge, sometimes deeply buried, in annual budgets without the opportunities for wider and more public discussion that accompany changes to public spending programmes. Publishing clear guiding principles and priorities for tax policy and better and more open and inclusive consultation are among the report's ten detailed proposals of particular value to opening up debate.

This helps to insulate fiscal discussion from the usual means of developing policy in spending departments, more so than in many other countries. The use of green and white papers to advance discussion of policy proposals and improve policy making is very rarely used instead of the 'rabbits-from-a-hat' technique of Budget Day. Moreover, moves towards a more structured approach allowing for some debate through shifting from March Budgets, implemented almost immediately, to Autumn Budgets, implemented in the following spring, have been disrupted by the COVID-19 pandemic. The effects of this shift in timing of the key annual fiscal event in the UK are yet to be really seen, as have their implications for the devolved governments' budgeting (who often have no more prior sight of Budget 'rabbits' than do the rest of us).

Furthermore, the efforts of those campaigning for reduced inequalities, and fairer, more generous policies for those briefly labelled as 'essential workers' in the early days of the pandemic, are handicapped by largely having to work from outside the budgeting process (Whiteley and Winyard, 1987). In contrast, many industrial, financial, property and other bodies, and many leading figures from such areas of business, have not only long been able to have regular meetings with ministers and civil servants but expect to be consulted about potential changes in their fields, and generally appear to be (Davis, 2022).

For others, it is not at all clear how much has changed since pre-internet days, when a welfare campaigner was told that the Chancellor of the

Exchequer had indeed seen their Budget representation. Along with many others, it had been piled on a trolley and wheeled through the office of the Chancellor who had been asked to look up and see it go past!

Whether such inequalities can be broken down while the Budget process persists in its present form is doubtful. What is clear from this volume is that tax policy making remains opaque, with no well-defined guidelines, subject to limited, often narrowly based consultation, to somewhat hasty parliamentary appraisal, which, as Himmelweit in particular observes (Chapter 11), impedes wider public scrutiny and consideration of gender, ethnic and other inequalities.

The need for wider discussion

This has been matched and assisted by the reluctance of HM Treasury and HMRC to share data and analysis, an issue, as Sinfield points out (Chapter 4), particularly demonstrated by the long resistance to publishing information on tax expenditures and the obstructions faced by attempts to investigate the work of fiscal administration (Hodge, 2016).

Meanwhile, the routine use by both these bodies of professional tax accountants and lawyers to advise on legislation results in their being left exposed to advice on tax planning and mitigation by the very same firms that have frustrated attempts to make changes, especially those concerned with inequalities, an issue highlighted particularly by both Pond and Farnsworth (Chapters 2 and 13).

Indeed, the strong impression gained by our authors is that HMRC and its controller, HM Treasury, have done little to provide a fuller and coordinated accounting of the many taxes that can hardly be described as 'a system' – in reference to their coherence at least – rather than very loosely linked ideas and concepts enacted at different times with political motivations and electoral calculations that may or may not have long-term value or consistency. As mapping the fiscal policy landscape indicates (Chapter 2), taxation in the UK continues to have neither a clear overall framework or logic to guide it, nor any suggestion of an underpinning 'master plan' of any obvious nature (see also Kay and King, 1990).

The degree of cooperation and coordination between the tax authorities in HM Treasury and HMRC and the spending departments too has remained very one-way. This detachment of the official tax agencies from other policy considerations is well illustrated in different chapters. Tax decision-making operates in contrast to public spending and has been largely insulated from the austerity regime from 2010. It is clear for instance that while basic social security benefits for those of working age rose by 3 per cent between 2012 and 2020, the personal tax allowance threshold was lifted by 46 per cent. In 2019/20 the boost to the higher-rate threshold was 4.6 times that of the basic allowance to all taxpayers (Lymer and Oats, 2020, p 126). In effect, the Exchequer cost of these tax changes was met by the 'austerity' saving on social security.

Furthermore, reliefs for various forms of wealth have continued largely unabated. In this regard, Rowlingson (Chapter 10) echoes Glennerster's conclusion that the long-term pattern of inequality reflects 'the Treasury's deeper concern – defending a mixed economy from the perceived destructive effect of major changes to the distribution of income and wealth' or, more radically, serving as 'the quintessential defender ... of the status quo' (Glennerster, 2012, p 247).

Beyond these barriers lie the many 'practical constraints' on more coherent links with social policy. These still include the major issue of how to take 'account ... of reasonable expectations that have become established' (Sandford et al, 1980, pp 231–2). Such obstacles to reform apply for instance to those who bought their homes in the context of a supportive tax regime whose house prices would be affected if a less favourable tack compared to other tenures was adopted (Chapter 9). Not surprisingly, vested interests are found to be at their strongest when change is mooted. This is also evident in the failure to increase National Insurance contributions for the self-employed for instance or in the attempts to reform the pensions system that produced little more than maintaining the status quo, constraining moves towards a level playing field in terms of provision and tax support (Chapters 5 and 6).

They also include the many administrative constraints touched on throughout this volume and especially in Chapter 3. There are many ways in which it is all too easy for discussions of taxes to become trapped within off-putting technical details. The result, as Himmelweit puts it (Chapter 11), is that those who do venture in may become too concerned with establishing better arrangements 'within the tax system' and less with 'whether the tax system works to create greater equality in society'.

Worryingly little of even independent discussion seems to have understood the importance of this distinction. Adding to this, it is necessary to recognise how impervious to each other the different divisions of tax and social policy have continued to be. In particular, and with few exceptions, the disciplines and professions concerned with taxation have proved very successful in treating and defending it as their own special preserve, not least in part because of the financial rewards that may be derived from advising on it.

Moving forward

With the benefit of hindsight, more than 40 years on from the publication of Sandford et al (1980), what is striking is not how much the debate has changed since the early 1980s, but how little the consideration of tax and its behavioural and distributional impact on the wider society has developed and become discussed more widely.

As Rowlingson stresses (Chapter 10), this reflects the ways in which such discussion has been framed and the continuing dominance of a broad neoliberal-inspired discourse on taxation. Often divorced from social policy concerns, this presents taxation negatively as an imposition transferring hard-earned resources from the deserving to the undeserving and as a burden on individuals and the economy. In this context, with political campaigning commonly focused on tax cuts and letting people control 'their own money', recent governments have proved reluctant, if not resistant, to support welfare services through raising taxes. Much of the media furthers this by focusing more on offering advice on how individuals could manage their finances to minimise tax payments rather than its social role. Such framing has also fed into low levels of public engagement with and understanding of taxation and its interaction with social policy.

In this longstanding context, many of the proposals and options for change considered in the 1980 volume are echoed in our chapters. Orton (Chapter 12) makes the point explicitly: '[I]ssues relating to local taxation retain a rather timeless feel. Concern, and even crises, arise periodically, but issues remain remarkably the same in terms of forms of taxation, options and so on.'

Many of our authors have also made the point that Atkinson (1983, p 36) put so crisply: '[T]he constraints lie as much in perceptions as in resources, and they are not immutable.' Such perceptions often flourish as a result of the many hidden wirings of taxation, clear examples of power 'at its most effective when least observable' as emphasised in Chapter 4 (Lukes, 2005, p 1). In differing ways, the chapters have brought much technical detail into view, countering elements of mythmaking and misperceptions of who pays taxes and how much.

One key to moving forward by building on this volume is to challenge the negative rhetoric around taxation and shift to a broader, more constructive view that recognises it as a collective investment in welfare, other public goods and the wider social and economic infrastructure. This would, as Rowlingson and Himmelweit respectively accentuate (Chapters 10 and 11), recast it 'as a positive contribution made by everyone to the benefit of all' and from which everyone benefits. It would also allow for a consideration of its 'wide-reaching behavioural, distributional and macro-economic implications' and the ways it might support a more equal society.

As other chapters also show, a concomitant key to moving forward is the furthering of social policy's consideration of taxation both nationally and locally (Chapter 12; Ruane et al, 2020). In the past, this tended to confine itself to tax measures directly focused on specific social problems. As Pond points out in Chapter 2, some form of Basic Income is perhaps the most common example. Even here, there has been less attention to the ways in which its financing will affect resources and relationships for those required to pay more on modest as well as higher incomes. Too little account has been taken of the many ways in which taxes other than income routinely affect people's living standards, health and quality of life and the development of communities and the common wealth. The fiscal incentive to build new housing in comparison to repairing and restoring is one example referred to in more than one chapter that clearly shapes the living environment as well as affecting carbon emissions.

Expanding social policy views of taxation

To fully encompass the interweaving of social policy and taxation alongside reforging views of the latter, what also emerges throughout is the need pinpointed by Sinfield to employ a triple framework in social policy analysis (Chapter 4). This involves adding the consideration of 'means-enhancing' to 'means-testing' and universal allocation of benefits and services. As many chapters make clear, the inverted, non-progressive pre–distribution of direct tax reliefs supports the better-off, often consolidating their affluence. Furthermore, the means-enhancement of taxation can be traced across the tax spectrum affecting people's opportunities and, as with corporate welfare, the wider society.

Factoring in this dimension and the role of tax in pre- and re-distribution would enable social policy analysts to draw on the work of those concerned with tax justice and human rights, further opening up consideration of issues of fairness beyond narratives of 'tax compliance', 'welfare abuse' and, especially, perceptions of tax as a 'burden'. It would also meet the need for a more sustained discussion of both the development of the dominant discourse that distinguishes the taxpayer and the citizen and alternative perspectives. In that theory, the taxpayer, an individual with self-interests defined by economic status, has an incentive to engage in tax planning in contrast to individuals and families with collective concerns and social responsibilities.

Today, this second view is often dismissed as far too radical, and many may be surprised that Beveridge took it for granted in 1948 when he wrote *Voluntary Action*. Often regarded as his retreat from his influential wartime report, it in fact underscores his objectives at that time. Titling the last chapter 'First things first', he pointed out that in 1942 he 'set out a practical programme for putting first things first. There was to be bread and health for all at all times before cake and circuses for anybody at any time, so far as this order of priority could be enforced by redistribution of money' (Beveridge, 1948, p 319).

Encapsulating a view mirrored across this book, the discussion of homes and housing (Chapter 9) also sets out the case for taxing that facilitates a broader, universal provision than protection only for those who can afford an asset: 'Tax policy, and the wider social responsibility associated with housing policy generally, must keep at its heart this motivation that all deserve to have a home. The desire to achieve that for all should be what drives housing policy.' In this, it reiterates another basic finding of Sandford et al (1980, p 230) that continues to be very much required – the need for far less 'ad hocery', greater coordination, simplification and above all 'a more systematic approach and a broader vision; in particular, viewing tax and social policy measures together'.

The need for this is made particularly clearly in Himmelweit's discussion of gender and taxation (Chapter 11), Taking account of 'tax changes without considering changes in benefits and other parts of the "social wage" gives a distorted picture. Because of their caring roles, women are more likely to be eligible for benefits and make use of public services.' Failure to consider the interaction of these different factors can lead to an underestimate of the gender equality effect of any change.

Proposals for more strategic, systematic reform of taxation are of course far from new and have been advocated, though as yet with little effect, many times since Sandford et al (1980), notably by the Fabian Society (2000), the IFS Mirrlees Review (2010, 2011) and other bodies (Rutter et al, 2017; Collins and Hammond, 2021; Adam Smith Institute, nd). Our authors clearly endorse a more strategic view but significantly call for actions that go further, stressing the importance of integrating fiscal, social security and other policies in bringing about institutional change that benefits the wider society. In doing so, they also signal the need for greater investment in boosting tax literacy, wider public engagement and more informed debate about tax/policy choices and trade-offs, including their implications for social disparities and fairness.

Needless to say, moving forward on these lines demands further, detailed research and less difficulty in accessing data. In a globalised environment, this should also involve more extensive comparative exploration of the role of taxation in social policy, including addressing not only issues such as the tax avoidance of multi-nationals and debates over corporate taxation but corporate welfare, as Farnsworth shows (Chapter 13).

Missed issues and opportunities

There are admittedly other social policy areas and focuses that could well have provided related analyses had we not been limited by space. A scan of areas such as education and training, childcare/early years provision and other forms of local social services has made it clear that they present similar issues to those running throughout the contributions to this book.

Specific examination of racial and ethnic issues would have added other important behavioural and distributional dimensions to consideration of tax, social policy and justice as Decolonising Economics' campaigning report, 'Tax as a Tool for Racial Justice' (2022), brings out vividly. It sets out a framework for tax research examining the many ways that white-dominated racial hierarchies have shaped current tax practices globally from the spider's web of tax havens and secrecy jurisdictions to national and local patterns and practices.

Further analysis of the organisation and operation of the different taxes examined in successive chapters would develop the mapping of the tax and social policy landscape in Chapter 3. This would also open up areas of interaction and the lack of it between taxation and social policy. Comparison of the issues could raise important questions for administration and training but also make more evident the different discourse used to discuss and evaluate policy and practice. The different tone and political tension of terms such as non-compliance and abuse deserve a new *Rich Law, Poor Law* (Cook, 1989).

In both tax and social policy, rapid digitisation and interactions related to obligations has become a significant emerging social policy issue, as Lymer points out (Chapter 3). While increased digitisation potentially may facilitate tracking and evaluating the impact of taxation and social security, open new ways of operating both systems with an improved social policy focus and enhance public understanding, much also depends on more effective tackling of the digital divides of access and capability that leaves those excluded from the better support provided online.

The broad issues of human rights and its many dimensions in relation to taxation, social policy and their interaction are raised in many chapters but could well have provided another chapter, if not a whole book (Lister, 2021, chapter 6; O'Hagan et al, 2021). Forms of Basic Income that are being tested by various pilots in the UK and abroad could also have been analysed more fully than in Chapter 2 (Standing, 2017).

Concluding thoughts

Any attempt to consider taxation and social policy together in a broad societal context clearly faces numerous challenges. However, there are signs of change. While there is still a long way to go to ease navigation of often labyrinthine documentation, HMRC for instance is beginning, as some of our chapters indicate, to make more information available, including administrative data, although there are still significant gaps. Bodies like the NAO, OBR, Office of Tax Simplification (until it ceased to operate in 2023) and some parliamentary committees too are opening up the bases for research. Though much depends on provisions to tackle the existing digital divide, increased digitisation has the potential to enable an improved social policy focus in taxation with better public understanding, as we have argued.

As we noted in the Introduction, there are also, crucially, signs of a new interest in taxation among social policy analysts and awareness of the subterranean fiscal welfare state more widely (Hacker, 2002; Hakelberg and Seelkopf, 2021; Harrop, 2022). The backdrop to policy formation is also starting to alter as the albeit limited devolution of tax and other financial powers across the UK has been encouraging a more accountable, open approach, widening the parameters of debate.

With cautious use of its narrow powers to set income tax rates as well as establish new land and other taxes, the Scottish government has already overseen a marked shift from the taxes of the rest of the UK. It is also seeking to reduce the distance between the Scottish Tax Authority and the public by spelling out tax principles and engaging more widely in roundtables and consultations deliberately pushed out to bodies outside accounting, fiscal and legal circles (Scottish Government, 2021). As Scotland takes on more responsibility for elements of the social security system, particularly relating to disability and child poverty, a similar approach is likely.

Wales and Northern Ireland also have potential to follow the direction of travel commenced by Scotland and use their lower tax powers to meet their governments' social concerns. In Wales, where a similar, more consultative approach is being pursued, this is beginning to occur in respect of land transactions and landfill disposal taxes, the raising of the maximum council tax on second homes and consideration of council tax revaluation. More may be expected in future as devolved (or more local) taxation follows regional differences more closely as the appetite appears to be increasingly developing to do so.

There are, moreover, indications of growing and widespread unhappiness with rising and persisting economic inequalities, increasing and deepening poverty and escalating wealth. This is demonstrated most notably for instance by the Institute for Fiscal Studies' Deaton Review of Inequality launched in 2019 that is beginning to provide valuable analyses (Delestre et al, 2022). Indeed, even the then Director of IMF, an organisation long a major supporter of market capitalism, acknowledged 'a better understanding that a more equal distribution of income allows for more economic stability, more sustained economic growth, and healthier societies with stronger bonds of cohesion and trust' (Lagarde, 2013 in Weldon, quoted in Chapter 10).

***

The UK faces an unprecedented conjuncture of pressures extending from the climate emergency, the ongoing fallout from the COVID-19 pandemic, spiralling living and energy costs, intensifying poverty, deep-seated health, educational and other inequalities to the under-resourcing of public services over more than a decade of austerity, demographic ageing, low productivity and low growth. All of these impact on the policy domains discussed here, as well as many others and the quality of life across society. They underline the need for a wider view of the operation and impact of taxes that takes into account the full resources of the economy and society and more structured coordination of the UK's spending and revenue generating arrangements.

Our authors have made it clear how working within what is seen as the 'cautiously feasible' has resulted in the failure to take proper account of relatively light taxation, its often-shrouded wiring and the ways in which the absence of taxes helps to shape society as much as, and sometimes more than, those enacted. The tendency to remain within the status quo has resulted in the neglect of resources that might otherwise have been deployed to the wider social good rather than more selectively to the benefit of the few at a cost that the global pandemic has made only too clear.

As we go to print in autumn 2022, the prospects for the UK society, economy and polity are unusually uncertain in the current political climate. The 22 September 2022 'mini-budget' is far from the 'carefully crafted package of reforms' discussed in Chapter 5, with much material, including public spending adjustments, not even published at the point of its delivery, and subsequent major retractions including the reinstatement of the 45 per cent tax rate. For some time following these announcements, each day brought more uncertainty and anxiety, underlining the message of this book that taxation and social policy cannot be considered in isolation from each other. These are too interconnected in the UK today to be so treated any longer. We hope that this text has helped draw attention to reform possibilities and will contribute to further research and debate.

Postscript

The fiscal experiences of the last quarter of 2022 have only underlined the importance of our conclusions emphasising the need for greater accountability and transparency from governments to enable a better understanding of the ways that taxation operates as 'an instrument of social policy'.

The astonishing Truss-Kwarteng 'fiscal event' of 23rd September 2022 came as we were about to send the text to the publishers. Described by IFS as the biggest tax cut in fifty years without any analysis of public spending and other implications (IFS, 2022), the political uproar that it created was accompanied by dramatically adverse reactions in the market sector that were clearly unanticipated by Prime Minister Truss and Chancellor of the Exchequer Kwarteng who had presented themselves as strengthening the market. Sterling slumped and UK gilt bonds were being sold off at alarming rates until the Bank of England acted. With widespread concern over rising energy prices and a growing cost of living crisis for very many, the proposal to abolish the additional tax allowance of 45 per cent for the best-off had to be withdrawn within ten days. We managed to take account of that tax change before submitting the book.

Change continued. Kwasi Kwarteng was replaced as the Chancellor of the Exchequer by Jeremy Hunt and his mini-budget on 17th October reversed most of the earlier changes although not the cancellation of the Health and Social Care Levy. Three days later Liz Truss resigned as Prime Minister to be succeeded by Rishi Sunak, a former Chancellor of the Exchequer, before the end of the month. Most last-minute changes to the text have had to be revised, if not reversed, after Hunt's mini-budget and his Autumn Statement eventually delivered on 17th November. The threshold for many tax allowances including the additional income tax rate of 45 per cent were reduced and/or frozen for longer.

These events underlined many of our conclusions on the low attention given by tax policy makers to social policy needs and the distributional impact of the changes across society, especially at a time when poverty and inequality were growing. After sustained pressure from many sides, the benefit uprating for April 2023 recognised the increased inflation of recent months and the increase to CGT planned by Sunak, when he was Chancellor earlier in 2022, was restored. But, the very regressive changes to pension taxes provided the 2023 Budget 'rabbit-out-of-a-hat' moment that only helped to reinforce inequalities.

Despite what was widely regarded as a broad economic and social emergency, the narrow range of areas and issues officially indicated as considered within all stages of the various tax changes gave little attention to many urgent issues including responding to the climate crisis. In addition the potential for various means of taxing wealth to ease fiscal pressures on the great majority of taxpayers raised in many of our chapters was not pursued. By contrast public and media discussion gave more attention than usual to the opportunities provided at a critical time to make more radical changes to taxing wealth and to promoting a greener approach to sustainability. If this continues, closer attention to the interaction of taxes and social policies of all kinds will be needed, as we have argued.

References

Adam Smith Institute (nd) 'Pro growth tax reform', Available from: https://www.adamsmith.org/policy

Atkinson, A.B. (1983) 'The commitment to equality', in J. Griffith (ed), *Socialism in a Cold Climate*, London: Counterpoint, pp 22–36.

Beveridge, W.H. (1942) *Report on social insurance and allied services*, London: HMSO.

Beveridge, W.H. (1948) *Voluntary Action: A Report on Methods of Social Advance,* London: Allen & Unwin.

Bradshaw, J. (ed) (2019) *Let's Talk about Tax*, London: CPAG.

Byrne, D. and Ruane, S. (2017) *Paying for the Welfare State in the 21st Century: Tax and Spending in Post-industrial Societies*, Bristol: Policy Press.

Collins, S. and Hammond, A.C.R. (2021) '20 tax laws to scrap: how to grow the UK economy', London: IEA.

Cook, D. (1989) *Rich Law, Poor Law*, Milton Keynes: Open University Press.

Davis, A. (2022) *Bankruptcy, Bubbles and Bailouts: The Inside History of the Treasury since 1976*, Manchester: Manchester University Press.

Decolonising Economics (2022) 'Tax as a tool for racial justice', Available from: https://decolonisingeconomics.org/wp-content/uploads/2022/09/Tax-as-a-Tool-for-Racial-Justice-report.pdf

Delestre, I., Kopczuk, W., Miller, H. and Smith, K. (2022) 'Top income inequality and tax policy: Deaton Review of Inequalities', London: IFS.

Fabian Society Commission on Taxation and Citizenship (2000) *Paying for Progress: A New Politics of Tax for Public Spending*, London: Fabian Society.

Glennerster, H. (2012) 'Why was a wealth tax for the UK abandoned? Lessons for the policy process and tackling wealth inequality', *Journal of Social Policy*, 41(2): 233–49.

Hacker, J.S. (2002) *The Divided Welfare State: The Battle over Public and Private Social Benefits in the United States*, Cambridge: Cambridge University Press.

Hakelberg, L. and Seelkopf, L. (eds) (2021) *Handbook on the Politics of Taxation*, Cheltenham: Edward Elgar.

Harrop, A. (2022) 'In the shadows: how "shadow welfare" has overtaken social security', London: Fabian Society.

Hodge, M. (2016) *Called to Account*, London: Little, Brown.

IFS (2022) 'Mini-Budget response', 23 September 2022 (includes forecasts), Available from: https://ifs.org.uk/articles/mini-budget-response

Kay, J.A. and King, M.A. (1990) *The British Tax System* (5th edn), Oxford: Oxford University Press.

Lister, R. (2021) *Poverty* (2nd edn), Cambridge: Polity.

Lukes, S. (2005) *Power: A Radical View* (2nd edn), Basingstoke: Palgrave Macmillan.

Lymer, A. and Oats, L. (2020) *Taxation: Policy and Practice 2020/2021* (27th edn), Malvern: Fiscal Publications.

Mirrlees, J., Adam, S., Besley, T., Blundell, R., Bond, S. and Chote, R. et al (2010) 'Dimensions of tax design', London: IFS.

Mirrlees, J., Adam, S., Besley, T., Blundell, R., Bond, S. and Chote, R. et al (2011) 'Tax by design', London: IFS.

O'Hagan, A., Hosie, A., Ferrie, J., Mulvagh, L. and Corkery, A. (2021) 'Advancing human rights through the Scottish budget process', SPA conference working paper.

Piketty, T. (2022) *A Brief History of Equality*, Cambridge, MA: Harvard University Press.

Pond, C. (1980) 'Tax expenditures and fiscal welfare', in C. Sandford, C. Pond and R. Walker (eds) (1980) *Taxation and Social Policy*, London: Heinemann, pp 47–63.

Ruane, S., Collins, M. and Sinfield, A. (2020) 'The centrality of taxation in social policy', *Social Policy and Society*, 19(3): 437–53.

Rutter, J., Dodwell, B., Johnson, P., Crozier, G., Cullinane, J. and Lilly, A. et al (2017) 'Better budgets: making tax policy better', London: Chartered Institute of Taxation, Institute for Fiscal Studies and Institute for Government.

Sandford, C. (1980) 'Conclusions', in C. Sandford, C. Pond and R. Walker (eds) (1980) *Taxation and Social Policy*, London: Heinemann, pp 228–36.

Sandford, C., Pond, C. and Walker, R. (eds) (1980) *Taxation and Social Policy*, London: Heinemann.

Scottish Government (2021) 'A framework for taxation 2021', Available from: www.gov.scot/publications/framework-tax-2021/documents/

Standing, G. (2017) *Basic Income: And How We Can Make It Happen*, Milton Keynes: Pelican.

Titmuss, R.M. (1968) 'Welfare state and welfare society', in *Commitment to Welfare*, London: George Allen & Unwin, pp 124–37.

Weldon, D. (2013) 'Miliband, Obama and Lagarde on reforming capitalism', Touchstone Economics, 19 February. https://touchstoneblog.org.uk/2013/02/miliband-obama-and-lagarde-on-reforming-capitalism/

Whiteley, P.F. and Winyard, S.J. (1987) *Pressure for the Poor*, London: Routledge.

Index